INDIA-CHINA

Underdevelopment and Revolution

INDIA-CHINA

*Underdevelopment
and Revolution*

NIGEL HARRIS

CAROLINA ACADEMIC PRESS
Durham, North Carolina

Published in the United States by

CAROLINA ACADEMIC PRESS
2206 Chapel Hill Road, Box 8791 Forest Hills Station
Durham, N.C. 27707

ISBN 0-89089-017-X

Library of Congress Catalog Card No. 74-30894

PRINTED IN INDIA

Introduction

The Indian Left faces a crisis. For those not on the Left, this might be a matter for rejoicing or indifference, except that the crisis of the Left is a symptom of a crisis facing the whole of Indian society.

It is now a quarter of a century since the attainment of Indian independence. The intervening years have witnessed the disintegration of hopes, the exhaustion of political and economic strategies. It is not simply a question of poverty. That was always there. But what seemed to make the poverty temporarily tolerable was the hope of economic development. It was assumed that once the drain of resources out of India to Britain could be staunched; once some elementary rationality introduced into the economy; protection brought in against predatory foreign capital and imports; some absurdly long overdue reforms passed; then the great engines of industry could begin to transform the Indian landscape. The cities would fuel the forward drive, and fertilizers, water and schools would sweep the countryside into the urban wake. Every Indian could be put to work, and could look forward to a real advance in the quality of his livelihood. A new economic giant would step out onto the world stage.

One of the arguments of this book is that even a most modest version of this optimism can now be seen to be utopian.[1] India has little or no chance of anything that can be seriously called economic development. Of course, all kinds of things can be done, from steel

[1] See Chapters 1, 8 and 10.

mills to hybrid seeds, but in terms of the mass of the population, it means virtually nothing. And in terms of world power, of "closing the gap" between rich and poor, the trend is in precisely the opposite direction.

This is not a peculiarly Indian dilemma. For it is becoming clear that scarcely any of the mass of backward—or in that hypocrite's word, "developing"—countries will be permitted to develop. All the popular claptrap about "take off," "sustained growth" and a permanent prospect of rising standards of living for all was a confidence trick to induce acceptance of a permanently unequal world. The millenium is not for the majority of the world's people.

Much of the Indian Left, consciously or not, accepted some version of the optimistic case. As a result, their activities were circumscribed to fit the politics of parliament. They tailored their behaviour to offering a kind of critical—but tacit—support to the *status quo*. Of course, they lashed with great vigour at all sorts of dark forces—the CIA, feudal landlords and so on—but that only indicated what they did not attack with the same verbal ferocity. The politics which informed their rhetoric was, by default, postponed to some distant future. Their practical application was devoted almost wholly to winning certain reforms, at best part of a gradualist perspective, at worst mere *ad hoc* actions without overall rationale. Being weak, the reforms they could win were not significant.

The combination of mildly reformist practice and much revolutionary bombast was not simply the product of India's domestic environment. The Indian Left was also linked to its ideological parents abroad, to Stalinism (the Communist Parties) and Social Democracy (the Labour and Socialist Parties). In both cases, what was meant by socialism had been steered very far from its historic moorings.

In the original version, the freedom of the majority could be secured only by abolishing the private ownership of the means of production, by the working class taking—by whatever means—control of economic power. In the later version, the extension of State power, of the public bureaucracy, was the essence of "socialization." The State was substituted for the majority; its power stood proxy for that of working people. The two versions were linked by a whole series of phrases designed to muddle rather than clarify. For in speaking of the State as "the nation," its policies as "the national will," what social class controlled the State was concealed. Nationalization without workers' power merely assists the preservation of the power of the existing ruling class by sacrificing one small section of private capitalism. This ideological "sand in the eyes" was designed to conceal the real change between the original and the later versions of "socialism"— namely, the reconciliation of Stalinism and Social Democracy to the existing distribution of power.

The power of the State is national. Its fiat runs only to its borders. So the socialism of the State was national socialism. In the original version, it was argued that the workers had no vested interest in the boundaries of the patch of land controlled by their ruling class, so that proletarian socialism was intrinsically inter-nationalist. Yet in the newer versions, the only kind of inter-nationalism permitted was either subordination to another State bureaucracy, that in Moscow, or the flabby pieties of the Socialist International. For the first, the stark nuclear terrors of the Cold War offered a convincing mimicry of the missing clash of the class war; the "armed camp" of the "Socialist Third of the World" demanded unflinching loyalties in the face of the enemy, regardless of whether that loyalty contradicted any serious prospect of working class revolution in a particular country. For the second, rhetoric bound no-one; it provided a discreet veil to conceal the reconciliation of Social Democracy to Western capitalism itself.

For the Communists, the extension of nationalization, State planning and loyalty to Moscow effectively encompassed the most important tasks for socialists. For the Social Democrats, extension of nationalization, State planning, and defence of "democracy" (for which read, association with the United States) was the essence of the struggle for socialism. In India, the pursuit of these aims plus economic development, provided there was no foreign intervention, would gradually bring the promised land. For most people, the foreign association—the Soviet Union or the United States—was all that remained of the great historic debate between Revolution and Reform. In practice, wherever the Social Democrats were strong—as in Europe—they remained politically where Lenin had so bitterly attacked them in 1914— wedded to the worship of the State and bureaucracy, to nationalism and modest reformism. Only now, those who claimed to follow

Lenin, the Communists, had crossed over to the politics, if not the organizational loyalty, of the Socialist International.

Perhaps no-one would have noticed or cared provided India's gross national product had reached a growth rate sufficient to make unemployment only a temporary problem. If the television aerials were already sprouting above the shanty towns, there would seem to many to be a future. If capitalism had still possessed the potential to develop the world, the Left might have remained either voices in their own wilderness—swallows without a summer—or charlatans, playing a Left tune but dancing a Right jig. The crisis of development, slowly growing more severe through the sixties, made that impossible. Even the verbal militancy of charlatans is liable to spark off revolt in deteriorating conditions. The unemployment level, the tangible poverty now without hope, the realization that after 25 years of sustained application there was still little prospect of serious economic change for the majority, all this cut away the optimistic perspective upon which gradualist parliamentary politics was founded. The Left was tested in a way that made evasion much more difficult.

The small craft of the Communist Party of India, never very strong, broke up on this unyielding rock. The Right unequivocally accepted—as the German Social Democrats had done in the more trying circumstances of 1914—that their future lay with the established ruling class, whatever criticisms they might carefully treasure. The Left, with no such clarity, swung from left to right and back again, dropping off small groups on each side, some to return with relief to the safe harbour of the Right Communists, some to strike out to revolutionary politics and guerrilla warfare.

Yet, was guerrilla warfare such a dramatic revolutionary break with the past? At times, to take off with a gun in hand seemed almost a way of evading the hard task of formulating a revolutionary strategy. It is a second argument of this volume that the two alternative strategies that have dominated the Indian Left most recently—Left parliamentary politics and guerrilla warfare—are two sides of the same coin.[2] Furthermore, both are now clearly exhausted: they cannot achieve the aims laid down for each. Both have been and are appallingly destructive of the Left and the cause of socialism in India. The development crisis is half the

[2] See Chapters 1, 2 and 11.

explanation for the crisis of the Left; the politics of the Left itself is the other half.

The origins of the politics of the Indian Left have not been examined here. To write that history would require us to examine what happened to the Russian revolution of 1917. For it is in the evolution of the Soviet regime that we see how State domination was substituted for working class power, Russian nationalism for proletarian internationalism, nation for class.[3] It was a transformation that destroyed physically much of the leadership of the Bolshevik Party. It was only made possible by the destruction wrought in Russia in the civil war, the aftermath of the First World War, the decimation of the Russian working class by war and famine, and the failure of the German revolution to bring relief to the beleagured garrison. Without a working class basis, the bureaucracy of the new Soviet State could pursue whatever policies appeared pragmatically to be in its own interests.

What interests were those? Despite a victorious working class revolution, Russia remained economically backward. It was isolated from the resources of economically developed western Europe by the defeat of the European socialist revolution. The new Soviet Republic survived under the constant threat of imperialist attack. The future of the Russian bureaucracy depended upon the future power of the Soviet Union, upon its military capability to repulse invasion. Military capacity is a function of industrial capacity. Industry can be built only by massive and sustained investment which, in conditions of economic backwardness, means forced savings, freezing—or even lowering—the level of consumption of the mass of the population. In Marxist terms, it means extracting as much surplus value from the workers as is possible in order to accumulate capital. To undertake such a process, the bureaucracy had to be entirely beyond the control of the masses who were squeezed, otherwise they would never agree to such a process. The bureaucracy had to assume a privileged position in relationship to the means of production. Industry might formally be "owned" by everyone, but it was controlled by the functionaries of the State with absolute strictness, not to say ruthlessness.

[3] The evolution of Marxism in Russia and Asia is examined in Chapter 9.

It was the specific role of Josef Stalin to eliminate the remnants of working class power, purge the Communist Party of those who remained wedded to the original conception of a working class revolution, and out of his bureaucratic clique fashion the nucleus of a new State capitalist ruling class. Once entrenched, the Soviet regime behaved like every other ruling class. It defended the privileges it had stolen from the workers; it used its monopoly of the means of mass education and propaganda to justify its rule to its own and other working classes and divert the threat of proletarian revolution.[4]

In that social process rather than in any intellectual revision lay the kernel of the degeneration of Marxism in the world Communist movement. Henceforth what Communist Parties strove to achieve was not working class power but State capitalism, a society where the working class—as a class, rather than as a few selected individuals—was consistently excluded from all organs of effective power. "Proletarian" was a word strictly for the propaganda agencies only. In practice, the "leadership of the working class" need include no actual workers at all, need have no organic links with working people nor involve them in the actual struggle for power. In eastern Europe, the agency of "revolution" was the Soviet Red Army mopping up the German occupation. In China, it was the People's Liberation Army, the instrument apparently of a "Four Class Bloc," not the Chinese working class. In practice also, the "internationalists" could be as nationalist as they liked, squabbling like any other set of petty principalities over some unimportant strip of territory. No international working class pulled each national ruling class into an international solidarity.

The results of the change in the politics of Moscow were rapidly apparent. The terrible defeat inflicted on the Chinese Communist Party in 1927,[5] the even more shattering defeat of the German Communist Party in Hitler's rise to power,[6] the destruction of the

[4] This is the argument developed at some length and in considerable detail in Tony Cliff's *Russia, A Marxist Analysis*, revised edition, London, 1964.

[5] For much the best account of this, see Harold Isaacs, *The Tragedy of the Chinese Revolution*, Stanford, 1938, revised editions 1951 and 1961.

[6] For Trotsky's brilliant contemporary account, see "Fascism, Stalinism, and the United Front, 1930-34" in *International Socialism*, 38/39, special double issue, August-September 1969.

Spanish revolution,[7] the failure to prevent the Second World War, and, when declared, the failure to transform it into the European socialist revolution, these were the triumphs of the Stalinist Comintern and its satraps. The whole line of development of modern history was reshaped by the degeneration of the Russian revolution.

The change in Communist politics did not mean that real alternatives were able to flourish. The great decaying monoliths of Stalinism and Social Democracy continued to cast long shadows across the working class movement until long after the Second World War. The terms of reference laid down by Moscow predetermined the limits within which radical socialists viewed the world until the 1960s and the creation of a New Left. All opposition outside the two major organizations was forced into being sects. On those rare occasions when a Communist Party did champion a popular revolt—in China, in Viet Nam, in Yugoslavia—it was only by rejecting the tutelage of Moscow, by openly courting Stalin's displeasure.

There had been a Marxist critique of Stalin's politics, provided by the Left Opposition of the Russian Communist Party. Yet despite the brilliance of their account,[8] and of the alternative they offered, despite the fact that their politics and the revolutionary cause of the working class—as opposed to the interests of the Soviet bureaucracy—were clearly fused, the Trotskyists remained impotent. They were unable to break through to serious influence in the working class movement. In the Soviet Union, they were hounded to death and concentration camps. Trotsky himself was murdered in his Mexican exile by the Russian secret police. In the countries where the working class was a majority, the hold of the Communists and the Social Democrats remained unshaken through all the disasters. Only in the sixties did this hold begin to weaken.

Yet Trotsky's appraisal of Stalin's policies—of "socialism in one country," of shifting reliance away from the working class,

[7] For the role of the Communist Party in Spain, see Felix Morrow's *Revolution and Counter-Revolution in Spain*, 1938, London, 1963.

[8] See Trotsky's writings from 1928, in particular *The Revolution Betrayed*, 1936; *Problems of the Chinese Revolution*, New York, 1932, paperback, University of Michigan, 1967, and *Permanent Revolution*, New York, 1931, London, 1962.

of the Popular Front, of collectivization, of the Comintern's China policy—remains the starting point for any serious account of what went wrong. It is a critique grounded in the development of the Soviet Union, not the accident of one man's opinions— whether this be Khrushchev's account of Stalin's "mistakes" or Mao's account of Khrushchev's "mistakes."

At the heart of Trotsky's account is the elementary Marxist argument that socialism, freedom for the whole of society rather than a small minority of the ruling class, is only possible after the basic material problems of society have been overcome. That is why socialism is possible for the first time only after the vast expansion of the means of production under capitalism. Socialism depends not upon some simple form of organization or personal morality but upon developed industry and a high productivity of labour. In an economically backward country, the working class may well be able to come to power more easily than in an economically advanced country—as happened in Russia. But the achievement of socialism is very much more difficult. Indeed, in such circumstances, a real advance to socialism can only be achieved by uniting the backward country to the resources of an advanced one—so making it unnecessary to squeeze the people of the backward country for the resources for capital accumulation. Such points were considered truisms to the Bolsheviks before the rise of Stalin to power. As Lenin put it: "We are far from having completed even the transitional period from capitalism to socialism. We have never cherished the illusion that we could finish it without the aid of the international proletariat. . . .The final victory of socialism in a single country is, of course, impossible."[9] Without the spreading of the revolution, without significant revolutions outside Russia in an advanced country, sooner or later the Russian revolution had to degenerate.

However, Trotsky was wrong in his assessment of how the degeneration would come about. He described the Soviet Union as a transitional society, torn between the restoration of working class power and a capitalist counter-revolution. There was no ruling class, only an isolated bureaucratic "caste" which had usurped the position of the working class. The bureaucracy was torn between the desire of some of its sections to restore capitalism

---

[9] V.I. Lenin in *Collected Works*, 26, Moscow, 1965, p. 465.

and the threat of the workers. He allowed—late in life—that the Second World War would settle the issue. The strains of mobilizing Russia and waging war would force a settlement one way or the other. In fact, the dilemma was not resolved. The Soviet bureaucracy emerged in 1945 stronger than it had been in 1939. The workers had not overturned the bureaucracy, nor had there been a restoration of the private ownership of the means of production.

The end of the Second World War brought other remarkable lessons. For it became clear that a workers' revolution was not required to achieve the sort of regime established in the Soviet Union. Much later, in Cuba, it was demonstrated that a revolution producing a Soviet-style regime could take place even without the participation of the Communist Party, let alone Cuban workers. The inherited traditions no longer permitted the analysis of such anomalies without retreat into logic-chopping, terminological quibbles and obscure confidence tricks.

Plainly, there had to be—at least in economically backward countries—some alternative other than either a workers' State or a bourgeois one. The social basis of this third alternative and its political orientation is explored later in this book and, in particular, how Communist Parties became the instruments for the State capitalist revolution.[10]

Some socialists have argued that, regardless of who it was who led the Chinese revolution—their social class—or how the revolution was achieved, it was so clearly a vast improvement over the preceding regime that it must be given complete support. China today, it is said, is "progressive." The argument appears on the surface to be so plausible that it is scarcely worth challenging.

Yet it conceals some important questions. Clearly, the mass of the Chinese people are now far better off than they were under the Kuomintang. But this could never be the simple basis for offering uncritical support. If it were so, presumably the Left should support modern capitalism in Europe or the United States because conditions for the mass of the population are so much superior to what they were in the past or what they are throughout much of the rest of the world. Again, what does "support" mean? Presumably, in any clash between world imperialism and China, we should

[10] See Chapters 8 and 11.

give unconditional support to the Chinese regime, as we should to any poor and oppressed country in a similar situation. But should we support the Chinese regime in its struggle to subordinate its own working class and peasantry? This possibility becomes a real one if we begin by saying it is of no importance what the social basis of the revolutionary party is.

However, the initial argument is not really about such simple matters. It is one which is derived from the history of Stalinism and the necessity of reconciling the contradictory interests of Soviet foreign policy and workers' revolution. For, to be "progressive" was quite simply to be aligned with the Soviet Union, itself supposedly the most progressive force in world history. Followers of China wish to make the same simple alignment with Chinese policy the criterion of "progressive." Of all the available world alternatives, is the present Chinese regime the one closest to historical progress, to the achievement of socialism? At this point it is clear the argument is absurd. For, China is extremely poor; in the fifties, it was far poorer than Russia in 1913, and its rate of development has been far slower than was that of the Soviet Union. Despite a more egalitarian distribution of consumption than most countries, the scale of its material resources relative to the now vastly enlarged tasks of industrialization are desperately small. Indeed, it is the poverty of China which makes impossible a Stalinist-style economic development programme; to extract such a high rate of surplus from the population would almost certainly produce a revolt. In the years since the revolution, China has shown no dramatically greater ability to industrialize than India. The generalization that economic development is denied the backward countries applies to China as well.[11]

If economic development is not possible for China, then the same kind of crisis faces the leadership of China as that facing India. What is more, there can be no talk of socialism. For the basic material problems which force the formation of a national division of labour, of a ruling class to administer the scarcity, remain whatever the regime does—unless there are revolutions in those countries controlling the world's resources. Mao may encourage people to be unselfish, but it was never the essence of

[11] For an early Marxist account of China's potential development, see Ygael Gluckstein's *Mao's China*, London, 1957; see also Chapters 5 and 10 here.

Marx's case that capitalism depended upon selfishness. Indeed, the strength of his analysis turns precisely upon the existence of a structure to society which will determine how it works regardless of personal characteristics—the structure determines personal attitudes rather than the reverse. It is entirely utopian—and philosophically idealist—to believe that mere personal unselfishness can somehow allow poverty to be evaded, that ideas can act independently of material reality. The critique of this central element in Mao Tse-tung thought is the concern of much of Chapter 9.

The degeneration of Marxism makes it possible for all manner of idealist, populist and anarchist politics to be counted as "Marxism-Leninism" today. For most socialists, there seem to be no clear criteria left for discriminating true and false. Any army general with a strong line in radical rhetoric can pass for a "progressive"; he needs neither a working class nor a revolutionary party to validate his claims, provided he swears at the United States and strengthens his State. Any terrorist can claim also to be the vanguard of socialism, even when he is fighting the army general. All the stormy debates on these issues between Marx and Bakunin, between Lenin and the Narodniks, are as nothing: the tradition has apparently become so dilute that it can offer nothing of substance to guide us.

In breaking away from Moscow and the parliamentary road, the habits of intellectual subordination to a mythical land abroad proved too strong for sections of the Indian Left. The majority of revolutionaries exchanged Moscow for Peking. Just as an earlier generation had systematically deluded themselves about the real nature of the Soviet Union, so now a new generation must invent a land of heroes and saints called China. For those who refused both Moscow and Peking however, too many chose instead Indian nationalism; they still found it necessary to cling to one or another State bureaucracy, rather than rethinking the class basis of their politics.

The Maoists replace the real China with a myth, the propaganda froth of Peking. They do no less with other societies. For example, the Maoists explain the clash between Russia and China as the result of the degeneration of the Soviet regime following Khrushchev's assumption of power. Somehow, unnoticed by the Chinese Government of the time, an entire counter-revolution took place in the Soviet Union when a particular clique attained power in the

Kremlin, producing a "social fascist" regime at home that pursued "social imperialism" abroad. That this fantasy can be accepted as an explanation of changes in Russian foreign policy demonstrates most vividly the enfeeblement of what passes for Marxist analysis. The temporary needs of Chinese foreign policy have come to determine entirely the analysis of Soviet society. In fact, of course, the terms no longer carry any scientific content. They are merely slang, government swearing. Other examples occur later in this book.

Given this level of analysis, it is hardly to be wondered that the picture of China itself is so like a fairy tale, so unlike any society of real men and women could be. For, despite the propagandists of Washington and Peking, China is a real country, not a myth, and the Chinese people are real people, not very different to the people who live in India. It is not a valid procedure to judge the two countries by matching Peking's rhetoric against Delhi's known reality, the slogans of the one against the known statistics and evils of the other. India does not look so bad if you consider only the propaganda of the Government of India. On the other hand, the real triumphs of the Chinese people are lost in the attempt to make it into an answer to everyone's dreams. The problems of China—like those of India—are the responsibility of all socialists; they are not at all the subject for complacency, self-congratulation and mere praise.

The differences between India and China are, in some respects, well-known.[12] In particular, the gross ostentatious consumption of the Indian upper classes in comparison to their Chinese equivalents is constantly noted, as also is the occurrence of scandalous poverty in India but only an egalitarian austerity in China. People sleep and die on Calcutta pavements, but not on Canton sidewalks. Many people on the Left regard these differences as the demonstration of a profound cleavage—between a modified capitalism in India and socialism in China; between a country at best a victim, at worst an open collaborator, of imperialism, and one which is the main bulwark against world domination; between one with a prospect of hopeless stagnation, and another with a perspective of great hope.

---

[12] See Chapter 8 for some discussion of the differences in the struggle to achieve national independence.

The truth is more complicated. For there are also striking similarities between India and China. Both are overwhelmingly dominated by a very poor rural population. Rural activities would "normally" provide the basic source for the surplus out of which would come capital accumulation—the type and pace of industrialization. The debate over the size and form of the rural surplus would then be the key to development. Yet both countries are so poor and so dominated by the political power of those who rule the countryside, rule the provinces (and resist relinquishing the surplus), that both national governments rely on urban activities to fuel development. Since the urban sector is so small, the costs of the government's "non-development" expenditure (including defence) so high any development is relatively small—and tending to decline.[13]

Both countries have been pushed by poverty and the balance of power at home and imperialism abroad into rejecting any conception of a rapid Stalinist development strategy. In its place, both have enshrined a Bukharinist perspective:[14] development shall take place at the speed determined by the slowest moving element in the national economy, peasant consumption. In fact, this shift was not so much a choice, as both regimes like to pretend, but rather was forced by urgent necessity. The transition from the second to the third five-year plans symbolized the beginning of the shift away from ambitious development aims. Today, that process has culminated in the virtual abandonment of national planning itself. Planning now covers only defence and large-scale national heavy industry. Of course, both Mao Tse-tung and Mrs Gandhi rationalize the sluggish pace as something they have chosen in preference to faster growth—equality, self-reliance, decentralization, these are of more value, they say, than mere growth. The necessities that shape Indian policy and guide the Chinese Government are not identical, but sufficiently similar to

[13] See Chapters 1, 5 and 10.
[14] On the application of Bukharin's case to China, see Tony Cliff's "Crisis in China", *International Socialism*, 29, summer 1967; on Bukharin's arguments, see A. Erlich, *The Soviet Industrialization Debate, 1924-1928*, Cambridge, Mass., 1960, and M. Lewin, *Russian Peasants and Soviet Power, A Study of Collectivization*, London, 1968; on the counter-case, see E. Preobrazhensky, *The New Economics*, Moscow, 1926, Oxford, 1965.

make the rationalizations, the cited "virtues" sound as though they have the same origin.

For a long time in China, and more recently in India, the preservation of national independence against foreign threats and of the regime against domestic revolt has been of more concern than development. Where the pace and character of development are sluggish, unemployment is a key index of the failure of the regime. Bayonets are needed to hold back the unemployed. In both Shanghai in 1967[15] and Calcutta in 1969,[16] the despair of many young people at the hopeless economic perspective set off events which brought into collision with the regime both workers and peasants. Events in Prague and in Paris in 1968 showed that the problems may be more extreme in economically backward countries, but they are not restricted to those countries.

Both regimes are currently more concerned with simply hanging on than with any dramatic attempts to force the pace of economic development. Hanging on in such conditions means allowing matters to deteriorate—allowing the rich peasants in India and the commune party cadres in China, the state governments and the provincial parties, to grow more powerful and entrenched in comparison to the national government; allowing a still smaller share of the national surplus to accrue to the centre; allowing a higher level of unemployment, and so necessitating a higher level of expenditure on army and police.

All kinds of radical and important changes can and must be made in India, and can only be achieved by a working class revolution. In China, the establishment of working class power is a precondition for a real mobilization of resources both to protect the country—by appealing to the Russian and American working classes—and further to advance popular welfare. But the keys to economic development, as opposed to important reforms, do not lie in the hands of either Indians or Chinese. They are held by a world system, more powerful and less yielding than at any time in its history. The resources which should be put to work to develop India and China have been carried off to Europe and the United States where, with the proceeds of the massive exploitation of their own working classes, the final results

---

[15] For an account of this, see Chapter 4, section VI.
[16] See Chapter 1.

of capitalism can be seen. The world is one place and capitalism is one system that dominates it. There cannot exist within it enclaves of an alternative power except as a temporary anomaly. Either the anomaly spreads until it provides the basis of the world economy, or it will be defeated, resubordinated to the overall system. Wherever the world socialist revolution begins, in whatever country, backward or advanced, private or State capitalist, it cannot rest alone without ensuring its own defeat. One national revolution is not the end of the struggle of revolutionaries, but the beginning. Unless the revolution spreads, the world system will sooner or later reclaim the part it has lost. Of course, when the part is reincorporated, the men who govern that country will not announce it; they will continue to use the quasi-revolutionary language of before, now however to conceal their reconciliation to the *status quo*. For too long simple nationalism has been accepted by socialists as socialism. Today, any nationalism is lost without a complementary internationalism.

The themes of this book are not at all original. They encompass the theoretical work of a British revolutionary organization, the International Socialists—expressed in various books and through the medium of the journal, *International Socialism*[17]— which is in its turn based upon the work of Trotsky and Lenin, on Marx and Engels. IS began with the slogan: "Neither Washington Nor Moscow, but International Socialism," and now perhaps it should add "Nor Peking." It argued that the heart of any struggle for international socialism must be the reunification of the socialists and the working class movements, of the political ideas and the day-to-day demands of working people. By "working class," IS actually meant men and women who work in factories, mines, docks and so on, not professional organizers of the Communist Party, nor peasants, nor professional soldiers, nor students. Some of its best theoretical work was in the area of analyzing the immediate industrial or other worker

[17] Now a monthly journal, IS began in 1960 (its current editorial address is: 8 Cotton Gardens, London E2 8DN). Its political positions have been expressed—apart from the journal—in *World Crisis, Essays in Revolutionary Socialism,* (edited by Nigel Harris and John Palmer), London, 1971, the weekly publication *Socialist Worker,* as well as in other citations here.

struggles, their relationship to socialist demands and perspectives.[18] However, even the best theoretical word cannot master the world without systematic aligned practice, a practice which then disciplines and guides theoretical work. Beginning in 1950, IS, particularly in the sixties, has put down roots among British industrial militants. It is now already in a position to contest with the Communist Party for leadership of the most militant section of the working class;[19] its weekly paper, *Socialist Worker*, has now the largest circulation of any Left-wing paper in Britain.

However, there is still very far to go towards the creation of a revolutionary socialist party. But for the first time for many decades, there is a serious chance that the task can be accomplished. The stability which world capitalism purchased by sustained high and continuous arms expenditure in the years of the Cold War is coming to an end.[20] The problems which so severely afflicted the backward countries through the sixties are only the harbingers of the crises to afflict the advanced countries in the later seventies and eighties. After the long secular growth phase which refashioned the political assumptions of the advanced capitalist world, issues which in the fifties seemed to have been long buried are now reappearing. Issues of colour, of sexual discrimination, of generational conflict, of family or personal morality are once

[18] For example, see T. Cliff and C. Barker (with an introduction by Reg Birch), *Incomes Policy, Legislation and Shop Stewards*, London, 1966; Tony Cliff, *The Employers' Offensive, Productivity Deals and How to Fight Them*, London, 1970; Chris Harman and Dave Peers, *Unemployment and How to Fight It*, London, 1971; Paul Foot, *How to Fight the Tories*, London, 1970; *Education, Capitalism and the Student Revolt*, Chris Harman and others, London, 1968; Paul Foot, *The Postal Workers and the Tory Offensive*, London, 1971; Mike Caffoor, *The Fight Against Racialism*, London, 1971; Hugh Kerr and John Phillips, *Tory Rent Robbery and How to Fight It*, London, 1972; etc. *IS* members are also involved with others in the production of a dozen or so rank and file newspapers for particular industries (e.g. *The Car Worker, The Collier, The Docker*, etc.

[19] For a general review of IS perspectives, with those of other political organizations, see my contribution "Britain: Prospects for the Seventies" in Ralph Miliband and John Saville (editors), *The Socialist Register 1970*, London, 1970, p. 179.

[20] These themes are explored both in the journal, *International Socialism*, and in Michael Kidron's *Western Capitalism Since the War*, London, 1970.

more becoming issues of immediate concern which cannot be pushed on one side. The violence intrinsic to capitalist society is once again being reflected in the violence of those who oppose it. Advanced society is coming more and more to look as it did before the First World War. Edwardian fashions, the decadence of *fin de siècle* terrorism, are not the sole signs of this "reversion to normal." And at the heart of this spreading cultural, moral and political ferment is the struggle of working people to control their own lives, to establish their control of society in the interests of all.

This time however, neither Social Democracy nor Stalinism provide that automatic obstacle to revolution which they once did. Certainly, in France in May 1968, the Communist Party bent all its efforts to preserving the Gaullist regime.[21] Certainly in Chile in 1973, it is the Communist Party that provides the strongest fetter on the radicalism of the Allende government. But even at the moment of apparent maximum strength, the decay can be seen. In France itself, new revolutionary groups occupy much of the new Left, and the Communist Party's decline is embodied in its aging membership. Every parliamentary success for the Communist Party drives another nail into the coffin of its claims to be the voice of revolution.[22]

This volume contains a selection of essays already published in Britain. It is written primarily for Marxists; that is, it does not seek to prove Marxist assumptions, but takes them for granted. The Indian Left is now undergoing a crisis of conscience, the fruit of its disastrous experience over the recent past. It is very important that socialists begin to re-examine radically the things they have so far taken for granted, the inheritance of the past. For that inheritance is mainly from Stalinism, and it has for too long been a system

[21] See Tony Cliff and Ian Birchall, *France: the Struggle Goes On*, London, 1968.

[22] As does every worker revolt in Eastern Europe—East Berlin 1953; Poznan, 1956; Budapest, 1957; Prague, 1968; Gdansk and Gdynia, 1970. For a superb Marxist analysis of the Polish State capitalist regime from the inside, see *A Revolutionary Socialist Manifesto (written in a Polish prison)* by Jacek Kuron and Karol Modzelewski, London, 1970; and on China, see the manifesto of Sheng-wu-lien (Hunan Provincial Proletarian Revolutionary Great Alliance Committee), extracts of which are republished in *International Socialism* 37, June-July 1969.

of false consciousness, inhibiting revolutionaries from under-standing and analyzing their own societies and the world system. Between the mindless militancy of simple activists and the parlour speculation of mere "theorists," there has seemed to be a gulf that rendered Marxism as a creative method impossible. Instead of the living tradition, we have had ritual, dogma, termino-logical hair-splitting, all designed to preserve the reputation of a foreign ruling class rather than promote the development of the only class which can liberate the world. The rationalization of past practice rather than the orientation of future action assumed primary importance—excuses rather than aims.

The restoration and reunification of theory and practice, of socialists and workers, is the vital task for the Indian Left in the coming years. This book is offered in the hope that it might assist a clarification of perspectives and the re-establishment of inter-national socialism—and thereby the struggle for the Indian revolu-tion.

London   NIGEL HARRIS
4 January 1973

Contents

Contents

PART ONE

India and the Crisis
in South Asia

1

India : Capitalism and Revolution

The people who live in the Indian subcontinent are about a quarter of the people of the backward countries. With the population of China and south-east Asia, this region constitutes the heart of the problem of backwardness. If the income per head in Asia could be raised steadily, then the world system could be shown not at all to have exhausted its potential. If capital accumulation could be seriously advanced here, if some perceptible development could begin (and by "development" we mean, not just increasing the stock of machines or the proportion of income generated in industry, but a clear and continuing shift of the labour force out of agriculture into industry) then perhaps world capitalism could look forward to another lease of life. The decisive confrontation could be postponed until the millions of Asia had been properly incorporated as proletarians.

Discovering why this perspective is unrealistic from the Indian end requires us to understand in some detail what has happened to the attempt by the new ruling class of independent India to raise the rate of capital accumulation. The attempt has foundered not simply on the immediate demands of predatory imperialist powers, but rather on a much less specific range of obstacles, all arising from the purposeless and sporadic development of the world market. The enormous potential of the world economy

This chapter was first published in *International Socialism*, 52, July-September 1972, and 53, October-November 1972.

cannot, in present circumstances, be fused to the demands of Indian development. The imperialist impoverishment of the past hangs over the present, making it—in conjunction with domestic circumstances—virtually impossible to develop.

The Indian ruling class set out in 1947 with high hopes of establishing an economically independent and expansive segment of world capitalism. Now India's rulers are being driven, step by painful step, to relinquish any such ambition. Each move they attempt to make, despite temporary successes, sooner or later comes face to face with either the intractable class stalemate at home or the intractable division of the world abroad. They are reduced to hanging on as the best that can be hoped for. To survive at all in such unpromising circumstances becomes a victory. Increasing military and police expenditure is the one area that really shows expansion.

Yet social paralysis and economic stalemate can continue for surprisingly long periods of time, particularly where one section of the ruling class feels that to settle with the other section will seriously jeopardize the entire social order. Despite an expanding labour force and increasing unemployment, despite increasing misery and hostility on the land, despite a rate of increase in the organic composition of capital that makes mockery of the sea of poverty in the country, despite a whole range of problems that seem insupportable, the existing order nevertheless survives. Indeed, some people regard the existing political order as stronger than it has ever been. For is it not correct that, after a debilitating economic crisis (the worst in the experience of India's rulers) and the virtual disintegration of the ruling Congress, Delhi has been able to undertake a war in East Bengal with resounding success and Mrs Gandhi has been able to annihilate her political rivals at the polls? Almost, it seems, both the main foreign and the main domestic challenges have been decisively beaten.

The appearance is only part of the surface phenomena. Underneath, things look very different. Indeed, the Indian ruling class is no exception in this respect. For the paradox—increasing weakness with an appearance of rising strength—only parallels the position of more powerful capitalist (private or State) countries. The similarities do not end there, since all the obsessions of the advanced capitalist countries afflict India. Within India, the decisive relationships of the world system are reproduced—the patterns of domination and exploitation, of technology and output. In certain respects, indeed, India is in advance. Being one of the weaker segments of the world system, the reaction of the Indian ruling class to crisis, to a weakening of its world position, forces it to innovate in ways less developed in more developed countries. The combination of truncheon and Left-wing rhetoric, edict and populism, as a mode of political control is well advanced in India, Ceylon, Pakistan and Bangladesh. The singularly vital role of the Communist Party in adding a "progressive" gloss to increasingly authoritarian rule also provides lessons for dominant powers.

I. The development of the Indian economy

The 1971-72 Annual Report of the Ministry of Industrial Development makes gloomy reading. It shows that the growth rate of Indian industrial production declined from 7.1 per cent in 1969, 4.8 per cent in 1970 to 2.2 per cent in the first nine months of 1971. After the severe recession of 1965-68, it had been generally assumed that the economy was climbing rapidly out of the trough. But now it is clear that expansion was temporary: the problem is much more deep rooted than just the result of the poor harvests of 1965-67. Even the 1969 performance was poor; the Indian economy ought without much difficulty to be achieving a rate of industrial growth of 10-15 per cent each year.

The government claims that the current decline is the result of shortages of vital industrial inputs arising out of the limited capacity in a number of key industries (steel, non-ferrous metals, tractors, cement, paper, fertilizers). Yet all the evidence points to a problem of *excess* capacity in most key industries. The Indian economy has consistently been plagued with the problem of the underutilization of capacity, and at the moment some two out of every five industrial enterprises are producing less than 60 per cent of what they could. The steel shortage—coinciding with a gross underutilization of the existing steel capacity in the public sector —has now been offset by the import of some two million tonnes, yet this has still not produced a dramatic upturn in the engineering industries. In any case, the greatest decline in output has been in industries that are not vitally dependent upon the key inputs listed by the government—leather and fur products (a negative growth rate, minus 15.2 per cent), transport equipment (minus 11.9 per cent), cotton textiles (minus 7.9 per cent). If anything, the metal industries (plus 10.3 per cent) have tended to pull the index of production up.

The government's argument is designed to show that the problems are temporary and will soon be eased. The official explanation of the downturn does not mention what appears to be the real source of difficulty. To understand that we need to explain what caused the earlier period of industrial expansion, roughly speaking through the second (1956-61) and third (1961-66) five-year plans. The second plan injected a massive dose of investment into the economy in a short space of time in order to build as rapidly as possible a capital goods industry. This investment pushed the whole modern sector of the economy forward. The limits of growth were set by the balance of payments on the one hand and the course of harvests on the other. The push was sufficient to raise general industrial output a great deal and industrial employment a little, but certainly not sufficient to establish "self-sustaining growth" (whatever that is) nor relieve the two main constraints.

In the sixties, defence expenditure—following the border clash with China in 1962 and the war with Pakistan in 1965—increased very rapidly (in money terms, by some 41 per cent per annum from 1961-62 to 1970-71). This, along with the failure of two harvests in the mid-sixties, forced a major cutback in public investment. The economy was pushed into slump. Neither the 1969 revival nor much improved harvests have been able to compensate for the continued slack in public investment.

The downturn forced the government to scrap the pretence, if not the rhetoric, of national planning. There was a "plan holiday" for three years before the fourth plan (1969-74) began. Even with the beginning of the fourth plan, public investment did not revive in the first two years of the plan, it was some 25 per cent less than in the last year of the third plan (1965-66). In any case, the plan was increasingly remote from Indian reality. For example, "black money"—money concealed from the taxman—has grown faster than the national income for a long time and now constitutes a parallel economy. A recent government committee estimated that in 1961-62, Rs 8,110 million (very roughly £405 million) escaped the taxman; in 1965-66, Rs 12,160 million (£608 million); and in

1968-69, Rs 14,000 million (£700 million) (a dissenting note to the committee's report argues that these figures are underestimates, and the real total for 1968-69 should be Rs 28,330 million and for 1969-70, Rs 30,800 million). Whatever the facts—and the estimates can never be accurate—the rough size and rapid growth of black money makes all financial statistics in India suspect. With a volume of cash of this size outside the planners' net, national planning becomes, even more than usual, inspired guesswork.

Defence expenditure has also eaten into development resources. The declared defence budget (as opposed to all the expenditure on defence which comes under other—apparently civil—expenditure heads) has risen from Rs 2,809 million in 1960-61 to Rs 14,084 million in 1971-72. Originally, this scale of expenditure was supposed to be designed to prevent Chinese and Pakistani military threats. No one now believes that the Chinese are likely to attack India, and Pakistan has just been decisively defeated. However, there is no question now of reducing the scale of defence expenditure. It has assumed a life of its own, and indeed there is boastful talk of supporting India's new role as a Great Power in south Asia with a defence budget of Rs 20,000 million. Whatever illusions some of the military planners might have, the present size of the armed forces of India will no doubt be primarily useful in holding down Indians. If that is the task, then the size of the budget becomes explicable. To assist the new Bangladesh Government against opposition within Bangladesh (as appears to have been guaranteed in the Indo-Bangladesh Treaty and currently executed in Indian military operations against the Mizos and tribal insurgents in the Chittagong Hill Tracts) or to help Mrs Bandaranaike put down her critics certainly would not require so much military expenditure.

Other forms of "non-development" expenditure have also increasingly robbed the plan of resources. Civil non-development expenditure has been expanding by some 37 per cent per year through the sixties. But in any case, the plan appears to be increasingly marginal to government activities, more an exercise in public relations rather than economic strategy. During the fourth plan up to the spring of 1972, the government had undertaken 30 industrial projects that were not part of the plan, abandoned 12 projects that were and made little or no progress on 55 other plan projects. It is hardly surprising that plan and expenditure diverge so widely;

for example, in 1969-70 some 26 per cent of the plan allocation for central sector organized industry remained unspent at the end of the year.

The decline in planning matches the decline in public investment. The cut in government investment between the third and fourth plans had the greatest effects on the industries created and sustained by the heavy industrial programme of the second plan. The capacity of the capital goods industries was expanded in the expectation that government demand would remain high. Yet with the end of the third plan, the government postponed even replacements and modernization, let alone expansion. The declaration of a "plan holiday" in 1967 was followed by a series of bankruptcies. The cut in the demand for steel not only afflicted the steel plants, it led to the financial weakening of, for example, coking coal mines (the government nationalized them in order to prevent unemployment). Machine tools and metal products were particularly badly hit, and are still operating at 50 per cent or less capacity. Railway wagon builders had expanded capacity to some 40 thousand wagons per year in the expectation of continued growth, but the railways then cut their purchases from 26 to 10 thousand per year. Formerly the government purchased half the national cement output and a third of paper production; now it takes a third and a quarter respectively.

The decline in public investment drove down private investment and savings (the rate of capital formation as a per cent of national income dropped from 13.2 in 1965-66 to 9.6 in 1970-71. This increased urban unemployment and so cut the demand for retail goods, for example, cotton textiles, leather goods etc. Inflation further hit working class consumption, producing an all-round contraction of the urban market.

Within the cities, these various changes seem to have produced a shift of income from workers, manual and salaried, to the self-employed, professional and business strata, a shift which is probably dramatically large if we had any idea of the black money flows. One estimate suggests that the real wages of factory workers fell by seven per cent between 1965 and 1970. By contrast, the expansion in upper class incomes has produced a boom in those industries catering for upper class consumption, in particular the consumer durables industries (the output of which has increased by some 50 per cent over the past six years). But these industries—refrigerators, fans, air conditioning, household appliances—account for only about five per cent of consumer expenditure, so that their growth could hardly stimulate the whole economy. Small though the upper income market is, the tastes of the rich play an enormously powerful role in the distribution of private investment, and in the distribution of public sector output (e.g. steel for cars). Public transport in India is appalling, yet private motor-car manufacture is receiving increasingly heavy priority (apparently regardless of the impact of the spread of cars on the urban transport system and the massive investment in roads that then becomes necessary). Of late, the government has licensed what it laughingly calls the "People's Car"; it will sell for a price (about £950) which, on the official income statistics, may just come within the purchasing range of less than a million of India's 547 millions. In political terms, the prosperity of the middle and upper classes has restored their morale and been a factor in Mrs Gandhi's electoral success.

More important in the perspective for Indian development than the shift between urban classes has been the shift between industry and agriculture, between city and country. Good harvests and high government prices have moved income into the hands of the rich peasants at the expense of the urban working class paying high prices for its basic foodstuffs and of the government. Yet the increase in rich peasant incomes—like that of the urban upper classes—has not been able to stimulate the overall economy. Increased returns have too often gone into hoards, speculation and conspicuous consumption. Taking the cash out of the circulation system is in effect a forced deflation of the urban economy. To that deflation have been added the effects of the government's policy in trying to damp down inflation by radically increasing taxes (three times in 1972, supposedly to pay for the refugees) to end deficit financing.

This outflow of income to the rural areas (or at least, to certain rural areas) is only the tip of the iceberg. For the struggle against the rich peasantry is rapidly becoming the most urgent single task in making possible any further phase of rapid development in India. The analogy is not exact but the second plan in India could be seen as Delhi's attempt at the Soviet first five-year plan—but without collectivization. The fourth Indian plan is the re-establishment of Bukharinism. Whereas Stalin broke unequivocally with the Russian peasantry in the first Soviet plan period as the precondition for rapid capital accumulation, the second Indian plan was an attempt to industrialize by stealth without taking on the rural ruling classes (of course, a serious attack on the rich peasantry—including here the landlords and large landowners—would seriously have jeopardized the social order; Nehru did not have a mass Communist Party as his instrument of power). The creation of a heavy industrial structure ought to have made it unnecessary to drain resources out of agriculture into urban industry; once it matured, the public sector should have generated resources capable of bearing the brunt of capital accumulation without taking on the peasantry. Indeed, in India's industrial strategy, the public sector ought to have played the role of those State farms that, in Russia's agricultural strategy, the Left opposition saw as the means to feed the growing cities without affronting the peasants.

However, the performance of the public sector has been nothing short of catastrophic. Far from providing a regular stream of savings on the basis of which further development could take place, the massive losses made by the nationalized corporations have been a constant drain on available resources, making further development even more difficult than would otherwise be the case. At the moment, for example, the public Ranchi heavy engineering plant is said to be unable to operate at over 20-25 per cent of capacity; the Durgapur and Rourkela steel plants work at 40 per cent of capacity; cumulative losses on the public sector steel plants reached Rs 1,300 million in 1970 on an investment of Rs 10,250 million. The rate of profit on capital employed in the public sector is said to be 2.5 per cent (give or take a few statistical tricks), a return that would prompt any ordinary capitalist to move his capital into something else.

Although agriculture was never neglected to the degree some people now suggest, nevertheless it seemed to the government that in the first three plans poor agriculture was the Achilles heel of the Indian economy. That agriculture needed a massive increase in inputs was a viewpoint which accorded exactly with that of the richer peasantry. The rate of growth of industry in the first three plans was nearly three and a half times that of agriculture. Now, however, the pattern has been reversed—in the five years, up to 1972, industrial growth has been only half that in agriculture

(6.5 per cent per year). Yet the expansion of agriculture has not done what the government said it hoped for—it has not produced rapid industrial growth, only a richer stratum of peasants.

The "green revolution" in India is almost a textbook example of the paradox of capitalism—each increase in output seems only to make conditions worse. Leaving aside the social effects of the expansion in wheat output, where it has occurred, it is difficult to see how agricultural expansion could be much of a stimulus to the overall economy. The returns from agriculture are concentrated in very few hands, too few to generate a real expansion in demand. Commercial crops have not been much improved by the recent changes, so there has been no decline in the price of industrial raw materials that might assist the industrial economy. In any case, industry has in the past 20 years moved further and further away from agricultural processing industries. As in the world economy generally, the creation of synthetic and substitute raw materials has decreased industry's dependence on agriculture. The weight of chemicals and engineering in total industrial production has increased from about 20 per cent in 1951 to nearly 40 per cent in 1965. Chemical substitutes (polyester, nylon, PVC, polyethylene) are displacing cotton, jute and wood products. In certain respects this trend is disastrous for the Indian economy, for it usually means decreased employment (for example, of peasants growing cotton) and increased imports of crude oil (for the petrochemicals industry). Plastic sandals at very low prices are afflicting the leather industy. On the railways, the rapid change over to diesel trains is displacing the indigenous coal industry, again to the advantage of international oil companies.[1] The

[1]The story of the relationship between the Indian Government and the international oil companies is only one of the more extreme examples of the relationship between international capital and backward countries. In the four years up to 1970, the oil majors in India remitted to their foreign parents some Rs 550 million (£27.5 million) in profits, dividends and gross remuneration on an aggregate capital employed of Rs 1,090 million (£54.5 million). Most of this profit was earned, not on refining or prospecting, but on marketing. In any case, the companies have illegally expanded their capacity from the permitted throughput of 2.9 million to ten million tonnes per year. On the past record, cf. Michael Kidron, *Foreign Investment in India*, London, 1965; Michael Tanzer, *The Political Economy of International Oil and the Underdeveloped Countries*, London 1969, and my review, "Aid—or a Golden Fleece?", *The Guardian*, London, 16 April 1970.

dominant pattern of the world economy is imposed on the internal economy, despite all contrary efforts.

Nevertheless, the Indian Government has put an increasing volume of its resources into agriculture. In addition, the terms of trade have moved against the cities throughout the sixties. The price of finished manufactured goods, as a percentage of the price of agricultural commodities, moved from a high of 130.1 in 1963-64 to a low of 71.5 at the bottom of the agricultural recession in 1967-68. The expansion of agriculture after this last year has not at all changed the situation. High food prices—sustained by the government purchasing system—with an industrial recession have only continued the drain out of the cities. Again, it needs repeating that only the narrowest stratum of rich peasants gain from this situation; the mass of peasants with very little or no marketable surplus remain as poor as before.

The government's declared aim of developing agriculture (which is why foodgrain procurement prices were originally set so high) fits exactly the views of entrenched rich peasant groups in each State Congress Party. It follows that conflict between agriculture and industry is reflected in the conflict between the states (the provincial governments) and the Centre, a conflict we will return to later. The logic of the second plan was to impose on the territory of India a geographical division of labour—for example, heavy industry was concentrated in the area of coal and iron sources in eastern India; Bombay became the main centre of petrochemicals and light manufacturing; Andhra, Punjab and western Uttar Pradesh were major foodgrain producers. But the growth of state-level power has steadily eroded any such division now. Food surplus states do not want to be dependent for industrial goods on other states; industrial states do not want to be dependent on other states for their foodgrain supply. As a result, the food surplus states are busy developing industry, whatever the cost, and food deficit states are developing agriculture. The two most recently proposed steel mills, for example, are to be located far from the supply of coking coal (and one of them is even far from a port to which coking coal could be brought or the output shipped out), both in food surplus states and remote from the main heavy industrial zone of India. On the other hand, Maharashtra —with a poor arid soil (but the Bombay industrial region)—is attempting at very high cost to reach self-sufficiency in foodgrains, regardless of the cheaper supplies of foodstuffs available from its food surplus neighbours. West Bengal, also an industrial state, is attempting to follow suit. The growth of state-level economic autonomy moves the development path away from that course which fosters the interests of the national capitalist class, the national government and the nationalist petit bourgeoisie,[2] and in favour of the interests of the local state petit bourgeoisie (including the rich peasantry). Given that the threshold concentration of resources required to launch and sustain development is rising all the time, this fragmentation of resources makes development increasingly difficult.

What makes the problem of the collision between the rural and urban ruling classes so urgent is the growth of unemployment.[3] For there to be stability, the Indian ruling class must be able to provide a steady and increasing stream of jobs, some semblance of hope. Yet the cost of providing one new job is rising each year as the technology of industry changes in accordance with the world system as a whole—petrochemicals displaces the cotton, leather, jute industries without making up anything like the employment. At the moment, a rate of growth of industrial output of eight to ten per cent per year will not absorb much of the existing reserve army of labour; very soon, a 20 per cent rate of growth will not do. The world economy's growth rate does not compensate for the domestic deficiency. Nor, despite the fond hopes of some people, is agriculture a place where surplus humanity can be shunted and forgotten. The prosperity of the rich peasantry (as well as its aggregation of the biggest chunk of resources put into the land) is likely to stimulate the introduction of labour-saving equipment on the land in the longer term, and that will force people out of

[2]These issues were discussed in "India : A First Approximation", *International Socialism* 17 and 18, Summer and Autumn, 1964.

[3]The notion of "unemployment" is difficult to define in a country like India so that there are no reliable statistics on the number of unemployed. The Register of Employment Exchanges covers only a small proportion of those actually out of work and is biased towards urban, educated, middle class, unemployed. Nevertheless, the number on the register has increased quite rapidly—from three million in 1968 to five million in 1971: the rate of increase per year has accelerated from 10 to 25 per cent over the same period. In addition, according to the census, the proportion of the population in the labour force is falling—from 39 per cent in 1961 to 34 per cent in 1971.

agriculture rather than making for more employment. More and more the modern economy threatens to degenerate into, on the one hand, the absurdly uneconomic public sector, sustained by taxing the cities and on the other, a small booming private sector for the high income market of the rich, rural or urban—a distant replica, on a very much smaller scale, of the US, European or Japanese consumer markets.

The government's response to the failure of the industrial economy to grow has been to nationalize anything which was threatened with closure and to relax the ban on the entry of private companies into certain areas reserved for the nationalized industries. In the former case, the government has taken over recently the Bihar coal mines, Indian Copper, a number of heavy engineering companies, some 41 textile mills (it is considering acquiring another 67 "ailing" textile mills). The public sector has become enormous within the modern economy. Of the 101 largest companies operating in India, 30 are publicly owned and include the nine largest companies; the 30 companies hold 60 per cent of the assets of the 101 companies. The largest private group (Tatas, with nine of the 101, including the largest private company in India, Tata Iron and Steel) has total assets of Rs 4,860 million; the largest company of all, the government's Hindustan Steel has assets of Rs 10,270 million (Tata Iron and Steel's assets are worth Rs 1,860 million). Twenty-seven of the 101 are foreign owned with combined assets of Rs 7,600 million (23 per cent of the total).

However the concept "private" is increasingly blurred. For not only are private companies now operating in fields reserved for the government, not only are "joint ventures" spreading (in joint ventures, few of the restrictions on private companies operate, but private profits are made with government money), but also an increasing volume of public money flows into private companies, usually without any particular obligations. The government, either directly or through public financial institutions, holds some 31 per cent of the equity in the three largest private companies; if it converted all its loans to equity, it would hold 60 per cent. On average, the government holds 16 per cent of the equity of private companies, but the proportion sometimes rises as high as 50 per cent.

Despite much empty rhetoric about curbing capitalist excesses, the Indian Government is heavily involved in ensuring that private capitalism continues to be profitable. Private business has not, by way of recompense, succeeded in restoring economic growth. For the private sector depends for its survival on public investment, on the kind of expansion of demand that took place in the second plan. But where are the resources for such an expansion to come from? Increasingly, for the private capitalists, agriculture is the only source for further capital accumulation. The rich peasants have been protected from taxation, their assets expanded at the expense of urban savings and their revenues enhanced out of urban tax revenue. The capitalists, rather than the socialists, are the people with the most powerful economic—if not political—interest in squeezing the kulaks.

The government by contrast refuses to take any clear positions. At most there is a rhetorical commitment to taxing agriculture, but in practice the issue is unlikely to be pressed very far. The government is trying to rationalize the failure of Indian industry to grow. In a "keynote" speech, Mrs Gandhi argued that for far too long India had sacrificed social justice to the ruthless pursuit of economic growth. Now the "abolition of poverty" must be the first target. She did not explain how poverty is to be abolished without economic growth. A Planning Commission document in preparation for the fifth plan repeats these brave phrases, putting the fleshpots of economic growth behind it. In practice, the strategy of the plan is unlikely to be much changed—there is to be more expenditure on rural employment and social service schemes. Since the allocation set aside in the fourth plan for these purposes was not fully used, it is difficult to see all this flurry—the "New Economics" as it is grandly called—as other than a more than usually cynical propaganda exercise. India has not achieved a high economic growth which can now be refused in favour of social justice.

II. Centre and states

The conflict between the agrarian and the industrial ruling classes, between rural and urban, is partly reflected in the collision between the Centre—the Government of India—and the states. Here there is space to mention only two elements in this connection—the financial relationship between the two, and the issue of agriculture's privileged position in the national economy.

Industrialization of the backward countries has pushed many of them further and further into debt. Repaying and servicing the debt consumes a larger share of export earnings, and this in turn often threatens to stifle all further development. Formally—but only formally—the internal relationship between Delhi and the states shows the position.

In March 1951, the states had an outstanding debt of Rs 2,450 million (roughly £122 million); by the end of the last financial year, the cumulative debt had reached Rs 87,580 million (or £4,739 million). The rate of increase is of the order of 165 per cent per year. Within this debt, loans from the Central Government have increased fastest—at about 195 per cent per year. However, the burden of repayment and interest payments has grown faster—they took 52 per cent of loans in 1965-66, 86 per cent in 1969-70. Last year payments to the Centre exceeded the size of its loans to the states.

The Centre's loans to the states represent its power of bribery. Resources generated in the urban sector are, through the Central Government, transferred to the states and thereby to the rural areas. From Delhi's viewpoint, its loans are a lever to influence the states' behaviour, so that if the rate of lending is negative, that represents a decline in Delhi's power rather than the stranglehold of international lenders over some backward countries. For Delhi, there are few sanctions against defaulters, and none against the aggregate of states. The Minister of Planning, alarmed at the size of the debt, tried to ban further loans. The only result was an equally alarming increase in the states' overdrafts on their accounts with the Reserve Bank. The overdrafts make a mockery of any attempt at monetary or credit control policies by the government. The minister, nothing daunted, banned an increase in overdrafts, but he cannot possibly hold such a ban and risk the bankruptcy of a state.

For an individual state, the situation can be alarming, and prompts various state Chief Ministers to demand greater economic autonomy. The non-Congress government of Tamil Nadu constantly complains of the "reverse flow of aid" and Karunanidhi, the Chief Minister, has talked threateningly of his party, the DMK, being a Tamil Awami League and prepared to lead a similar struggle to that which took place in East Bengal. The Kerala

State Government which includes Congress, has made similar threats, demanding that the state's debts be written off and the financial neglect and strangulation of the state be ended or a new Bangladesh movement will arise to free Kerala. There are similar threats in other states, and the Communist Party of India (Marxist) has taken up the same position in West Bengal.

Yet they are only threats for the real balance of power lies ultimately with the aggregate of states. Individual states may feel—rightly—oppressed, but they are more interested in bargaining than breaking with the Centre. For they need the Centre. Each local bourgeoisie struggles to secure its unchallenged domination in each state against national forces, but also needs national forces to protect itself against the possible revolt of its own local people. The threats are attempts to squeeze more out of Delhi in competition with other states, not the first step in secession. As will be seen later in the case of West Bengal, the intervention of the Centre can be vital in protecting the local ruling order against challengers.

Where the real power of the states is most clearly seen is when they combine against the Centre, when their nearest interests are at stake. In particular, agriculture—part of the sphere of responsibility of the states—touches all most sensitively. The powerfully entrenched position of the rich peasants within each State Congress has ensured that land reform legislation has largely been ineffective, that agriculture has been kept largely untaxed and that a significant flow of resources has been diverted into rich peasant hands.

In the sixties, particular rural groups have grown strong on this rich diet. In Punjab—on the basis of the new wheat technology—annual income per head has increased from Rs 307 (1961) to Rs 854 (1970), and if that is the *average* figure, the rich farmers must have done very much better (Punjab's foodgrain output has increased from two million tons in 1950-51 to 6.5 million tons in 1969-70). Nor is this phenomenon simply the result of the new hybrid seed, for in Andhra Pradesh the larger rice growing farmers are very prosperous. It is said that tractors are now replacing bullocks even among the smaller farmers (who find it cheaper to hire a tractor for short periods than keep bullocks all the year round). Army officers and civil servants have been induced to retire into farming because it is such a lucrative way to make money and escape taxation. Congress ministers are not averse to dabbling in land speculation (contravening the land reform laws at the same time) either in their own names or that of their wives.

The prosperity of the richer farmers is purchased in part at the expense of the poorer farmers. The growers of hybrid seed have been favoured with the lion's share of irrigation water, fertilizers, pesticides and so on, all of which deprives the poorer cultivator of his share. The market is so favourable, also, that landlords and richer peasants are eager to grab as much land as they can. The violent incidents between sharecroppers or labourers and larger farmers seem to be increasing. In November 1971, for example, ten sharecroppers were shot dead, four burned alive in their huts and 35 wounded when thugs in the employment of local landlords set out to teach them a lesson; the sharecroppers were trying to prevent the landlords seizing a piece of their land. The granaries can be full while there are starving people. In 1972 there was famine among the poorest tribal people of part of Bihar State (the Paharias), but Bihar State announced it was within sight of "self-sufficiency" in foodgrains.

To lower the permitted size of land holdings (the "ceiling"), it has been argued, will make available land for large numbers of landless peasants. To introduce the stringent taxation of the rich peasant agriculture will produce a flow of resources for development without a radical restructuring of Indian society. To lower the present price at which the government buys wheat—indeed, to eliminate government wheat purchases altogether—will simultaneously save the Central budget a considerable sum and force the rich farmers to grow crops neglected in the present agricultural boom, either commercial crops or other foodstuffs vital for the national diet (e.g. pulses). But to achieve any or all of these desirable ends requires the Centre to subordinate the State Congress parties and compel them to execute Delhi's wishes.

Mrs Gandhi's victory in the last elections was seen as achieving this subordination. Before the March elections in some 16 states, the Prime Minister supposedly vetted the leaders and candidates of every State Congress, securing in each case loyalty to her programme (to lower the land ceiling) and dismissing any who seemed doubtful in loyalty. At the same time, the government's Agricultural Prices Commission (APC) produced a report (which every year seems to reach the same conclusion) arguing that the highest production cost for wheat in India is about Rs 50-55 (and the lowest Rs 38) per quintal, yet the government's purchase price is Rs 76; the APC urged that the government's procurement price be cut, depending on the type of wheat, by between four and eight rupees per quintal, scarcely a very dramatic reduction.

It was thought the combination of Mrs Gandhi's purge of Congress (and humiliation of State Congress leaders) and her election victory would ensure that the wheat price, the land ceiling and the agricultural taxation proposals would be easily achieved. Yet very little had changed in reality. The basic balance of power remained the same. Mrs Gandhi may have increased the loyalty of her party members to herself, but only on condition that she refrained from injuring the interests of their supporters. Immediately after the election, Mrs Gandhi's personally-selected Chief Minister of Punjab announced that the Punjab Congress would not be lowering the land ceiling in that state. Four days later, the Chief Ministers met in Delhi. Despite the Finance Minister's alarm that the total government wheat bill had increased recently from Rs 350 million to Rs 1,200 million, the Chief Ministers threw out the proposal for a cut in the wheat price. Indeed, the irrepressible Punjab Chief Minister argued that, since it now cost Rs 80 per quintal to produce wheat, the procurement price ought to be *raised*.* The meeting went further, for it successfully extracted a promise from the government to increase the proportion of the wheat crop it was obliged to buy and refrain from unloading government wheat on the market without consulting the states.

Only three states grow wheat in significant volume, but the others—with the exception of West Bengal, now the most loyal of the loyal—rallied round to support the threatened agrarian interest. In return, no doubt, the three wheat growers will support other states on issues close to their interests (for example, Gujarat's demand for the government to guarantee the price of raw cotton). Outside the Chief Ministers' meeting there was remarkably little dispute about the wheat price; none in the lower house of the national parliament; in the upper house, members—regardless of political party—condemned the APC recommendation. So far as the government is concerned, it looked as though it recognized the inevitability of its defeat beforehand and put up no real fight.

*This was written before the partial failure of the 1972 grain crop shifted the basis of the argument about grain prices.

Mrs Gandhi did not put her reputation to the test by attending the meeting and fighting for the APC proposals.

The balance of power revealed by this encounter means little can be expected of the proposal to lower the land ceiling or increase agricultural taxation. The government has already shunted the former proposal into a committee of enquiry as if information was the main obstacle to taxing the kulaks. In 1971 the Chief Ministers refused to accept an agricultural tax to pay for the Bengali refugees, so it is doubtful whether a committee report this year will soften their obduracy. They have a powerful ally in the Central Minister of Food and Agriculture. He has recently performed sterling service on the land ceiling issue. The ceiling to be most drastically lowered was to apply to "perennially irrigated" land and the minister kindly defined this as land irrigated for at least ten months of the year from *government* canals and wells. The rest of the land—including land irrigated from private water sources (mainly tubewells)—is accounted as "dry" and therefore subject to much more generous land ceilings. On this definition, "perennially irrigated" is rare and proportionately becoming rarer. At the moment, about 22 per cent of India's cultivated land is irrigated (though probably not for anything like ten months per year), and about half of this from government water sources. The expansion of private tubewells has been a boom industry for the past ten years, all through the years of so-called harvest failure. Government and banks have pushed the financing of private wells hard, and rich peasant profits have also assisted. Indeed, the spread of tubewells is something of an index of the prosperity of the richer peasants—at the end of the third plan, there were something like 80,000 private tubewells in the country; in the years of slump and harvest failure (1966-69), another 175,000 were built; and during the fourth plan, yet another 190,000. So the minister's definition must have caused an audible sigh of relief in rich peasant households round the country (the minister's explanation—that this was the definition standard in all the previous land reform legislation—only made matters worse).

III. West Bengal

The impact of the crisis of the sixties on the working class has been most powerful in the State of West Bengal. Of all the states, this is the one most dependent upon the national economy for its prosperity. It is also the state where the left was strongest and yet now has been most decisively defeated.

West Bengal and its immediate environs were designed to be the heavy industrial zone of India. Five major steel plants, the major part of the coal and iron ore mining industries, heavy engineering plants and a very large chemical fertilizer plant, railway wagon and repair workshops were all concentrated here. In the Calcutta Metropolitan District, a quarter of India's engineering capacity is located, much of it in heavy engineering. Vast sums have been poured into the area to sustain the growth of the capital goods industries. Between 1959 and 1965, investment in the larger factory sector (units employing 50 or more workers with power, 100 or more workers without power) increased at a compound rate of 21 per cent per year (by contrast, income increased by 12 per cent per year and employment by five per cent per year). Capital per worker has consistently been high and increasing rapidly; it increased by 147 per cent in the same time period. The other major employer in the West Bengal industrial sector is jute, an old and declining industry.

The result of this industrial mix is that what was a serious recession in India in the last half of the sixties was a slump in West Bengal, or rather in the industrial heart of West Bengal, Calcutta. It inflicted grave damage on the working class, its organization and morale.

Registered factory employment in the Calcutta Metropolitan District (CMD) fell by nearly 100 thousand between 1965 and 1969,[4] whereas it rose by nearly 16 thousand in West Bengal as a whole. Of the decline, engineering lost 29 thousand, jute 55 thousand. Even the upturn of 1969-70 scarcely affected engineering at all and at the end of 1971 still only 40-50 per cent of capacity was being used. The jute industry, strongly assisted by the war in East Bengal (the other major jute producer, then part of Pakistan),

[4]If we count "lost employment" as the difference between the actual employment in 1970 and what would have been total employment in 1970 if the trend between 1951 and 1965 had continued, then 326,000 jobs were lost; cf. A.N. Bose, *A Note on the Economic Development Programme for the CMD* (mimeo), 1972, paper for the Regional Studies Association conference, Calcutta, 1972.

did make some recovery in 1970-71, putting on 20 thousand new jobs (the rest of the CMD lost two thousand jobs at the same time). If Bangladesh's jute manufacturing industry recovers soon, however, it may mean a return to slump for West Bengal's jute industry.

In addition to unemployment, wages have not at all kept pace with price inflation, particularly the increase in food prices. The total real wage bill in West Bengal is said to have declined by 7.5 per cent between 1965 and 1968, and per capita real wages by 3.3 per cent. The large inflow of refugees in 1971 cannot at all have improved the situation since food prices must have been further inflated and wages depressed by the willingness of refugees to work for virtually any pay. There has not been much improvement. In the year ending October 1971, registered unemployment increased by 220 thousand which, on the normal ratios used, suggests a total increase in unemployment of three quarters of a million.

Worker reaction to this catastrophic economic performance has been to wage a bitter and savage struggle for survival against the attempt by employers to offload their problems on to them. The physical decay of Calcutta, now notorious as an example of neglect, only exaggerates the open class warfare that has occupied the city for the past five years. Take for example the number of workers in dispute as a percentage of all workers in registered factories; this proportion was about 14 to 15 per cent in the fifties; it rose to 18 per cent in 1966, 32 per cent in 1967 and 1968, and 85 per cent in 1969. Or take the percentage of man days lost to total man days worked; this rose from under one per cent to nearly five per cent in 1970 (both sets of figures include lockouts; nearly half the disputes involved lockouts, and the average duration of lockouts—45 days—was three times that for strikes). Or take the rate of political murders: as officially estimated (or almost certainly under-estimated), these rose from 108 in 1969 to 1,169 in 1971, the year of the Congress "clean-up" of Calcutta.

The government has devoted less and less of its attention to trying to raise the economic level of West Bengal, more and more to trying to beat opposition into the ground. Thirteen battalions of the Central Reserve Police—the Central Government's special police force—along with several thousand local police and, from time to time, army units have been required just to hold the CMD together. West Bengal's expenditure on the police has risen from Rs 160 million in 1966-67 to Rs 450 million this year. This scale of spending means little can be raised for development. Maharashtra State (the other most industrialized state) raised Rs 2,250 million for its 1972-73 development plan; West Bengal has raised Rs 750 million.

The Central Government has now begun to push in some cash to the CMD economy (during President's rule in 1971 and with the help of the abolition of Calcutta Corporation). With its simultaneous policy of massive physical repression, it is hoped the state can be restored to "normal." So far the government's policy has been successful, and indeed has been ratified by the substantial increase in its popular vote at the elections last year. Factory disputes, violent clashes on the streets, political murders, all seem to be declining. The number of *gheraos* (locking up the managers in their offices until they agree to negotiate) at the notorious trouble spot, Durgapur steel plant, has declined from 517 in 1969 to 20 in 1971.

The possibility of a revolutionary situation in Calcutta Metropolitan District depended entirely on the revolutionary political forces available. The objective conditions could hardly have been more favourable. Calcutta, with the right cast, could have played the role of Petrograd. That it is absurd to say this shows how remote the prospect was. Calcutta came nowhere near imitating Petrograd because of the available political organizations. In fact what revolutionary movement there was, crumbled against a ruling class far shrewder and tougher, far better organized and far more clearly aware of its interests than any of the Left alternatives. By comparison, the revolutionaries appeared to be only playing with words. The invasion of Bangladesh by the Indian army has made India the Great Power of south Asia. The much less publicized domestic baptism of fire took place in West Bengal.

What were the available organizations on the Left? The Indian Left is dominated by the two major fragments of the old Communist Party of India.

IV. The Communist Party of India and the Communist Party (Marxist)

In 1964, the Communist Party split. The lines of the division had existed for quite a long time. In part, the dispute was about the domestic strategy to be pursued, separating those who thought the best way forward was in alliance with the Congress Left, and those who wanted one or another of the more radical alternatives. The divide also separated the local bases of party support and its rural organization (the Left), and the party bureaucracy, members of Central and state assemblies and the trade unions (the Right). What made it impossible to hold the party together was partly the Sino-Soviet dispute, but more immediately the border clash between India and China in 1962.[5]

The smaller fragment of the split, the pro-Moscow Right under S.A. Dange, retained the party name, the Communist Party of India (CPI). The larger group which carried off the main geographical areas of CPI strength—in West Bengal, Kerala and Andhra Pradesh—called itself the Communist Party of India (Marxist) the CPM. Later on, the CPM also split, or rather crumbled on its Left wing, to produce a third Communist Party, avowedly against parliamentary politics altogether; this was the Communist Party of India (Marxist-Leninist), CPML.

The developing crisis in West Bengal—and also in Kerala—as well as the vagaries of the simple majority electoral system, brought the CPM and its allies increasingly close to a majority in the state assembly. While the CPM was a minority party, it could sustain both parliamentary politics and revolutionary rhetoric while evading the question of what was the real method of attaining power. But the strangulation of West Bengal thrust the CPM forward into the position where it could attain parliamentary power. In 1967, when the West Bengal United Front (which included both the CPM and the CPI, along with 12 allies) won 51 per cent of the vote (as against 41 per cent for the undivided Congress), the CPM could no longer evade the question of its attitude to forming the State Government. It succumbed to the temptation and led its forces for some five years into the marsh of—not

---

[5]For an account of the early phases of the split see "India: A First Approximation", *IS* 17 and 18, summer and autumn 1964; for more recent events, see the two books by Mohan Ram, *Indian Communism— Split within a Split*, Delhi, 1969, and *Maoism in India*, Delhi, 1971, both of which contain much useful information if poorly organized; the author counts himself as a supporter of rural guerrilla warfare (a sympathizer of the Andhra Naga Reddy group).

merely parliamentary representation—but pursuit or defence of State *Government* power.

The United Front government fell in late 1968, after which President's rule (that is, direct rule by the Central Government without a state assembly) lasted until new elections were held in February 1969. In that election, Congress—again with 41 per cent of the votes—secured only 55 seats, whereas the CPM with 20 per cent of the votes, won 80 seats. The ensuing CPM-led coalition governmentl asted until March 1970 when another bout of President's rule intervened until new elections in March 1971. It should be added that, in late 1969, Congress split between Mrs Gandhi's Congress (R) and Congress (O). In the 1971 elections Congress (R) won 28 per cent of the vote but secured 105 seats; the CPM with its highest voting score — 32 per cent—won 113 seats. A weak Congress-led coalition was formed and lasted until June of 1971 when President's rule was again introduced. Delhi ruled until the elections of March 1972 when Congress (R) won its highest proportion of the votes in West Bengal's history—50 per cent—and 216 seats. The CPM's vote went down to about 28 per cent (a drop of only 4 per cent on 1971) but the number of seats dropped disastrously from 113 to 14. The Right Communists, the CPI, allied with Congress (R), won 12 per cent of the vote and 35 seats, giving the governing alliance 251 seats in an assembly of 280.

The only reason for giving these figures is that, in the sometimes random variations in number of seats, much of the articulate political middle class has lived a hectic, indeed frenetic, political life over the past five years. Yet from the variation in the vote— with the exception of the effects of the 1969 Congress split on the 1970 Congress (R) vote—it is clear that although there have been changes, these have not necessarily reflected any very powerful shifts of opinion. Congress vote has remained around 40 per cent throughout; the CPM vote has climbed from around 20 per cent to 30 per cent and now seems to have fallen back a little. The seat swings give CPM followers the excitement so signally lacking in the actual behaviour of the party; it seems as if hot and bloody class war is being fought out in the polling booths.

Politically, the Right Communists, the CPI are now little more than a pressure group for the Soviet Union within the ruling Congress. CPI politics—simple, hardly even Left-wing, Social

Democracy—distinguish the party in no way from the rhetoric of Mrs Gandhi's Congress apart from its curious addiction to things Muscovite. Nevertheless, its politics and behaviour have some kind of coherent rationale. The CPM, by contrast, has failed to find for itself any clear role. What it has achieved over the past five years is the destruction of any serious revolutionary upsurge in West Bengal (or anywhere else). It has set back the possibility of a revolutionary movement a long way. Yet it has still not found any coherent kind of role—for example, pressing for "structural reform," so beloved by Left parties seeking to escape revolutionary politics.

V. The class nature of the Indian revolution

In 1967, the CPM decided (in *New Situation and the Party's Tasks*) that a political crisis was maturing which might lead even to a non-Congress coalition in Delhi. The CPM, it said, should participate in various non-Congress governments, not because participation could lead to any serious reforms, but because the party must win allies and support—"it is imperative," it said, no doubt with sceptical members in mind, "that our party realises that its immediate future in no small way depends on how it plays its worthy part in running the two State governments of Kerala and West Bengal."[6] It argued that the Central Government was the organ of the class rule of the bourgeoisie and the landlords, led by the big bourgeoisie in alliance with foreign capital. The big bourgeoisie, because of its alliance, refused to complete "the democratic anti-imperialist tasks of the Indian Revolution," one of which is the replacement of the government by a "State of People's Democracy" led by the working class (viz. the CPM).

The CPI on the other hand regards Delhi as the "organ of the class rule of the national bourgeoisie as a whole which upholds and develops capitalism." For the CPI, the national bourgeoisie and its government is basically progressive, but threatened by the monopolists and "feudal elements." All progressive forces must rally round to support the progressive national bourgeoisie—Mrs Gandhi, no less—in order to create a government of "na-

[6]For a critique of this turn see "Again, hunting with the hounds", in Chapter 2 here.

tional democracy" where power is jointly held by the working class (viz. the CPI) and the national bourgeoisie.[7]

Neither party believes that it is practicable to struggle for the socialist revolution. The disagreement between the two is over how progressive Mrs Gandhi's Congress is. The CPM argues that "the basic and fundamental task of the revolution in today's context cannot be carried out except in determined opposition to and struggle against the big bourgeoisie and its political representatives." The CPI seeks rather to "transform Parliament from an instrument serving the bourgeoisie into a genuine instrument of the people's will."

For the CPM, there is no chance of transforming parliament. Parliamentary and non-parliamentary methods of struggle must be combined to "push forward" the movement. State Governments, it argues, can do little to solve fundamental problems. For example, United Front governments should be "treated and understood as instruments of struggle in the hands of the people more than as governments that actually possess adequate power that can materially and substantially give relief to the people."

This position permits the CPM to sustain a radical rhetoric—denouncing those with illusions in parliament—with a surprisingly conservative practice. When the CPM led the State Governments of West Bengal and Kerala, it simultaneously initiated popular demonstrations against the Central Government—but feared to use its power as State Government to in fluence the national government. Elementary reforms—or even trying to achieve elementary reforms—were neglected because supposedly this would lead to reformist illusions. Yet in practice, the CPM has become completely identified with the attempt to secure parliamentary power, and having secured it, keep it whatever the political cost.

[7]The CPI leadership is not unaware that this position can prompt people to question the need for a Communist Party at all; for the members might well feel it more sensible to support the progressive national bourgeoisie by joining Congress (R) and dissolving a separate party (a problem that has persistently afflicted the Praja Socialist Party). The CPI's *Political Report and Political Resolution* (for the Ninth Congress, Cochin, October 1971), p. 113, notes "serious shortcomings" in the party and a drift into reformism and ideological dilution; it says the party has a tendency to get "too bogged down" in elections and parliamentary politics; as a result, the "demarcation between the CPI and the Congress has got blurred,"

Whatever the CPM leadership says, in practice on various occasions it has been nudged very close to the CPI. In the national parliament in late 1969 for example, when Congress split—to the delight of the CPI which was able then to identify Mrs Gandhi's Congress (R) as the progressive national bourgeoisie—the CPM was forced to decide whether or not to support Mrs Gandhi's minority government or write it off as indistinguishable from the rival Congress. In fact, it decided Congress (R) was the lesser evil and offered support. In the Presidential elections the CPM supported Mrs Gandhi's candidate, Giri. President Giri is the man who twice since the CPM gave him their support has imposed President's rule on CPM-led State Governments.

VI.   Bangladesh and the CPM

In 1971, the CPM performed the same ideological acrobatics on the issue of Bangladesh. It had decided by then that Mrs Gandhi's government was "semi-fascist" since Congress thugs were beating up and murdering CPM members, instead of just concentrating on the cadres of the Communist Party of India (Marxist-Leninist). Yet the CPM gave unconditional support to Mrs Gandhi's "semi-fascist" government in its approach to East Bengal. It argued that war was threatened (before it actually broke out) by the Pakistan military dictators against "our country" because India had helped the refugees and supported the independence struggle. "It is India's duty and right to support this freedom struggle....India must do this to safeguard her own independence and democracy [presumably a semi-fascist democracy, NH]. And if war is imposed upon us for doing this, it is war to defend freedom and democracy, a just war."

The CPM trade union federation—CITU—accordingly promised to avoid strikes, continue production without interruptions through the war, see all disputes were settled quickly through negotiation and cooperation with the government. Unilaterally, it agreed to stop all strikes currently in progress, to accept government arbitration terms even when these were not satisfactory and collect funds from the workers for National Defence and Bangladesh relief—"Workers in every factory should contribute a day's wages and get the employer to contribute an equal amount,"

Presumably Mrs Gandhi's government had become "progressive semi-fascist."[8]

The CPM leadership's line is designed—as before—to assist unity, to carry both the chauvinists and the radical opponents of Congress (R) on the Bangladesh issue. But on occasions the muddle incites opposition. The CPM tried in 1967-68 to avoid taking a position on the Chinese case in the Sino-Soviet dispute in order to hold the party together, united in their opposition to the Soviet position. A draft document (the *Madurai Document*) of mid-1968 rejected all the positions (except one) advanced by the Soviet Union but said nothing on China's arguments. As a result, the Andhra Pradesh and Kashmir units of the CPM threw the document out. Nevertheless it was accepted by the national party at its Burdwan plenum. Some 60 per cent of the Andhra CPM then walked out of the party to form an explicitly Maoist group.

Only when Peking itself directly attacked the CPM did it make any kind of reply, and even then its response was eclectic rather than coherent. It supported the Russian invasion of Czechoslovakia in 1968, warmly praised the Soviet attitude to the struggle in Bangladesh and also the Soviet position on Kashmir (a "domestic problem for the Indian Government"; the Chinese are for the right of national self-determination of the Kashmiris). These gestures did not evoke any olive branches from Moscow so the CPM has tried to establish a "middle affiliation" between Moscow and Peking. The CPM leaders now take their holidays in Roumania!

VII.   The CPM split

The ambivalence of the CPM as well as its participation in two

---

[8]Of course, in comparison to the CPI's position, the CPM is clearly proletarian internationalism! The CPI *Election Manifesto* for 1972 speaks of the "glorious victory...our country has won in the brief war thrust upon us by the military junta of Pakistan through aggression, aided and abetted by US imperialism and the Peking regime. These victories are truly the achievement of the nation as a whole, of its patriotic, secular and democratic forces....The CPI shares the thrill of our people at the magnificent victory of the liberation forces of Bangladesh and the gallant armed forces of our nation which repulsed the Pak aggressors. It shares the pride of our great people who went ahead to do their duty, despite the moving in of the US Seventh Fleet [*sic*] and the threats of the Maoists," etc, ete.

State Governments inevitably affected its more revolutionary members. What the CPM leadership called the "ultra-Left" became increasingly important through 1967 and 1968. A whole range of revolutionary groups appeared on the Left flanks of the party, and this affected not only the local standing and tactics of the CPM but also its international standing. China was happy to accord the CPM a certain benevolent neutrality (which tended to keep the CPM's Left moderately happy) while there was no alternative.

Already in early 1967, two movements, of agrarian revolt were underway—in Naxalbari (whence "Naxalite") in north Bengal and in Srikakulam, Andhra Pradesh. Indeed, the attitude of the Andhra party to the *Madurai Document* was partly conditioned by its involvement in Srikakulam, a development which seemed quite inconsistent with the CPM's aspiration to government power. In Naxalbari, it was the activity of CPM cadres, in particular Kanu Sanyal, which generated the movement.

The CPM's participation in the 1967 West Bengal State Government persuaded the Communist Party of China that the CPM was not its chosen instrument in India. On the basis of the Naxalbari movement, Peking announced that India was now objectively ripe for armed struggle; only a Communist Party was lacking. On behalf of the CPM, Basavapunniah detected the hand of the big bourgeoisie—and subsequently the ubiquitous CIA—in the Naxalbari movement, claiming its was a conspiracy to discredit the CPM. However, at that stage the CPM was still trying to temporize; it denounced police violence and intervention in Naxalbari (the minister in charge of the West Bengal police at that time was Jyoti Basu, the chief of West Bengal CPM) and called for negotiations. Subsequently, it was less discreet in its attempts to root out Naxalism by force.

Whatever successes were won in Naxalbari, they were temporary. The lessons that Kanu Sanyal drew from the failure of the north Bengal agitation (*Report on the Peasant Movement in the Terai Region*) were that it lacked a strong party organization, it failed to build a powerful mass base and was guilty of "old line thinking." None of this however moderated Peking's adulation. It praised Naxalbari to the skies and did not mention its failure, let alone discuss the reasons for this. It was anxious to attack the CPM through the Naxalbari movement; in Andhra where the

CPM was not participating in the government, the Srikakulam agitation at this stage received much less Chinese attention.

The CPM scattered on its left flank a number of groups committed to rural guerrilla warfare. Some of these came together to form a coordinating committee in West Bengal and start a journal, *Liberation* (*Deshabrati*). In November 1968 an All-India Coordinating Committee of Revolutionaries was formed (subsequently "Communist" was inserted in this unwieldy title, hence AICCCR), but it still probably included only a minority of the Maoist groups in India (it did not include one of the largest groups, the Andhra group of Naga Reddy).

The leading theoretician of the AICCCR was Charu Mazumdar, a former old-time CPM district leader from north Bengal. He argued—in contrast to the positions of the CPI and CPM—that the chief contradiction in India was between the peasantry and the "feudal order," a contradiction that could be overcome only by armed peasant struggle against the landlords. A party would be formed, he said, out of the youth of the working class, of the peasantry and "the toiling middle class," *after* the struggle had begun. The armed struggle was supposedly the first step in seizing the state, but in practice its main driving force—in so far as peasants were involved—seems to have been to seize crops and land.

VIII. The Communist Party of India (Marxist-Leninist)

In March 1969, the secret rural-based West Bengal AICCCR launched an open public rally in Calcutta to proclaim the formation of the Communist Party of India (Marxist-Leninist) (CPML). The new party not only excluded the Andhra group but a number of others, all of which were denounced by the CPML. In July the CPML received official recognition; the Peking *People's Daily* acknowledged the CPML as the only genuine Communist Party in India. The party had neither programme nor constitution. Instead of a strategy, it had a political resolution which committed its members to maintaining an organization which was secret, rural and dedicated to armed struggle. There was no provision for building mass organizations, rural or urban, and indeed, Mazumdar implied that work in mass organizations would make difficult the party's aim of remaining secret. In any case, it was suggested, mass organizations would inevitably permit the domination of rich peasants and lead to "revisionism." Only a secret organization could properly secure the leadership of the landless peasants in the movement. Mass organizations would become possible when particular rural areas had been cleared of class enemies (Peking did not contradict this argument although it was clearly quite inconsistent with Mao's tactics—open mass organizations should precede, not follow, armed rural struggle).

Secrecy, as operated by the CPML, was inevitably elitist. The party was dependent on a few reliable cadres, and that increasingly prevented the involvement of those, the peasants, who were supposed to be emancipating themselves. Secrecy is necessary in all kinds of situations, but it is tolerable in a revolutionary organization only where there are already organic links with the class the organization claims to lead. Without this, the organization isolates itself and becomes increasingly marginal to the class concerned. Originally, CPML squads of cadres—usually students from Calcutta—were to organize the peasants to act against landlords and police. But it became safer for the squads to attack the landlords themselves, without involving peasant support (quite often, the peasants were probably far too shrewd to get involved in what was clearly gangsterism, although they might be quite happy to share the rewards after the event). This is the origin of the notorious "annihilation tactic" that Charu Mazumdar unveiled as his particular contribution to the corpus of Marxism-Leninism in February 1969. Cadres must win the support of the landless peasants by systematically murdering the most hated landlords and so clearing areas of class enemies.

The police net closed in with increasing rapidity wherever the CPML cadres undertook any kind of action. The Calcutta students were usually easy to identify in the rural areas. After a phase of demoralization in the police when the United Front government dithered, the forces of the law used the inexperience of CPML cadres as a training ground for counter-insurgency which will stand them in good stead in future.

Yet the worse the situation became, the fewer lessons Mazumdar seemed prepared to learn. He argued now that guerrilla warfare could be started anywhere (not just in remote areas), mass organizations were always a hindrance in waging guerrilla warfare, and guerrilla warfare depended for success on first liquidating the "feudal classes" in an area (*Peking Review* in 1969 gave some kind of sanction of this position although carefully emphasizing at the same time the importance of mass participation). In late 1969, Mazumdar announced that the party was on the verge of forming a People's Liberation Army and beginning a civil war. By early 1971, he said, the army would begin its triumphant march across the plains of Bengal.

IX. The turn to urban terrorism

In the year up to the spring of 1970, the CPM-led government had been trying to establish an unchallengeable monopoly of political support in Calcutta. The CPM used its government power to try and eliminate Congress support—and indeed support for any other political party, including its allies in the government —first in the police and bureaucracy of the state, then among organized workers and in rural areas. The era of open violence had already begun.

It was in this situation that, in mid-1970, Mazumdar began to shift the centre of CPML activities out of the countryside into Calcutta city in order, he said, to unleash a "red terror" against the "white terror" stalking the city. To assist the campaign, the CPML recruited a motley gang of footloose thugs. Open street warfare ensued with considerable bloodshed on all sides.

In Calcutta, the CPML tried to have a mini-Cultural Revolution. It attacked educational institutions, government offices, burnt pictures and books, smashed statues. Retrospectively, Mazumdar said, the campaign constituted the students destroying the super-structure of society while the peasants attacked the base. However, very few peasants were doing any attacking outside the daydreams of the CPML leadership. In July of 1970, the Calcutta district committee of the CPML decided on the murder of class enemies in the city—policemen, military personnel, capitalists, black marketeers. In practice, this usually meant policemen, and finally policemen who were known supporters of the CPM. Peking did not criticize the new turn, it ignored the CPML completely (from October 1970 to October 1971, *Hsinhua* was silent on the vast Indian revolution which, until then, had reportedly been sweeping all before it).

Mazumdar's reversal of policy is difficult to explain. Perhaps it was a tactic of despair, after all attempts at a rural revolt had failed. Perhaps he calculated that the mass following of the CPM would respond to a sustained CPML campaign and replenish his reserves of cadres. Or perhaps the cadres, hunted continually in the rural areas, just voted with their feet and fled home to Calcutta as the only retreat safe from police search. Another argument has it that Mazumdar had in fact become a police agent or at least had entered into some kind of deal with Mrs Gandhi.

Perhaps this story is malicious slander. It was certainly in the interest of the CPM to put about such stories: the CPML and the Congress (R), it could claim, were part of one conspiracy to destroy the only real revolutionary alternative. But even in CPML circles, the "explanation" of the failure of the hallowed tactic of guerrilla warfare could be simplified if Mazumdar was a traitor; the explanation would require no radical reappraisal of the whole strategy. In any case the CPML was wrested from the control of Mazumdar by another group, the Bihar-Orissa Committee (the leadership of which includes Ashim Chatterji and is largely in gaol); Mazumdar himself was captured in July 1972 and died in prison.

Evasion characterizes Peking's attitude. Having given uncritical support to Mazumdar's line of pure terrorism, *Hsinhua* has now moved over—without explanation or critical scrutiny of the record—to praising the Bihar-Orissa Committee (of Chatterji) and its emphasis on the role of mass organizations.*

In the autumn of 1971, the Chatterji group produced a document that acknowledged the CPML's mistaken attitude to mass organizations, to the recruitment of lumpen proletarian elements (the Calcutta thugs who practised annihilating class enemies) and to the "annihilation tactic." However, in the same document, it also argued on the Bangladesh issue that since Peking supported Yahya Khan, all true revolutionaries must do likewise; Yahya, it said, was an anti-imperialist figure like Prince Sihanouk. By contrast, Mazumdar's document acknowledged no mistakes

---

*More recently, a letter purporting to represent Peking's real view of Mazumdar's line has been published by six prominent leaders of the CMPL (all now in gaol). For a copy of this, see Peking and CP (ML), *Frontier*, November 4, 1972, p. 15. Its authenticity is not beyond dispute.

but did say all true revolutionaries should support the struggle for an independent Bangladesh (perhaps Bangladesh was the issue that changed Peking's mind).

The disastrous politics of Maoism remains unchanged by the debacle. Indeed, there are still areas of armed struggle, or at least rural agitation, in the country; in particular, the Revolutionary Communist Committee of Andhra Pradesh continues its operations in the Andhra forests; it opposes the "annihilation tactic," tries to build mass organizations and is fairly cautious in approach to the authorities.

In West Bengal, doubts have certainly been expressed about China's foreign policy vis-a-vis Bangladesh, but where Maoism is at its most vicious and destructive—in the domestic struggle —there are still few criticisms. Perhaps two or three thousand political activists have been murdered; the government claims to have 7,000 CPML supporters in gaol. Yet the radicals of West Bengal cling to the politics of Peking. It took all of that loss to learn the primitive lesson that "when party warfare replaces political action, it provides a powerful reinforcement to Right reaction."[9]

X. The repression

The new Congress government of the spring of 1971 tried to deliver the final blows in eliminating the CPML and the CPM. It is said that large numbers of CPML members crossed over to Congress to form the nucleus of the Congress youth organization (Chattra Parishad); another story is that the government offered to release 800 "Naxalites" provided they agreed to work for Congress. The Youth Congress has certainly been the spearhead in trying to eliminate the CPM. Jyoti Basu claimed in January 1972 that 600 CPM activists had been killed in the preceding 18 months. The attacks continued through the period of President's rule, culminating in a drive to ensure the CPM was defeated in the last elections. The constituency of Baranagar in Calcutta had been held by Jyoti Basu with a very handsome majority since 1952; in March he lost the seat to the CPI (Congress ally) by 39,000 votes.

[9]Banerjee, in *Frontier*, November 20, 1971.

The violence did not stop with the election victory, for the Youth Congress is now busy carving out a place for itself at the expense of both the CPM and perhaps also the CPI and some elements of Congress itself. The Chattra Parishad has been trying to break up the CPM trade union organization and establish itself in its place.

In February 1972, the CPM trade union federation, CITU, appealed plaintively to employers to protect their workers against Congress and police attacks—no talk of workers militia here.

Both the CPI and the CPM rejoiced originally at the destruction of the CPML. *New Age* (the CPI "central organ") in March crowed publicly at the liquidation of the CPML, the "ultra left"—"It has paid dearly for its politics of terror, disruption, opportunism and clandestine liaison with the grand alliance of reaction." Yet what has been done to the CPML and continues to be done to the CPM, can equally well be done to the CPI should it ever show any signs of independence.

The CPM has learned no lessons. At the ninth party Congress in July 1972, the Political Resolution was carried without major opposition and the leadership congratulated for steering between Right reformism and Left adventurism. The leadership explained its loss of so many seats at the last election—its radical defeat in pursuit of what, by default, must be seen as its primary tactic—by blaming all its troubles on Congress gangsterism and manipulation of the vote (Congress intervention was not very successful, in this case, since the CPM vote was not cut so radically). Jyoti Basu and the CPM have now emerged as the most passionate defenders of Indian "democracy" against Congress' "anti-democratic" actions. The party boycotted the state assembly by way of protest (but not, it should be noted, the two houses of the Central Parliament). Basu's complaints, along with the CPM's characterization of Congress as "semi-fascist," might be taken as arguments for the party going underground. The rhetoric of the CPM leaders occasionally suggests such flights of fancy, but reality is less exciting. It is clear the party leadership is pathetically dependent on the existing parliamentary set-up. Without elections and parliament, what is it to do? The CPM leadership is old and tired (at the Congress, of the 408 delegates, only 57 were said to be under 35 years of age); it could not become revolutionary by small stages. If Mrs Gandhi will not allow it to be a parliamentary opposition, it no longer has any *raison d'etre*.

The CPM is not now a cadre organization. Nevertheless, it is better organized than most Indian political parties and in its heyday had roots in the organized working class of West Bengal. Yet the real force of its support came from the Calcutta lower middle class whose hopes and fears, for a short time, seem to have been embodied in the party. Both the CPI and the CPM draw support heavily from the educated. The last election however showed that such support provides no sure bulwark in elections. Only a small proportion of the CPM vote needed to swing behind Mrs Gandhi's Left nationalist rhetoric to exaggerate the effect of the Congress offensive and the vagaries of the simple majority system.

XI. The lessons

The politics of the CPML embodied the attitudes of a particular social group and, as a result, attracted recruits and support from the same social group. This was both cause and effect of the perpetuation of these attitudes. For the party never recruited a significant number of members from any stratum other than the student-intelligentsia milieu of Calcutta.

The political confusion, incoherence, implicit elitism and unashamed romanticism of the party's politics were, in essence, Narodnik, and not accidentally. The CPML and the Narodniks were drawn from the same social source, embodied the same kind of frustration and idealism, and were attracted to certain similar kinds of activity. Where the power of a major social class is lacking, terrorism has an obvious attraction for the dedicated middle class revolutionary.

If one stratum of the Indian middle class reaches instinctively towards terrorism (and there is a significant terrorist tradition in India), yet another demands the carefully circumscribed opposition of parliamentary radicalism, full of exciting rhetoric but not actually oversetting the existing order of society; raising the spectre of revolution, not to destroy society, but rather to blackmail the Establishment into conceding more. This tradition is a more powerful one in India than that represented by the CPML, and has included a whole generation of those who struggled for independence and, afterwards, against Congress Raj. But, like the membership of the CPM, it is ageing, and the certainties upon which controlled opposition depend—above all, that development, progress, is taking place, even if in an unfavourable way—are dissolving. The development crisis knocks away the *raison d' etre* of parties like the CPM, for it means that only a real revolutionary force can tackle the problems.

So far in India, the Left has followed the sterile alternatives of rural guerrilla warfare, of terrorism, and parliamentary politics. The CPML's adherence to the first is the mirror image of the CPM's pursuit of the second. Both represent courses of action open to middle class radicals (even if drawn from different strata) that require neither conscious class politics nor identification with class interests. Both preserve the "independence" of the radicals, that is, allow them to operate in accordance with their own social attitudes rather than with the interests of the classes they claim to represent (peasants or workers). Because of this "freedom," it is possible for activists to swap between one alternative and the other without apparently any great political transition. The instability of the Indian Left reflects the shallowness of its social roots. It is outside the main arenas of class struggle and sees little necessity to be inside, except as a temporary foray to secure an audience or a stage army for a demonstration. For the most part, it dismisses the battles fought as no more than "economism"; in doing so, it gives up all opportunity of making itself the real leadership of the classes in struggle, of rooting itself securely. In exchange, it preserves its sectarianism, its voluntarism, its volatility and, for the most part, its irrelevance.

The social basis of the revolutionaries is also the source of the theoretical poverty of the Left. To know what Indian society is as a prelude to changing it requires the revolutionaries to be identified with the working class. Of course, all Indian socialists talk about the proletariat, urban or rural, but the word is largely detached from any real workers or real peasants; the concept is a puppet in the revolutionary's private show, rather than embodying real people with wills and interests that cannot be automatically read off from some pre-existing formula, but are revealed only by joining in the ongoing struggle. The outworn formulae of Stalinism and Maoism fill the vacuum, and much ingenuity and talent is devoted to trying to give meaning to these formulae rather than examining Indian reality. For example, the term "feudalism," rarely defined or explained in any rigorous form, is in much vogue, even though it is doubtful whether any serious sense of the term could ever have been applied to India. A belief in the existence of Indian feudalism becomes a matter of faith, rather than a question for scientific enquiry. Conceptually, India cannot be allowed to be capitalist because that would put socialism on the agenda, and, after all, China has only just had its "national democratic revolution."

Politically, the argument is double edged. For the danger of "feudalism," of reactionary forces, is one of the arguments for the CPI lining up with the "progressive national bourgeoisie." Of course, in parts of India there are relationships which may disappear with the further growth of Indian capitalism, but to make them of central significance is to divert attention from the important tasks. The kulaks are not a feudal class but a rural capitalist class, and in so far as "feudal" elements survive, they are part of the rich peasantry.

The tyranny of concepts does not end even when, as with the CPM, the socialists break with foreign patrons. The CPM's alternative to loyalty to Moscow or Peking is not political independence but Indian nationalism and a reformism without reforms. It does not lead the party to root itself more securely in the working class, but to become even more free floating, blown by the temporary winds of middle class politics. The CPM, in practice, is the instrument of the section of the "toiling middle class" which invariably sees itself as "the people." And "the people" are a vast nameless throng, suitable for demonstrations and voting, but not as the instrument of self-emancipation and the government of society.

If the lack of a serious working class base impoverishes theory, it also makes a strong disciplined organization impossible. Disciplined sects are certainly possible, but not an organization that is politically significant, operating in the centres of power rather than on the margins of society, a village or a parliament. Yet the daily battle is still being fought out in the cities of India, and a force could be built there from which base it would make sense to attempt to create peasant organizations. Without that base, peasant work leads back to the same sterile alternatives.

Even those alternatives are scarcely worked out with any clarity. Where Marxism, in isolation from working class struggle, degenerates into a system of false consciousness, a style of talk which masks rather than clarifies and guides political purposes, revolutionaries can provide no clear direction or coherent leadership. On the Indian Left, there are enormous resources of idealism and self-sacrifice, but existing without any coherent political framework or serious revolutionary organization. The vacuous ranting of politicians—ever onward and upwards—consoles the defeated and prevents the learning of lessons that might challenge the politicians. Indeed, in such circumstances, clarity itself is seen as defeatism. Even after the experience of the past three years in Calcutta, some of the so-called revolutionaries can still argue that it was all for the best: omelettes need egg breaking etc. The bombast of Peking's propaganda provides a good example of this quite undiscriminating attitude toexp erience. For the Chinese Communist leaders, their propaganda is not important, for they are not called to account, nor required to pay for their mistakes. Peking cares little for what happens in India, and has no serious interest in a coherent revolutionary alternative there. It requires only an echo, a few sycophants who can substantiate the Chinese claim to represent all the oppressed people of the world.

The Indian working class is the only force that can decisively wage war on the rulers of India. That the weakest link of West Bengal, in the last crisis, did not snap is partly attributable to the fact that the revolutionaries did the ruling class the favour of removing themselves from the working class centres and going into voluntary exile in the villages.

In China (and also Viet Nam) two decades were required to build a rural alternative. Time on that scale is something that will not be available in the coming phase. The rich peasants are soaking up the surplus that should go to industrialization. The Indian bourgeoisie will almost certainly not be prepared to push its demands on the rich peasantry to the point of open social collision, simply because an open confrontation could produce a radical social breakdown. Imperialist domination of the world market makes it impossible for Indian capitalism to develop the country without an agrarian transformation. The result is a stalemate, accompanied by increasing corruption and social decay. The mass of the population will pay the costs. Increasing unemployment and shrinking mass consumption, now exacerbated by high rates of inflation, will generate successive sporadic revolts by the desperate. To curb rebellion will demand an increasingly authoritarian regime, modelled in the first instance on West Bengal. The army and the police will drain off an increasingly large chunk of resources, so making development—and job creation—even more difficult.

The need for a revolutionary alternative in these circumstances could hardly be more urgent. The vicious downward spiral of defence and unemployment can be broken only by a revolution that challenges the kulak at home and imperialism abroad. But to challenge these requires also a frontal assault on Indian capitalism. Only the Indian working class, with the help of sections of the peasantry, can break out of this stalemate and secure the concentrations of power against both the bourgeoisie and the rich peasants.

2

A Parliamentary Road
to Socialism ?

The letter of the traditions espoused by the Communist Party of India (Marxist) do not explicitly condemn participation in governments in non-revolutionary times, but the spirit does. The debate about "Millerandism"—participation in non-socialist governments—comes close to condemnation, but such tactical questions in the last analysis must be decided in the light of specific circumstances. The same is true of a party decidingto go under ground to espouse guerrilla warfare. We postpone considering that side of the coin until later in this book—in Chapters 6 and 7.

Our concern here is with the participation of Communist parties—or Marxists—in established governments, without that participation being the act of revolution itself. Communist parties round the world are now more and more seeking simple participation, without conditions. Of course, this has always been a tactic of some note for Communists ever since the Popular Front movement in the thirties. By and large, however, they have been kept out of participation in governments not by their own politics or principles so much as by the desire of established ruling classes to preserve the Communist Party as bogey-man-in-chief. Now, however, many ruling classes find it increasingly useful to have Communists in the government, particularly in the ministries of labour and agrarian reform. The Allende government in Chile has provided a focus for radical hopes in Latin America, consoling revolutionaries for the signal failure of ural guerrilla warfare over the past decade. Despite the formal adherence of both China and Cuba to guerrilla warfare as the sole means to revolutionary power, both are now supporting Allende as the best that can be hoped for. In Italy and France, various attempts have been made and continue to be made to decorate the *status quo* with red flags. The headlong rush of Communists into not even Left-wing Social Democracy makes it seem that government power at any cost—and regardless of any real political achievements that might result—is the only thing left. The paper tiger continues to eat with dreary regularity the paper revolutionaries of the Communist Party.

Nowhere is the trend new. In south Asia, it is becoming almost a convention. The CPI's devotion to Mrs Gandhi's Congress has already been noted in the last chapter. In Bangladesh, the so-called pro-Moscow wing of the former National Awami Party loyally garnish the unappetizing meal of the Awami League government. In Ceylon, not just the Communist Party, but the erstwhile Trotskyists, the Lanka Sama Samaj Party, are part of the national government. The 1967 entry of the CPM into the State Governments of West Bengal and Kerala (like the earlier entry of the united CPI into the Kerala State Government) might almost seem, by comparison, to be a mild error.

In both these last two cases, however, not even simple calculations of political profit and loss seem to have intervened between the supposedly revolutionary parties and their patriotic obligation to form the government. This was not necessarily some question of historical precedent or high principle—the sectarians argue the first, the anarchists the second. But rather what was at stake was the survival of the party as a serious political alternative. The CPM sold its modest birthright most cheaply, and almost happily fulfilled the wishes of the Indian ruling class. The Lanka Sama Samaj Party performed signal services for the Establishment in Ceylon, and all for such trivial rewards—a few leading members in office. In 1964, Mrs Bandaranaike first induced the Lanka Sama Samaj Party to act as her loyal retainer, and what follows is a comment on this written at the time. Following that is a description of the losses to the Indian Left when the CPM decided to follow the same path in West Bengal in 1967.

I. Ceylon : Hunting with the hounds, 1964*

Comparisons should not be pushed too far, but there are striking similarities between the current situations in Italy and Ceylon. For different reasons, both face a windy inflation of crisis proportions, generating simultaneously a sharp challenge from labour (which, unless it produces a revolution, helps to hump up inflation even further) and a series of balance of paymentsd isasters. In both cases, the proponents of sound finance demand immediately that prices and profits be allowed to remain stable by holding down wages—workers alone must bear in their day-to-day standard of living the full cost of inflation.

In both, the tactic offered is to bring in the Left to do the government's dirty work on the assumption that punishment administered by a member of the Left will not be thought of as punishment. Let a trade unionist or socialist be the Minister of Labour or Finance. Let him be the strike breaker, turn out the troops, lead the way to an "agreed" wage freeze. In Italy, the results are clear, and all power to the anti-coalitionists. In Ceylon, the issues are more complex, but the principle is the same.

Consider the advantages to Mrs Bandaranaike of having the Left in her Government. The Sri Lanka Freedom Party (SLFP), a classical coalition of rural conservatives and urban radicals, only secured the government in 1960 through its alliance with the parties of the subsequently formed United Left Front (ULF). ULF self-denial allowed the SLFP to win 30 or 40 marginal seats that would otherwise probably have gone to the rural and Right wing United National Party (UNP). The SLFP polled 1,022,154 votes and won 75 seats; the UNP polled 1,143, 290 votes and won 30 seats. Since then violence and inflation have destroyed whatever unanimity once existed between the government and the ULF. To survive, the ULF has had to represent fully the fierce opposition of labour to the government's failure to hold the price line. The result has been a rash of strikes culminating in the Emergency in March and the proroguing of Parliament for three months to safeguard the government from imminent defeat in the House of Representatives. In terms of pure party politics, Mrs Bandaranaike urgently needed allies if her government was to survive through

*First published in *International Socialism*, 18, Autumn 1964.

to the General Election in 1965, and those allies would have to seem leftist if she was to keep urban loyalties.

Economically, her need was even greater. Sooner or later, wages and salaries will have to be faced. The rice subsidy, now running at a quarter of the budget, will have to be cut. Not that this will solve the problem, since Ceylon's payments crisis is primarily a product of the world market. The declining prices and revenue of exports (tea, rubber, coconut) along with an astonishing rise in the price of imports (notably sugar) is the cause. Efforts to Ceylonize or nationalize private business (nationalization of petroleum outlets and insurance, two of the most profitable enterprises in Ceylon, was completed by the beginning of 1964) have frightened off foreign capital and aid (notably American and West German) and dried up the sources of government borrowing. The government has freely created cash to bribe its way to domestic stability, with a commensurate increase in the money supply, thus adding to inflation. Strict import restrictions only help to inflate the prices of formerly imported consumer goods. A drastic strike in Colombo port produced a backlog of 100,000 tons of cargo, prompting foreign shippers to double freight charges for shipment to Ceylon, a further heavy strain on costs. By January, the exchange reserves were down to an all-time low, and a former IMF loan was just coming up for repayment. With an estimated record of 800,000 unemployed, with white-collar workers chafing, with the UNP advancing both in September's Colombo municipal elections and by-elections in the winter, the drastic nature of the spring Emergency can be understood as well as the government's active attempts to divert attention to the non-Sinhalese as the cause of all troubles.

And if there is dirty work to be done, who better than a leftist to do it? The "Trotskyist" trio (Perera, Moonesinghe, Goonewardena) that Mrs Bandaranaike has grabbed, have at one move solved a series of government headaches—they have shored up the government majority, prepared for a repetition next year of the alliance that won it the 1960 election, split irreparably the only serious Left opposition (the ULF), and purchased a small breather from the harrying tactics of the trade unions commanded by the Lanka Sama Samaj Party. In March 1964 the LSSP defied the Emergency to hold a mass trade union demonstration to demand more pay (the now dead "21 Points"), but now the three LSSP leaders troop to a Buddhist temple to say prayers and party propagandists stress the blood links between Perera and Moonesinghe and popular Buddhist figures. The ULF remains a ruin, five factions instead of three parties—two LSSP fragments (the pro- and anti-coalition factions), the literally national-socialist MEP, and the two Communist splinters (Moscow and Peking).

The cost is very high. What are the rewards, apart from the Ministry of Finance for Perera? The 14-Points Programme agreed by the government and the LSSP as the basis for coalition is just a face-saver for the Left and includes nothing that the government had not already planned or which can be achieved in the short stretch remaining to this Parliament. Policy since the coalition began remains the same—the attack on the Tamils and Indians continues (no universal brotherhood of man, let alone of the working class, here). The Ceylon Chamber of Commerce has exchanged compliments with the new Finance Minister; Perera has promised to toughen the implementation of the plan through monthly departmental checks, to consult the trade unions, to create "Soviets" or rather committees of trade unionists, to "advise" the government, a suggestion of how far the revolution is becoming merely verbal. Goonewardena is gunning for racketeers among public works contractors, and Moonesinghe has introduced a new welfare and pay structure for Colombo dockers to try and get the accumulated tonnage moving. Ceylonization in industry and land ownership proceeds as before and the government, as promised before the coalition, will extend control and ownership over the import-export trade; due place has been guaranteed to Buddhism as the majority religion, and to Sinhalese (opposed firmly by the Tamils) as the majority language. Most recently, Perera's long-awaited budget has declared a moratorium on all profit, dividend and interest payments abroad for one year. Given that much of this was coming anyway, this is mild stuff. No wonder that, despite all its earlier grumbling, Mrs Bandaranaike's right-wing has settled down in the new cabinet with three Trotskyists without a murmur. Perera will pull all their chestnuts out of the fire.

The LSSP ministers promise radical efficiency within Ceylon's mobile *status quo*, and certain verbal changes along corporatist lines. Anti-foreignism can be substituted for anti-capitalism—Tamils are fair game for cheap radicals. Ceylon is not 1917 Russia or even 1962 Algeria, and Mrs Bandaranaike is neither Lenin nor

Kerensky. Tears and all, she is tougher and wilier than most and needs more than three Trotskyists to shove her into socialism. Meanwhile, the pro-Peking Communists will have a field day in the trade unions, both pulling in and outdistancing the anti-coalition Trotskyists to become the sole mouthpiece for urban labour—and Perera will be left to be the strike breaker. The cost to the Ceylonese Left is terrifying and tragically high, and for little more than Perera's ambition or tiredness.

II. India : Again hunting with the hounds,1967.*

The worst that can befall the leader of an extremist party is to be compelled to take over the government at a time when the movement is not yet ripe for the rule of the class he represents . . . He who gets himself in that false position is irredeemably lost. (Engels, *The Peasant War in Germany*, 1850.)

The Indian Left is drawn almost entirely from the urban middle class and, in particular, those employed or associated with the national State. Thus, as a political tendency, it has always found it difficult to reconcile either the divergent trends within the middle class or, more important, the divergence between the demands of its own origins and the demands arising from its fluctuating popular support in the urban and rural masses. On the one hand, the pressure towards State capitalism—a Stalinist solution to India's backwardness—and the impotence of the urban middle class before the power of the dominant peasant castes and national big business, vies with pressure from below for a working class and peasant movement that will both reach down to the roots of Indian society and overcome the fragmentation of India instigated by the castes dominant in each state. On the other, the Left strategy of pressure within existing parliamentary institutions for an expanded State sector, pressure either within Congress as carried on by the old Krishna Menon-style Left, or within state and national assemblies as pursued by the non-Congress Left parties, competes with a contradictory strategy of fighting in the factories and on the land. The second has usually been no

*Originally published in *International Socialism*, 30, Autumn 1967.

more than an adjunct of the first in the past, and so relatively sporadic, weak, and, given the very uneven distribution of the Left parties, fragmentary.

The issue of popular struggle or pressure within the citadels of power can be fudged for quite long periods with impunity. The experience of the Indonesian Communists (PKI) up to the abortive *coup* of 1965 demonstrates this, as do successive episodes in the history of European Labour or Social Democratic parties. But sooner or later, a choice has to be made: either to help run the *status quo* properly or focus fully on the creation of a radical rank-and-file movement, for which Parliament may or may not be a temporary but very subordinate outlet for publicity. The price of a failure to choose can also be seen in Indonesia and the terrible destruction wrought upon the PKI once the house of cards fell apart (cf. "The Notebook", IS 24, Spring 1966); the disaster to the Chinese Communist Party in 1927 when the Kuomintang fell upon it comes into the same category. Point is added to this dilemma in India when it is recalled that politics there have been moving Rightwards for the past half decade.

The Indian Left could perhaps evade a choice until the February 1967 General Elections. Brutal and incompetent as Congress rule has been, in those elections its vote declined only marginally (from about 43 to 40 per cent of the total poll). As before, the cities were fairly solidly hostile to Congress, but the dominant rural castes ensured its real base remained secure. However, the oddities of the simple majority system of elections and the united front tactics of the opposition parties (plus a series of important, if not particularly Left, revolts within Congress) produced a change of government in six states (three more have created non-Congress ministeries since then), in two of which, Kerala and West Bengal, the Left is the dominant force: in two others, Bihar and Uttar Pradesh, the Left is of importance. One need not follow the Right Communists (CPI) in their strategy of a "national coalition government" (in yoke with the party of big business and the old princely families, Swatantra, and that of lower middle class Hindu chauvinists, Jana Sangh) to see the grave dangers implicit in the situation.

India is currently suffering its worst famine for a very long time, concentrated most heavily in the food deficit states—Bihar, West Bengal, Kerala and eastern Uttar Pradesh. The third five-year plan is now officially regarded as a failure, and the fourth has faded into nothing before it even began: what the national state loses, big business will recoup. The economy is in severe recession (worst in the most industrialized zones—for example, West Bengal), with little hope of strong revival until famine passes and Washington relaxes its grip on the purse strings of aid, currently manipulated in the interests of US foreign policy and those American companies hoping to profit in India. Overall, Congress survives by permission of the US PL 480 foodgrains programme, and is progressively overshadowed by its own and foreign big business and the dominant rural castes of the states.

In such a situation, when, as *The Call* (organ of the Revolutionary Socialist Party, April 1967) puts it, "neither in West Bengal nor in Kerala can the people be regarded as ready for a socialist transformation. The class struggle of the workers and toiling peasantry in these two States are far from reaching that stage, whether by utilising the forum of Parliament and legislatures or outside them"—in such a situation, the non-Congress Left has decided to assume responsibility for the disasters that must inevitably occur by forming non-Congress governments. The Rightward moving perspective for India might include at some stage a military *coup* to maintain "law and order," particularly as Congress State Governments fall. In that situation, the articulate Left faces at worst physical annihilation—as in Indonesia—or mass imprisonment—as in Greece. Yet, with one marginal change in votes, the Left parties have accepted responsibility for administering this Rightward-moving *status quo*, for the starvation in the countryside and the unemployment and sheer human misery in the cities—the employers are currently intransigent on the question of mass redundancies. Whether planned beforehand or not, these issues are and will be exploited to the full by Congress as a means to discredit the Left in power.

The arguments advanced to justify participation in the government concerned indicate the absence of any coherent analysis of the situation facing the Left and the Indian working class. *The Call* (*ibid*) speaks of a "progressive democratic programme" to attack the bourgeois capitalist order, and of the Left having "now one advantage that they can do so from positions of constitutional and legal authority and with the effective sanction of militant mass movements behind them." Either this is a revolutionary situation and participation in the government is at best an irrelevance or distraction, or it is not; and if it is not (as *The Call* admits), for what purpose is the Left holding power: to create a revolutionary situation from the vantage point of the Chief Minister's office? When a Calcutta police station beat up a former Left MP, followed by the new West Bengal Minister of Revenue (of the Left CPI, namely, the CPM), the irony of seeking "constitutional and legal authority" for revolution became painfully clear.

To survive, the Left must subordinate itself to the same logic as any other party seeking to administer the *status quo*. And in India, at the state level, that means helping the disintegration of the country by pressing the state claims above any national ones. Bihar has threatened to refuse coal exports from the state unless Delhi sends more food; E.M.S. Namboodiripad (Left CPI), Chief Minister of Kerala, has threatened to deny Delhi foreign exchange earnings on the state's exports unless Kerala gets more food, and very early on, he breakfasted with G. D. Birla (one of the largest and most hated of Indian big businessmen) to beg some private investment funds for his state; Kerala's Labour Minister has condemned *gheraoes* (strikes where workers occupy the factory and prevent the management leaving) and threatened strong police retaliation; and in West Bengal, the police and army have put down both striking workers and peasants in revolt—in early July, Bengal's Chief Minister despatched 1,000 police to suppress the Naxalbari peasant revolt in the north, saying the police had full power "to use tear gas, *lathi* (truncheon) charges and shooting to crush the pro-Chinese free zone." This sounds like the language of counter-revolution, whether spoken by a Communist or not.

The Left CPI, by far the largest Left element in the two main states concerned (52 in a 133-seat house in Kerala and 44 of 280 seats in West Bengal) has no clearer perspective than *The Call*. Its explicitly Maoist Left elements certainly dragged their feet about entering the government, but the broad bloc of the centrists (neutral as between Moscow and Peking) which includes both the Calcutta section led by Jyoti Basu (now West Bengal Finance Minister) and Namboodiripad, Kerala's Chief Minister, have been eager to participate in the spoils. One Left CPI leader has sought some rationale—the elections, he said, would "unleash new forces, even within the ruling party and among the capitalist class" which would enable India to adopt "genuine and national policies" (viz. land reform, more progressive taxation, selective nationalization and the ending of foreign aid). At best, this is ingenuous, at worst, positively fraudulent—"new forces" and a "new phase" are conjured out of a hat to cover a vacuum of opportunism. There is no word as to why the Indian ruling class should accept anything at all because of an electoral quirk. Certainly the Left's popgun is no match for the armed divisions standing behind Congress.

The hunger of the starving is offered an end to US foodgrains aid, the peasant more land (although no mechanism to achieve this is cited, given the flop of Congress land reform), and the middle class more jobs in the expanded public bureaucracy. Meanwhile, the leadership of the Left is swallowed up in the decorous antics of government, and the class issues at stake are absorbed in empty phrases. The rationale is old—Millerand's attitude to participation in a bourgeois French cabinet; the Mensheviks' attitude to Kerensky's Provisional Russian Government in 1917; British minority Labour governments, and today, in India, the attitude of the Right CPI and social democrats (Praja and SSP).

However, some have learned. The Left CPI Politburo meeting in Calcutta last May complained of ultra-Left splinters in six states; in West Bengal, four government members resigned in June, and 19 Left CPI State Council members were expelled for "ultra-Leftism." And in Naxalbari, north-east Bengal, one of the first full peasant revolts since the 1947 Telengana outbreak, has broken surface among the tribal people, partly engaged on the tea plantations; there have been echoes westwards as far as Bihar and southwards to beyond Calcutta. No doubt the Left CPI will argue that the revolt has been permitted to develop as it has because it is in power, despite pressures for suppression of the rebellion from its major partner in government, Bangla Congress (a group of defectors from Congress, based on the rural bourgeoisie of one district, Midnapore). But this is a transparent rationalization, contradicted by the government's present attempts to suppress the revolt. The West Bengal Government cannot "succeed" unless it puts down "anarchy" in the shape of this revolt, and in putting it down, it destroys what should be its own popular base. The revolt has taken place in the face of efforts by the Left CPI to stifle it, and has precipitated the sectarian splintering of the Left CPI itself. More to the point, despite the cheering off-stage by Peking (cf. *Peking Review* 29, 14 July 1967, p. 24), the Indian army under Delhi's command can annihilate both the State Government and the rebels (as it did in Telengana) as soon as Delhi is confident the short-term food crisis is over and that therefore it is creditable for Congress to resume power. It is the Left that will bear the responsibility for famine and suppressing popular protest, for interposing itself between the two millstones of rulers and ruled.

The argument is not, as many Indian socialists seem to think, about whether revolutionaries should cooperate with the Muslim League or Bangla Congress or anyone else. It is about what the Left can most effectively do to build its rank-and-file strength and guard against complete destruction as the Rightward movement continues, about safeguarding and building organizations of real workers and peasants (rather than the empty abstractions that feature in much Indian socialist writing). At no stage in this process does the donning of ministerial fancy clothes help; on the contrary, by confusing the issues, by putting the Left leadership in a position in which it cannot help but attack its own followers or "fail," it is a positively retrograde step. The main hope in India is that the governments in which the Left participates can be defeated by Congress quickly to free the Left for more important matters.

3

South Asia in Crisis

India is not an isolated case. Its problems are common to most countries of Asia. Indeed, south Asia in particular is a most sensitive seismic zone of the world economy. When there is generalized pressure in the system as a whole, it bursts out with explosive force here. The regimes that border the Indian Ocean round into the South China Sea reveal the sudden sharp cracks and fissures of the system as a whole. It is always the weakest segment of the world economy—like the weakest segment, the backward regions, of each constituent part—which shows the problems of the whole in its most extreme form. The problems of south Asia are not generated from within it, but are forced upon it by the world.

The effects of periodic stagnation in the world economy—particularly in the late sixties—are exaggerated in Asia by the dominant tendencies in imperialism. For the advanced countries more and more inhibit the possibilities of capital accumulation, of economic development. The level of capital required to launch an economy into sustained self-transformation has risen far beyond the reach of most backward countries. Each year the price rises even further, sometimes by gigantic leaps. The poverty of the mass of the population makes it impossible to raise the rate of accumulation by a significant increase in exploitation. The surplus each year is too small to charge the economy with real power. The capital goods needed for industrialization are more and more expensive, while the market for the goods the backward countries produce is dammed and restricted by the domination of the advanced capitalist powers. Each backward country finds itself locked in a vice, the handle of which is held abroad. The vice makes it impossible to accumulate capital at a rate sufficient to change the balance of power between the country and the world. Indeed, it scarcely makes it even possible to stop the drain of resources out of the country, whether in terms of cash, profits and dividends, interest on loans, or in terms of the brain drain of expensively educated workers.

The crisis is a developing one and will be the central concern of a later chapter. There are ups and downs, temporary boosts and periodic slumps, but overall the gap between the advanced and the backward grows wider. The development crisis grows steadily more severe.

Each ruling class in the underdeveloped world responds to the external vice by imposing the same repressive system upon its own people. In the old united state of Pakistan, Karachi imposed its own form of neo-colonial oppression upon East Bengal. The levels of poverty are such that these mechanisms produce vast social differences with some scarcely having a toehold on life itself, others worrying about the problems of obesity, affluence and pollution.

The mere force of nationalist rhetoric cannot hold together such worm-eaten structures. The hoops on the barrel are police and military power. Each state must steadily increase its military preparedness, not so much to guard against its predatory neighbours, but to keep its own people in check, and particularly those with least hope but most life to look forward to, the young. Military expenditure in south Asia has risen from half a billion US dollars in 1949 to something over two billion dollars today (constant prices). There are some eight million men permanently under arms in Asia.

The more resources are diverted to arms, the less there remains for capital accumulation, for industrial and agricultural development to provide the jobs which will offset unemployment. The domestic threat to the State from the unemployed, the underemployed, the miserably low-paid and the hopeless, increases with each year as new generations enter the labour force faster than the old leave it. With that increase, the need to divert even greater resources to military expenditure rises. A downward vicious circle drains resources out of production into so-called defence. At the end, not even a military regime can keep the national wreck afloat.

The wrecks that dot the Asian scene demonstrate how fierce the crisis is becoming. At the heart of the situation is the great open wound of Viet Nam. But alongside are other appalling disasters —half a million slaughtered in Indonesia in 1965 following the military *coup*; countless thousands lost in the typhoons along the East Bengal coast, natural disasters that could be prevented; yet further thousands slaughtered or starved to death in the repression of the Pakistan military. Perpetual war in Laos and now Cambodia, race riots in Malaysia, military and presidential *coups* in the Philippines, South Korea and Thailand, the slaughter of a generation of the young in Ceylon. And all producing no resolution, only at best a postponement of yet further disasters. The achievements of imperialism in south and south-east Asia today already far exceed those legendary atrocities of European colonialism. Political independence was granted but without any of the means to make that independence work.

In 1971, there were two vivid and extreme examples of the crisis of south Asia and of the struggle of people to be free of the crisis. In Pakistan, Bengal and Ceylon, the oppression and the battle for emancipation conjoined, so that for a moment it looked as though the whole of the south Asian *status quo* might be thrown into the melting pot. It was the first surge of hope in the lives of many people, and it went far beyond the tired priorities offered by the established parliamentary Lefts. The challenge of the rebels in Ceylon and Bengal was explosive precisely because it seemed they could no longer be fobbed off with claptrap about nationalizing the banks and insurance, measures which in no way shifted the balance of class forces, let alone ameliorated the terrible poverty of the masses.

The explosion in Bengal threatened the ruling class not just of Pakistan, but even more important, of India. The Indian Union could not withstand the modest demands of the Awami League on the Pakistan state if made by its own numerous minorities. Once the Indian house of cards began to slide, there would be hope for all other movements, whether in Pakistan or Ceylon or elsewhere. Otherwise, the Indian Government would use—as in fact it did—all means available to stifle revolution on its borders. It backed the Awami League in Bengal precisely in order to destroy the possibility of a "workers and peasants socialist republic of Bengal."

Yet the movements in Ceylon and Bengal failed to break through. Mrs Bandaranaike won in Sri Lanka, and Mrs Gandhi won in Bangladesh. Their victories underline the desperately weak political perspectives of the rebels. In the whole of Asia, revolutionaries have adhered for many years to a loose Maoist-Populist-Anarchist political combination that—as with the Naxalites in India—is disastrous in terms of programme, activity and organization. It encourages no clarity, no identification with real class interests, no serious analysis of the target and the strategy. Elitism, masquerading as populism, places entire emphasis upon small groups of students or others outside the main classes. These issues are explored in greater depth in Part Three of this book.

Above all, this political perspective is nationalist, and the revolutionaries aspire to establish a national State capitalist pattern of development. This in its turn isolates the revolutionaries in the actual struggle. It inhibited the revolutionaries of East Bengal from seeing an important priority in building a common alliance with the workers of Karachi—to check the military Mafia in both East and West—and with the workers of Calcutta—to check Mrs Gandhi's military games. The lack of a serious class basis meant that the Ceylonese rebels could not invoke support from Colombo workers in order to check Mrs Bandaranaike's oppression. The social and international issues—as opposed to the national—were of decisive significance in both struggles if there was to be a real chance of victory.

The external lessons are easier to draw than the domestic. The role of China in both cases and of the Soviet Union in Ceylon has been shown in the least complimentary light. It is only possible to believe that either of these powers plays some "progressive" role in the world by deliberately ignoring what happened.

Let us take, as an example, China's role in the Bangladesh struggle. China has been publicly supporting the Pakistan military for some ten years, and President Ayub Khan deliberately used that support to undercut his Left critics at home. Indeed, at one stage

Maulana Bhashani was induced to offer critical support to the President because of Peking's devotion to the General. In the actual war, China's role was never in real doubt since its central foreign policy aim is to defeat or neutralize Soviet influence, and the Soviet Union was already set to establish close and cordial relations with Pakistan (in June 1970, President Yahya Khan made a State visit to Moscow and was rewarded with much aid, including the promise of a steel mill). An all-weather highway was opened from Sinkiang in China to Karachi in April 1971 and, it is said, a 100 lorries a day from China funnelled military equipment into Pakistan *en route* for East Bengal. They also brought newsprint to break the Bengal strike which had halted newsprint shipments from Chittagong through much of March and April. Chou En-lai also sent fulsome greetings to Yahya Khan on Pakistan's National Day, assuring him of China's full support for Pakistan's struggle to safeguard "national independence and state sovereignty." Throughout, China insisted on seeing events in East Bengal as mainly the result of Indian intervention.

Of course, any regime has at times to undertake actions which seem inconsistent with its declared principles. But any serious revolutionary regime would explain why it felt compelled to take the action it did, particularly for the benefit of its foreign followers and supporters. The fact that Peking is happy or indifferent to the confusion it produced throughout south Asia among revolutionaries is a more striking testimony to its lack of serious revolutionary purpose than what it actually did, which was bad enough.[1]

In the following two accounts, the struggle in Ceylon and in East Bengal are examined. In both cases, battles—and fairly serious ones—have been lost but the campaign cannot be ended. For the crisis of development means that the revolt will have to go on. The survivors in both cases will regroup, sadder and wiser, to take up the fight once more.

[1]China's foreign policy is examined in greater detail in my: "China's Policy", *International Socialism*, 48, June-July 1971, and the Soviet Union's aims and behaviour in Asia in: "China and the Russian Offensive", *International Socialism*, 41, December-January 1969/70. *See also* Chapter 5 here,

I. Ceylon 1971*

The ruling class of Ceylon has been baptized in fire. Until last month, a certain grudging toleration hung like a mist over the relations between the classes. Today, the real class struggle has been revealed. The Leftish phrases, the fog of rhetoric, has dissipated. Cynical and brutal, the rulers of Ceylon will go to any lengths to preserve their position.

This revelation of the real state of power has been forced by the steadily worsening crisis of Ceylonese capitalism. The "Left" government of Mrs Bandaranaike which won a quite unexpected landslide victory at the polls in March 1970 has been, as always, long on promises and short on delivery. But the balancing game— between revolutionary slogans for the mass audience and strictly conservative action for the foreign financiers and domestic capitalists—has become progressively less easy to maintain. Both audiences were less and less convinced that Mrs Bandaranaike was not the creature of the other. To escape, she needed to find and hunt a scapegoat, preferably on the Left so that the Right would be impressed and extend·credit and support to her government. The Left critics would also be silenced by the invention of an "ultra" challenge.

(*a*) The crisis of Ceylonese capitalism is only an extreme version of the problems facing many developing countries. Sixty per cent of Ceylon's foreign exchange earnings come from tea (and a further 30-per-cent-odd from rubber and coconut). World tea output increases two to three per cent per year, but world demand for tea has been stagnant for years. For Ceylon, the price of its imports is rising, but the revenue it receives from exports is sluggish or declining. The widening gap can only be plugged by foreign loans, but on steadily more and more restrictive terms.

For Ceylon's economy even to survive as it is, industrial equipment and raw materials, and agricultural inputs (e.g. fertilizers) have to be imported. And a quarter to a third of the Ceylonese staple diet, rice, is imported, as well as fish and a number of other vital elements in the food supply. In time, many of these imports

*Original version published in *International Socialism*, 48, June-July, 1971.

could be substituted at home. Successive governments have tried to do just this (the government before Bandaranaike claimed to have nearly doubled domestic rice output and that Ceylon would be self-sufficient by 1973). But plans of this kind take a very long time to succeed. In the meantime, any government's survival depends on keeping the imports rolling in and the population, at least in part, fed. So foreign aid has been used, not to develop industry and agriculture so that jobs are increased, but to buy foodstuffs just to survive. The new government slashed non-essential imports —mainly middle class consumer goods—and tried to borrow abroad once again.

Ceylon already has debts to foreigners of more than £108 million (this sum has tripled in the past five years, and servicing the debt now takes a fifth of Ceylon's export earnings). Foreign lenders— Western governments, the International Monetary Fund, World Bank etc—are less and less inclined to extend more capital until they are sure of their profits, sure that Ceylon's economy is going to grow fast enough to repay the loans. As a result, the terms of each new loan get stiffer, and the government is less and less able to resist the demands of foreign lenders for control or influence over the Ceylonese economy. In opposition, the Bandaranaike coalition radically attacked the terms of loans clinched by the former UNP government; this time, Minister of Finance Perera (of the formerly Trotskyist Lanka Sama Samaj), refused to publish the terms of his deal with the International Monetary Fund. The latest World Bank report on Ceylon says that the balance of payments problem of the country is now more disastrous than ever before in Ceylonese history; the country's foreign reserves are "practically nil."

Using foreign aid just to survive—and to fulfil Mrs Bandaranaike's election promise to double the rice ration—piles up the problems for the future. The economy is not expanded, and new jobs for the rising labour force are not created. Between a half and one million are said to be unemployed (out of a total population of 12 million), many of them in the age group 15 to 25. The government announced a crash programme to employ 100,000 of them, but this scheme will take a long time to produce any results. Instead of tackling employment, the government concentrated in its election platform on pure demagogy—it would take over the tea industry (the biggest employer, with 800,000 workers),

the import trade and the banks; it would set up "people's committees" to represent popular interests in districts and workplaces.
But all this was just noise beside the central problem.

In the short term, tea cannot be touched without wrecking the
British-controlled market outlets in London. It would be useless to
be able to produce the tea but not sell it, especially in one of the
world's biggest markets, Britain. To appropriate tea would almost
certainly cut export earnings, which would cut the volume of
imports available (and so cut into popular consumption) unless
foreign aid (from the Eastern Bloc) filled the gap. In practice, the
government was more circumspect. The "Speech from the Throne"
in June 1970 promised boldly that Ceylon would become a republic, nationalization of the banks would be completed, and state
agencies would assume direction—but not ownership—of the trade
in tea, rubber and coconut. But in the autumn, an austerity budget
showed the real state of play after all the talk (and even that budget
was based on an assumed rate of aid that has in fact not
materialized). But the all round increase in taxes did nothing to
help the rising tide of inflation for the mass of the population,
particularly given the appalling level of unemployment. Taking
over the tea-box import trade and the graphite industry,
abolishing the Upper House of Ceylon's Parliament (where there
was an anti-Bandaranaike majority) filled few stomachs. But
the government did make a substantial increase in the police
force.

If the mass of the population was denied any hope of improvement, Mrs Bandaranaike was not winning friends among the ruling
class of Ceylon. What nationalizations there were, plus an incomes
ceiling, a compulsory savings scheme to limit dividends, the general
spurious populist furore of the government, all induced upper class
anxieties about the rising tide of Bolshevism. And behind the
government lay even more substantial threats. Industrial output
has been falling, the workers increasingly prone to strike. In
September 1970 strikes in the petroleum and electricity industries prompted the government to introduce a state of emergency
under which the army took over petrol and paraffin distribution.
But with all these troubles, the government looked after its own.
Allowances for MPs were increased. They—unlike the rest of the
upper classes—can import foreign cars. And their expensive trips
abroad soften the hard edge of sacrifice.

(*b*) The Bandaranaike government was threatened on every side. From abroad came demands to cut the rice ration, increase rice prices and scrap plans to change the ownership of Ceylonese assets—as conditions for the loans which seemed to be the sole means of survival for Bandaranaike's administration. Domestic capitalists were terrified that the government was going to extinguish them. And the mass of the population was more and more aware that all the promises of a radical new deal made during the elections were being betrayed in intrigue and petty manoeuvres. Something was needed which would simultaneously defeat all these threats, and provide the pretext for a generalized attack on popular living standards (increasing prices, cutting social services, halving the rice ration). The youthful and fragmentary revolutionary Left was just the opportunity Bandaranaike and her "Trotskyist" and "Communist" allies needed.

For some years, there have been "men training with arms" in the hills. And no doubt they would have continued there if Mrs Bandaranaike's need had not been so great. There are a number of radical opposition organizations—including the largest, the People's Liberation Front (Janatha Vimukthi Peramuna, JVP)—but none of them was of a significance capable of worrying the government. Indeed, the JVP supported the Bandaranaike coalition at the time of the election, and had not—except rhetorically—raised the question of seizing power in Ceylon. By August 1970, the JVP had reached the stage of mass meetings to criticize the government, and the government in its turn harassed JVP militants. JVP membership was drawn primarily from students and the educated unemployed. Despite the fog of rumours and government inspired fables, there is no evidence that the JVP was very large, nor that it was preparing seriously to attack the government, nor that it had connections with any foreign powers (in the early days, it was said, "vast" arms caches of foreign weapons had been discovered; in fact, it turned out, the only weapons discovered were those lifted from the army and police in Ceylon; the North Koreans were expelled as a scapegoat, although there is no evidence they were seriously involved with the JVP or any other movement).

The government's imagination was lively, if inconsistent. Last October, the police claimed that there were 15,000 men preparing an uprising. By March, the number—according to the government

—had climbed as high as 85,000 which —for the benefit of foreign arms suppliers—was happily contrasted with the tiny armed forces of Ceylon (25,000). Other official estimates asserted that there were 4,000 "hardcore" rebels, and 10,000 "active supporters"; or 20-30,000 "hardcore" members (that is, those with weapons), excluding other supporters in the cities. And so on. This is the stuff of upper class nightmares, not of Ceylonese reality. There are of course at least 100,000 *potential* rebels in Ceylon, but there can at most be only a few thousand actual organized rebels. Yet when the government set out to use the second as a scapegoat for its failures, it discovered the first. It accidentally stumbled upon a sea of hostility which, at least briefly, frightened it.

The official explanation as to why the Emergency was called was as diverse as the estimates of rebel strength. The police said the JVP had been planning an armed insurrection for "several months" and that they had attacked the US embassy in March. In fact the attack on the embassy has all the marks of a provocateur's action: the attackers called themselves the "Mao Youth Front," an unknown group, and the JVP entirely rejected the accusation that it had been involved. But the incident gave the pretext for the arrest of the JVP leadership. On 16 March the government claimed that there was a plot to kidnap the Social Services Minister, and introduced the Emergency. On 18 March Mrs Bandaranaike argued that the JVP and others had planned an armed uprising for mid-April. On the 23rd she said it was a plot to seize public buildings and steal guns.

The truth may never be clear. But the government used the opportunity to slaughter as many of the overt or potential opposition as they could. And the sheer ruthlessness of government forces added desperation to the hunted, so that what began as a demonstration of Mrs Bandaranaike's power ended as a bloodbath. The numbers killed will probably never be known. The army claims to have made 3,000 arrests (75 per cent of those arrested were between the ages of 13 and 22); another thousand are said to have surrendered under the amnesty. Yet still some of the rebels fought on, with amazing heroism and tenacity. And in reply, the government escalated its brutality. In late April, one foreign correspondent observed: "Though clearly on the wane, the insurgency had become a cockerel in the hands of the government forces who, not satisfied with wringing its throat, now sought to tear out its giblets as well."

The ruthlessness of the army and police—like that of the West Pakistan military in East Bengal—is designed to achieve the most vivid effect on the minds of the mass of the population in the shortest time possible. What was left of the opposition was concentrated in those areas of the centre and south of the island from which the government draws its main support, from the rural Sinhalese Buddhist areas (not from, for example, the Sinhalese Christian or Ceylon Tamil districts).

The government has crossed its Rubicon. It can no longer play the Left rhetoric waltz to charm its mass audience. And the more "Left" the cabinet member is supposed to be, the more he has been required to stand up and be counted in these troubled times for Ceylonese capitalism. Leslie Goonewardene, Lanka Sama Samaj Minister of Communications, proclaimed in *The Nation* that the rebels were "right-wing reactionaries," a view echoed by Colvin Da Silva (LSSP Minister of Plantations). Pieter Keuneman, Communist Party Minister of Housing and Construction, went a little further and dubbed the JVP "new style fascists." Government ministers proclaimed, not the struggle for socialism, but their firm intention to "protect democracy and the democratic way of life which the people of Ceylon have cherished and preserved through the years." But a "Left" government does make some difference; originally the last massive onslaught on the militants still fighting was timed for the end of the amnesty on 1 May, but the government felt it would be indelicate to launch such a repression on international labour day, so they postponed the attack for a few days.

Few others have emerged with much more credit. However, the Parliamentary Secretary to the Minister of Planning (R. D. Senanayake) was arrested quite early on. And an LSSP MP, (Vasudeva Nanayakkara) leader of the party's youth organization, was arrested for "complicity" in the revolt which might suggest that some of the LSSP youth sympathized with the JVP. The private secretary to the Minister of Information (R. S. Perera) also appears to have been detained. Outside the government, all the leading members of the Ceylon Broadcasting Corporation were arrested or dismissed.

(c) The JVP militants have now a clear idea of who their friends at home are. And abroad the picture is no less clear. There was an unseemly rush to prop up the Bandaranaike regime and provide it with the instruments of repression—six US helicopters, six Russian, four Indian and two Pakistani; six MIG-17s and 20 armoured cars—with Russian staff—from the Soviet Union; a quick injection of small arms and 18 army scout cars from British imperialism; and five Indian anti-submarine frigates patrolling the coast.

The Indian army guarded Colombo airport—so that Pakistani planes could fly troops and munitions through to East Bengal! Russian MIGs went immediately into service on arrival and were used to strafe rebel areas in the north-central region. More assistance came from Yugoslavia, Egypt and Australia. China restrained its no doubt strong desire to be counted among Mrs Bandaranaike's warmest admirers; but it is already a major supplier of assistance to Ceylon, and is, after Britain, Ceylon's biggest trading partner. Rumours have it that it was Chinese pressure which persuaded the very hard-pressed Generals of Pakistan to divert two helicopters from Bengal to Ceylon as a gesture of Sino-Pakistani solidarity with Mrs Bandaranaike. However, the Chinese cannot afford to be complacent, for the Russians do seem determined to secure a military foothold in Ceylon to offset the Americans at Diego Garcia and the British at Gan. In late April, the Chinese Government wrote to Mrs Bandaranaike, congratulating her on successfully destroying her young opposition and offering a long term, interest-free loan of £10.7 million.

(*d*) The government seriously underestimated the potential for revolt and overestimated the army's capacity to suppress the Left. The JVP underestimated the ruthlessness and cynicism of Mrs Bandaranaike, and were caught relatively unprepared. For the JVP and other revolutionary groups, the lessons are hard and bitter. Despite enormous heroism and tenacity, the Left has received a setback. Without links with organized workers of Colombo, the revolutionaries were unable to threaten the government from behind its back. The opposition has been forced into the more isolated areas, and it will take time for it to recover, if it does recover (in Malaya and the Philippines, the guerrilla opposition never did recover after its defeat in the fifties). But when it re-emerges, the crisis of Ceylonese capitalism will have reached a much more extreme state.

On the one hand, Mrs Bandaranaike—for short-term political gains—has created an army that will not, as it has in the past, passively accept its role as watchdog to the civilian government. Defence expenditure has tripled through the emergency; the resources going into defence will mean there is less for development, for job creation, which means there will be more opposition, and so the need for more defence expenditure. On the other hand, the cost of the military operation has made the immediate economic prospect, critical before the emergency, now catastrophic. The tea and rubber trades have been brought to standstill, and the rice output has been cut: export earnings and the basic food supply of the population are simultaneously threatened. The middle and upper classes have no doubt been terrified into supporting Mrs Bandaranaike, and perhaps foreign lenders have been impressed with her commitment to defend the Ceylonese outpost of world capitalism, but at fearful cost. She has delivered such a crushing blow to the economy that the class struggle is bound to escalate even more dramatically in the future. And then the only force capable of holding the country together will be the army, no doubt also tricked out in Leftist rhetoric. But the army cannot solve the central problem either. Only if Russia wants to buy Ceylon lock, stock and barrel, or if there is an international revolution from a Ceylonese source can that happen.

II. Bangladesh 1971*

Rarely have the policies of a contemporary government been such an unmitigated disaster as those of the West Pakistan military. Despite the utmost savagery, the rulers of Pakistan have lost well over half the population, not to independence, but to their most consistent rival, India. The institution around which the whole concept of Pakistan was built, the army, has suffered a crippling defeat in what it claimed was its main reason for existence, fighting Indians. Even on the western front, it has lost far

*Original version published in *International Socialism*, 50, January-March 1972.

more territory than it gained, and is in no position at all to bargain for what it hoped would save its face, a bit of Kashmir.

The new Pakistan is a dwarf beside the Indian giant. Yahya Khan directly assisted in the creation of the giant's power. The Indian army has demonstrated its military superiority. The Indian Generals have grown to be nine feet tall, and increasingly their shadows will grow long, not just over India and Pakistan, but over the whole of south Asia.

Politically, the new State is broken-backed. One General— Yahya Khan—has fallen. As he did, his Prime Minister and Deputy Prime Minister, with a host of others, led the way in denouncing him as little better than an Indian spy. In this way, they hope to inherit the peace. But what they inherit could just as easily destroy them. The Pakistani people have been fooled for a long time by anti-Indianism and militarism. Bhutto has nothing to offer them except the same brew with more pepper. But in a very much smaller cup.

East Pakistan was required to help support a military establishment of 392,000 men, costing—officially—53 per cent of the budget of the unified Pakistan. The costs of the war, of the loss of East Pakistan as well as the cumulative foreign debt of Rs 3,200 million (equal to a fifth of all the foreign exchange earnings of the unified State where East Pakistan produced about a fifth of the exports) will not just force a brutal contraction of the military. It will also make very difficult any expensive Leftish adventures by Bhutto. In any case, Bhutto's rhetoric has already frightened parts of the army and the conservative ruling order. He will have to make considerable concessions to them to be trusted. Meanwhile, his own following might develop more intransigent ambitions.

However, the circumstances of massive military defeat for a people still passionately committed to war on India are hardly promising for a revolutionary movement of opposition. That chauvinism which has always robbed radical movements in West Pakistan of their most powerful weapon against the ruling class still reigns supreme. The military may be radically altered. The Generals and Bhutto may find it necessary for their own survival to make more or less fierce growling noises at the 22 families that control Pakistan capitalism—may expropriate some or all of them—but all this will not produce popular power, only rhetoric. Meanwhile, the aspirants for power in the ruling class can play leapfrog in *coup* and counter *coup*. Without a coherent organized revolutionary party that has unequivocally abandoned Pakistani chauvinism (and what that entails, military force), there can only be one or other version of Bhutto.

On the other side of the border, Mrs Gandhi emerges with a position of power unrivalled since independence. She has, at very little cost, executed the central aim of Indian foreign policy since 1947, the reduction of the threat of Pakistan. She has also escaped with glory from the dangers facing her at home. For her massive electoral victory in March 1971—on a programme of radical reforms, including a major programme to reduce unemployment— was no more than an opportunity for her to deliver something to the mass of the population. The fate of Mrs Bandaranaike in Ceylon in April, also with a massive electoral victory behind her, must have been instructive in Delhi. For, like Ceylon, the ailing Indian economy can deliver very little in present conditions.

If Mrs Bandaranaike had had ten million refugees thrust upon her, no doubt she would have been able to escape the criticisms inevitable when she failed to honour any of herpr omises. Mrs Gandhi, full of virtue and weeping all over the poor Bengalis, sailed through triumphantly. War and victory will, at least temporarily, swamp any domestic critics, while allowing her complete power to squeeze, rather than increase, mass consumption.

The Indian Left (including the Communist Party of India, Marxist) were loyal to Indian chauvinism to the end. There were no challenges to Mrs Gandhi's war policy. At first it was supposed to be for the refugees, but in November Mrs Gandhi suddenly announced that the presence of West Pakistani troops in East Bengal was a threat to Indian security—for the first time since 1947. She went further. Just as Yahya Khan denied any independent role to the Bengalis by saying the whole revolt was the result of Indian intrigue, so Mrs Gandhi began to argue that the refugees had been driven out of East Pakistan by the army to force India to concede Kashmir.

The attitude of the Left meant that only minor criticisms could be directed at, for example, the reintroduction of the Preventive Detention Act last June (ever squeamish, some critics changed the name to the Maintenance of Internal Security Act), the even more far-reaching Defence of India Act, the arrest of countless "undesirable elements," the escalation of inflation and military expenditure, the cancellation of the state assembly elections (originally scheduled for next February) and so on. On the first day of the Lok Sabha winter session, Mrs Gandhi prevailed on the opposition parties to withdraw their censure motions. All have been bent not to rock the boat (to end strikes, withdraw "excessive" pay claims, work harder etc). The army the Left has been supporting in East Bengal will now turn upon Indian socialists if they dare to be impertinent.

If the refugees were the pretext for war, the Mukhti Bahini guerrillas were the decorative facade. The real purpose was not left in doubt. Indeed, it would be exceedingly strange for an Indian Government to be so passionate in support of the principle of national self-determination in East Bengal when it has bloodily and consistently tried to deny that right in Kashmir, in Nagaland and the Mizo country; when it has outlawed demands for secession to head off challenge by the Tamils, the Punjabis and others.

The guerrillas were, whether they knew it or not, Mrs Gandhi's public relations men. But even then they had to be carefully controlled (at least, those in India) lest they be infiltrated by revolutionaries. The Indian army directly supervised the guerrilla training camps, and the Indian Government both propped up the Provisional Government of Bangladesh in Calcutta and supervised its relationships with other bodies. Indian pressure was exercised to prevent the creation of a united National Liberation Front, admitting only Bhashani's fragment of the NAP, the pro-Moscow NAP, and some insignificant groups. The important sections of NAP—armed, under Maoist leadership and fighting inside East Bengal—were firmly kept out lest a common Naxalite strategy develop on both sides of the border. When the campaign started, the guerrillas were there to act as runners for the Indian army, not fighters for independence.

Listen to the authentic tone of the Indian Generals—General Jacob (*Times*, 18 December report) to the Mukhti Bahini leadership:

'I want this transfer of power to go bloodlessly and without incident'. When they answered that they would try to do their

best, the general roared: 'Don't just try—do it. If not, I'll
start shooting you fellows'.

or a nameless Brigadier (*Sunday Times*, 19 December):

> We are taking territory and are not ashamed of it. Bangladesh
> must simply be ours if it is to remain stable. Some semblance
> of democracy can be created but no one in Delhi or elsewhere
> pretends that is the real reason we are here. Bangladesh will
> be like Calcutta, which we keep firmly under our thumb from
> Delhi, with no nonsense of local autonomy.

The new State is born in the most unpromising circumstances.
Before the events of March 1971, it was one of the poorest
countries in a poverty stricken continent. Now, it has not
recovered from 1970's cyclone (200,000 dead), let alone 1971's
succession of civil war, savage Pakistani occupation, and
now, Indian invasion and occupation. On top of that, the
Indians will be trying to shove back into East Bengal ten million
refugees when their land and homes have already been scooped up
by someone else. The political force created in a real struggle for
independence might have been able to establish some stability in
these desperate circumstances, provided itw as clear the threat of
Indian domination was already being neutralized by a revolutionary movement in India. But no such force has been created.

The sleek gentlemen from Calcutta who have travelled to power
in the admin tail of the Indian army cannot create their own power
by magic. They are eager to establish their position, but that
depends entirely upon the Indians. Independence by proxy is no
independence at all. Indeed, so weak is the new government,
it must inevitably continue to rely for a long time on Indians, in
the army, the senior administrators and policemen now temporarily drafted into East Bengal by Delhi, and on Indian
handouts. The only hope is that Bangladesh will prove to be a
sharp bone sticking in Delhi's throat.

The small inner core of the Mukhti Bahini can no doubt be
absorbed in the new State as army and police, although the
Indians will severely circumscribe their power and prerogatives.
But the mass of young men with guns cannot. The Indians know
it and are moving rapidly to try and disarm them. For these

young men, resentful that they, who fought inside East Bengal, are now offered only a return to their old life whereas those who went into exile have inherited all, learning the lessons will be hard. If, like the Maoist cadres in the countryside, they already see the drift of events, they will prepare for the long and bitter struggle against Indian domination. But without a political awareness, they can become only armed gangs, as much bandit as nationalist, marauding the countryside, adding only further misery to the lot of their countrymen.

The border with India is too long for the Indians to be able to bottle up Bengali poverty outside of India. Gun-running across the border and the exchange of political cadres—the other side of the coin to the flood of Indian carpetbaggers into East Bengal— could and almost certainly will spread the chronic infection into India's heartlands.

China could well be of assistance here. Before the Indo-Pakistan war, China was busy trying to mend its fences with India, perhaps uneasily aware that its old ally, Pakistan, might well turn out to be the loser so that new friends were needed. The danger was greater because the Soviet Union already holds an entrenched position in India. Chou En-lai sent a warm and friendly letter to Mrs Gandhi in mid-November, the first formal communication from China for years. Mrs Gandhi replied by suggesting the two countries raise their diplomatic representatives to the status of ambassadors and begin talks on disputed border questions. Even as late as 30 November, the Chinese Government is said to have protested to Mrs Gandhi unofficially that China had never publicly denounced Sheikh Mujibur Rahman or the Mukti Bahini, only foreign intervention in Pakistan's affairs.

It was far too late to do more than injure Pakistani feelings. The outbreak of war made China's attempt to do what the Russians did at Tashkent after the 1965 Indo-Pakistan war, establish a role as independent mediator, impossible. China could do nothing except support Pakistan, albeit only with words and arms supplies. Its policy went down to the same defeat embodied in a massive Russian victory in India's triumph. Perhaps now, the only means available to China—despite its desperate attempts to be a respectable member of the United Nations—to challenge Soviet power in south Asia is to support the guerrillas in Bangladesh. It is too much to expect that the guerrillas, having been coldly repulsed by

China to date, will learn any lessons from Chairman Mao's sudden change of heart.

The independence of Bangladesh has not at all been won. The appalling repression by the Pakistan military has indeed been ended. But that—despite the joy of the crowds in Dacca—is not the same as independence. The Indian Government will be delighted if the Bengalis are satisfied with an "independence" which means no more than the trivial symbols of a State—a flag, a President, a seat in the United Nations. Those are things the Indians, if not the Pakistanis, can easily concede. But the right of Bengalis to decide the affairs of East Bengal, regardless of the Indian ruling class, is quite a different matter. Indeed, in the final analysis, the new government has only Indian power to protect it from Bengalis. The war will not produce an independent government, only a puppet on strings pulled from Delhi.

Indeed, independence is now further off than it was before the Indians converted the struggle into an Indo-Pakistan war.[1] For now the struggle for an independent Bangladesh is completely locked in the general struggle of Indians against the Indian ruling class. At the moment, that battle is less promising than the old war of Bengalis on the Pakistan ruling class.

---

[1]For the background to the crisis in West Pakistan and the relationship between East and West Pakistan, cf. my pamphlet, *The Struggle for Bangla Desh*, Pluto Press, London, 1971.

PART TWO

China and the Struggle for
National Liberation

4

The Chinese Cultural Revolution

I.

The *detente* between Washington and Moscow, the partial
"thaw" in the cold war, permitted the expression not just of
nationalistic polycentrism between nation-States, but polycentrism
within each nation-State. The forces of revolt were expressed not
merely in a Gaullist foreign policy against NATO, but also in
France's May 1968 revolt against De Gaulle himself. Nowhere has
this double process been more vividly illustrated than in China
where the basic problems of survival for the majority are greater.
Between the slack expansion of agricultural output and the inexorable pressure of a rising population, in a world overshadowed
by the industrialized powers, by the military threat of the United
States and the Soviet Union, there is almost no room for manoeuvre. China, like the other underdeveloped countries, is trapped
in a stifling strait-jacket where despair and bold rhetoric mingle
on equal terms.

But just because it is an underdeveloped country, China's
economy can survive much of the Cultural Revolution when it
is isolated in a few urban centres. The rural majority continues
its life much as before. The economy does not depend in the same
way upon a single integrated structure. The villages depend much

This chapter was first published as "China : Let a Hundred Flowers
Bloom", *International Socialism*, 35, Winter, 1968-69.

less upon the cities than in a more developed country. Thus, in some of the wilder talk about "civil war," one must be careful to see how many people and places were really involved. Sometimes, it seems, a minor scuffle between two bands of teenage thugs has been duly reported with solemnity on Red Guard posters as a major struggle, and thence transmitted to the world press as a collapse of the social order. The information emerging from China is more fragmentary than that on any other country in the world, and must be treated with a certain initial scepticism.

By late 1968, the Cultural Revolution was drawing to a close. It would still be a long time before the entire country was once more at peace, but the leadership was committed to establishing peace. Nothing had happened since the climax of January 1967 to change the basic balance of forces in the country. Up to that time, the central party leadership held the initiative and set the pace. It was able to escalate its war against opposition forces in the party in successive phases, until it virtually abandoned the party altogether. The climax was reached when the students, the Red Guards, were shown to have failed in their task of remaking the party, and the Peking leadership appealed to the workers and peasants to "bombard the party headquarters...to seize power." It thereby released a host of new forces which rapidly came to threaten itself. Despite many short-term zigzags in policy, after January 1967, the leadership was trying to draw back from the abyss. It had been forced to devote itself to the problems raised by its campaign, rather than to the purposes of the campaign itself. It first sought to use the army (PLA) to impose a single unified order on the country, and then, when this proved inadequate, to promote conservative deals with whatever local provincial leadership, in collaboration with the army, would cooperate.

But to do this was to deny the earlier rhetoric of the Cultural Revolution, to rehabilitate the discredited party cadres and reject implicitly the competing demands of Red Guards and Revolutionary Rebels. Peking had too little power over the whole country to secure its will, and sudden spasms of violence and conflict swept through provincial capitals as new and old groups competed for first place in the new order. Despite the merciless exposure of the old provincial party leadership, many of them returned to power. The stalemate between Peking and the opposition could not have been illustrated more vividly. Neither side could defeat the other, and in their common interest in domestic order against the mass of the population, both were forced back into cooperation. The crucial problem—namely, the balance of power between Peking and its provinces—remained unsolved. Indeed, if anything, the Cultural Revolution has immensely exacerbated the problem rather than approached its solution.[1]

As the campaign proceeded, it connected different layers of the population and party in different areas at different times. This immense complexity of issues and loyalties is the background to the twists and turns in Peking's policies. Once opened, the contents of Pandora's Box threatened to take control. But each change in policy ran the risk of inciting new groups of people to begin to compete for the prizes, and ultimately, a real— rather than rhetorical—class war. There are some signs that a few of the rebels made the transition from attacking "a handful in the party taking the capitalist road" to war on "the Red Capitalist Class," a phrase from the manifesto of a Hunan rebel group Sheng-wu-lien.[2] The rise and fall in Peking's attacks on the "ultra-Left" and "anarchism" gives an indirect indication of how serious the threat at times has been, and, perhaps, still is.

The twists and turns in policy embody Peking's search for an agency to replace or reform the party, to sidestep localized webs of power in each province, and thereby impose a new centralized regime. On the "Left" swings, it tried to use new forces—Red Guard bands, Revolutionary Rebel groups; on the "Right," it brought in the army (PLA) in the first instance, and then the party cadres themselves once again. The PLA is only three million strong, unlike the 17-20 million cadres in and around the old party, and provincial PLA units in any case are likely to have loyalties to the province concerned. The stresses within the PLA threatened the sole remaining coherent framework in the country as a whole, as well as exposing China's vulnerability to Soviet or American threats. In the end, Peking was reduced to trying to rehabilitate the party itself. Nothing was solved; two and a half

---

[1]For earlier material on the Cultural Revolution, cf. "The Notebook", *IS* 26, autumn 1966; Nigel Harris, "China: What Price Culture?" *IS* 28, spring 1967; and Tony Cliff, "Crisis in China", *IS* 29, summer 1967.

[2]January 1968: the Manifesto of Sheng-wu-lien is reprinted in English, with an introduction by Tony Cliff in *International Socialism*, 37, June-July 1969.

years had been lost with nothing to show—except, perhaps (for 1967 alone) 86.4 million copies of Mao's *Selected Works* and 350 million Red Books.

II. The centralization issue

The Cultural Revolution was an attempt to overcome the sluggish rate of China's economic growth, and one of the results of that sluggish rate, localized power groups which inhibited central direction. At the beginning of the campaign, the most important of the localized groups were in control of provincial administration. At the end, new groups had blossomed at every level, and, indeed, outside the administrative structure altogether.

The battle is, then, over the distribution of scarce resources. It is partly between town and country, between different provinces, between the provinces and Peking; it is also partly between workers and managers of party cadres, and, in some areas, between peasants and party cadres. The first kind of conflict is one between different geographical areas; the second, between different national classes (or fragments of such classes). Territorial conflict is endemic in most underdeveloped countries, and has been central to the pre-industrialization history of the developed countries. However, in developed countries today, interdependence between the different territorial parts of the economically centralized nation-State has long since superseded conflict. There are, of course, some kinds of regional conflict still—Welsh and Scottish nationalisms are currently embodying certain regional demands. But these are only possible on the margins when social and class conflict is relatively mild. When class conflict rises, it tends to eliminate much of the significance of regional clash in modern developed countries. Rather than Welsh employers and workers combining to fight London; Welsh, Yorkshire, Scottish and other miners combine to fight the National Coal Board, part of an employing class which includes Welsh, Scottish and so on employers.

In a backward country, national interdependence is weak, for the economy consists of much more independent segments. National classes are therefore very underdeveloped as well. The ruling class is "embryonic"; that is, its members have not all identified a common class interest, and particular groups are prepared to press their opposition to the national centre to the point of open rebellion. Thus each territorially defined ruling group is open to pursuing its own narrow interest at the cost of the national ruling class interest; the final stage in pursuing this narrow interest is to secede altogether and create an independent State. Whether or not a group does this depends upon its assessment of its strength (how far it is economically independent in fact, how far its own subordinate classes will follow it) and its assessment of the strength concentrated in the parent-State (if the parent-State has a monopoly of military force and is willing to use it, the local group is unlikely to rebel except where it can get foreign assistance on a comparable scale).

An exacerbating condition in this relationship is the demand the parent-State makes upon the local ruling group to relinquish a share of the surplus generated in the group's territory. If the group's territory is economically advanced, its surplus is likely to be an industrial one; in return, it may receive foodstuffs, without which it cannot survive. Thus, the industrialized areas are likely to have, initially, a greater interest in a strong national centre which can provide them with adequate foodstuffs. By contrast, the food surplus areas are likely to resent central control since their product is taken; yet, in conditions of high accumulation, they see few returns in terms of manufactured goods. If foodstuff is plentiful, these tensions may be minor ones, the real debate surrounding the national distribution of investment resources—which area gets the next steel mill. The foodgrain surplus areas have power to influence national investment distribution when food is short; the food-deficit areas, often (but not always) the industrialized areas, can attract the major share of investment resources when food is easy to obtain because they already provide an infrastructure of previous investment which will maximize the use of such resources.

On the other hand, every local ruling group has some interest in securing as much as possible of the surplus its territory produces in order to strengthen its own power within the territory.

This is a very oversimplified account of a complex issue. There are many other factors at stake in the bargaining between different areas, and the national centre—for example, whether or not the area is also an international boundary; or whether or not communications and distance preclude the centre actually moving force against a recalcitrant province. In China, Peking has, in the short term, to trust the Lhasa administration because it cannot move large numbers of troops into Tibet rapidly.

Peking needs to maximize the rate of capital accumulation if China is to develop as a national economy. To do so, it must secure unimpeded control of the surplus generated in every province. To do this, it must prevent provincial parties skimming the provincial surplus for their own purposes, and distribute the national surplus as it thinks fit. If Shanghai can make the best use of new investment, then that is where new investment must go, even if it deprives the poor provinces and increases regional differentials in terms of income and power. However, a number of features over the past decade have steadily strengthened local power and thereby progressively inhibited Peking's ability to plan. Overcoming these inhibitions cannot indefinitely be postponed. The longer entrenched enclaves of provincial power are permitted to stand against Peking, the more powerful they become, the more difficult Peking finds it to accelerate the overall rate of development. Thus, the Maoist stress upon the need for poverty and self-sacrifice is a stress on the need for a common subordination to central control, a common sacrifice of consumption to national accumulation.

In Imperial China, the conflict between provinces and centre was one important theme at different times. When the Imperial dynasty was strong, it sought to inhibit the creation of a provincial opposition by keeping the mandarins in circulation between provinces. Provincial mandarins were supposed never to have sufficient time and opportunity to build up a proper base within the province. This circulation of officials has not happened in Communist China. The provincial administration of 1965 was still manned by many of the people who originally took power in the province after the fall of the Kuomintang, and the regional bureaux are still, broadly, the original occupying armies.

Between 1948 and 1957, the country as a whole was steadily centralized, a process culminating in the period of tightest central control during the first five-year plan. Yet the unity of the country still depended upon the local party cadres: indeed, holding the party together meant holding China together. But there was in this period room for Peking to manoeuvre. A respectable rate of economic growth and rising foodgrains output made central control tolerable. This does not mean there were not provincial tensions. For example, in the 1953-54 rectification campaign (which, at the national level, purged Kao Kang and Jao Shu-shih), the first secretaries in six provinces and two autonomous regions were changed. Again, the purge of 1957-58 affected 12 provinces and autonomous regions. It seems there had been much grumbling among provincial leaders during the speed-up in collectivization in 1956-57, and the purged were accused of favouring a slower rate of economic growth and qualifying national directives. In Honan the party first secretary was said to have argued: "Honan is different from Peking and Shanghai, and what is marked out by the central leadership can serve only as a guide."[3] Small personal cliques were said to have seized control of some provincial parties for their own benefit, the cliques appealing to provincial loyalties. For example, the purged Governor of Shantung is alleged to have said: "I am a native of Shantung, I am for the people of Shantung and the cadres of Shantung"; by implication, against the Pekinese. He was accused of packing the party with his own supporters and blocking national directives. But the purge in practice affected mainly the middle ranks of the provincial parties rather than its top leadership. During the Cultural Revolution, others have been accused in identical language—for example, Peng Chen, the Peking Party leader until 1966, was accused of making Peking an "independent kingdom, watertight and impenetrable."

Perhaps one of the motives of the central leadership in the Great Leap Forward was to break the provincial leadership's power by decentralizing the economy to the under-province level, to the county (*Hsien*) and commune. Peking relinquished substantial controls over management, finance, grain procurements, price control and planning. There was some decentralization of control over new capital projects, and in some parts of the economy, control was divided between the province and the centre ("dual control" of the railways, for example). Peking remained in control of interprovincial grain balances, even if not of grain procurement.[4]

From 1960, Peking tried to reverse the results of this disastrous loss of power which, far from destroying the provincial leadership,

[3]Cited by F. Tiewes, "The Purge of Provincial Leaders", 1957-58, *China Quarterly*, 27(*CQ*) July-September 1966, p. 21.
[4]The details can be found in Audrey Donnithorne's *China's Economic System*, London, 1967.

had only strengthened it. But the agricultural disasters of 1960 61 made it, in the short term, even more dependent upon provincial cooperation. Any slight variation in local administrative control could produce famine in such conditions. Peking concentrated on a cautious, conservative economic policy, described earlier by Cliff as a phase of "neo-NEP."[5]   The margins were far too narrow to gamble, even though permitting the situation to continue only made it more difficult to solve later on. Differentials between rich and poor, advanced and backward areas, town and country, between social strata, widened, sustained by the provincial party's toleration of its own friends and supporters. The longer Peking permitted local power to continue unhampered—or rather, checked by little more than Peking's propaganda rhetoric as in the "socialist education campaign"—the more powerfully entrenched provincial leaders might become, the more slippery Peking's grasp of provincial surpluses. The threat implicit in the shifting power balance was that Peking might become just a servicing centre for real power groups in the provinces or the front for a coalition of powerful provinces. Indeed, it has been argued that Peking's purchase of grain on the world market was not so much to meet a general deficit at home as give it an edge in the hard bargaining over the distribution of interprovincial grain balances.[6] Peking imports about six million tons of foodgrains a year, which is a mere three per cent of China's total grain output, but 12 per cent of central procurements and probably much more of interprovincial balances. The grain is not solely for domestic use; it has been used as an instrument of foreign policy—grain was exported to Egypt in 1967 so that China could compete with Soviet foreign policy.

However, breaking the provincial leadership is only one part of the problem. Once the web of control at the provincial level is broken, it might merely be that a multiplicity of groups would be created at the under-provincial level, each vying for power in the province, each exhibiting what the Peking press calls a "mountain stronghold" or "small group" mentality. At least, in the old situation, Peking had only to deal with 29 local authorities (provinces, autonomous regions, autonomous municipalities). Destroying that

[5]Cliff, *op. cit.*
[6]See the evidence of Audrey Donnithorne to the Joint Economic Committee of Congress, *Mainland China in the World Economy*, Washington, 1967, pp. 46-50.

level of administration could create thousands of different groups to be dealt with. In addition, both the central and the provincial leaderships were not necessarily united. At the centre, within the small leadership group, different perspectives were available, and as the struggle outside developed, so it connected with this inner struggle, fragmenting the inner cliques, which in turn fragmented the forces outside. At every level, factionalism threatened to dissolve what unified structure remained, producing an immensely complex picture where easy identification of the forces became impossible. And the disagreements came to range over the whole spectrum of foreign and domestic policy—from the best way forward for the economy, to China's relationship to Russia, the US and Viet Nam.

The PLA seemed to be the sole force left to hold the whole together. Securing the sowing and harvesting of crops was one of its persistent responsibilities. Yet it was too small to take up the burdens of the party properly. If the rural party administration weakens, the peasants may fail to relinquish the grain. Honan radio, for example, rebuked selfish peasants for hoarding grain, for "economism," in mid-1967. But once the grain is hoarded, a force as small as the PLA cannot possibly find it. Fortunately, 1967 seems to have been a very good year—officially ten per cent above 1966's output. But the limitations of PLA control were vividly illustrated. The centre, of necessity, had to begin the process of rebuilding the party, whatever the economic cost.

The central leadership—or the dominant faction within it—closed all educational institutions in mid-1966 in order to make available an extra-party scourge of the cadres. It was ironic, since earlier Mao had said the youth was the weak factor in China's progress since it had not experienced Kuomintang rule. At every stage, the Red Guards needed official encouragement and support for survival—for transport, telegraphic services, food, accommodation, newsprint, etc—and were subject to subversion by different factions in the central and provincial leaderships. By November 1966, it was clear the Red Guards were no longer a useful instrument for the central leadership, but, on the contrary, merely engendered factionalism and violence. From that date, the Peking leadership began the long task of trying to get the students back to school and university.

In February 1967, primary schools were officially reopened, with secondary schools and universities supposed to open in March: all, despite earlier promises, unreformed. By June, it was clear work had not been resumed in the schools. They were used as faction headquarters, as dormitories; the teachers were often too demoralized to risk returning to work; university textbooks had been denounced, but no new ones written. One correspondent[7] estimated that on average a half to two-thirds of all school pupils attended school for one or two hours per morning to read or sing Mao quotes and undergo military training.

The summer violence of 1967 sucked in the Red Guard groups once more and made them, at particular times and places, briefly important. The campaign in the party had little effect—the Red Guards were determined to get their foot in the door before the old order returned. Hsieh Fu-chih, Minister of Public Security, reproved the youth for squabbling in October;[8] and said some of them might gain admission to a reformed party after a probationary period.

None of this had very much effect, and the summer of 1968 found bands of Red Guards again awaiting the opportunity to participate in the struggle for power. However, throughout 1968, the central leadership shifted its emphasis almost entirely away from youth—the "working class" should now be the main element in the Cultural Revolution. The party recruited squads of "workers and peasants" to do the task the PLA had failed to do, and moved them into all educational institutions to reimpose discipline. The first such team entered Tsinghua University in late July, and was rewarded with a basket of mangoes from Mao himself.[9] A much greater stress appeared in the party press on the errors of "intellectuals," and the need for them to submit to discipline.

However, there were some suggestions that the more radical

[7]Harold Munthe-Kaas, Peking correspondent, *Sunday Times*, London, 25 June 1967.

[8]24 October 1967, published in the *Cultural Revolution Bulletin*, 11 December 1967.

[9]The mangoes were originally a gift from Pakistan, but immediately deified by their contact with the Chairman. They subsequently circulated China—one is said to have been deposited in the strong vault of a bank in Shanghai. Giant models of the mangoes were displayed on the National Day march in Peking, 1 October 1968.

elements in the Cultural Revolution Group in Peking still saw the youth as a possible replacement for the party. On 7 September a rally to celebrate the end of the long agonizing process of forming Revolutionary Committees in all provinces was held in Peking. But it was not held before the famous Tienanmen, nor did Mao or Lin Piao attend. And Chiang Ch'ing, Mao's wife and one of the most important members of the Cultural Revolution Group, gave a most curious speech to the assembled students which included the following ambiguous comment on her predecessor's speech: "You will notice that—unlike Chou En-lai—I have pointedly omitted to mention the workers and peasants who are trying to break you up." It had other waspish asides, and ended with an injunction to the audience to keep its spirits up. Clearly, someone had been defeated.

III. The Cultural Revolution in 1967 and 1968

The brief climax to the Cultural Revolution in January 1967 was followed by an immediate and rapid retreat by the central leadership. A central directive of 21 January ordered the PLA to intervene and restore order, seeking to create conservative coalitions, the "triple alliances," between the PLA, reformed party cadres and Revolutionary Rebels (the "worker" successors to the Red Guards) in all provinces. However, whatever the rhetoric about triple alliances, at this stage military control was the first priority to overcome urban disorder and stiffen the administration for the tasks of spring sowing in the countryside. The PLA instructions were very wide:

In all institutions where seizure of power has become necessary, from above to below, the participation of the PLA and militia-delegates in the temporary organs of power of the revolutionary triple alliance is indispensable. Factories, villages, institutions of finance and commerce, of learning (including colleges, secondary and primary schools), party organs, administrative and mass organizations, must be led with the participation of the PLA. . .where there are not enough PLA representatives available, these positions should better be left vacant temporarily (*Red Flag*, 10 March 1967),

Press and radio urged the peasants to concentrate on the sowing and *Red Flag* (22 February) even criticized those who launched indiscriminate attacks on all persons in authority—such a policy "robs the nation of the mature political and organizational skills of experienced men." On 6 March it reported that the Central Committee (which had not, apparently, met) urged all rural party cadres to take the leadership in the spring sowing: "Those cadres who have made mistakes," it said, "should redouble their efforts in spring farm work to make amends."

However, the more the PLA extended itself, the more *it* became the target for criticism rather than the old party order. In particular, the rebel group it failed to choose as its partner in a triple alliance sooner or later appealed over its head to Peking for arbitration. Sheer military involvement made the PLA vulnerable politically. In Peking itself, the PLA was midwife to a revolutionary municipal committee (the sixth "triple alliance" formed to that time; 23 to go) of which Hsieh Fu-chih, Minister of Public Security, was chief; two of the four vice-chairmen and 14 of the 97 committee members were from the PLA.

On 6 April, the Party Military Affairs Committee issued a directive forbidding PLA units to suppress any rebel faction or to use force to secure order. It was to be a free for all, and through the summer, the maximum violence and disorder of the Cultural Revolution occurred. The scale of the violence is impossible to estimate reliably, for the evidence is fragmentary and from biased sources. One Red Guard source retailed a speech by Hsieh Fu-chih in which he is supposed to have said that production in Peking fell by seven per cent in April because of "armed incidents." However, it is unlikely that the statistical services of Peking were up to any such precise estimate so soon after the event. He is alleged also to have said that between 30 April and 10 May, there were 130 armed struggles around the city, involving 63,000 people in all, with 50 to 100 casualties *per incident*.

Radio and press continuously appealed throughout the summer for an end to violence, to attacks upon soldiers and interference with public property.[10] The PLA was probably at the limit of its tolerance when the Wuhan incident in July dramatically

---

[10]For example, the 6 June order, signed by the Central Committee. State Council, Military Affairs Committee and Cultural Revolution Group.

illustrated its vulnerability and the central leadership's dangerous dependence on the PLA. The Wuhan Military Region commander was Chen Tsai-tao, a veteran party soldier who had commanded the 4th Army in 1934 and become a full General in 1955. In the formation of Wuhan's Revolutionary Committee (the "triple alliance"), he backed the One Million Heroes rebel group as his collaborators. A coalition of seven Red Guard groups appealed to Peking against this, saying that the One Million Heroes was just a front for the old "capitalist roaders" of the provincial party. Hsieh Fu-chih and Wang Li (head of the party propaganda department) visited Wuhan to plead for the excluded Red Guards, and were promptly arrested by the PLA. Demonstrations against Chen in Peking, furious protests from the centre, rumours of the personal intervention of Chou En-lai, of paratroop drops on Wuhan and gunboats being sent from Shanghai up the Yangtze to Wuhan, finally secured the release of Peking's emissaries. The air force was said to have taken over security functions in Wuhan. Most of the military command acknowledged their errors and returned to the fold, although Chen himself was replaced by an officer from the Peking Garrison.

The details are suspect, but the substance of the incident dramatically revealed the weakness of the PLA as a substitute for a popular revolutionary force. Attacks on the capitalist roaders in the PLA followed (e.g. *Red Flag*, 17 August), but briefly, since to turn the attack on the PLA itself was to threaten the only safeguard left to the existing leadership, the sole framework for holding together the country. Lin Piao is said to have restricted himself to urging patience upon the Generals who met in military conference in Peking on 9 August. However, there were contradictory tensions within the national leadership. On the one hand, some leaders sought to protect the PLA; on the other, some of the Cultural Revolution Group were said to be pressing for selected Red Guards to be armed to help safeguard public property. It was perhaps the second group which sponsored or encouraged the attack on the Foreign Ministry in the same month and the attacks on foreign embassies, culminating in the sack of the British Charge d'Affaires office on 22 August.

But the violence was not restricted to Peking. "A wind of armed struggle is developing in several regions," the *People's Daily* noted on 19 August, and the New China News Agency reported opposition to the formation of Revolutionary Committees in eight provinces. Ceaseless adjurations and edicts from the central leadership seemed to have little or no effect. Tougher measures were required to repudiate the wilder men. On 20 August, Wang Li of the Cultural Revolution Group was dismissed, and others immediately around him accused of being Kuomintang agents. The honour of the PLA had received its sacrificial victim. On 25 August, the national press launched a campaign: "Support the army and love the people," and the PLA was ordered at all costs to restore the tattered urban administration to order. On 5 September, Red Guard sources reported that Chiang Ch'ing had publicly defended the central leadership, the Revolutionary Committees and the PLA against "a gust of foul wind" on the ultra-Left and the Right among the Red Guards.

In the same month, Mao toured some provinces in order to examine the situation at first hand. His verdict stressed the need to re-educate the Red Guards and Revolutionary Rebels lest they turn to the extreme Left. They must stop trying to be active in reforming society as a whole, and return to their schools and work-places to form triple alliances there—where, we might add, the dangers were much less, and in any case, overseen by the PLA. It was clear that the situation had to be stabilized as rapidly as possible, the glaring gaps in ruling class solidarity closed lest it incite outsiders to try and get in. However, the party adminis-tration could not just be restored in its old form or the opponents would redouble their efforts to destroy it and might, in addition, destroy the Peking leadership as well. Revolutionary Committees must be created as rapidly as possible, even if in practice it meant no more than a new name for the civil administration of the PLA or the old party organization itself. Revolutionary Committees must be created in the remaining 23 provinces by January 1968, it was announced. Where disputes occurred, fac-tions should send representatives to Peking for arbitration. As it happened, only seven more provinces received their Revo-lutionary Committees by the deadline, suggesting how difficult the stalemate had become in many provinces.

One major source of grievance, then, was who was to share in the prizes of the new order. In October, Hsieh Fu-chih offered some clarification to the aspirant groups in announcing a new Party Congress in 1968—in May or June, or just before 1 October.[11] The Congress, he said, must be organized from the top downwards lest the old guard dominate it: "Inth is way, it will be possible to ensure that the rebels among the party members will be in a majority." And it should be much larger than past Congresses, not 1,000 but 10,000 representatives. This would be a Congress with a vengeance, swamped with Peking nominees and incapable, by reason of its size, of deciding anything of significance. The 8th Congress was held in 1956, and under the constitution, Congresses were to be held at four-year intervals. Yet the 9th, so long delayed, was not mentioned again in 1968, and one must presume that, with all safeguards, the Peking leadership still could not be sure of a majority.

With the winter, activity tended to fall. The Peking press concentrated on conservative themes, and the joint New Year editorial of the *People's Daily*, *Red Flag* and *Liberation Army Daily* stressed the need to consolidate, to complete the rectification of the party organization and strengthen it. In order of precedence, the party and the Young Communist League (supposed to have been disbanded in 1966) appeared before the Red Guards. This did not mean that there were no dissonant voices at all. In Shanghai, troubles were reported, and in February, the press was once more taking to task "anarchism," indiscipline and disobedience among workers and students. It was clear also that the events of 1967 had created a subterranean network of contacts and communications in particular areas which defied the Peking attempt to reimpose silence.

A further 12 Revolutionary Committees were set up by April, but many of them were little more than PLA-cadre fronts. Increasingly, criticisms were levelled at over-hasty rehabilitation of those disgraced—the "mass organizations" were under-represented, and many of the old cadres were sneaking back into the new order, cadres which were "Left in form but Right in essence." Mao's current instruction (reported, *People's Daily*, 12 April) described the opposition to the Cultural Revolution as the same as that of the Kuomintang. The hardening of the line was a prelude to further violence. It came with the first intimations of spring, and blossomed in the summer heat. Yet it did not reach the proportions of mid-1967, perhaps because only one faction of the

[11]*Cultural Revolution Bulletin, op. cit.*

central leadership was supporting a greater role for the Revolutionary Rebels, the others being more concerned with the restoration of order.

The 1 August Army Day editorials unequivocally demanded absolute obedience by all to the PLA. On 5 August the *People's Daily* denounced domestic polycentrism and demanded absolute obedience to centralized control (the paper said it was merely reiterating instructions contained in orders issued on 3, 24 and 28 July). The agency of social change, the leadership of the movement, was the "working class" (*People's Daily*, 15 August). In practice, this meant the recruitment of teams of workers and peasants to take over detailed execution of policy from the hardpressed PLA units—to assume control of schools and universities, factories and urban administration.

The PLA remained in command, but its agents now became squads of civilians under military and cadre supervision. In the cities, teams of vigilantes were able to fill the gaps created by the erosion of the old public security organs. Kwantung boldly set the target of one million men to join such teams, and Kweichow announced that up to ten per cent of the workers in any one factory could participate in the takeover of educational institutions. Mao's instruction on such teams stated that they "should stay permanently in the schools and colleges, take part in all the tasks of struggle-criticism-transformation there and always lead these institutions."[12] Either there was a great deal of surplus labour in the factories, or overall production was likely to suffer by cutting the labour force.

At different stages, the leadership had tried to control the Red Guard factions—by placing them under PLA command, by sending them to the communes for labour and, even, for a brief despairing moment, on fruitless Long Marches. The shift to "the leadership of the working class" can similarly be seen as a way of ridding the labour force of Revolutionary Rebels, shunting the worker factions into detailed and isolated work which would permit the restoration of order under PLA control. The Chinese working class has no independent class organizations with which to identify itself, to crystallize its policy. It exists in the Maoist teams by permission of the party leadership. No doubt De Gaulle, test-

[12]*Peking Review*, 42, 18 October 1968, p. 5.

ing the mild temperature of "participation," would quite like to create teams of "working class" youth to bloody student noses, but nobody should be misled into thinking that this is somehow an authentic proletarian act. As will be suggested later, wherever authentic proletarian organization has in fact appeared, the central leadership has been quick to try and crush it.

On 5 September it was announced that the last two Revolutionary Committees had been formed. The national press returned to the point from whence the Cultural Revolution began in the spring of 1966—a critique of journalists and "some intellectuals." Liu Shao-chi remained the prime casualty, the scapegoat and warning to all the other cadres now to be rehabilitated. On National Day (1 October), the Peking press said that the "handful of capitalist roaders" had now been overthrown and power returned to the proletariat (the same claim was made, somewhat prematurely, by *Red Flag* on 1 July). On 15 October, Peking radio said that China's Khrushchev had been deprived of all party posts, although presumably he still remained President of the Republic, and on 1 November, Liu was for the first time publicly named by the radio in a broadcast reporting the decisions of an enlarged plenary session of the Central Committee, meeting since 13 October. Liu had been formally deprived of all powers and rank and expelled from the party.

Is this all it was supposed to be about? For two and a half years, the party's power had been systematically eroded, for no better reason than "an extremely small handful" of "renegades, spies, counter-revolutionaries, and cadres taking the capitalist road," led by Mao's erstwhile heir, now described as "the main traitor, workers' thief and Kuomintang running dog." It would strain the imagination too far to think so much had been gambled for so little. While the Red Guards rampaged in Peking streets, Liu and the party Secretary, Teng Hsiao-p'ing, remained untouched in their government residences. Liu was still not officially destroyed in 1968, since only a full Party Congress could ratify his expulsion from the Party, and a National People's Congress his dismissal as President of the Republic. Such devotion to constitutional niceties suggests how vulnerable the leadership feels itself to be: violence against an important member of the Party can be the precedent for violence against those that inherit.

IV. The provinces

The provincial level is the crucial area to observe the Cultural Revolution, and yet it is the area where there is least information. The essential issues have been decided here, rather than in the Peking leadership clique. What follows are some notes on Sinkiang, Szechuan and Tibet, not at all because they are representative—indeed, they are among the least representative provinces of China—but because they illustrate some features of the opposition.

(*a*) *Sinkiang* is in the far north-west, with a long common border with the Soviet Union and a large non-Chinese population (Turkic tribes, who inhabit also the adjacent Soviet territory). From 1955, the head of the administration was a Hunanese, Wang En-mao, controlling the provincial party, government and Sinkiang PLA units. The last is particularly important, since there are said to be 600,000 troops in Sinkiang along the Russian border. Lop Nor, the main nuclear testing site, is in Sinkiang, as well as plants of nuclear significance; the main gaseous plant producing enriched uranium is at Lanchow in neighbouring Kansu.

The Red Guards in Peking launched successive poster and press attacks on Wang in 1966, accusing him of brutality in controlling his fief. He is said to have repressed Red Guard attempts to enter Sinkiang—turning their trains round and despatching them back to Peking, gaoling others, and even driving some to a death by starvation in the Gobi desert. The attacks did not meet their target. Wang is said to have been received amicably at Mao's court in Peking on 31 December; and in February 1967, the Cultural Revolution was officially suspended in Sinkiang on the grounds that it was a sensitive border region. The suspension coincided with a rumour that Wang had threatened to seize the nuclear installations in the north-west unless he was left in peace.

However, in June there were reports of fighting in Urumchi (Sinkiang's capital), and again in August. In between—in early July—again it was rumoured there had been a settlement between Wang and Peking. The Red Guard verbal attack continued unabated, as did reports of more trouble through 1968. Certainly, Sinkiang was one of the last provinces to establish a Revolutionary

Committee. In the Peking announcement of its creation, Wang, the chief leader of the province since 1955, was not included among the list of "capitalist roaders" ousted during the Cultural Revolution, but he was included as "third vice-chairman." However, when an important Albanian delegation visited Urumchi in October 1968, it was Wang who met them on behalf of the province and made the main address of welcome. He was described as vice-chairman of the Revolutionary Committee and Political Commissar of the PLA Sinkiang Military Area Command.[13] In practice, very little appears to have changed in Sinkiang, whatever the rhetoric.

(*b*) *Szechuan* is in the south-west, adjacent to Tibet. It is vital as a key grain producing area. It is also what the Red Guards called the heart of the empire of the south and south-west. The former party head, Li Ching-chuan, the "local emperor," came under heavy attack. Kweichow Radio (Kweichow is a neighbouring province) permitted a former Party Secretary from Ipin in Szechuan, Liu Chieh-t'ing, to broadcast his criticisms of Li (presumably he could not broadcast them in Szechuan itself). He accused Li of seeking to maintain Szechuan's grain capacity as a bargaining counter against Peking; of suppressing Peking's instructions to collectivize agriculture and create Communes; of giving collective agricultural property over to private peasant production; and of gaoling him, Liu, for two years for criticizing the way the province was administered.

Liu, like many of the rebels, had his own fortune to think of —regicide is one way of trying to inherit the crown (Liu and his wife were subsequently both named as members of the Szechuan Revolutionary Committee). So the truth of these accusations cannot be taken for granted. However, there was a fairly violent struggle for power in the province. In May 1967, fighting was reported in Chengtu (the provincial capital), and also in June. On 11 June Red Guard sources alleged that 300 had been killed on 7 June in Chungking because the PLA political commissar had led 30,000 workers in defence of the old guard and against the attacks of 800 Red Guards (the figures seem very un-

[13]*Ibid.*, p. 4 and p. 29.

likely). Peng Chen, the Peking chief purged in the spring of 1966, is said to have visited Szechuan for talks with Li, to create, as the posters said, "a stronghold of opposition" for the capitalist roaders. When Marshal Peng (purged in 1959) was re-arrested in 1966, it was in Szechuan.

In early July, a Peking team visited Szechuan, and also Yunnan province in the south; the leadership of Yunnan was said to be in league with Li to control the whole south-west. The visit did not settle the issue, for further fighting was reported in August, and also in the summer of 1968. A Revolutionary Committee was not established until May 1968, one year after the announcement of a Preparatory Committee. All this, despite the fact that the strong-arm General of Tibet, Chang Kuo-hua, was transferred to Szechuan in late January 1968 (he subsequently became Chairman of the Revolutionary Committee).

(c) *Tibet* is certainly the most backward and barren province, geographically isolated from China proper and yet crucial for defence purposes by reason of its long and troubled border with India. Given the border problem and the Tibetan history of sporadic revolt against Chinese rule, the PLA has inevitably played the dominant role in Tibet. Tensions between the immigrant Chinese and the Tibetans are, however, probably less important for the Cultural Revolution than friction between the military rulers and the immigrant workers, exiled from their homes to work impossible hours in impossible conditions.

The conflict in Tibet, according to Red Guard sources, was between the rebel headquarters, supported by the mass of Chinese workers in Tibet, and the Great Alliance, sustained by the PLA under General Chang Kuo-hua (appointed in 1951). Very few Tibetans seem to have been involved at all. Chang was accused of suppressing the Red Guards and supporting the local party leaders. In early February 1967, the old guard was said to be in control of Tibet, and the PLA to have declared martial law. On 17 February, some 120 were said to have been killed in fighting in Lhasa, and on 18 February, Lhasa radio reported that three PLA divisions had been drafted into Tibet. Simultaneously, Red Guard sources said the Cultural Revolution in Tibet—as in Sinkiang—was suspended. The Military Affairs Committees of the party in Peking issued a statement saying that Chairman Mao fully supported General Chang, and Chang's critics were evil liars.

Some disturbances continued in 1967, and in August some 500 Tibetan refugees crossed into India (the highest figure since 1962, when the border dispute with India broke into hostilities) with lurid accounts of persecutions. Again, Tibet's Revolutionary Committee did not make its debut until the very last minute. Yet, Peking must have felt moderately confident when it transferred Chang out of Tibet in January 1968 to become Commander of the Szechuan Military Region; although not so confident that it appointed a successor—Chang remained in *de facto* control of the Tibetan Military Region and head of its Military Control Commission.

Other provinces also had bitter and sustained conflicts, although the exact alignments are not always clear. In Kwantung, for example, there have been persistent reports of violence from Canton, of clashes both between workers and students, and between rebels and the PLA. Canton's proximity to Hong Kong makes it particularly subject to inflamed rumours, transmitted by excitable travellers. But there are more objective indices of some disturbance—the 90 per cent fall in passenger traffic between Canton and Hong Kong in August 1967; the 41 bodies washed up in Hong Kong in June 1968. On 8 June the Canton *Southern Daily* said that some "class enemies" had "fanned the evil wind of economism on a large scale in order to corrupt the combat spirit of the revolutionary masses. Some have incited the reactionary ideology of anarchism and sabotaged socialist labour discipline.[14] On the other hand, the Canton international trade fairs have continued on schedule, and food and water supplies to Hong Kong have not been dramatically interrupted.

V. The People's Liberation Army

The PLA has been an additional casualty in the Cultural Revolution. Spread too thinly over too wide a range of duties, its military capabilities can only have been weakened. The Peking Garrison has provided senior officers wherever needed to fill provincial

[14]BBC Summary of World Broadcasts, III, 2799, cited *CQ* 35, July-September 1968, p. 186.

gaps—for example, to head the Inner Mongolian Revolutionary Committee or take over Wuhan. It has also been purged, as when the deputy commander, Fu Chung-pi, tangled with a Red Guard faction and was dismissed.[15] The PLA generally has had also to submit to factional onslaughts—as Chiang Ch'ing put it in September 1967, when she rebuked the Red Guards for attacking the PLA: "Everywhere we seized their guns, beat them up and reprimanded them. But they did not strike back or argue."[16] If they did not strike back, then the experience must have been a demoralizing one for the troops.

The administrative tasks constantly expanded, and PLA senior officers were expected to take the initiative in setting up and manning the Revolutionary Committees.[17] On the other hand, the supply of officers was pruned by purges.[18] As the PLA seemed almost to be dissolving into a civilian administration, so the US escalated its war in Viet Nam, the Russians were said to have installed missile sites along the Chinese border, and Moscow indicated how far it was prepared to go in subjugating critics by invading Czechoslovakia. The pressure within the PLA and the party leadership to call a halt to the Cultural Revolution so that the army could resume its military role must have grown steadily stronger.

[15] *Survey of Mainland China Press* (SMCP), 4169.

[16] Quoted *CQ* 34, April-June 1968, p. 6.

[17] Up to August 1967, the Revolutionary Committees (six in number) were headed by three PLA men and three party cadres; the 18 Vice-Chairmen included six from the PLA, seven party cadres and five "others" (presumably from rebel groups). Of the nine Revolutionary Committees created up to February 1968, seven were headed by PLA men, two by party cadres; and of the 37 Vice-Chairmen, 23 were from the PLA, ten from the party and four "others."

[18] On the purge in the PLA—three of the seven Vice-Ministers of Defence fell; the Director and two of the five Deputy Directors of the PLA General Political Department; the Chief of the General Staff (and the subsequently appointed acting Chief of Staff) and four of his eight deputies; the commanders of the armoured force, the artillery and the railway corps; four of the 13 military region commanders; nine of the 13 first political commissars; 13 of the 25 military district commanders; 17 of the 25 military district political commissars; all are said to have been dismissed. The figures are, of course, collated from doubtful sources, and it is quite unclear how many have in fact been permanently discharged, and how many temporarily rusticated.

VI. The workers

Since the Cultural Revolution was primarily an urban pheno-menon, the industrial working class inevitably played an important role. In the older cities, there is now a settled core of urban indus-trial workers with a relatively long history. It is a group which is highly privileged relative to newcomers to the city, and even more so relative to peasants. The core of the urban industrial working class still includes men with political experience which long pre-dates Communist rule, and possibly, for a few, stretches back as far as the great general strike of 1927. Such experience was at a premium during the turmoil of the Cultural Revolution, perhaps suggesting what the party leadership attacked as "ultra-Leftism."

Theoretically, the settled core of industrial workers is protected by movement controls from massive dilution with new rural immigrants, but in practice, urban working conditions are so much better than rural that there is constant pressure from peasants try-ing to get into the city. The municipal authorities through check-points at railway and bus stations, on incoming highways, by use of the ration card, try to prevent illegal entry or the expulsion of illegal immigrants. Any breakdown in the administrative structure allows both new immigrants to enter the city, and those previously exiled to distant provinces (where labour is scarce) to return.

Officially enterprises are permitted to recruit labour only through local labour departments and, where rural labour is concerned, only with the agreement of the city and rural commune authori-ties. When the economy is slack the pressure to recruit labour is weak, and the problem of the authorities is how to expel the un-employed from the city. But every increase in the tempo of indus-trial activity tends to threaten the control system—enterprises have a strong incentive to evade the regulations in order to employ cheap rural labour. Over a long period, migration raises the urban population well beyond the employment capacity available when the economy is slack. For example, after the disasters of 1960-61, the government officially sought to cut the urban population from 130 million to 110 million up to 1963, and banned the recruitment of rural labour. The effects of these proposals were probably not dramatic, since it is beyond the capacity of the urban adminis-tration to check everyone (despite the organization of "Street

Committees," District Committees, and so on, designed to check the urban population). In any case, the steady expansion of the economy since 1963 has probably prompted enterprises to recruit rural labour once more. If the urban labour force were not diluted in this way, the labour scarcity would become such that there would be a substantial pressure to raise wages.

If individual enterprises have an incentive to evade the controls on recruitment, the government itself is also seeking to squeeze industrial costs. It has proposed the "worker-peasant" system to span the credibility gap. This system is supposed to overcome the distinction between town and country, but in fact it is the revival of a rather nasty capitalist tactic to employ cheap labour on temporary contracts from rural communes, while sending expensive permanent urban workers out to the communes. Rural labour is not a charge on the city, receives few fringe benefits (housing, medical services, old age pension), and urban labour is paid by the rural commune (if the worker is old, the city avoids the cost of his pension while he is retired and therefore unproductive). However, rural labour is suitable only for a limited range of jobs, particularly seasonal and unskilled work (such as loading and unloading on the railways, in ports, mines and lumber plants). The clash between temporary and permanent workers and their mutual attack on the party officials that sustain the system is one thread in the Cultural Revolution as it affected the cities and key industries, particularly the railways.

At the end of 1966, there were reports of large-scale sackings among temporary and contract workers in Shanghai.[19] Retrospectively, we might guess this occurred because the Shanghai Party officials feared a purge and sought to appease the grievances of permanent workers and damage production in order to discredit the Cultural Revolution. Peking ordered the reinstatement of such workers, and this, in conjunction with massive immigration of Red Guards into Shanghai, precipitated a wave of industrial disputes, including strikes, demands for increased pay and fewer hours. Just before Christmas, a harbour strike had begun, and the railways subsequently went on strike: together, this could have provided the beginning of a general strike. Some party officials are said to have raided the banks to pay increased wages and year-

[19]*People's Daily*, 26 December 1966.

end bonuses as a means of safeguarding their own position against a purge threat.

In the middle of this, some 11 Revolutionary Rebel organizations combined in the Shanghai Revolutionary Rebel Headquarters to seize the city administration. In retrospect, it seems, this *coup* was executed not so much by workers as by the faction that hoped to replace the existing party administration (and probably included a good many ambitious cadres) but was frightened by the appearance of a complete collapse in order. For the city was not only flooded with thousands of Red Guards, but also youth returned from exile in the provinces or rural areas, and peasant immigrants. Strikes threatened to paralyze the entire city, different factions were fighting openly for supremacy, and thousands of workers took the pretext of the Cultural Revolution to down tools and take free trains to visit Peking and complain of their conditions.

The revolt in December and January, according to *Wen Hui Pao* (21 January 1967), "swept over the whole city and quickly spread to the rural areas with temporary crushing success." In the middle, "hundreds of thousands" of temporary and contract workers demonstrated against the system of their employment, imposed, according to instant official explanations, by the evil capitalist roaders. Chiang Ch'ing offered the same explanation when she met a delegation of contract workers on 26 December.[20] Yet the new Revolutionary Municipal Committee made no move to rectify the anomaly, and a bold statement of the All China Federation of Trade Unions in mid-January went so far as to say existing policy on contract employment was to remain as it was.

Temporary workers did not give up. Despite a ban on the independent organization of temporary workers,[21] they continued to organize and agitate. Red Guard sources even said that one organization of temporary workers launched an attack on the Shanghai Revolutionary Municipal Committee, saying that conditions for workers were no better than in Kuomintang days. The unemployed held a rally on 20 February, demanding that they be permitted to keep their jobs in order to help the Cultural Revolution. The Municipal Committee, now firmly in the saddle

---

[20]Cited by Colina McDougall in "Second Class Workers", *Far Eastern Economic Review* 19, 5-11 May 1968, p. 306.

[21]Central Committee and State Council Order, February 1967.

and protected by the PLA, sternly rejected their demand and ordered them to leave their jobs; it reproved them for "egotistical ideas" and "economism."

The Revolutionary Rebels were not in the main ordinary workers, and, indeed, there was much friction between workers and rebels. *Wen Hui Pao* (3 May 1967) urged the rebels not to "regard all workers as conservatives and to fight 'civil wars' against them. We must be aware," it went on, "that, except for a few diehards, most of the workers misled by conservative groups are our class brothers." In June, press and radio continued to attack "economism" and also what appeared to be the formation of embryonic independent trade unions, officially stigmatized as workers' "guild organizations." These "guild organizations" had earlier featured in a *People's Daily* article[22] where it was said that they were extending to cover busmen, cooks and technical school students, and were designed to "formulate economic demands and raise the egotistical interests of particular groups." The *People's Daily* would not have attacked such organizations if they had been solely restricted to the Shanghai area.[23]

In July, the Shanghai Municipal Committee again denounced a second wave of demands for higher wages, improved welfare facilities and a changed labour system. It accused some of a conspiracy—"they even put pressure on the new revolutionary order by threatening to slow down work or refuse work assignments."[24] Again, in December, the Shanghai *Liberation Daily* condemned "some persons (who) are once again demanding greater benefits and higher wages" and others who were trying to organize temporary workers. Early in the New Year, *Wen Hui Pao*[25] attacked "civil wars" among "proletarian revolutionaries" in Kiangsu, Chekiang and Anwhei provinces. These battles, it said, had started in January 1967, and in some cases had not yet ceased. In particular, it mentioned a plot to seize the railways—"These few people (the plotters) were so mad as to make out a plan for first controlling the towns and villages along the Shanghai-Nanking railway lines, occupying south Kiangsu, and advancing to control Shanghai and Chekiang." Forces, it said, were assem-

[22]Reported *Le Monde*, Paris, 16 March 1967.
[23]See also *Wen Hui Pao*, Shanghai, 11 March 1967.
[24]Shanghai Radio, 6 July 1967.
[25]10 January 1968.

bled in south Kiangsu, and included former party cadres.[26]

The railways were a particularly sensitive area throughout 1967 and 1968, a sector most easily sabotaged since there are very few lines and what there are, are crucial for the economy. In addition, the railways must have been very overburdened with traffic, since Red Guards and Revolutionary Rebels had been using them free since mid-1966. The authorities persistently warned railwaymen to stay at work, to prevent sabotage and resist all attempts to stop trains running. In August 1967 troubles were reported from Canton, and in the following January, a conference of railway workers was called in Peking to discuss the problems of keeping the lines open. In the following months, stoppages, disputes and fighting were reported on the route to Lanchow in the north-west, in Kwantung in the south, and, in particular in Kwangsi on the route to North Viet Nam. On 9 August Red Guard sources mentioned an instruction issued to railwaymen to end all violence along the Kwangsi route, to dismantle all factional strongholds along the Kwangsi line, return materials stolen from the shipments to Hanoi, and return arms lifted from the PLA (the order was supposed to be dated 3 July and to repeat orders issued by the Kwangsi provincial authorities on 13 June). Again, another conference of railwaymen met in Peking in mid-May, and Chou En-lai is said to have pinpointed the place of maximum difficulty on the railways as Liuchow, a point on the line from Nanking in Kwangsi to Hanoi. On 11 August Peking radio celebrated the victory of its supporters over the faction that had seized the Liuchow line.[27]

Some of the major oil, coal and steel centres were also said to have been affected by spasms of revolt. It has been estimated

[26]BBC Summary of World Broadcasts, III, 2665, cited *CQ* 34, April-June 1968, p. 163. See also Shanghai radio broadcast, citing report of Security Command Headquarters, PLA Unit 6410, *ibid.*, III, 2788, *CQ* 35, July-September 1968, p. 182.

[27]An unofficially published version of a document supposed to have been issued by the Finance and Trade Front of Kung Ko Hui, Canton, contains what is called a transcript of the Peking meeting between Chou En-lai and representatives of Kwangsi factions. The transcript includes charges that in June and July 1968, whole trains intended for Viet Nam were highjacked by factions, the Grand Rebel Army of Liuchow and its rival, Lien-Chih, for the internal power struggle; the loot included 11,800 cases of ammunition and 16,000 rifles.

that two-thirds of the mining labour force is "worker-peasant." In 1967 clashes affected the main steel centre, Anshan, also the industrial city of Wuhan, as well as Paotow, Shanghai and Chungking. The leading role of the "working class" was embodied in factory reorganization to set up "collective control" of production. Again, this was a "revolution from above," designed almost certainly to inhibit authentic revolt rather than enshrine it, and to prevent wage pressures. It was said collective responsibility had replaced individual responsibility, wages had been made more egalitarian, and the clerical staff heavily pruned.[28]

The overall evidence is fragmentary in the extreme, but it does suggest that some workers have been stirred into activity by the Cultural Revolution. The sediment will not settle in the coming years.

VII. Stability

China is a very large country, and thus quite capable of supporting apparently large conflicts in a few isolated places without this affecting the majority of the population or even being seen by visiting foreigners. Thus, there is a grave danger that the impact of the Cultural Revolution will be exaggerated. Probably the mass of the peasantry (excluding those immediately around large cities) has been untouched, and the rural cadres only slightly affected. The 1967 harvest is officially rated as very good, and there is no evidence of real hunger in the accessible parts of the country (although some reports have stressed the increase in the urban black market over the past two years). The middle level cadres in the cities have probably suffered much more, with significant effects in terms of urban administration, the demoralization of the urban party, and a probable decline in official initiative. Yet even here one must not exaggerate. Many of the important local cadres have probably learned to swim in the new tide of the Cultural Revolution, and learned to swim on top.[29] Perhaps around the cities, peasants have been affected, and possibly there has been more

[28]For a report on the new order in Shanghai No. 3 Iron and Steel Works, see *Peking Review* 43, 25 October 1968, p. 16.

[29]For a case study, see Neale Hunter, "Three Cadres of Shanghai", *Far Eastern Economic Review* 231, 1 June 1967.

peasant hoarding of foodgrains (both because the procurement administration is weaker, and because the black market offers high incentives to those prepared to risk trading on it).

The speed with which the last Revolutionary Committees were created suggests that the process was not much more than the re-baptism of the old order. That order has kept the countryside moving, and kept up the foodgrain output, without which the cities could not have made "revolution." The concessions made to the peasants in 1960-61—for example, the right to cultivate private plots for a private market—have not been withdrawn.

The trade figures show no dramatic variation over the two-and a-half years of the Cultural Revolution, and the export figures (from non-Chinese sources) are some indirect index of the state of agriculture. In 1966 exports to the West reached a record level for the fifth year in succession. In 1967 exports to the non-Communist world fell by 12 per cent, but imports were roughly the same. Sales to Hong Kong in the first half of 1968 were slightly below the comparable period for 1967; the lowest point in 1967 in sales to Hong Kong was reached in September, and affected textiles and livestock the worst. This is fairly mild stuff beside some of the wilder accounts of the Cultural Revolution. It means that important communes and factories have kept up output, and transport has shifted the goods.

The Canton trade fairs have continued to attract foreign businessmen, and routine trade negotiations have been sustained (Chinese trade missions visited Bonn and Paris in the spring of 1967, and Sino-German negotiations continued over a three million ton steel rolling mill). China's purchases of gold on the London market continued—a routine shipment of £49 million bullion left London for Peking in May 1967. External assistance also continued—to Nepal, wheat to Egypt (50,000 tons), the promise of £100 million to Zambia for the Zambia-Tanzania railway.

Quite clearly also the nuclear programme continued. Although no scientific publications have been received from China since October 1966, and the fate of university science departments is unclear, the government research staff have been excluded from the Cultural Revolution.[30] China's sixth H-bomb test took place on

[30]Point 12 in the Central Committee programme for the Cultural Revolution, August 1966.

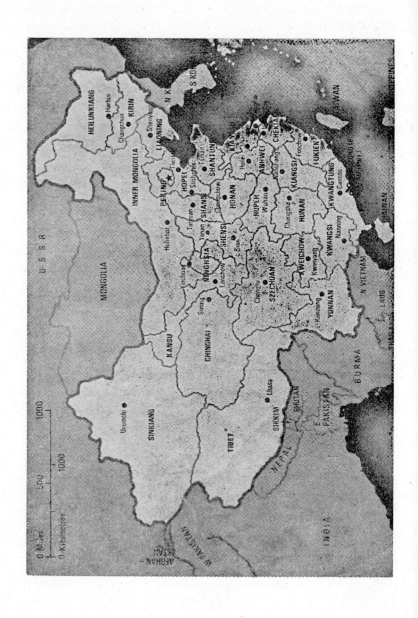

17 June 1967, and a seventh was suggested by foreign seismographs on 24 December although not officially confirmed (the Japanese also alleged a further test on 13 July). This does not just mean that the nuclear sites, plants and labour have been free of trouble, but also that the massive inputs of power from the national economy have been available. When US diffusion plants were working full blast to stockpile Uranium 235, they consumed an eighth of national electricity supply. Although China may have found a cheaper way of doing this, it must still impose a major demand on national energy resources, a demand that must have been met despite any disturbances. In the longer term, the programme might be affected by the decline in the output of appropriately skilled manpower from the institutes of higher education.

Industrial output in 1968 is compared favourably by Peking with 1966, which suggests that possibly 1967 was a poor year. Foreign estimates propose a 15-20 per cent drop in total output in 1967, but a slow expansion in 1968. Virtually nothing has been said officially about the third five-year plan, of which 1968 is, theoretically, the third year. Other projects have been completed in 1968—for example, the Yangtze bridge at Nanking was completed in October, some ten years after it was first begun under Soviet guidance.

Thus, although this evidence is indirect and fragmentary, there have been narrow limits to the Cultural Revolution. In particular areas, there have been major changes, but these have been perhaps relatively isolated. In Peking, in the Central Party leadership, the limits have been least. One estimate suggests that, of the 11 members and alternate members of the Politburo active in 1965, eight have been dropped; of the 11 active members of the Party Secretariat, three have survived; of the ten known Directors of Central Committee Departments, only one seems still to be active; 52 and 40 per cent of the Central Committee membership have been attacked during the Cultural Revolution.[31]

VIII.

The Cultural Revolution was an attempt by a section of the

[31]C. Neuhauser, "The Cultural Revolution and the Party", *Asian Survey*, VIII/6, June 1968.

Central Party leadership to re-establish central control over the whole country, perhaps as a prelude to accelerating the rate of overall economic growth. To do this, it had to destroy opposition at every level of the party. It secured a monopoly of all official propaganda agencies, but it did not secure victory. On the other hand, the opposition remained (so far as one can tell) fragmented.

The national crisis which originally precipitated the Cultural Revolution remains as before. China's rate of economic growth is too slow to give any assurance that it will ever catch up with the advanced powers, that it will ever be able to institute a tempo of growth which will submerge domestic cleavages and integrate the country. What was lacking to institute Mao's order was an agency for social change sufficiently powerful and diffused throughout the country, sufficiently separate from the old party, to execute his will. The central leadership was forced to rely on the army, and then, to rehabilitate the party, lest disorder sweep away both sides in the conflict. Yet this retreat has settled none of the important issues, and indeed, it has exacerbated the solution of those issues. The party administration, bowed but unbeaten, remains the sole effective guarantee of China's unity and continued output. That administration has been itself fragmented by the Cultural Revolution, and perhaps, in part, demoralized, so that although it is the only framework holding the country together, it is now even less likely to take bold initiatives in development.

Outside the party, the youth and some sections of workers have been involved in action, have seen the local ruling class completely discredited, have read reams of dirt on all the bureaucrats, and have perhaps glimpsed freedom. They cannot all be bought off with places on Revolutionary Committees, for there are too many of them. Subterranean communications survive, and pockets of resistance will continue, probably through to the next explosion. For Mao's defeat is a defeat for Chinese development, and he will once more be forced to take up the same issues again if Peking's power is to survive. Next time he tries, he may find an authentic revolt on his hands.

Thus, as China returns to silence once more, a legacy remains. On the one hand, a stalemate within the fragmented ruling class; on the other, a legacy of simmering hostility among the other urban classes.

5

China : Decentralization and Development, 1973

The face which the People's Republic of China presents to the world is truly an astonishing one. At one moment, China is rotten with resurgent capitalism, the decay reaching as high as the top leadership of the Communist Party and some of its most trusted members. A short time later, the capitalists turn out to be the tiniest group of people, easily excised to reveal once again the picture of a happy China, a sort of continuous Methodist Sunday School (no wage pressure, no strikes, no riots, so appealing to the visiting representatives of foreign ruling classes). At one moment, continuous political discussion is the only way of saving China; all remnants of private enterprise must be rooted out; Red Rebels in the factories must revolt against all who seek to impose "capitalist" norms. At another, the *People's Daily*—without so much as the hint of a blush—calls for an end to time-wasting meetings and discussions (23 October 1972), praises the peasants' private plots (22 October 1972), and demands punishment for those who resist managerial authority and discipline in the factories (30 May 1972). It must be a strain for even the most agile cadre to know what is correct.

Suddenly all the old slogans have become "ultra-Left." And the fears as well—the creeping shadow of Japanese imperialism across east and south-east Asia which a short time ago seemed so worrying for Prime Minister Chou En-lai has suddenly disappeared. Once Japan's Prime Minister had been able to exchange a few diplomatic words with Chou on his visit in September 1972, it was all cleared up. They signed a treaty, of which Chou—without batting an eyelid—said: "The new relationship is not directed against third parties. Neither of us is seeking hegemony in the Pacific region, and both are opposed to those who are." Imperialisms pop up and fall down simply on the nod of the Chinese Prime Minister, it seems.

Yet there are casualties in this zigzag policy which moves so rapidly from "ultra-Left" to the most conservative orthodoxies. Prominent leaders of the party turn out to be insufficiently "flexible." There are now only two effective members surviving from the 1969 five-man Standing Committee of the Politbureau (Mao and Chou). A third of the Politbureau itself seems to have been purged in the past 18 months, and of the remaining 14, only eight are active (that is, neither very aged nor ill).

Then there are those foreign Maoists and pro-China liberals who bravely defended all things Chinese through the difficult years of the Cultural Revolution. Now they find much of what they defended was "ultra-Left," and some of those whom they praised now purged. Even that little Red Book, bravely waved by so many millions, now turns out to have been part of the wicked plot of Lin Piao to embroil his modest master in the cult of personality. If those supporters were right then, they must be wrong now, or vice versa. And if they are right now, but mistaken in the past, how can we be sure that next year they will not decide they were wrong now? One must be a little shameless to act merely as an unpaid public relations agent, regardless of all twists and turns.

Between the leadership and their foreign acolytes are many millions of young Chinese who believed Mao's promises, but have now been betrayed. They did not inherit power. They have been whipped back to school or exiled to remote rural areas. A small minority of them—perhaps 20,000—last year defied death to break through the Chinese border controls and swim to Hong Kong. The rate of illegal immigration to the city is now higher than in any year since the famine exodus of 1962. Half the swimmers are young people banished to rural areas, and a quarter are regular young farm workers.

The key factor in the period since the end of the Cultural Revolution that has produced this great swing to the Right has been the behaviour of the Soviet Union. In 1968 Russia invaded Czechoslovakia. In 1969 it launched border attacks on China in the north,[1] and for a time it looked as though it might push matters to war. At that stage, the Chinese army was ensnared in administering China, since efforts to restore the administrative capacity of the Communist Party had not been successful.[2] The first priority for the government was therefore to restore the army—or a significant part of it—to its military functions, and rapidly improve and develop its weaponry, equipment and transport. To do these things, the party had quickly to be restored to administration, trade expanded (to import materials for stockpiling and defence production), and State civil expenditure radically reduced to make room for an expanded defence budget. All these things, as well as the Soviet border threat itself, required most urgently a return to domestic peace, an end to faction warring and real attempts to soothe the feelings of the mass of the population, to give people something worth defending.

The economy

To make room for an expanded defence programme, the government has radically cut its financial obligations and made extensive changes in economic policy. There has been a general campaign for economy in the Central Government bureaucracy. Edgar Snow reports from his interview with Chou that the employment of cadres in the Central Government had been cut from 60,000 before the Cultural Revolution to 10,000 by December 1970, and this shrinking has continued. Those sacked have been bundled off to rural areas rather than being allowed to join the urban unemployed; the communes have to support the redundant bureaucrats, although admittedly at much lower rates of pay and without the obligation to provide the welfare provisions customary for urban workers. The Red Guards were similarly broken up and despatched to the countryside—some ten to 20 million of them. All the young people who got back into the city, will now have

[1] See "China and the Russian Offensive", *International Socialism*, 41, December-January 1969/70.

[2] For the development of this point, *see* Chapter 4.

been expelled again. Wuhan, for example, a city of three million people, claims to have sent 220,000 of its young people to the countryside over the past three years. To encourage the communes to accept these unlooked-for mouths, some public authorities are said to be offering subsidies of Y200 to Y240 per head.

Second, the State has drastically cut its expenditure on education, health and culture (a quarter of the central budget in the 1950s). The length of compulsory schooling has been cut from ten to seven years; all pupils must simultaneously work in a factory or on the land, and their education is subordinate to the demands of their work. More important, education must now be financed and supervised by the production team in the villages (production teams vary in size, but roughly correspond to a small village) and factories in the cities (formerly, it was financed by the Ministry of Education). The same is true for health, cultuie and administrative services. Whatever this saves the central budget, it will inevitably produce an increase in inequality between districts. The most backward areas will have the most backward services for they will be deprived of the subsidies which formerly came from the richer areas through the central budget. In education and health, the general decline in standards in much of the country could be dramatic. On the other hand, the richer areas—like the city of Shanghai—will improve their services and in the longer term, their relative superiority. In higher education, no one can now go straight from school to university without a few years' work in between; in the physical sciences, this could also produce a radical lowering of standards. Introducing social criteria for selection and putting selection in the hands of local authorities also means anybody who tends to raise awkward questions in the locality is unlikely to get higher education.

Third, the communes and factories have been told to be increasingly self-sufficient. Communes should use any surpluses they have to manufacture simple light industrial and consumer goods to meet their own needs (producing such goods on the communes will be much cheaper in wage terms since the peasants will not be paid urban industrial wages nor be granted urban welfare standards). The constant theme reiterated in the national press in connection with "self-reliance" is that it is absolutely wrong to ask for financial assistance from the State, which again fits "decentralization" into a general economy drive. The government claims that "local industry"(that is, on the communes) is now a major component in the economy—producing 60 per cent of the national output of chemical fertilizer, 40 per cent of cement, a third of steel.

Industrial decentralization was originally justified on strategic grounds—dispersed industry would be protected from Soviet attack. But the policy was also perhaps a recognition of the existing state of affairs after the Cultural Revolution and of Peking's inability to recentralize the economy. For the middle—provincial—levels of the party had been destroyed, leaving the local cadres very much to get on as they might. Local self-sufficiency is one way of trying to insulate one's bit of territory from the fluctuations beyond its borders. Decentralization is also a means of inducing the support of the commune leadership—or, in Indian terms, the rich peasants. It is a common mood in almost all developing countries, particularly in backward regions that feel neglected by the development process. Breaking up industry and distributing it round the country seems to be a logical and desirable process to the leaders of backward areas. In Chapter 1, Maharashtra's intention to grow more food on the Deccan, and Tamil Nadu's decision to build steel capacity was mentioned in this respect.

In China's case, decentralization saves the State a lot of money, might tap commune savings that would otherwise not be available, forces the use of raw materials and labour that would otherwise not be employed, and produces goods that are a net addition to the stream of commodities produced in the Chinese economy. But it can have other effects as well. Where raw materials are scarce, the policy can—as in the Great Leap Forward—be very wasteful, and deprive efficient national industry of its inputs in order to supply inefficient local industry. Shanghai which grows no cotton can be deprived of its supply of raw cotton so that primitive mills can produce at much higher cost inferior goods in the cotton tracts. Furthermore, where raw materials are scarce, communes are likely to stock up with raw materials far in excess of there immediate needs so that production will not be interrupted later; the same goes for producer goods, transport and so on. The result of that is a lot of unutilized capacity going to waste in conditions where everything that can be used should be used. The central justification of central planning is just to avoid such waste, to avoid the duplication which is inevitable with a mass of small competing private firms.

The same points apply to investment. If the savings would not otherwise have been used, local industry is an excellent way of tapping resources. But it is more likely that, of the available supply of investment, communes will now be diverting a larger proportion of it into relatively uneconomic—because small—and badly run plants (badly run because there are few on the communes with the appropriate industrial skills). The commune leadership is likely to use its power within its own territory to ensure its own goods are sold, and competing goods from outside the commune kept out, which simultaneously robs national industry of its market and forces inferior goods on to the commune's captive market. The commune leadership can set its own prices so that it may well try to maximize its profits on the goods it manufactures so that more savings will be available for further investment. The last stage in this process is when the commune leadership tries to produce more than the commune can take, and exports the surplus at much lower prices than the price of national industry's output (it could not otherwise sell the goods outside its own borders).

At this point, each commune is behaving like a small country, increasing its exports and trying to reduce its imports. Each country pursues an import substitution policy, even though it is clearly cheaper and more efficient to produce some things elsewhere in the national economy, to specialize, to develop a division of labour. Of course, "dumping"—selling cheaply abroad, dear at home—would be modified by the development of a black market. With each commune behaving like a separate country—or, at least, a separate private firm—the whole national economy suffers. If each factory has to grow its own rice, both its rice growing and its factory production will be relatively more inefficient than if it specialized while someone else grew the rice. All the advantages that come with development, which make possible the enormous productivity of an advanced economy—an elaborate division of labour, specialization, concentration, planning—are deliberately abandoned. The loss grows more serious the more developed and complex the economy becomes.

"Decentralization" is reactionary in the strict sense of the term (as opposed to the emotive sense): it tries to drive the economy backwards into a sort of feudalism, it disperses the resources that need concentrating if development is to take place. It makes it impossible for there to be effective planning, for the power to plan is now vested in the mini-countries. No economy can remain without coordination if it is to survive, and if a national plan does not coordinate the units, the revival of a market most certainly will. The trading relationships become the method of coordinating the economy. In the long run, that would mean a very slow moving capitalist economy whose dynamic would be competition between the communes and other districts, in contrast to the State capitalist economy of the Soviet Union which operates, very roughly, as one consolidated conglomerate.

Marx and the Marxists have always been great centralizers. For without centralization, mankind could never escape backwardness, never put together the enormous power at its disposal. Always, the dispersal of resources and power would make all equally weak. The same would be true after a socialist revolution: the only possibility of democratic control is if power can clearly be located at one place and subjected to popular check; if power is dispersed, there is no power with which to do anything. Mao is not checked by the thought that his scheme is associated with the name of Proudhon and the conservative anarchists who wanted not that power should be used in the interests of all, but that power should be abolished altogether. Localized self-sufficiency has always been the ideal of the petit bourgeois, the peasant with his small patch of land or the small capitalist or craftsman with his little workshop. In economic ruin, the search for "independence" has often become a frenzy for such people so that they run away to build a utopia in new lands, or turn to unmitigated violence as the expression of how little dependent they are upon society.[3]

All this is far from China and the Chinese leadership. Mao is less interested in the ideological aspects of the turn to the Right than the economies to the State in trying circumstances. If he were interested in the ideas, he would not have remarked to Edgar Snow in his last interview that "China must learn from the way America developed, by decentralizing and spreading responsibility and wealth among 50 states." This is such compounded nonsense as a comment on US capitalism and imperialism that it can only

[3]See the recent volume, *Marx Engels Lenin: Anarchism and Anarcho-Syndicalism*, Progress, Moscow, 1972, and my review, "The Anarchist Argument", *International Socialism*, 54, January 1973.

indicate an almost complete indifference to the political issues of importance to revolutionaries.

There is some evidence that already the leadership has begun to check "excessive" decentralization, perhaps as part of the drive to economize on raw materials and prevent the loss to the State of local investment resources. For Peking tried initially to alleviate some of the financial strain on local bodies of setting up industrial units and taking over educational, health and administrative services by leaving more of the tax revenue in the hands of rural communes and raising public revenue almost entirely from urban areas. This has been a trend for a long time—certainly since 1958 —and places the main burden of financing the State on the exploitation of urban factory labour rather than peasants. It has a paradoxical resemblance to other regimes—for example, India—that do not tax the conservative rich peasantry in order to assure its political support. The Chinese Finance Ministry recently claimed that whereas in the early 1950s, the Central Government took 13.2 per cent of farm incomes, now it takes around six per cent. Of course, that only gives the figure for the Central Government— not the Provincial Government, *hsien* (county) or commune administration. And it concerns only direct taxes, not the surpluses taken from the communes in compulsory State grain purchases, indirect taxes etc. In the past, a sizable part of government revenue has come from profits and taxes on the processing and sale of agricultural products. The relaxation of control during the Cultural Revolution may well have changed the terms of bargaining between commune and government. Audrey Donnithorne[4] argued recently that it was no longer practicable nor politic for the State to compel the peasants to deliver up enough grain under the compulsory sales system to meet the needs of the State, despite good harvests; this was why Peking continued to have to import significant quantities of grain. The government, as always, makes a virtue of necessity; it has claimed that it is deliberate policy to change the terms of rural-urban trade to favour the peasantry; farm produce prices have been increased while industrial prices were lowered over recent years.

Leaving more in the hands of the communes, restoring material incentives for work, allowing the peasants to cultivate private

[4]"China's Cellular Economy: Some Economic Trends since the Cultural Revolution", *China Quarterly*, 52, October/December 1972.

plots and sell the produce for profit, all help to soothe the commune leadership after the "ultra Left" excesses of the Cultural Revolution. Perhaps this is also the reason why—despite continued calls for austerity, discipline and increased savings—there seems to be more colour in the cities, a modest revival in music and the opera, and the end of some of the sillier slogans (see the Red Guard cry: "Making Love is a Mental Disease Which Wastes Time and Energy").

Strengthening the peasant market forms the vital part of a Bukharinist economic strategy which is said to be embodied in the unpublished fourth five-year plan (said to have begun on 1 January 1971). Bukharin[5] was one of the main protagonists in the great debate on economic strategy in the Soviet Union between 1924 and 1928. He argued that industrial development should be geared to the expansion of agriculture, to the rate of growth of the rural market and of the supply of agricultural commodities. Everything should be done to encourage the peasant to expand his output. Nothing should be done which smacked of draining resources off the countryside into industry. The opposition to Bukharin's argument, particularly in the work of Preobrazhensky,[6] said that it would lead to the strengthening of the rich peasantry to the point where it could precipitate counter-revolution. Rather must the State use all means—without alienating the peasantry—to accumulate capital in its own hands, to build an industrialized economy which would no longer be dependent upon peasant goodwill for survival and could begin to build socialism.

The debate in China has scarcely challenged the basic Bukharinist orientation that has dominated Chinese policy since the Great Leap Forward. Admittedly there seems to have been some dispute about the place of defence in the government's priorities and what kind of defence expenditure it should be (i.e. men and munitions or technically sophisticated weapons, missiles etc). But the discussion on the main direction of the eco-

[5]On the application of Bukharin's case to China, see Tony Cliff, "Crisis in China", *International Socialism*, 29, summer 1967; on Bukharin's case. Cf. A. Erlich, *The Soviet Industrialization Debate, 1924-1928*, Cambridge Mass., 1960, and M. Lewin, *Russian Peasants and Soviet Power, A Study of Collectivization*, London, 1968.

[6]For Preobrazhensky's argument cf. *The New Economics* (Russian original, Moscow, 1926), Oxford, 1965.

nomy has not been between supporters of heavy industry and of peasant agriculture, but rather between those who see agricultural mechanization as the first task, and those stressing the development of local light industry. The press by and large did not argue so much as assume Bukharin's case (for example, see *Red Flag* through July 1971): only agricultural prosperity could make possible industrial advance; light industry serving agriculture should be the key link transmitting peasant demand into the growth of heavy industry. However, unlike Bukharin, no one pointed out that such a strategy made rapid economic development impossible; for industrial growth would be determined by the speed of increase of peasant consumption, the slowest expanding element in the national economy and the one least susceptible to rapid expansion. As Bukharin put it with characteristic but foolhardy—so far as the later Stalinist strategy was concerned—honesty: "We shall move at a snail's pace, but...we shall be building socialism."

The main aim of the leadership in the Cultural Revolution—to restore central control of the provincial surpluses so that accumulation could be geared to a new high level—was defeated. Now, accumulation—economic development—is to be sacrificed, on the one hand to defence, and on the other, to standing still at a politically tolerable level. But even the latter depends upon the good grace of the weather. The harvests in 1970 and 1971 were good, but the 1972 output was severely affected by droughts and floods. With the population increasing by nearly 15 million each year, a quirk of the weather can spell disaster. Even in good years, the increase in grain is hardly a hair's breadth ahead of the increase in population. The room to manoeuvre is very small.

The Soviet intervention of 1969 drew a very clear line for Peking between the need for a domestic purge and the costs of instability. Unlike the US war in Viet Nam, China could not ignore the Soviet attack and just continue with its home concerns. The defence budget and the weather have become the two central factors which determine the operation of the modern Chinese economy. Neither is likely to do much for economic development.

Foreign policy

The 1969 attack made the Soviet Union China's "Number One

Enemy," and revealed to Peking how far its diplomatic isolation had gone during the Cultural Revolution. The regime set out to find friends, anywhere and everywhere, but especially wherever the Russians were. This sudden flurry of activity coincided with US efforts to escape from the Viet Namese war. The two could therefore collaborate to mutual advantage (remember Foreign Minister Chen Yi's 1965 declaration? "Peaceful coexistence with US imperialism which is pushing ahead its policies of aggression and war is out of the question"). As a result, all other cold war relationships changed—China entered the UN, the Foreign Ministers of France, West Germany, Britain and many others searching for markets dutifully followed Nixon to Peking. Finally, Japan mended its fences with the People's Republic.

In 1964-65, the Chinese leadership had already tried to build an alliance in the "intermediate zone"—that is, all countries between itself and the United States. As Mao put it to a startled French parliamentary delegation in 1965: "France itself, Germany, Italy, Great Britain—provided the latter stops being courtier of the United States—Japan and we ourselves: there you have the third world." By 1973, the US is no longer the main enemy, and the revived intermediate zone is now directed against Russia and Russian influence. To this end, Chou En-lai offers public support to the European Common Market (and British entry, regardless of the stand of British labour) as a counterweight to Soviet influence, and opposes the security talks between the European powers and the Soviet Union lest they reach agreement. He even went so far as to modestly approve the five-power Commonwealth security arrangements for policing south-east Asia and the US military presence in Asia (excluding Viet Nam) as a means of keeping Russian influence—and its notorious Asian security pact—out.

The same principle has guided Chinese foreign policy round the globe. The cases of Pakistan and Ceylon have already been mentioned (see Chapter 3). Chou is currently wooing Iran—the Shah's sister and wife have both made recent state visits to Peking—even though the Iranian secret police, SAVAK, has only recently carried out a massive purge of all opposition including the summary execution of rural guerrillas. China's long-standing association with the notorious Emperor Hailie Selassie of Ethiopia is not troubled by the Eritrean National Liberation Front fighting him. Chinese aid assists the stability of the Ethiopian regime, assists the maintenance of its capacity to root out armed opposition. Former association with the United States is no obstacle to Chinese friendship—after all, Pakistan was a member of both CENTO and SEATO during the years of association with China, and Iran is still a pillar of CENTO. Thailand is currently being wooed by China, partly to prevent Soviet influence, as also is the Philippines. So is Malaysia, and Peking has even made soothing noises to Taiwan since the Soviet Union sent there an unofficial emissary. Nor is this just a matter of polite diplomacy. When the pro-Soviet group in the Sudanese Government made a bid to oust President Nimairy, it was the Chinese-Sudan Friendship Society which organized demonstrations in Peking in support of Nimairy—following this up with the offer of $ 45 million aid.

So far Peking has—largely for public effect—refused to consider Western aid, but this is not a point of principle despite appearances to the contrary (see Chou En-lai's coat-trailing statement to the 1956 National People's Congress: "We have no objections to economic aid by Western countries to economically underdeveloped countries.") The stockpiling of 1969 certainly seems to have produced a deficit in China's balance of trade, and all the Western countries are now vying with each other to offer attractive terms for their wares. It has always been clear to the Chinese leadership that a quick increase in the capital stock of the country was possible by borrowing on the right terms; China's current needs are on such a large scale that the terms could be relatively favourable, certainly much more favourable than Ford offered Lenin when he explored the possibility of US investment in the Soviet Union. China is currently buying a great deal abroad—grain, Tridents, Concordes, petro-chemical and vehicle plants—and giving a lot of aid to win political favour with other backward countries (much more than is currently offered by the Soviet Union; China committed itself to long-term aid of $700 million in 1970, over three times the Russian commitment), so that it seems likely that sooner or later Peking might well bite the bait.

The party

Successes abroad do not do much to console people inside China for the continuing political vacuum. Despite massive efforts, the new provincial administration is still dominated by the army. It is supported by rehabilitated party leaders, but almost always in second place. Real newcomers among the RedRe bels of the Cultural Revolution seem to have no role in administration.

At the centre, the situation is little short of disastrous. It is astonishing enough that the second-in-command of the regime, Head of State and respected party leader of many years standing, Liu Shao-ch'i, and the General Secretary of the Chinese Communist Party, should be found secretly scheming to restore capitalism in China. Yet no sooner had a successor been found, a man notorious for his slavish devotion to Mao, then he too turns out to be rotten. Yet Lin Piao's name was enshrined in the 1969 constitution as the sole legitimate heir to Mao. Now what is left of the Politbureau has to summon another Party Congress to ratify the destruction of Lin. No replacements have been appointed to the posts of those purged—Head of State, Party Secretary, Minister of Defence, Chief of the General Staff (Huang Yung-sheng), Commander of the Air Force (Wu Fa-tsien), Political Commissar of the Navy (Li Tsa-pang), and many other senior officials and officers. If it is true that Lin's group, along with Politbureau member, Mrs Lin, was in the plane which crashed in Outer Mongolia in September 1971, it is a staggering commentary on the stability and integrity of the Chinese regime that the top leadership of the armed forces had been induced to flee to the Soviet Union. Chen Po-ta, for 35 years Mao's private secretary and appointed by him as Chairman of the Cultural Revolution Group that directed the Cultural Revolution, fourth in precedence in the leadership, has also apparently been purged.

In contrast to Stalin in the 1930s, Mao has been able to rid himself of his rivals, but not to appoint successors, nor ratify the changes under the existing State and party procedure. Only a quarter of the ministers and vice-ministers of 1966 are said to have survived through to 1969. Yet the present leadership still cannot summon the fourth National People's Congress (scheduled originally for 1969) to ratify the changes and replacements. Even the leadership line-up on Tien-an-Min Gate has too many embarrassing gaps—so the traditional national parades (May Day, 1 July anniversary of the foundation of the party, 1 October National Day) have had to be abandoned. All the leading bodies of the party appear still to be in disarray, and despite the border clash, only the army is the thin line between the ruling class and chaos.

Economically the country is standing still; politically it is still in stalemate. This is in vivid contrast to the picture presented by Western journalists recently on visits to China. Many write as if they were 20th century Columbuses just discovering America (and finding it strangely not populated by unbelievable monsters). The gap between the domestic reality and the external image of the country has probably never been greater, although it has always been very great in the case of China.

It is the domestic stalemate which will determine future reactions by China's leadership. That will make necessary further campaigns against both "revisionists" who are apparently after all the events of the past eight years still operating within the party, and the "ultra Left" that continues to resist the army-old party carve-up. For the moment, the leadership is forced to tolerate the recreation of some form of market economy and a kind of kulak class, the cadres who run the communes. This positively encourages people to seek private solutions—speculation, embezzling, profiteering, black marketeering, all current targets for press attack. Having raised so many hopes of a new deal in the Cultural Revolution, it will now prove most difficult to hammer out of people ambitions quite impossible to fulfil within the present *status quo*. For the mass of people there are few private solutions—whether it is profiteering, private plots or flight to Hong Kong. Cynicism and bitterness are the likely responses of the majority.

The retreat forced on the leadership by the collapse of the party and the Russian attack leave unsettled all the outstanding issues. Indeed, the retreat makes matters worse. The more Peking restores the old party bosses and relies on them, the less is the flexibility and the possibility of a real mobilization of resources for development. That is the reason why Mao or whoever it is who runs China will be forced to make the present pause temporary. Then the attack will have to begin again. Watch the Western liberal sympathizers, then jump yet again on the new swing of the roundabout, just as their predecessors jumped every time Stalin changed line in the 1930s. The real target for their attention ought to be world imperialism that subordinates the struggle of the Chinese people to the needs of the Soviet Union, the United States and all the rest. But that would mean opposing their own ruling class here and now instead of myth making about dreamlands,

A Rural Guerrilla Road
to Socialism?

If India's ruling class offers a "Parliamentary road" to socialism, China's offers a rural guerrilla one. In much of the world the two alternatives are seen as the only ones, the alternatives of reform or revolution, capitalism or communism. This chapter looks briefly at two questions, postponing the more general topics to Chapters 7 and 8. First, what has been the experience of guerrilla warfare in Latin America? Second, can we assume an identity of interests between guerrillas, peasants and the struggle of the proletariat for socialism? If the peasants cannot achieve socialism, and the guerrillas cannot lead the self-emancipation of the peasants, what happens to the struggle for socialism?

Clearly, socialists must support every real struggle against imperialism. In the case of Viet Nam, this means unconditional support for the National Liberation Front. But the struggle against imperialism is not identical with the struggle for socialism; the interests of the peasants are not the same as those of the working class. Much of Lenin's work is devoted to drawing the sharpest possible line between these two things. Without a clear separation there could be no "alliance of peasants and workers," and certainly no working class leadership. Blurring these questions means blurring the class basis of the revolutionary movement—rural banditry, student revolt, urban terrorism, anything can act as a substitute for the working class movement. Nor is approval restricted to purely violent opposition—in Latin America, the exhaustion of the strategy of guerrilla warfare through the 1960s has prompted Fidel Castro (and Mao Tse-tung) to offer public support to reformist governments, Allende's administration in Chile or the military in Peru. Significant Chinese economic aid is now being extended to the Generals of Peru, and that aid—as happened in Pakistan—will serve to bolster up the government *against* its own rebels, to give credibility to the politics of the army. In Chile, Castro has lent his considerable reputation to Allende; on his visit to that country, indeed, he urged copper workers to end their strike and return to work on behalf of the President.

The lightness with which the erstwhile proponents of guerrilla warfare shifted their support to reformist governments suggests how lacking in seriousness their original strategy was. It was all purely "pragmatic," not rooted in the necessities of a real mass movement. A revolutionary movement which is simultaneously battling for power and fighting the day-to-day battles which face workers has its room for opportunism severely circumscribed. A group of middle class revolutionaries organized separately from any class struggle has no such imperatives imposed upon it. It can do as it wishes, shifting with speed from rural to urban guerrilla warfare, from guerrilla warfare to parliamentary reformism. It does not matter what promises it made to its peasant supporters in the first phase, to its urban followers in the second, to its consti-tuents in the third: it can betray them all in pursuit of its private aims. Here is no self-emancipation by a whole class of society; here is only a clique, whose integrity is not ensured by its subordi-nation to a mass movement, only by its inner morality. Every Latin American—or Asian—*caudillo*, Right or Left, asks for no more than popular trust.

I. Guerrilla warfare : the Latin American case*

Rural guerrilla activities—like those of their closest precursor, rural banditry—inevitably seem remote from the broad political

*Original version, "The Guerillas: Old and New", published in *International Socialism*, 43, April-May 1970.

or social changes in society as a whole. The tradition of guerrilla warfare and social banditry is much older than the particular motives of those currently fighting. And the fight seems to have little effect at all on the society in which it takes place except on very rare occasions. Thus rural guerrillas seem to lead a sub-terranean existence, without great gains and yet, without being completely wiped out; in a sense, they are independent of the society within which they operate.

Urban terrorists, on the other hand, are intimately related to broad movements in mass consciousness; they are produced by such changes, and they cannot survive without the willing collaboration of many urban dwellers. Thus urban terrorism is directly linked to changes in political and social events. The terrorists are the revolutionary anarchist edge of popular dis-content and radicalism, forerunners or substitutes for mass political movements.

The shift from a rural to an urban location by important guer-rilla groups in Latin America is thus of some importance. Nece-ssarily changes in recruitment and, above all, in politics, have been involved. The political ideas of the group concerned become much more important than its military ingenuity, and "guerrilla action" (if action in an urban area can any longer be called that) becomes only one small part in a political campaign.

The aim of rural guerrilla warfare—associated with the names of Che Guevara and Regis Debray—was, as a first priority, to create a rural base, independent of the national or urban political scene and, indeed, independent of the population of the rural areas as well. The establishment of a rural military base would itself begin to transform the political balance, but essentially, politics was subordinate to military tactics. The aim was to build a guerrilla army and secure popular approval or acquiescence by showing the vulnerability of the armed forces of the ruling class, not to build a revolutionary party among the population. The guerrilla army, it seemed, made a popular revolutionary force redundant. In any case, the revolutionary party could not be built, it was argued, as the history of the communist parties showed. The city was a corrupting influence; the cadres had to be quarantined against the urban virus. Tough material conditions and military discipline in the most remote rural areas would prevent corruption among the guerrillas; isolation and insulation would keep at bay "bourgeois society" until the moment came to destroy it.

But to be properly effective, the guerrillas had to be serviced from somewhere. Until they had secured a base capable of meeting their own needs, and were able to capture arms and ammunition in adequate supply from the police or militia, someone had to assist them from outside. In the event, Havana was cast in the role of outside sponsor; it filled the vacancy left by the guerrillas' rejection of their own local cities.

Three things have happened to make this strategy doubtful. First, in the classic test case for the strategy in Bolivia, Guevara and his comrades were wiped out, and the Bolivian army was thereby able to secure 18 months' relative domestic peace. Second, rural guerrilla activities elsewhere—in Peru, Argentina, Brazil and Guatemala—have also consistently failed to achieve any major results. And the failure can be traced to the strategy itself. The guerrillas were isolated from the rural inhabitants, often by language, colour and culture. The traditional Communist Parties in the cities did not support the movements. So the armies of the Establishment, well armed and financed, proved fully capable, if not of wiping out the guerrillas, certainly of rendering them harmless. Finally, Cuba proved unable to give adequate material support to the guerrillas. By 1969 Cuban policy had shifted away from trying to foster revolution in Latin America and towards concentrating on domestic economic development. The veteran Venezuelan guerrilla leader, Douglas Bravo, has accused Havana of "working solely to strengthen its economy, and having suspended all help to Latin American revolutionary movements."

It was clear from 1968 that Castro was gradually withdrawing material support from the guerrillas. Cuban policy was returning to the position originally outlined by Guevara before the United Nations Assembly in 1964, when he stressed that "We have argued, over and over again, that revolutions are not exportable, that revolutions are created in the hearts of the people." Castro himself repeated the same point in July 1969, when he said that the Cuban leadership was not impatient, but would wait almost indefinitely for revolutions to develop independently in other Latin American countries. By inference, it can be seen that the Cuban attempt to offset Soviet tutelage by expanding the Cuban revolution in Latin America has now been given up in favour of what Moscow wants—"peaceful co-existence." Not that this is the end of the road, for Cuba will no doubt be tempted to go further than "peaceful co-existence" and offset its dependence upon the Soviet Union by reopening friendly relations with other Latin American countries, and perhaps even trying to secure re-entry to the Organization of American States. The Cuban revolution is being nudged into the same historical niche as the Mexican revolution—events of purely domestic significance.

An element in this change of emphasis by Havana is likely to be a reappraisal of other regimes in Latin America. Of particular importance here are the actions of the military regimes in Peru and Bolivia, both of which have nationalized major US interests in their respective countries. Since the Bolivian Generals, however radical they might be, are implicated in the slaughter of Guevara, reconciliation with Bolivia will take time. But on Peru, Castro made a particular point of recognizing that "The most notable feature of the case is that in the bosom of a traditional army, of an army that was the bulwark of reaction and of repression in Peru ... there has developed a military movement of quite distinct significance ... that has nationalized a US company, proclaimed an agrarian reform, and expressed clearly the proposal to develop at any cost the Peruvian economy." The Soviet Union has sent trade missions to try and recoup some of what the US has lost, so that there may be Soviet pressure added to Havana's wish to find some way back into Latin America by orthodox means.

This, then, is the background to the movement of guerrillas back to the city. For former Guevarists, this means a new stress on the importance of political work, of work among the urban masses, and of depending on local material assistance, all of which supports a turn to nationalism. But urban guerrillas—or terrorists—are not at all a new phenomenon in some Latin American countries. Even revolutionaries strongly influenced by Cuba have in some cases felt the need for an urban base. Carlos Marighela persuaded his comrades in the Brazilian Revolutionary Communist Party in 1967 that a campaign in the cities of Brazil was vital, and—until he was murdered—worked mainly in the cities. Better known and of earlier origin are the Tupamaros of Uruguay (named after an 18th century Indian rebel, Tupac Amaru).

Created in 1962 among northern rural sugar workers, the Tupamaros quickly saw that in a country like Uruguay, all the parts of which are easily accessible to military forces, they must move for survival to the "300 square kilometres of buildings" in the capital, Montevideo. In July of the following year they began their preparatory work by seizing arms from the Swiss colony's Club de Tiro. Preparation lasted until August 1968, when they began more direct political actions. They kidnapped the president of the State Factories and Telephones Agency, Ulises Pereira Reverbal (a landowner, friend of, and economic influence on, the Uruguayan President, Pacheco Areco). In June 1969, they destroyed the General Motors administrative building as part of the continent-wide welcome accorded to President Nixon's emissary to Latin America, Governor Nelson Rockefeller. In September they kidnapped the director of a major bank, Gaetano Pellegrini Giampietro, during a long strike by his employees as deliberate attempt to secure support among trade unionists. And in October, in a spectacular *coup*, 150 guerrillas seized the city of Pando (32 kilometres from Montevideo), attacked its four largest banks, and held the place for 24 hours. The seizure of Pando, however, evoked a massive reaction from the government, and for the first time police arrests managed to break a major part of the secret cell organization of the Tupamaros.

The Tupamaros aim was explicitly to change the political consciousness of the urban masses, and to do so by directly influencing strikes and the trade unions. Elsewhere, this aim is less clearly spelt out, and many urban guerrillas are only contingently operating in the concrete jungle. In Brazil, the kidnapping of US Ambassador, C. Burke Elbrick—in exchange for 15 political prisoners—is only the most spectacular of the *coups*, but the long-term strategy of such actions is unclear. In 11 Latin American countries (including Bolivia) last year there were urban terrorist actions—bank robberies, bombings, sabotage, kidnapping. Even in Guatemala where what is left of the guerrilla base seems to be still rural, after the 1967 wild slaughter of Left-wingers by army units and Rightwing-vigilante groups under this year's winner in the Presidential elections, Colonel Carlos Arana Osorio, the guerrillas have increasingly sought to intervene in the urban areas.

Two US military attaches and the US Ambassador (on 28 August 1968) have been assassinated. During the elections, the Foreign Minister and the US Labour attache were kidnapped to secure the release of guerrillas held by the government.

In Chile, the sudden appearance of the Movement of the Left (MIR) startled the Christian Democrat Government's composure. The police claim, from captured documents, that the MIR are following the same phases of development as the Tupamaros— that is, first a phase of preparation by raiding banks and seizing arms, then political kidnapping, assassination and sabotage, finally, the creation of a National Liberation Army and a clandestine government in the mountains. Thus, for the MIR—unlike the Tupamaros—the urban activity is only a prelude to the creation of a rural base, a sort of geographical "dual power." This is called a Viet Namese strategy, as opposed to a Guevarist. But even here the social basis has changed. It is no longer aimed to unite a student leadership with the most backward rural elements, so much as—as Luciano Cruz of MIR puts it, "to initiate a major and prolonged war which would permit it (the MIR) to mobilize around itself the most combative sections of the workers, peasants and students." In addition to these elements, some urban guerrillas aim to recruit important sympathizers in the ruling class, in the police, civil service and business. As with the Russian Narodniks, securing such support is vital for the survival of the guerrillas, for the tip-off which prevents capture.

Thus, the change from rural to urban needs to be heavily qualified. The change is not one which leads inevitably to proclaiming the necessity for the proletarian dictatorship. But at least, some of the socialists have abandoned the *cul-de-sac* of rural self-destruction. Their urban activity could elicit a proletarian response of greater significance, or at least provide the occasion for workers to begin to consider political alternatives. It is most unlikely that the doctrines of urban guerrilla warfare can "evolve" into Marxism—after all, it needed the destruction of the Russian Narodniks to produce the Marxists—but some of the guerrillas may begin to see the limitations of minority heroism as the Narodnik Plekhanov did. The possibility of this turns very much on the behaviour of Latin American workers, and thus on the overall perspective for Latin America, as well as the behaviour of workers elsewhere.

II.   The War in Viet Nam*

Whatever the outcome of the present situation it cannot detract from the amazing continuous affirmation of NLF strength and resilience. Few on the Left can now seriously doubt the reasons for that strength: the strong roots of the NLF in the southern population. There is no magic about the strength of these roots—the NLF and only the NLF represent a credible new deal for almost all South Viet Namese, pillaged by 20 years of war and the robbery of successive foreign powers. Above all, the NLF represents a new deal on the land, and in a peasant country in Viet Nam's situation, this is political dynamite for those who resist change on the land. Thus, the power of the NLF turns not upon what help it receives from elsewhere but upon its politics—just as the farcical weakness of the Saigon regime also turns upon its politics, even if that weakness is some-times clad in the borrowed garments of American military power. The existence of the NLF, and its immense triumph reaffirms one of the basic premises of the Left everywhere: people and their consciousness, not property or armaments, in the final analysis determine the operation of power.

However, to say this and no more is to evade some of the thornier issues of a socialist's attitude to the war in Viet Nam. We have argued (and continue to do so) for an immediate Ameri-can withdrawal from Viet Nam; necessarily this means support for the NLF and a North Viet Namese victory, and it would be dishonest to pretend otherwise. Yet, does this position not con-tradict many other things we have also said? For example, that State capitalism of the Eastern Bloc is not intrinsically superior to the private capitalism of the Western: neither Washington nor Moscow, but international socialism. In the lucid absurdi-ties of the cold war, does not our support for Hanoi, negative or positive, mean we are in fact abandoning the possibility of a third alternative and coming down on the side of Moscow—or, at any rate, adhering to the full programme of the North Viet Namese regime?

The result does not follow. For the Viet Nam war does not fit neatly into the pattern of incidents between East and West since

*Originally published as "Neither Washington, Nor Moscow—But Vietnam?", *International Socialism*, 32, Spring 1968.

the war. Such incidents were most often the result of direct confrontations between the major powers, each jostling for military or strategic advantage along the undemarcated border between their respective empires—the raw wound that ran through central Europe and straight through the city of Berlin, the Balkans, the Middle East and south-east Asia. Clearing up the open points along the border was part of the unfinished business of the Allied wartime conferences that divided the spoils of victory. In practice, both sides accepted the division and thus implicitly rejected the aspirations of those victims whose misfortune it was to inhabit the border zones. Both sides accordingly reserved their response to the other side's suppression of social or national liberation movements to rhetoric (as in Greece, as in Hungary).

The Korean war was both the most inflamed confrontation between the two sides, and not atypical. There were indeed elements of an indigenous national liberation movement in the south of Korea, but the outbreak of fighting in 1950 had little if anything to do with these. Rather was the war no more than an extension of the global jostling for power between Russia (now joined by China) and the US. The first hoped to prevent Japan falling under US hegemony to protect its eastern flank, to secure a strategic position on the Pacific seaboard, and to keep China within the Eastern Bloc. The second sought to complete its control of the Pacific seaboard, to keep that ocean as an American lake, to hold what it had as the prize of the Second World War—and, incidentally to push Congress into advancing funds for rearmament, thereby creating the permanent arms economy of the 1950s. The war ended in stalemate, when neither side could see strategic gains in the continuation of war. Only the Koreans paid a real price—in blood and in the loss of national independence.

The Viet Nam war has certainly not been immune to the same jostling—indeed, it would have been over in the early fifties if outside powers had not intervened. But the jostling is different, particularly because the Soviet Union has not permitted itself to become directly implicated (its own interests, now detached from those of China, have little direct relevance in Viet Nam) nor has China, since, without the Soviet nuclear umbrella behind it, it is too weak in military terms to risk such a confrontation with the United States. Thus, the Eastern end of the seesaw is very light. The war could not have been waged at all if there had not been a genuine popular movement to replace the absent military power of the Eastern Bloc. This circumstance has made the war both more bitter, more long drawn out and more difficult to settle—even though the North Viet Nam leaders have not consistently been unwilling to subordinate themselves to the strategy of others (as they did at the Geneva Conference in 1954). Sometimes the NLF (or those who created it) has had to act despite the wishes of Hanoi—as with the 1956-57 outbreak of peasant revolt in the south. The war in the south has not been turned on and off at the whim of the rulers in Moscow, Peking or Hanoi—indeed, if it could have been turned off, certainly Moscow, and probably Peking, would have turned it off rather than risk the present involvement of American military power. Quite rightly, help has been accepted from outside (as the Vietminh accepted help from the Americans in the closing years of the Second World War), but the outside help should not conceal the politics feeding the movement—land and freedom, not global power politics.

However, to say that the NLF is a genuine popular movement is not to say that the NLF—much less the more developed regime of the North—is either socialist or will lead to socialism, or is no more than the authentic embodiment of the aspirations of the workers and peasants of Viet Nam. The programme of the NLF is consciously one for a popular front, as was that of the Vietminh, appealing to "Rich people, soldiers, workers, peasants, intellectuals, employees, traders, youth, women. . . ." As with the Chinese Communist Party in its rise to power, the Lao Dong Party leadership is overwhelmingly drawn from the old middle and upper classes, not from the poor peasantry or workers. If it were not the case that the concept of a bourgeois revolution is no longer meaningful in contemporary developing countries, then we might deduce that the regime in the North is bourgeois, and that what is happening in the South is the attempt to install a bourgeois regime against the old order allied to imperialism. But "bourgeois" carries the connotation of the private ownership of the means of production whereas in almost all countries of the third world today the radical drive is towards State ownership, and it is the attempt to create a State-class, not a private or bourgeois class, that is spearheaded by the NLF and has already been instituted in the North. The aim is, however, the same: capital accumulation to build an independent nation-State. Just as in the bourgeois revolution the bourgeoisie came to represent the interests of all except the aristocracy, so now in the new revolutions of the third world, the group which is striving to constitute itself as the new State also represents the interests of nearly all—and in particular, of the peasants, to secure a new land settlement; and of the old petty officials, mandarins and intellectuals, to build a new State which can, in conditions of freedom from foreign intervention, begin the process of development, of building a national enclave of substantial power. Often, in such countries, the industrial proletariat is so small that it cannot, as the historic agent of socialism, exercise much political role. The process can be seen with clarity in a range of countries which, in other terms, seem diverse—from China and Cuba to Egypt and Syria. The agency which often has alone proved capable of overcoming the heterogeneity of different strata of population, of connecting the aim of national independence to the force of the peasant's demand for land, of providing the nucleus for the new State, is the Communist Party.

Of necessity, the political programme of such a force is very different from a socialist platform. Most important, the programme must be nationalist, not internationalist, populist not class-conscious. The coalition of forces is held together only temporarily for a limited and specific end, and the very achievement of power begins to separate out once again the constituent interests, despite possibly radical reforms to sustain the momentum of the movement and undercut some of the more obvious interests. In North Viet Nam, the separation began in 1954 and exploded briefly in 1956. The general crisis which affected the Eastern Bloc in 1956 found its echo in the peasant revolt against Hanoi in Nghe An.

Not that the Vietminh leadership consistently pursued the broad interests of the coalition even before 1954. They tried in 1945 and 1946 to do a deal with the French which would have robbed some of their most important sectors of support of what they were fighting for. Indeed, Ho Chi Minh's willingness to compromise was one major cause in the subsequent outbreak of fighting again. Those who opposed the settlement, including the Trotskyist leaders in Saigon, were murdered by the Vietminh. Again, after 1954, while thousands of opponents of Diem were being ruthlessly hounded, interned and shot in the South, the North did nothing but make verbal protests. The Russian line in pressing for the admission of both Viet Nams to the United

Nations stemmed from the same attitude as that in the North after 1954—an acceptance of the permanent partition of the country. The claim that the fightback in the South began independently of Hanoi is not mere propaganda—it is an indictment of the policies pursued by the North. Indeed, Hanoi was forced into intervening, since if it had not done so it would have lost all control and influence over the southern revolt.

Thus, in supporting the victory of the NLF, we do not thereby mistake its significance, its class politics, and thereby mistake its possible future role. In the same way, socialists were required in the 19th century to support bourgeois liberal movements against feudal or absolutist regimes—without crossing over from Garibaldi to Cavour, let alone Palmerston who also supported some nationalist movements. In Tsarist Russia, Lenin was particularly precise on this question: "We support the peasant movement to the end, but we must remember that it is a movement of another class, not the one that can or will accomplish the socialist revolution." Or again, writing in 1909 on the Social Revolutionaries, he said: "The fundamental idea of their programme was not at all that 'an alliance of the proletariat and the peasantry is necessary', but that there is no class abyss between the former and the latter, and that there is no need to draw a line of class demarcation between them, and that the (Marxist) idea of the petty-bourgeois nature of the peasantry that distinguishes it from the proletariat is fundamentally false."

Thus there is no contradiction between support and realistic appraisal. We must oppose the terrorism of US intervention in Viet Nam, and we must defend unconditionally the right of Viet Namese to be left free of outside intervention—to do so, in the circumstances, is to offer unconditional support to the NLF. But Ho Chi Minh is not thereby made some genial uncle, nor the NLF merely the Viet Namese YWCA—the fog of cosy sentimentality with which Communists seek to cloud the issue must not mislead anyone. Of course, when the issue of American power is settled, we know what kind of regime and policies the NLF will then choose—and be forced to choose by the logic of their situation. But that is, for the moment, another fight, the real fight for socialism. Socialists must support every genuine struggle against imperialist and capitalist oppression—whether it be by workers of the advanced countries or by all classes in the backward.

PART THREE

Issues in Marxist Theory

7

The Revolutionary Role of
the Peasantry

The sheer diversity and immensity of the rural population in the world's backward countries makes general discussion of "the peasantry" very difficult. However, certain important generalizations can be made, but it must be borne in mind that such generalizations may have different implications for groups as different as owner-occupier peasants, subsistence tenants, share croppers, landless labourers—for the serfs of Latin American *haciendas*, for the depressed small tenants of south Asia, or for the tribal farming groups of sub-Saharan Africa.

But, on the other hand, the sheer size of the peasantry in the world suggests something of its possible political importance. What that political importance is, however, is the subject of considerable disagreement. In particular, this chapter is concerned with the debate between those socialists who identify the industrial proletariat as the *sole* agency for the achievement of socialism (the Marxists), and those who identify other groups or classes —including the peasantry—as capable of achieving socialism. The debate is an old one. Its themes are an important element in Marx's disagreements with Bakunin and the anarchists, in the critique by the Russian Marxists (in particular, Plekhanov and Lenin) both of the Narodniks (Russian Populists) and the Social Revolutionaries. And they recur again in the debates

This chapter was first published in *International Socialism*, 41, December-January 1969-70, p. 18.

within the Comintern in its early years. The themes are certainly important today—even if in a distorted way—in the Sino-Soviet dispute, in the repressed disagreements between Moscow and Havana; and, much more generally, between the "Third World" socialists and others.

However, in the past the Marxist position has been reasonably clear. Supporters of "peasant socialism" have, quite rightly, seen the Marxists as critics and, in some circumstances, as opponents. Today, so great is the muddle about Marxism after its systematic perversion in the Soviet Union and China, that Marx (and Lenin) has been called in as supporter both for peasant socialism and against it. It is ironic that the Maoists and their sympathizers call themselves "Marxist-Leninist," with so little knowledge of how sharply Marx—and even more so, Lenin— condemned some of the most favoured positions held by the Great Helmsman. Thus it is important to restate—even if crudely —what the Marxist view of the peasantry has been,[1] and why the proletariat—that is, the industrial working class—was identified as the *sole* agency for the achievement of socialism.

1.   Marx on the peasants

In analyzing the perspective for socialists in France and Germany, Marx noted that in countries where the peasantry constituted a majority of the population, the peasants held the power to decide whether or not the proletariat could win and keep power. Where the peasants were solidly conservative, then the proletariat would not be able to hold power indefinitely. But in Germany, the peasants were fighting the feudal aristocracy on their own account, to establish freehold land rights and rid agriculture of feudal restrictions. The peasantry were waging the bourgeois revolution. The proletariat accordingly must win the support of the peasantry in the proletarian struggle against capitalism by supporting the peasant struggle against feudalism. The two battles must be synchronized for either ally to win its aims.

But clearly a common struggle would include contradictory

---

[1] This is dealt with in detail by Tony Cliff, "Marxism and the Collectivisation of Agriculture", IS 10, Winter 1964-65, pp. 4-16.

elements, and socialism could not be won unless the proletariat was clearly the leader of the struggle. The leadership of the proletariat was essential because the nature of the peasantry made it impossible for it to lead, and in any case, the peasants were aiming at ends not necessarily consistent with the achievement of proletarian aims. What was this "nature of the peasantry"? Perhaps Marx's best known outline of an answer to this question—in relation to the small French peasantry—occurs in *The Eighteenth Brumaire of Louis Napoleon*, and it is worth quoting at some length:

> The small peasants form a vast mass, the members of which live in similar conditions but without entering into manifold relations with one another. Their mode of production isolates them from one another, instead of bringing them into mutual intercourse. The isolation is increased by France's bad means of communication and by the poverty of the peasants. Their field of production, the small-holding, admits of no division of labour in its cultivation, no application of science, and, therefore, no multiplicity of development, no diversity of talent, no wealth of social relationships. Each individual peasant family is almost self-sufficient; it itself directly produces the major part of its consumption and thus acquires its means of life more through exchange with nature than its intercourse with society. . . . In so far as millions of families live under economic conditions of existence that divide their mode of life, their interests and their culture from those of other classes, and put them in hostile contrast to the latter, they form a class. In so far as there is merely a local interconnection among these small peasants, and the identity of their interests begets no unity, no national union, and no political organisation, they do not form a class. They are consequently incapable of enforcing their class interest in their own names, whether through a parliament or through a convention. They cannot represent themselves, they must be represented.[2]

It is true that we cannot jump directly from this description of the

[2] Karl Marx, *The Eighteenth Brumaire of Louis Napoleon,* in Karl Marx and Friedrich Engels *Selected Works,* 2, n.d., p. 414.

small French peasantry in the middle of the 19th century—a peasantry with half a century's experience of relatively unfettered private ownership of land—to the rest of the world's rural population at all times and places. But certain key aspects of the conditions of material existence of virtually all peasants are outlined in this quotation, and it is these aspects which underlie the Marxist position.

II. The nature of peasant life

The peasants are isolated from national society, isolated physically in villages which have little consistent need for continuous communications both with each other and with the cities. At most, the peasant is likely to be aware of his district, within which members of his own family meet or secure marriage partners, and of the local district town, perhaps the source of the merchants who buy his crop, the market place, the site of the police station and so on. Second, the peasant is dependent almost entirely upon himself and his family for his way of life. He is not part of—or at least, is not aware of—a complex interdependent national division of labour. Since there is little division of labour outside the family, there is little specialization, and as a result, production is primitive, the peasant is poor, the cultural and technical resources of the village are most backward.

The peasant's important relationships are not to a wider economy of which he sees himself as a constituent part, but rather to nature, to the rhythms, to the arbitrariness of soil, weather and season. The production unit is the family, and personal relationships are thus also production relationships. Family relationships, rather than competence and technical specialization, determine the primitive division of labour within the family (the relationship between man and wife, between man and his eldest son, his youngest son, his aged father, and so on), and the production relationships exaggerate and intensify the family relationships. The desperate family feuds within the village exhibit the intensity generated within what is simultaneously the basic personal, production and property unit. The rural family embodies all the exploitative relationships of the wider society, and it is the peasant household father who is of necessity the agent for the worst forms of exploitation of the members of his own family; the agent which sustains all that is worst in pre-capitalist society in terms of personal relationships. The violence locked up in the family is matched by the violence between families, the violence intrinsic in the gross subordination of the peasantry as a whole.

Thus, if achieving a socialist revolution were merely a function of the savagery of exploitation, then undoubtedly the peasantry would always have pre-eminently qualified for the role of agency of the revolution. But revolution requires also collective organization, a mass division of labour, a concentration of advanced technical and political abilities. And it is these which the peasantry—by the nature of its way of life—cannot produce. It cannot, as a class, produce the abilities required to operate a society with a collective division of labour. It can only duplicate the ideal of its own members, the small peasant holding. The aim of peasant rebels thus becomes, not the advance of society as a whole, but no more than a just sharing of a common poverty. This is certainly egalitarianism, but it is the egalitarianism of communalists, of independent identical participants, not the egalitarianism of collectivists, of interdependent people organized in a social division of labour. The peasantry cannot, as a class, constitute itself the ruling class in order to realize the full economic potentialities of society. On the contrary, it can, on its own, only drag society backwards into the poverty of the past.

III. Peasant opposition

It is for these reasons that the revolt of the peasant is so often a purely localized occurrence, restricted to the district he knows. His enemy is the local landlord or landowner, the local moneylender, policeman or merchant, not a national ruling class of which he is inevitably only very dimly aware. But without destroying the national ruling class, the local peasant's cause is lost. The destruction of only the local minions of the ruling class will invoke massive reprisals on a scale with which the local peasant cannot cope. Indeed, so muddled may be the peasant's view of the world outside his district, he may completely exonerate the ruling class for responsibility for the crimes of its local officials. In Tsarist Russia, the peasants often certainly hated their local noblemen, but they worshipped the Tsar as the "Little Father," explaining that the Tsar did not know the crimes committed in his name by his noblemen. For them, there was no "system" within which Tsar and noblemen fitted as complementary elements within a common exploitative class. Thus when the Narodniks assassinated Tsar Alexander in 1881 with the expectation that this would precipitate a peasant revolt against the regime, the peasants were appalled, and blamed yet again the evil nobles for depriving them of their only defender. Lewin suggests that Stalin was similarly exonerated by the Russian peasantry for the communist rape of the countryside during collectivization.[3]

Thus, historically, the peasant is a figure of the utmost tragedy. He is grotesquely exploited, forced into self-subjection, forced into preserving all that is most backward and reactionary. And yet he makes his own strait-jacket. He cannot, by his way of life, conceive of a real alternative. He cannot emancipate himself, and self-emancipation is one of the preconditions for socialism. His opposition to his exploitation, when he is solely dependent upon his own resources, is thus either purely negative, or marginal to the system—that is, the opposition does not challenge the existence of the system so much as check certain practices within it. The most common form of this opposition—and the least effective in revolutionary terms—is social banditry. Small bands of armed men prey on the forces of authority, acting as Robin Hoods to take from the rich and give, at least in principle, to the poor. The small size of such groups, their great mobility, and the willingness of the dispersed peasant families to protect and supply the rebels as a sort of "counter police" force, make them almost invulnerable to counter-attack by the authorities. Hobsbawm has described the features of such forces in parts of southern Europe,[4] and perhaps these features are shared with the Indian *dacoits* and similar bands which operated in China. Hobsbawm also notes the similarities between social banditry and guerrilla warfare, and how the second sometimes absorbs the first (thus, no one should be shocked to find that the guerrilla forces of the Chinese Communist Party incorporated erstwhile bandits[5]).

---

[3] M. Lewin, *Russian Peasants and Soviet Power, A Study of Collectivisation*, London, 1968, p. 452.

[4] E.J. Hobsbawm, *Primitive Rebels*, Manchester, 1959.

[5] Some cadres also moved into banditry, cf. Harold Isaacs, *The*

Banditry is the most primitive form of taking sanctions against the system, where self-interested criminality is scarcely distinguishable from socially conscious rebellion, and where the sanction is no more than a marginal irritant to the system.

The sporadic riot in densely populated agricultural areas has more possibilities. Here, rural Luddites directly attack the symbols of immediate oppression—the merchant hoarding grain, the big farmer cutting his labour force or the wages he pays, the State reducing the price it regulates for wine. If such riots are a response to a general condition on the land, the riot may spread. And if it coincides with movements in the towns, it may provide a contributory element in a movement for radical change. But it is only one tributary to the river. Alone it can do little. When Wat Tyler's rebels took London, as when Zapata's warriors reached Mexico City, they did not know what to do with it. Finally they could only retire back to the world they knew, to the village and the dispersed land holding. They left the real power of the ruling class, chastened perhaps, but not destroyed.

Of course, if the status quo is already under threat from other sources, the possibility may exist for a temporary enclave of peasant power. Makhno and the Green armies in Russia relied on the civil war raging around them to defend their islands of power. And in China, the decay of the Manchu dynasty under the corrosive forces of imperialism, permitted the Taiping rebels similarly to establish their own domain along the Yangtze. But once the wider issue is settled or moderated, the national ruling class can react with a force capable of destroying the enclave.

More effectively and more characteristically, the peasantry can in certain conditions control much more massive sanctions of a purely negative kind. They can refuse to obey the law, and if this spreads far enough, the ruling class has insufficient power to garrison the whole countryside. But the organization capable of coordinating such a strike usually can only be found in the cities. The intellectual formulation of this tactic is clearest in the doctrine of passive disobedience as advanced by Tolstoy in Russia and Gandhi in India.[6] But what is to be done when the countryside is

---

Tragedy of the Chinese Revolution, (2nd Edition), 1961, pp. 328-329 and 348.

[6] This point is made by Theodor Shanin, along with much else of interest, in "The Peasantry as a Political Factor", *Sociological Review*, V/XIV/1, 1966, pp. 5-27.

paralyzed? It is at this point that again the strategy breaks down, for the peasants have no positive alternative to present. The same applies to a similar tactic: withholding the food on which the survival of the cities depends. This is unlikely to occur normally, since the peasants also depend on the cities for certain goods, and many need to sell their crop quickly to meet their debts. But in Russia between 1927 and 1929 when the cities could not supply the goods the peasants wanted, there was something of a strike which produced a major crisis in the society as a whole. The strike was *not* an organized act, one of collective solidarity and depending on political consciousness.It was a simultaneous reaction to a market situation. And the peasants had no defence when Stalin launched his counter-attack and set about destroying the Russian peasantry once and for all.

IV. Rural strata

What is lacking in all of these examples is the role of a national class for itself. In the citation from Marx, he makes this point explicitly. The peasantry as a class of men certainly exists. But by the nature of its way of life, it cannot become aware of itself as a class, a body of men sharing a common class interest which extends throughout society. In the sense of recognizing a common interest, peasants are normally only a class in one district. And the peasants of one district may regard those of another with as much hostility as representatives of the ruling class. In some cases, the hostility is greater, for at least they know their own rulers in the district, and the known generates fewer fears than the unknown.

Some Marxists have tried to apply a class analysis to the countryside to overcome some of these problems. They have identified poor, middle and rich peasant strata (with other, more complex, patterns as well), landlords and landowners, and argued on the basis of the conflict of interest between these strata, for identification with the poor peasantry. In a feudal land-distribution system, socialist identification with the peasantry as a whole against the large landowners is reasonably straight-forward. Again, in certain circumstances, and in some locali-ties, a proletarian alliance with the poorer peasantry may embody a real class struggle. Indeed, on some occasions, the poor peasantry has attacked its rich brethren, as seems to have been the case in the Telengana revolt in India in 1947 (to the horror of the Maoist sympathizers in the Indian Communist Party who wanted an alliance of all peasant strata). But these cases are not necessarily the standard ones, particularly where the land distribution system is a complex one. For some peasants may also be landlords, and the social mobility (up and down) of peasant families may be high. Thus, a rich peasant father with many sons may divide his land among them all, making all his descendants poor peasants. There may be constant interchange between strata —the landless move into and out of cultivation; the small peasants into labouring, or, if their families are small for a couple of generations and there are no outside crises, into the ranks of the middle or richer peasantry. And one peasant family may fit into several strata—it farms some land, it rents another small piece, it works as labourer on someone else's land, at different times of the year. With such complexity, it makes little political sense to identify the "natural allies" of the proletariat *in general*.

The peasant situation itself can also make nonsense of such identifications. The poor peasants, like the landless labourers, are the most depressed group—less analogous with the proletariat than with the lumpen proletariat. And the poor peasant's natural sense of identification is more usually upwards, to the richer peasant strata the poor peasant aspires to join, rather than out-wards to poor peasants in other—unknown—districts. The rural society is bounded by the district boundaries, and it is within these boundaries that the strata can be identified most accurately. Outside the district, one usually has only statistics, not a political strategy. The instability of the lower strata has prompted socialists and communists more frequently to rely on the middle and richer peasants for radical organization, for they are the village leaders and, as such, most likely to be more aware of the outside society. In times of relative peace, a "poor peasant movement" is likely to be a myth of urban politics. For identical reasons, radical attempts to set up all-India alliances of the lowest castes have always proved abortive. The natural identi-fication of village Untouchables is, sadly, with the dominant peas-ant castes of the village (even when they murder some of them) rather than with the millions of Untouchables in other districts. To know of the existence of those other Untouchables, to recognize a common interest, is already to be part of another—urban, and so national—world.

Thus, the peasant revolt needs the intervention of parts of other —national—classes to take it beyond its prescribed role. It is not accidental that the peasantry has always been more oppressed than any other class, has a history of revolt, and yet has so few successes. Success comes when other ambitions are allied to peasant grievances. In classical China, peasant revolt was success-ful when members of the nobility came to lead it, came to use it in order to establish a new dynasty. On rare occasions, peasants themselves became members of the new ruling order, but only on terms which negated any real revolutionary transformation of Chinese society. In the bourgeois revolution, the struggle of the bourgeoisie to establish its own political power borrows heavily from the peasant struggle to destroy the great feudal estates, and is the precondition for the success of the peasants.

V. The crude materialist case

Socialists who have seen the peasantry as an agency for the achievement of socialism—leaving aside what could be meant by "socialism" in this context—have usually been impressed by the violence of peasant struggle,[7] by the complete alienation of the peasant from the forms of urban (or "bourgeois") life. But the violence is a function of the backwardness of the peasantry and its relative weakness, the lack of political means to change other than violence, rather than revolutionary fervour or vision.

Such socialists also often utilize a particularly crude material-istic explanation of political militancy. This materialism does not, however, rule out a simultaneous romantic idealism about the possibilities of human action whatever the material circumstances. The case runs something like this: revolution is a function of explo-itation; so that those who are most exploited will be the most

---

[7] Consider, for example, Frantz Fanon's comment: "In colonial countries, the peasants alone are revolutionary, for they have noth-ing to lose and everything to gain. The starving peasant, outside the class system, is the first among the exploited to discover that only vio-lence pays. For him, there is no compromise, no possible coming to terms...." Fanon, *The Wretched of the Earth*, London, 1965, p. 48.

revolutionary; those who are the most exploited are the poorest; thus, the poorest peasantry, the most backward tribal groups (in some countries), the lumpen proletariat, are all candidates for the agency of revolution.

There are obvious surface similarities to a Marxist case, but a major difference lies in the obscure word "exploitation." In this case "exploitation" means impoverishment. In the Marxist case, "exploitation" means "the degree to which surplus value is appropriated." Thus, for the Marxist, sheer poverty is not a necessary index of "exploitation," nor is it a guide as to the agency of revolution. If Marx had believed that poverty of itself was the source of revolution, then it is a signal failure on his part not to have identified the 19th century peasantry (or the lumpen proletariat) as the agency of socialist revolution: the peasants were undoubtedly poorer than the proletariat. Again, within the proletariat, the poorest strata would obviously be more revolutionary than the richer, the unskilled more than the skilled. In fact, for Marx as well as historically, revolutionary political consciousness tended to develop in exactly the reverse order. More to the point, Marx actually allowed for an increase in the real consumption of the working class, a decline in its absolute poverty, without this affecting his case. He writes, for example:

> If, therefore, the income of the worker increases with the rapid growth of capital, the social gulf that separates the worker from the capitalist, increases at the same time, the power of capital over labour, the dependence of labour on capital, increases at the same time....Even the *most favourable* situation for the working class, the *most rapid possible growth of capital*, however much it may improve the material existence of the worker, does not remove the antagonism between his interests and the bourgeois interests, those of the capitalist (Marx's emphasis).[8]

The dimension missing in the crude materialist case is power. Skilled labour is not only more "exploited" than unskilled, the proletariat than the peasantry, but it is clearer to skilled labour how much capitalism depends upon it, just as it is clearer to the

[8] Karl Marx, "Wage-Labour and Capital", *op. cit.*, 1, p. 273.

proletariat how much the whole of society is sustained by its efforts. There is thus a real, daily, contradiction between the economic power of the proletariat, and its political impotence— the proletariat *is* the economy, but it does not run the economy. Thus, it is exploitation in the Marxist sense, not in the sense of "impoverishment," and the contradiction of power and impotence rather than depressed consumption, which are the driving forces for the revolutionary mission of the proletariat in the Marxist scheme.

VI. The proletariat

One can take the case further than this. For on all the criteria mentioned earlier in relationship to the peasantry, the proletariat is contrasted. It is heavily concentrated in great cities, and within those cities, in particular districts; not dispersed over an enormous area, and isolated in small units. Daily, the workers operate the most advanced sectors of the economy, where innovation and change are constant dynamic elements destroying the in-herited customs of the past. They have forced upon them, as part of their very daily existence, a mass division of labour which includes high specialization, including the most advanced techni-cal knowledge, and elaborate interdependence. Of necessity, the workers are a collective, covering the whole of the most important parts of the economy, not a community of independent producers. By their daily work and daily struggle, they are aware that society as a whole is the arena, not one district, nor even just one factory. The employer is part of an employing class, standing in a certain relationship to the State and its agencies.

Of course, in practice, many different levels of perception exist among workers and make for many variations from this rather abstract pattern. However, the difference between the proletariat and the peasantry is that, in principle, workers can comprehend society as a whole, and given the Marxist perspective for the deve-lopment of capitalism, will be driven to do so. The peasantry, in principle, cannot comprehend society as a whole, and are not driven to do so by the nature of their way of life. On the contrary, the peasant who acquires a knowledge of society as a whole is an anomaly, someone who has to fight against the intrinsic conditions of his way of life rather than being led necessarily by those conditions in that direction.

Where the proletariat is a majority, its own emancipation is within its own power, and its self-emancipation is the emancipation of society as a whole, including the peasantry. Thus, the role of the proletariat is not an optional element in Marxism. Without it, Marxism becomes nonsense, and we have to start from scratch all over again. Whatever form of "socialism" could be formulated on different grounds could not, validly, borrow from Marxism except by changing the essential meaning of the words involved (as we have seen is the case with the term "exploitation").

VII. The worker-peasant alliance

In countries where peasants are a majority of the population, Marxists have had to formulate what should be the relationship between the proletarian struggle and the peasantry. Marx himself always supported the small peasant struggle against large feudal owners—a constituent element of the bourgeois revolution—but he opposed the struggle of small property owners against large capitalist concerns—a counter-revolution.[9] Large-scale capitalist enterprise had to be preserved for collective ownership, for it was the source from which the wealth of socialist society would come. When the proletariat begins its battle against capitalism, making socialism for the first time possible, large-scale production was not to be broken up among the producers. In the 1850 programme for the Communist League in Germany, Marx proposed that the Royal and large feudal estates should *not* be distributed to the peasants, but preserved under State ownership.[10] Similarly the Bolshevik programme in Tsarist Russia demanded the nationalization of commercially important landed estates, *not* their redistribution among the peasants. In this, the Bolsheviks went flatly against the demand both of the peasants and their main political champions, the Social Revolutionaries.

In the event, the Bolshevik programme was irrelevant, since the peasants just seized the land, and the Bolsheviks could do little

[9] For further discussion of this, cf. Cliff, *op. cit.*
[10] Karl Marx, Address of the Central Committee to the Communist League, 1850, p. 166, in *Selected Works*, I, *op. cit.*

about it except ratify the seizure. But in seizing the land, the peasantry created a new class of owners of private property. It was an albatross around the neck of the Soviet regime. The regime only freed itself by Stalin's Final Solution of the peasant question, the complete destruction of the peasantry in collectivization.

Implicit in both Marx's and Lenin's writings is a stress upon the inconsistent aims of peasant and proletarian, their *different* targets. Many populist socialists have refused to accept this sharp distinction, even though the distinction is a crucial line between libertarian socialism and the autocratic State socialisms which occur when outsiders ride the back of the "People" into power. Since the peasants are not a national class for themselves, they cannot control their own leaders, they must be represented (cf. the quotation from Marx above). When these leaders are intent on ends other than those of the peasants—ends such as industrialization, national unity, and so on—the populists can be the worst dictators of all.

Thus, the distinction between peasant and proletarian is not a pedantic aside, a piece of irrelevant sectarianism. It defines different roads to *different things*. Lenin was particularly emphatic in stressing the difference, in refusing to muddle all the issues in the "People." He constantly criticized the Social Revolutionaries for doing just this. For example, in 1909, he wrote of the Social Revolutionary programme:

> The fundamental idea of their programme is not at all that 'an alliance of the proletariat and the peasantry is necessary', but that there is no class abyss between the former and the latter, and that there is no need to draw a line of class demarcation between them, and that the (Marxist) idea of the petty-bourgeois nature of the peasantry that distinguishes it from the proletariat is fundamentally false.[11]

The peasant movement was indeed fighting, but not capitalist relationships so much as pre-capitalist relationships. The complete

[11] This is translated from the Russian edition of the *Collected Works* (Vol. 9, p. 410); the English equivalent is in "Revision of the Agrarian Programme of the Workers' Party", March 1906, Volume X, *Collected Works*, p. 191.

victory of the peasant movement "will not abolish capitalism: on the contrary, it will create a broader foundation for its development."[12]

This does not mean that peasants will not play an important role in the battle for socialism, but that role is only possible under leadership from the proletariat. Without that leadership, the peasant struggle leads to other things. Of course, like Lenin, we must "support the peasant movement to the end, but we must remember that it is a movement of another class, not the one that can or will accomplish socialism."[13]

VIII. China and the peasantry

If the foregoing case is broadly true, then it becomes important to explain a number of modern revolutions which have been claimed as "peasant revolutions." What follows mainly concerns China, although elements of the analysis could also be applied to other countries, for example, Cuba.

[12] Useful comparisons can be drawn between current socialist attitudes to the struggle in the backward countries, and, for example, views expressed by Marx on Bolivar in the struggle for the freedom of Latin America, and by Lenin on Sun Yat-sen in China. For Marx on Bolivar, cf. Hal Draper, "Marx and Bolivar: A Note on Authoritarian Leadership in a National-Liberation Movement," *New Politics*, VII/I, Winter 1968, pp. 64-77. Lenin on Sun Yat-sen is contained in "Democracy and Narodism in China", July 1912, *Selected Works* 4, p. 305. Lenin writes: "They (viz. the Chinese nationalists) are subjectively socialists because they are opposed to the oppression and exploitation of the masses. But the *objective* conditions of China, of a backward, agricultural, semi-feudal country, place on the order of the day, in the lives of a nation numbering nearly half a billion, only one definite historically peculiar form of this oppression and exploitation, namely feudalism." p. 308.

[13] V.I. Lenin, "Petty bourgeois and proletarian socialism", Nov. 1905, *Selected Works* 3, p. 150. Compare Marx, p. 160, Address of the Central Council to the Communist League, *op. cit.* : "The relation of the revolutionary workers' party to the petty-bourgeois democracy* is this: it marches together with it against the section which it aims at overthrowing, it opposes the petty-bourgeoisie in everything by which they desire to establish themselves." *This "comprises not only the great majority of the bourgeois inhabitants of the towns, the small industrial businessmen and guild masters, it numbers among its following the peasants and the rural proletariat,"

The leadership of the Chinese Communist Party was drawn in the main from urban classes, particularly from the urban intelligentsia. It utilized different segments of the population in its advance to power, but undoubtedly the bulk of its support was drawn from the peasantry. The struggle for power was, for various reasons which cannot be cited here, not a *class* struggle in the Marxist sense. It was not primarily a struggle taking place between elements of the contending classes within the same production unit. Rather was the struggle a military-territorial battle, while the social struggle—which certainly occurred—was no more than a supporting element for the military operation. Of course, the final phases of any revolutionary movement may be a military-territorial struggle—the civil war in Russia was just such a struggle. But in China, the essence of the movement was military-territorial, and the direct class struggle marginal from 1928 through to 1948.

The party used different demands in different localities to build up its support, demands designed to build not a class force so much as a national force, drawing on different sections of the population. Nationally, the party restricted itself to demands for relatively mild reforms in order to carry the whole coalition against the main target. Thus, the party opposed the demand for land reform up to 1945 in order not to frighten the larger land holders, and its only concession to its poor peasant supporters was the reduction of rent and interest to be paid to landlords. Even after 1945, it appears now that it was the discredited Liu Shao-chi who championed land reform in the face of the opposition of Mao Tse-tung who resisted such "sectional" demands in the interest of national unity. All that Mao would concede was that "excess land" should be compulsorily purchased.

Thus, the Chinese Communist Party cannot be seen as the agent of the Chinese peasantry, and indeed, cannot be seen as the agent of any class. It sought to operate *outside* the peasant social structure, drawing support from all rural strata. It was not responsible to any particular segment of the population, nor yet to the peasantry as a whole. No section of the peasantry controlled the party. Rather did the party and the People's Liberation Army control sections of the peasantry.

If the party had not operated outside the peasant social structure, it would have been infiltrated by the richer peasants and subordinated to their interests, a change which would have led to the disintegration of the party between different districts. At times the party was threatened with this. For example, Mao complained in 1933 that 80 per cent of the central district of the Hunan-Kiangsi Soviet was controlled by the landlords and rich peasants.[14] Again, in the early fifties, when peasant communists returned from military service to their homes, the rural party threatened once more to become no more than a rich peasant organization. The peasant cadres expected to be rewarded for their services, and to be left alone to till their new land after the sacrifices of war. The rural party was used to make cadres rich peasants, and rich peasants became cadres as a means of advancing their position. Kao Kang in 1952 castigated cadres who had become exploiters, lending money and hiring labour:

If no active steps are taken . . . to lead the peasants towards the path of co-operative economy rather than to the rich peasant economy, then rural village government is sure to deteriorate into a rich peasant regime. If the Communist Party members all hire labour and give loans at usurious rates, then the Party will become a rich peasant party.[15]

The same phenomenon occurred in the Soviet Union during the New Economic Policy, rendering the rural party useless as an agency for change.[16] It is a striking demonstration that the

[14] Isaacs, *op. cit.*, p. 344, writes:

Mao Tse-tung, president of the 'Soviet Republic' wrote : Many landlords and rich peasants put on a revolutionary coloration. They say they are for the revolution and for the division of land . . . . They are very active and rely on their historical advantages—"they can speak well and write well"—and consequently in the first period they steal the fruits of the agrarian revolution. Facts from innumerable places prove that they have usurped the provisional power, filtered into the armed forces, controlled the revolutionary organisations, and received more and better land than the poor peasants.

Mao estimated that this was the case in '80 per cent of the area of the central district, affecting a population of more than 2,000,000'. (From Mao, "Re-examination of Land Distribution in the Soviet Districts is the Central Task" *Red Flag*, 31 August 1933).

[15] Kao Kang, "Overcome the Corrosion of Bourgeois Ideology : Oppose the Rightist Trend in the Party", *People's Daily*, January 24, 1952, cited *Current Background*, 163, March 5, 1952.

[16] Lewin, *op. cit.*, p. 121 passim.

Chinese Communist Party is *not* a peasant party that it did not degenerate in the way Kao Kang feared. It was possible for the party to purge its rural organization and to whip errant cadres into line simply because it was *not* a peasant party.

Thus, the Chinese Communist Party was not a "peasant party" in the sense in which we might speak of a "proletarian party," or, indeed, a "bourgeois party." Certainly people of peasant origin provided the bulk of the party rank and file, but even then, such recruits had usually long since left the land to become professional cadres or soldiers. The party's ability to transform China depended upon it being independent of peasant interests, and in this respect it was largely successful. Rather was it the case that a section of the urban intelligentsia organized peasant discontent. And even then, success depended heavily upon the occurrence of the Japanese invasion and the Japanese policy of ransacking and burning villages in the wake of their advance. By and large, peasants do not seem susceptible to nationalist demands—unlike the urban middle class, and for fairly obvious material reasons— unless such demands are closely linked to demands of immediate concern for peasants, demands over land, or, in this case, sheer survival. It is open to doubt whether the sections of the Chinese peasantry which did respond to Communist appeals would have done so if the party had not provided the only real opposition to the Japanese whose actions directly affected the existence of some of the peasants. In India, certainly, tying the demand for independence to the demand that those who supported the British, the landowners, should be expropriated and their land redistributed among the peasants, was a vital factor in eliciting peasant support. And in Viet Nam, without the Vietminh and National Liberation Front's land reform programme, it is unlikely the war against the American army could have been waged.

Because the leadership of the Communist Party in China was not securely tied to the interests of any class, it was able to act as an elitist force, and its politics have striking similarities with the elitist flavour of much populism (and, including in this, some brands of anarchism). Populism can be roughly defined as a passionate belief in the spontaneous energies of the "People," and a powerful elitist belief in one's own necessary role in bringing enlightenment to the "People."[17] But rejecting identification

[17] This definition is taken from Meisner's biography of an important

with any particular class is rejecting responsibility to any class. It leaves the leadership free to pursue whatever ends suit its tactics. In Maoism, populism includes a powerful nationalist element, a belief that anything and everything is possible within one's own national boundaries, that nationalism encompasses socialism. Everything is possible because there is no given objective society— if hearts and minds can be changed. Thus the target becomes souls rather than a definite ruling class, and no objective laws of capitalism or anything else can, it is said, defeat this infinite voluntarism. There are certainly aspects of Marxism which lend themselves, in isolation, to a populist revision,[18] even though such a revision also directly contradicts Marxism.

IX. Backwardness and socialism

None of this bears directly on the kind of problems which face Marxists in backward countries. Thus: is the thesis of permanent revolution, and in particular, the role of the proletariat, still relevant in backward countries today? If it is not, then what should be the role of Marxists in backward countries? These are major questions which demand separate answers, one of which is advanced in the last chapter of this book.[19] Suffice it to say at this stage that, even if the proletariat can no longer be seen as the agency of revolution in backward countries today, this does not change the validity of the points made here. It means only that proletarian socialism cannot be achieved in the backward countries on their own today. But then it never could. Socialism is not possible in one country or one region, particularly when these are the most backward. Certainly, imperialism can be defeated at various points in backward countries—but not destroyed in the world as a whole. Certainly, important and progressive changes can be

---

Chinese populist, Li Ta-chao, one of the two founders of the Chinese Communist Party. Cf. Meisner, *Li Ta-chao and the Origins of Chinese Marxism*, Cambridge, Mass., 1967, p. 251.

[18] On this, cf. the extended discussion in Chapters 9 and 10.

[19] For another attempt at this, cf. Tony Cliff, "Permanent Revolution" *IS*, 12, Spring 1963. An American non-Marxist author has attempted some comparisons—cf. Ernst Halperin, *Proletarian Class Parties in Europe and Latin America*, Cambridge, Mass., 1967.

made in backward countries—but these changes do not constitute socialism. No amount of rhetorical elan can convert poverty into wealth, can give men in a backward society the basic conditions of life already secured in an advanced one. Indeed, the rhetoric alone should make us suspicious. Where objective conditions permit little rapid improvement of material circumstances, governments have often seen the next best thing to real progress as trying to persuade people that there is really progress anyway, that the things of the spirit are so much more important than the next bowl of rice.

What one must not do is to bend one's estimate of objective reality to accommodate short-term tactical considerations. Thus, the progressiveness of the revolution in China leads on to arguing that the Chinese "model" is the sole means to achieve socialism, and all things Chinese are, by definition, progressive. The Left intellectuals of the 1930s played the same game with the Soviet Union, and ended being taken for a ride. Moscow came to equal socialism, and all criteria for judging Moscow on a socialist basis disappeared. The sympathizers ended as apologists for the Russian State (of course, it is also true that the Chinese revolution has not played nearly so important a role in the political awareness of non-Chinese socialists as did the Russian revolution, or has Mao achieved anything like the international significance of Stalin?).

Progressive steps are important, even if they are not the final step. But in present conditions, whatever happens in China— or anywhere else—is continuously threatened by the continued existence of the imperialist powers. In Viet Nam, the American forces may be defeated, but this will not end the existence of Washington. The existence of the advanced capitalist powers, private and State, makes the prospects for any sustained economic development in the backward countries grim. Thus, the future of the backward countries, like the future of the peasantry, depends, not upon one defeat of one element of imperialism, but its global destruction. And it cannot be destroyed globally in Viet Nam, nor can it be destroyed by the world's peasantry. It can only be destroyed in the advanced countries themselves, and only by the proletariat. Thus the issue—peasant or proletarian—is not about who can achieve "socialism" in one country, but about the emancipation of mankind as a whole.

Lenin and Imperialism
Today

A majority of the world's population has always lived in poverty. But the difference today is not just that the contrast between the rich and the poor, on a world scale, is so much more extreme, but that the productive resources available to the world could in principle conquer poverty. There is no shortage of technique, no shortage of technicians, no shortage of capital. The problem arises because human need and the supply of resources exist in isolation from each other. And those who possess the resources are in the main preserved from experiencing poverty. In Watts, in Parisian bidonvilles, in decaying Durham villages, in the Appalachian mountains or the Brazilian north-east, in Lagos or Manila, Calcutta or Szechwan, the poverty is trapped where the PR men cannot see it, except properly mediated by the photographs of colour supplements. Even where sheer material poverty is hidden behind net curtains, as much spiritual poverty—generated by the emptiness of man's role in the production machine—pervades the life of all but a fortunate few.

Sometimes the poor, for so long staring and wondering in silence, penetrate the hypocrisy. But the occasional riot is more a flash of bared teeth by the hunted than a strategy for changing the world; the violence is that of despair as much as of hope. But the violence does, like lightning at night, suddenly reveal the true

This chapter was first published as "Imperialism Today", *World Crisis, Essays in Revolutionary Socialism* (edited by Nigel Harris and John Palmer), Hutchinson, London, 1971, p. 117.

landscape. The privileged reach for their guns, for "law and order." In the United States, the threat of the poor is more tangible, and the powers-that-be more explicit about the dangers:

> ... unless the Administration and Congress launch a vastly expensive and 'full-scale war on domestic ills, especially urban ills' ... the central cities of the United States will in a few years ... become 'fortresses' in which the wealthy live in 'privately guarded compounds', people will travel on 'high-speed patrolled expressways connecting safe areas' ... 'private automobiles, taxicabs, and commercial vehicles will be routinely equipped with unbreakable glass and light armour' ... 'armed guards will ride shot gun on all forms of public transportation' and protect all public facilities such as schools, libraries, and playgrounds'; and 'the ghetto and slum neighbourhoods will be places of terror with widespread crime, perhaps out of police control during night time'.[1]

This form of repressed civil war in the middle of the "rule of law" is no more than a microcosm of the coming world. The Fortress islands of America and Europe will face a sea of discontents, with tiny colonies of the rich policing the further extremities, linked by the tenuous life-line of air travel. But for the moment, even the privilege of being feared is denied the majority of the poor. They live and die far from the eyes of most of the rich. And in Calcutta or Manila or Saõ Paulo, the local representatives of the world's rich are braver in bearing the offensiveness of poverty. Hearts less stout would crack.

Poverty is sustained by the inability of the world productive machine to employ the human resources available at an adequate wage, and by the unwillingness or inability of our rulers to transform the machine so that it accords with human needs rather than the interests of their own power. The interests of the rulers are fragmented among a multitude of petty local ruling classes, each more concerned to defeat its rivals than answer the central problem. The little principalities of the world, a sort of medieval

---

[1] United States National Commission on the Causes and Prevention of Violence, *Report* (on Violent Crime, Homicide, Assault, Rape and Robbery), November 1969, as reported in the *Guardian*, 25 November 1969.

Germany, squabble; the clerics pursue the higher verities; and the poor wait. The rivalry drives the machine apparently further and further away from the needs of the available population, so that the standard solution to all problems of economic backwardness or oppression—"economic development"—recedes like a mirage the more we seem to approach it.

In the last half of the 19th century, the forward thrust of capitalism swept into its wake the rest of the world. But today, the enormous expansion of capitalism appears to have fewer and fewer effects on the great mass of poor satellites. Certainly, since 1948, advanced capitalism has been in a frenetic, headlong rush of growth. But the spin-off seems weaker and weaker. In the same way, the ripples from the growth of the American economy are more and more sluggish as they approach the black ghettoes. Having dragged the backward countries pell-mell into the market place, having fleeced them, the rich are now fleeing back to their fortresses. They will sit on their heap of treasure, and when there is time from adding more booty to the pile, pity the less fortunate.

The problem of world development has to be a *central* concern for any socialist strategy, not a charitable after-thought if we have something left over. Talk of human emancipation and of freedom is so much parlour prattle while the experience of the majority of men, women and children is such an appalling prospect of hunger and oppression. But to make world development central to any strategy demands that we grasp the nature of modern capitalism and its relationship to the rest of the world. It may be useful to show the hypocrisy of Western governments in concealing the real impact of their societies on the rest of the world, but on its own, it is not a strategy. Describing the evil does not necessarily go any way to overcoming it. Indeed, in isolation, it may merely encourage cynicism or apathy. After all, the scale of the problem is so gigantic, what could possibly be done about it? A strategy requires not just the identification of the problem, but putting it in context and showing how the problem can be overcome and by whom. What is to be done, how can it be done, and who will do it?

More than 50 years ago, it was one of Lenin's remarkable achievements to answer all three questions. The influence of his answers still pervades the Left, so that any new strategy has to start by coming to terms with Lenin. The Left has added remarkably little to *Imperialism, the Highest Stage of Capitalism.* Yet the rate of change of capitalism has, if discontinuously, accelerated over the past half century. In many respects, the backward countries have also been transformed. It would be most unlikely if the relationship between the two had not also been radically changed. Yet the assumption of much of the writing on the Left is that nothing of substance has changed, and that any attempt to identify changes only betrays the cause. We must cling to the symbols, lest innovation betray the substance; lest the baby leave with the bath water.

But this cowardice nullifies any serious attempt to outline a clear strategy. Myths and phrases become the substitute for serious thought. Fudging the issue is at a premium. And muddled criteria make it impossible to understand clearly a whole range of different issues—what happened to the Russian revolution, and what safeguards are there against the degeneration of any regime which breaks with world capitalism? The muddle confuses communists in trying to detect "true socialism" in such diverse phenomena as Czechoslovak managerialism, the Yugoslav market economy, in the dead weight of Russian bureaucracy or the rhetoric of China, or even Albania. It dogs the heels of any attempt to understand the Chinese or Cuban revolutions. It subtly blurs attempts to characterize the military regimes of Egypt and Algeria, and the former leaders of Indonesia and Ghana. For the young, it becomes impossible to understand nationalization in backward countries, and leads them to wonder whether one party regimes, "democratic" dictators and all the fraudulent paraphernalia of incipient or fully-fledged tyrannies are really symptoms of a higher human emancipation or a deeper freedom. The Left is robbed of its independence, becoming no more than public relations outriders for one or other official State. For those with no vehicle of their own, fellow travelling becomes a way of life.

The account which follows deals separately with the two central issues of concern: the nature of modern imperialism, and some of the means by which imperialism could be overthrown.

I.   The economics of imperialism

(a) Lenin and Imperialism

Lenin described imperialism as "the highest stage of capitalism," the stage preceding the socialist revolution. It was a different stage of capitalism because its characteristics contrasted with the preceding phase of growth. Those new characteristics now compelled capitalism not merely to increase domestic exploitation, but to intensify its control of the rest of the world. Internal changes within particular capitalist economies and the external extension of capitalism were part of a single process.

Very crudely, Lenin identified the new characteristics as: (*i*) The creation of monopolies and cartels in all the main branches of capitalist production, and an increased concentration of capital. As a result, the price discipline of open market competition between many small rivals tended to be replaced within each capitalist economy by monopoly-administered pricing, leading to very high profits, made even higher by the control of empire. (*ii*) Within each capitalist economy, production was increasingly controlled by banks and financial institutions, by the lending capitalist (the *rentier*) rather than the producing one (the *entrepreneur*):

> Imperialism, or the rule of finance capital, is that highest stage of capitalism in which this separation (between the *rentier* living entirely on income obtained from money capital, is separated from the *entrepreneur* and from all those directly concerned in the management of capital) reaches vast proportions. The supremacy of finance capital over all other forms of capital means the rule of the *rentier* and of the financial oligarchy; it means the crystallization of a small number of financially 'powerful' states from among all the rest.[2]

Financial control, based upon the control of individual firms, had come to control whole capitalist States, and thus the rest of the world.

(*iii*) But the monopolistic financial control of particular markets did not end competition within capitalism. On the contrary, rivalry now became much fiercer between the leading capitalist States. And as competition tended to be replaced within each economy by administration, so it tended to be replaced internationally by open warfare.

[2] Lenin, V. I., "Imperialism, the Highest Stage of Capitalism", *Selected Works*, V, London, 1936, p. 53.

The two limitations on the system which simultaneously drove it outwards internationally and threatened it with disaster were the search for raw materials and for outlets for "surplus" capital. The rate of expansion of capitalism depended upon an increasing inflow of materials, and the search for materials drove capital out to the rest of the world. In doing so, it created outlets for capital which otherwise would have been able to find no profitable forms of investment within the advanced capitalist economies themselves. Capital was "surplus" because of the very high rates of profit characteristic of monopoly capitalism, and because the limits of profitable investment had been reached at home; it could not be diverted into improving the conditions of the mass of the population or developing agriculture—if capitalism did these things it would not be capitalism; for uneven and wretched conditions of the masses are fundamental and inevitable conditions and premises of this mode of production.[3]

Here capital was necessarily driven outwards to the rest of the world, both to seize territory from its capitalist neighbours and to colonize "new" territory. The rivalry between the capitalist States punctuated economic competition with phases of open warfare: war had become an essential element in the highest stage of capitalism.

The long-term effects of the new system would be to convert the most advanced capitalist countries into financiers for the rest of the world which would, in turn, increasingly take over the functions of commodity production. The financial State, the "Bondholder State" was increasingly revealed as a purely parasitic element on the production process of the backward countries— "the world has become divided into a handful of money-lending states on the one side, and a vast majority of debtor states on the other."[4] Finally, the vast profits made by the *rentiers* gave them the resources with which to bribe their own working classes, to buy off the proletarian revolution, and this "sets the seal of parasitism on the whole country which lives by the exploitation of the labour of several overseas countries and colonies."[5]

Given that this is inevitably a crude and oversimplified restatement of Lenin's analysis, how does it stand up today? Clearly, the

[3] *Ibid.*, p. 56.
[4] *Ibid.*, pp. 92-93.
[5] *Ibid.*, p. 92.

concentration of capital, the degree of monopoly, has gone much further than it was in Lenin's day, and the conclusions Lenin drew from increasing concentration apply with even greater force today. Furthermore, the relationship between capital and the State, and between economic rivalry and warfare, has gone even further. In Lenin's day, the State was by modern standards ill-prepared for war; today the Western States are in a state of permanent preparation for war. Since the Second World War, in particular, defence expenditure in peacetime takes an unprecedented share of public revenue. In 1937, the per capita military expenditure of the Great Powers was $25 per year; in 1968, the same figure for the United States—at 1937 prices—was $132 dollars.[6]

However, on "finance capital," Lenin seems less reliable. For the hegemony of the *rentier* did not survive. The power of finance as an independent part of the ruling order depended upon the free flow of funds internationally, on the pre-World War I Gold Standard. But as well as giving finance its international power, it also made it independent of its State of origin abroad. The extension of empire by the State and the free flow of finance internationally were not necessarily matched. Indeed, the figures Lenin used to illustrate the export of capital did not identify the destinations involved, so that we do not know from these figures what proportion of, say, British capital went into the British empire and what elsewhere. From other sources, we know that the dispersion of British capital before the First World War was very wide—to Latin America, Japan, Russia, eastern Europe, the United States and so on. On the face of it, the demands of finance could only have been a very subordinate interest in the extension of empire. The search for raw materials was probably more important for some parts of empire; for other parts, straight political competition between the advanced capitalist powers seems to have been the main motive. The argument might well have been: seize the territory first, and then try and find some raw materials, rather than locate raw materials and then seize the territory. And seizing the territory was in many cases motivated by the attempt to prevent the French or the Germans or someone else getting in first.

Nor is it clear that empire was related to a high rate of growth for a metropolitan country. If it were so, we would have to explain

[6]Calculated by Harry Magdoff, "Militarism and Imperialism", *Monthly Review*, XXI/9, February 1970, p. 8.

why British capitalism—with the largest empire of all—was in relative decline, while German capitalism—with hardly any empire at all—was ascending. Empire was a vital component in the struggle for power between the advanced capitalist countries which culminated in the First World War, but it did not explain the differing rates of growth of different capitalisms.

What transformed capitalism, its relationship to finance and to empire, was Lenin's third characteristic of the "highest stage" —war. Not just the First World War, but the clash of capitalist rivalries embodied in the slump of them iddle inter-war years, the Second World War and the following phases of localized wars, and the creation within capitalism of a permanent arms economy, transformed the system. It made possible the post-1945 growth in real mass consumption (without necessarily changing the proportions of real income accruing to different classes), and a rapid growth in agricultural output, both of which were ruled out by Lenin. The growth of agriculture in Britain was directly the result of the development of economic nationalism, of the attempt to become independent of imports.

Between the First and Second World Wars, capitalism underwent a period of long drawn out stagnation, in which individual States slowly adjusted themselves to the imperatives of military, as much as economic, rivalry. The adjustment shifted the weight of the industrial structure, the flow of resources and the distribution of power. And the wings of finance capital which had permitted it to go where it pleased were effectively clipped in the aftermath of the 1929 collapse. The State intervened in all capitalist countries to prevent, curtail or circumscribe the export of capital, except for purposes expressly sanctioned by the State. In Britain, leaving the Gold Standard robbed the City of its independent power, and forced it back into the role of "national capital." The State was not acting as an independent force. It pursued the salvation of British capitalism, and to this end, sought to force domestic savings into domestic industry rather than permit it to be loaned to foreign competitors. And slowly, over time, it had some success. Between 1928 and 1935, the proportion of available domestic funds going into domestic investment increased from 60 to 89 per cent. In the longer term, there were major changes in the role of capital exports within the British economy. Capital exports declined from about eight per cent of the gross national product

in the period preceding 1914 to about two per cent now; then capital exports took about 50 per cent of domestic savings, now under ten per cent.[7]
Tariff walls, protection and direct State assistance, aided the process of the concentration of capital. And capital concentration, with the decline of the *rentiers*, made the characteristic capital export, not indirect investment by *rentiers* but direct investment by the largest British companies seeking to escape foreign tariffs on British exports. Protection also made the role of the State vital in the domestic economy. In alliance with corporate capitalism, the State began the process of replacing the *rentier* in order to force up the rate of domestic savings. Neither the State nor the largest companies had any love for the *rentier*. Certainly, they did not follow the audacious prescription of Keynes and pursue the "euthanasia of the *rentier*"[8] but State assistance to the "entrepreneur," even its differential tax rates between "earned" and "unearned" income, all had the effect—intentional or otherwise—of reducing *rentier* power. Indeed, the State substituted its own taxes as a means of securing a large part of what formerly went in dividends. Between 1938 and 1956, taxation increased from 14 to 39 per cent of net company income; dividend and interest payments fell from 68 to 35 per cent. Dividends as a percentage of profits fell from 67 per cent in 1912 to 23 per cent between 1949 and 1956.[9]
The State intervened to strengthen national production in the economic war on the foreigner. Necessarily it had to destroy the international aspirations of the *rentiers*. That the State was able to undertake such a task demonstrates that it was not simply the creature of the *rentiers*. Of course, the changes introduced only made the *rentier* even more parasitic in appearance, and this had useful political benefits. For the *rentier* could always be held up as a scapegoat for anti-capitalist feeling. Both the Communists and the Labour Party leadership—not to mention Adolf Hitler and the extreme Right (where Jewish finance played the key role)—used the evil *rentier* as a substitute for capitalism itself, the murder of Shylock would expiate the guilt of "healthy" capitalists.

[7] Figures cited by Michael Kidron, "Imperialism, Highest Stage of Capitalism But One", *International Socialism*, 9, Summer 1962.
[8] Keynes, J. M., *General Theory of Employment, Interest and Money*, London, 1936, pp. 375-376.
[9] Kidron, *op. cit.*

If the thesis of finance capitalism appears incorrect today, so also must some of Lenin's other conclusions. Read in isolation, his account might seem to imply that the world division of labour was being transformed in a way which would culminate in the world's proletariat being concentrated in the backward countries, while the population of the advanced would be entirely concerned either with financial operations or servicing the financiers. In practice and in the rest of his work, Lenin did not frame his strategy around this implication nor argue that in the future, only revolt in the backward countries would threaten capitalism. His concern with the "weak links" of capitalism was the result of a political analysis, rather than designed to deliver simply an *economic* death blow to the system. In practice, he concentrated on the backward countries of Europe where the political implications were strongest, arguing that:

> The struggle of the oppressed nations *in Europe*, a struggle capable of going to the lengths of insurrection and street fighting will sharpen the revolutionary crisis in Europe infinitely more than a much more developed rebellion in a remote colony. A blow delivered against the English imperialist bourgeoisie by a rebellion in Ireland is a hundred times more significant politically than a blow of equal weight delivered in Asia or Africa (VIL emphasis).[10]

Since Lenin's time, the division of labour in the world has not led to the backward countries becoming the producing sector, and the advanced simply the lending and consuming sector. The advanced have only increased even further their share of production, as well as consumption and lending.

If finance capital does not accurately identify modern capitalism, we have to formulate a new description so that we can understand why one phase of economic expansion demanded empire, and another, the dissolution of empire. Only then can we begin to understand the present position of the backward countries, and so, how it can be changed.

---

[10] Lenin, V. I., Discussion on self-determination summed up, *Selected Works*, V, London, 1936.

(b) Decolonization

A number of socialists have argued the thesis that the backward countries are vital for the economic survival of advanced metropolitan capitalism. Advocates of this position who are economically sophisticated no longer argue that the backward are vital for the capital exports of the advanced, simply because the available information directly contradicts this, but they do usually imply that it is the raw material needs of capitalism which make it not only dependent upon the backward, but increasingly so. We shall return to this thesis later, but here our only concern is with Left explanations of decolonization. For if the advanced are increasingly dependent for survival upon raw material imports from the backward, how was it that the imperialist countries could ever bring themselves to grant political independence to their imperial possessions?

John Strachey of the British Labour Party argued that British decolonization occurred as a result of the Labour government of 1945 to 1951 (but not, for some reason, as a result of the two earlier Labour governments). For the first time, he says, the working classes came to power, and immediately began the task of freeing nations ensnared in the British Empire,[11] presumably in ignorance or disregard of the economic dependence of Britain upon its colonies. But the case smacks of wishful thinking, not least because the relationship between working class wishes and the policies of Labour is tenuous in the extreme. In any case, Strachey's explanation does not help us to understand world decolonization, only British, nor why economic domination was not ended at the same time as political independence was granted, nor why successive Conservative governments continued the same policy throughout the 1950s. Strachey raises more questions than he answers.

Others, using the opportunity to embellish the image of the Soviet Union much as Strachey wished to embellish that of the British Labour Party, have suggested that it was really the threat of the Soviet Union which compelled war-weary western Europe to relinquish its imperial holdings. The evidence is even thinner here, for Moscow showed little more than propagandist interest in the colonies of her Allies. Indeed, in Viet Nam, both the

[11] cf. John Strachey, *The End of Empire*, London, 1959, p. 135.

Soviet Union and the French Communist Party either supported or acquiesced in France's attempt to re-establish control of Indo-China.[12] In any case, much of the decolonization took place in the fifties when Europe was not "war-weary" but rather in boom. Even after the Second World War, unusually large numbers of British and American troops were scattered throughout Asia, in just the position to secure the Allied empires. In Saigon, British troops indeed did just this for the French. War-weary France may have been in 1945, but it did not prevent the French army waging a bitter and brutal war in Viet Nam up to 1954, followed by seven more years of savage warfare to hold Algeria. But the French case—like that of the Dutch in Indonesia, or much later the Belgians in the Congo—was the exception. The overwhelming majority of imperial possessions were granted political independence without anything like this scale of struggle. And the Soviet Union played scarcely any role at all in this.

A different argument states that it was the heroic struggle of the population in the backward countries which forced the end of political control. This is obviously much more plausible, but it is still not enough on its own. For, in the majority of cases, there was no popular anti-imperialist struggle at all. Even in some of the cases where there was—as in India, for example—independence was conceded without the imperial power really waging an all-out war to retain control. And in some cases, the imperialists merely scuttled as quickly as they could.

Certainly, American pressure played an important part in the granting of independence. The European imperialist powers were heavily dependent upon the United States, both in waging the Second World War and in coping with the problems of its immediate aftermath. And the interests of American Liberalism in ending imperial tyranny—in advancing the rights of national self-determination—neatly coincided with some of the interests of American business in wanting to prize open protected imperial markets. But, again, the behaviour of France in Viet Nam and Algeria, and of Holland in Indonesia, showed how far the European powers could go if they really calculated their colonies were vital for their economic survival. And the United States did

---

[12] There are numerous accounts of this, but, by way of example, cf. Ellen J. Hammer, *The Struggle for Indochina, 1940-1955*, Stanford, 1966.

not deny assistance to France as a reprisal, since it also needed European support once the Cold War began. On the contrary, Washington in Viet Nam demonstrated its willingness to take up part of the White Man's Burden.

In some of the explanations, there is obviously much which is valid. It is also true that, as many on the Left have pointed out, political power was conceded to independent regimes without conceding economic power. Backward countries remained subject to the domination, control or influence of foreign capital, foreign finance and foreign commodity markets. But it would be quite wrong to infer from this that nothing at all changed, or that conceding independence was no more than a devious conspiracy to conceal even greater foreign domination. Political independence did make metropolitan capital less secure in the backward countries; very often, it permitted the nationalization in whole or part of foreign interests, even by the most conservative regimes in backward countries. If the metropolitan countries were indeed economically dependent upon the backward, granting independence was a rash gamble.

The gamble paid off. Western capitalism entered a phase of unprecedented growth at the same time as it dismantled its different empires. Any explanation of decolonization has also to explain this phase of growth. For, on the face of it, it seems that decolonization was conceded because the metropolitan powers were economically less dependent upon their colonies, not more. The price of retaining empire steadily exceeded the returns on empire. And the possibility of surviving without an empire seemed reasonable. The explanation for the change lies in the mutation of the industrial structure of capitalism. Old style capitalism contained much more powerful interests whose survival depended upon the maintenance of political control of colonies. The more powerful those interests, the more the survival of capitalism itself depended upon empire. But post-war capitalism needed to the same degree neither those domestic interests nor their external extension—empire.

The imperial powers in the post-war period could have made a run for it. The scale of military operations undertaken by them in Korea, for example, as well as the resources sunk in the maintenance of the defensive walls of NATO, CENTO, SEATO and so on—directed not against the "Third World," but against

"International Communism" (and the two, despite the best efforts of Washington and Moscow, are not the same thing)—show how far the Western powers could go when they felt themselves seriously threatened. The backward countries, neither economically nor politically, could threaten capitalism on this scale. The high growth rate of capitalism sustained its military capability, and the expansion of its military capability had a crucial boosting effect upon its growth rate. A by-product of economic expansion was increased economic domination of the backward countries. But increased economic domination does not necessarily mean increased dependence. It remains true that imperialism does produce wars; but not so much between the advanced and the backward as between the advanced themselves. And this is true even where the backward countries are the scene of the war.

(c) An Alternative Account

(i) Capitalism, Old and New

During this century, the centre of equilibrium within each capitalist economy has shifted away from the old core of 19th century industry—the extractive industries (particularly coal, iron and steel) and industries concerned with the relatively primitive processing of raw materials (for example, cotton textile production). It has shifted towards manufacturing proper, and in particular, to the most technically advanced sectors of manufacturing, the metal-using, electrical and petro-chemical industries. The change was from more extensive forms of production to more intensive ones, from a process ultimately limited by the supply of raw materials and labour to one limited rather by the technical ingenuity of the production process itself. The intervening stages in the industrial process between raw materials and final output has become longer and longer and increasingly complex.

The changed technology, which is sometimes seen as the cause of the transformation, was in fact the result of the rivalries bred by "the highest stage of capitalism." The struggle for power between the advanced capitalist countries, and, in particular, those characteristic features of imperialism, war and the permanent arms economy, continuously forced the evolution of technology into particular channels. The shift was not a smooth adjustment from one phase to another, but a piecemeal, *ad hoc*, twisting and turning change, impelled by the fluctuations in the relationships between the rivals, none of them being able to establish sufficient control of their environment to begin to plan deliberately their own self-transformation.

The shift in part transformed capitalist society. The labour force required by the new forms of production had to be much more highly educated, and to sustain the drive to raise its productivity it needed both higher real incomes and an elaborate complex of welfare provisions. The characteristic figure of the old labour movement, the unskilled manual worker, went into slow decline; the new white collar worker, demanded by the much more highly concentrated and therefore bureaucratized public and private companies, rose to new importance within the labour movement. Politically, the old capitalism was not divested of power by the new without a long transitional period and much disturbance to the inherited order. In other countries, major crises and new regimes were the backcloth to the shift in political power impelled by the crisis of capitalism.[13] But in Britain, it was power in the British Conservative Party which slowly changed hands between the regimes of Bonar Law and Churchill in 1951.[14] The overall shift —misleadingly summarized in the tags "managerial revolution," the creation of a "mixed—or Social Democratic—economy," the "Welfare State," "People's Capitalism"—seemed to change the appearance of capitalism dramatically. The robber barons and their sweat-shop colleagues gave way to the faceless corporation men.

Appearances overdramatized what had happened. For the system remained driven by forces generated within it—the endemic rivalries of capitalism—and yet beyond its control. The glitter of its achievements still only imperfectly concealed the damage it left in its wake. And nowhere was this more true than in the backward countries. For the shift away from a capi-

---

[13] Although now out of date, the account of R. A. Brady is still one of the best available on this subject; cf. *Business as a System of Power*, Columbia, 1943.

[14] cf. my *Competition and Corporate Society, British Conservatives, the State and Industry 1945-1964*, Methuen, 1972.

talism heavily dependent upon the relatively primitive processing of raw materials was catastrophic for those historically
snared in the role of raw material suppliers. The earnings
which raw material exports generated had purchased the simple
low priced output of advanced capitalism. But now the exports
had declining power to earn, and advanced capitalism produced
increasingly complex and high priced goods, suitable for sale on
a large scale only in high income markets, in markets within
other advanced capitalist countries. The terms of the exchange—
however unfavourable they were before—now began to break
down.

For the inter-war slump, the balance of payments difficulties of
each capitalism, a whole era of economic nationalism, had compelled each national capital to conserve its domestic resources,
to minimize imported materials. As a result, dramatic economies
in the use of raw materials were made; [15] substitutes for imports
were found; and out of the ingenuity and diversity of the petrochemicals industry, thousands of synthetic materials were created,
at first more expensively than the raw materials imitated, but
finally more cheaply. Quite accidental factors suddenly released
new resources—just as today, the anti-air pollution programme
may generate, as one by-product, the retrieval of sulphur from the
smoky atmosphere, and so undercut the raw material export of
every sulphur exporter. In some cases, the raw materials imported
were used in startlingly new ways that, in the end, could be used as
replacements for a different range of imports; British Petroleum
is building factories at the moment to manufacture protein as a
by-product from oil, at a price which could undercut the world's
fisheries and soya bean plantations.[16]

[15] As an example of the economies in the use of materials, see for
example, the decline in the average amount of coal burned to produce
one kilowatt hour of electrical energy in the United States: 1902: 6.4 lbs.;
1920: 3.4 lbs.; 1944: 1.3 lbs.

Statistical Abstract of the United States, Washington, 1946, Table 531,
p. 475. Raw materials are also increasingly re-used after extraction from
scrap: "The reclamation and recycling of secondary materials represent
about 35 per cent of the total U.K. consumption of copper; 25 per cent
of zinc; 55-60 per cent of lead; 30 per cent of aluminium; and 5-10 per
cent of tin"— T. W. Farthing, *Financial Times,* supplement, 19 May
1970.

[16] cf. report, *Economist* 6-12 December 1969, p. 104.

Rising real incomes in the advanced capitalist countries provided expanding markets for the increasingly sophisticated and highly priced output. And it ensured the profit rates on new investment that continuously sucked in an increasing proportion of the world's new savings. Both labour and capital were dragged out of the backward countries to service the economies of the advanced. The trade between advanced capitalist countries provided the dynamo for an unprecedented expansion in world trade and output in the period after 1948, and for an even greater concentration of capital in the hands of the richest countries. What had been seen by the imperialists as the division of labour in the world between the manufacturing advanced and the raw material exporting backward countries was overtaken by a division between the relatively self-sufficient advanced enclave and a mass of poor dependents.

In the context of the shift in capitalism one can begin to understand decolonization. Political power could be conceded precisely because the group of metropolitan countries was becoming less dependent upon the commodities produced in the backward countries. The old colonial companies producing raw materials for their metropolitan parents needed political control for the stability and survival of their operations. They had a vested interest in empire. But such companies have been in steady decline since before the First World War. Now the companies operating in backward countries are international ones, whose dependence on any one backward country is slight, whose interest is less in the search for raw materials and more in jumping tariff barriers to exploit the small internal market of any particular backward country. For political independence permitted new governments to restrict imports from the advanced. Direct investment in the backward country overcomes this obstacle, and though the profits are small in absolute terms, the rates are high. One of the results of this is the outflow from the backward country, not of raw materials, but of profits from foreign marketing operations, and the expansion of imports demanded by the foreign operator. Hence the balance of payments becomes the main restriction on the expansion of the backward country. This would be partly alleviated if the foreign companies really did bring capital into the country. But in most cases they bring relatively little, relying for their expansion either on abnormally high local profit rates or local borrowing. For example, a Philippines Government report on 70 per cent of the American companies in the Philippines estimates that between 1956 and 1965, 84 per cent of the capital used by US companies was borrowed locally.[17]

Even with high profit rates, foreign Western investment flows to the backward countries sluggishly. In general, the flow is stable, hardly increasing very much, and heavily concentrated in the areas known to be safe, because they are directly accessible to Western political or military power. Latin America has received more than all the other backward regions put together.[18] Wherever it goes, favourable government concessions—in some cases, amounting to a quasi-monopoly—keep the profit rates at a level where either the balance of payments is continually strained by the repatriation of funds, or the proportion of the local economy under foreign control is continually increased (leading in the course of time to an even more massive outflow of funds). Foreign investment, because of its changed purposes, produces few exports (often the

[17] Government of the Philippines, *Aspects of U.S. Investment in the Philippines*, Memorandum to the Staff Secretariat of the Working Committee on the Laurel-Langley Trade Agreement of the National Economic Council, reported in the *Far Eastern Economic Review*, 26 May 1969, p. 529.

[18] On the distribution, by region and activity, of accumulated direct investment (December 1966, estimate), cf. Chart 4, p 100, and Table 13, Annex II, p. 376, of *Partners in Development*, Report of the Commission on International Development (the Pearson Commission) to the International Bank for Reconstruction and Development (World Bank), London, 1969.

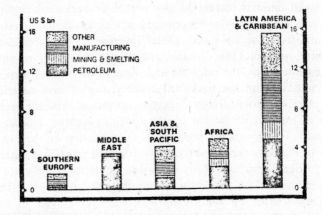

affiliate of an international company is forbidden to export lest this compete with the output of the parent company), and tends to increase the volume of imports, and in time, the outflow of funds. In India, for example, it has been estimated that in 1951 to 1952, foreign companies exported 70 per cent more than they imported (the 1952 figure, which more clearly excludes the exceptional effects of the Korean war boom, was 42 per cent); by 1956-58, the foreign sector had a net annual *import* surplus of ten per cent; and by 1964-65 to 1966-67, of 330 per cent.[19]

Because the companies concerned are often international ones, their global interests are less in creating small scale manufacturing plants in backward countries (although they may do this as the price of keeping up the sale of their parent companies) and more in finding ways to market their home production. Because they are very large, they can afford to refuse to invest in a backward country if the terms are not to their liking. And the government of the backward country is very limited in the sanctions which it can take against such a company once established, short of nationalization. Behind the international company, those who supply aid, credits, military assistance and so on, Western governments and international agencies use their power to ensure the "liberalization" of the world economy for private—Western—capital. Even if the government of the backward country tries to offset foreign control by developing local manufacturing, this may only increase foreign intervention as has happened in Latin America.[20]

The relationship between backward and advanced appears to have changed and to be changing in a way which steadily exacerbates the problems of backwardness. But in the raw material field, there are obvious exceptions, of which oil is the pre-eminent one. Of the direct cumulative investment of the advanced capitalist countries in the backward (December 1966), 40 per cent was in oil, and only nine per cent in other minerals and in smelting (the rest, 51 per cent, was invested in manufacturing, utilities and services). Not all of this investment in oil was in the extraction of resources; a great deal of it went into refining crude oil imported

---

[19] Calculated by Michael Kidron, unpublished paper, *Pearson on Foreign Investment,* 1969, p. 9.

[20] cf. the account by Osvaldo Sunkel, "National Development Policy and External Dependence in Latin America", *Journal of Development Studies,* 6/1, October 1969.

into backward countries with relatively poor local sources of crude. On the other hand, foreign investment certainly does not indicate anything like the raw material imports of the advanced, even if it gives some indication of the relative profit rates in the eyes of foreign investors.

Decolonization was certainly a dangerous exercise in countries producing raw materials of importance for Western capitalism. But it was offset in important ways. First, sources of the raw materials were, wherever possible, diversified so widely that it was hardly conceivable that all exporters could combine to pressure Western buyers. Oil is a good example. The seven "majors" which, by their control of the cheapest sources of crude oil in the Middle East and of the most extensive marketing outlets, maintain a position of supremacy against both the oil-producing countries and the smaller independent oil companies (as well as the Soviet Union), have led the way in trying to secure a foothold in every important oil find. Diversification of oil sources is the trump card in cartel control,[21] for the organization of oil exporting countries (OPEC) can never hope in the long run to discipline all producers to present a united front. Second, exploration for minerals in the advanced countries has been pushed hard in order to offset dependence on any particular backward country. The mineral strikes in Australia and Canada are particularly important here, and the United States Government is quite explicit as to why it is particularly interested in the oil, natural gas, coal, uranium and electricity of Canada—to offset dependence upon sources in politically unreliable or unstable backward countries.[22] Finally, alternative sources of raw materials or energy are sought—whether this is of relatively marginal significance like the reopening of Cornish tin mines, or the exploration for North Sea gas, or the development of atomic energy, or the recycling of already used materials.

It is the price of raw material supplies, and the security and

[21] The point is made explicitly in the "Portrait of British Petroleum" by Barton William-Powlett, *Times Business News*, 5 January 1970; cf. also Tugendhat, *Financial Times*, 3 December 1969, and Michael Tanzer, *The Political Economy of International Oil and the Underdeveloped Countries*, London, 1970.

[22] cf. for example, the speech by Hollis Dole, Assistant Secretary of the Interior (for mineral resources), US Government, to a conference on natural resources, Oregon State University, 9 March 1970, reported in *Financial Times*, 10 March 1970.

stability of supply, which determine the decision to import from one source rather than another, or to find local sources or substitutes. The United States, for example, through the sixties has steadily increased its import of iron ore (reaching about 44 million tonnes in 1968). Half of these imports come from Canada, and about a quarter from Venezuela. Australia, given the right price, could also be a major producer. The dependence is not upon exclusive sources in backward countries; on the contrary, the availability of supplies round the world makes the backward producer dependent upon the US market. If the price of imports gets too high, new domestic resources will suddenly become economic. Iron ore has recently been discovered in Nevada (Nevada State says the strike could be up to 1,000 million tonnes), but the US steel companies are reluctant to undertake the investment required to get it out at the present price of ore.[23] An increase in the ore prices demanded by any backward country could prompt a shift to purchases from sources in other countries; and if world prices as a whole rose, the US steel companies would have an incentive to develop home sources.

The manufacturing emphasis of modern capitalism promotes its technological ingenuity. Far from the advanced becoming more and more dependent on the backward for raw materials,[24] the system appears to be becoming more and more flexible, more and more adept at substituting one input for another. No one raw material exporter, any more than any one group of skilled workers, can regard their contribution to production as indispensable. The concentration of technical skill in the advanced countries ensures this flexibility as well as the paramount position of the advanced capitalist countries in the world economy. It is an "almost impregnable foreign monopoly of advanced technology that comes from concentrating research and development in the world's industrial heartland."[25]

Indeed, the argument could go in exactly the opposite direction

[23] cf. report, *Financial Times*, 19 December 1969.

[24] As argued, for example, by Pierre Jalee—"Imperialism does not pillage the Third World diabolically or for fun, but because of *vital necessity*, because it could not survive otherwise" (p. 131, PJ emphasis)—*The Third World in World Economy*, London, 1969 (translated from the French by Mary Klopper).

[25] Kidron, *Pearson op. cit.*, p. 13.

—that the backward countries are more and more dependent. In so far as the backward industrialize, they become increasingly dependent on the advanced, not just for imported capital equipment and technology, but also in part for primary produce and raw materials. The advanced countries export nearly double the volume of food and raw materials that the backward export.[26] The periodic dependence by some backward countries on foodgrains from the United States, Canada, Australia and France illustrates one element in this relationship. For minerals, many of the backward countries remain dependent upon the world market. For example, in 1969—a boom year for base metals in world commodity trade—demand for copper, lead, as well as special steels, all at unusually high prices, was significantly affected by the very large purchases made by China. And China, by reason of its size, is one of the richer backward countries in terms of indigenous resources. Indeed, in the case of copper, it was Chinese purchases which prevented a surplus of copper depressing the world price. The same is also true of natural rubber, where the 1969 price was significantly affected by China's purchases (China is the fourth largest buyer of natural rubber from the largest producer, Malaya).[27]

Expansive though the demand of industrializing backward countries is, it has still not prevented the deterioration in the respective shares of world trade held by advanced and backward respectively. Between 1953 and 1964, the industrialized countries increased their share of world trade from 37.1 to 45.5 per cent. Up to 1967 the share of the backward countries fell from 27 to 19 per cent (and if oil is excluded, this last figure falls to 12-13 per cent). Forty per cent of the doubling in world exports between 1958 and 1968 went to West Germany and the United States alone. Even in the best year for the exports of backward countries since 1945—1968—they increased their exports by nine per cent (compared to three per cent in 1967), in comparison to the 11 per cent increase in the exports of the advanced countries. The divergence in rates of growth appears to be too consistent to be any short-term factor: the rich are consistently getting richer, the poor poorer.

[26] Colin Clark, *Lloyds Bank Review*, January 1970.

[27] cf. John Woodland, *Times Business News*, 2 January 1970, and report, Communist purchases absorbed 1969 copper surplus, *Financial Times*, 25 February 1970.

The flows of capital follow the same paths as those of trade—to other advanced countries. For if direct investment to exploit markets is becoming the characteristic form of private investment abroad then it is the size of the market, the income level of the population, which determines how large the flow of investment is to be. Nor is it true that cheap labour, as an inducement to foreign capital, compensates for the smallness of the market. Modern manufacturing requires a highly skilled labour force—for which, abundant unskilled labour cannot be substituted—sophisticated manufactured inputs, specialized ancillary services (power, transport, communications) and a stable scale of output beyond the size of most markets in backward countries. Even where unskilled labour can be substituted for skilled, the costs may be significantly higher per unit of output.

High profits are made in backward countries but, as often as not, this is the result of domestic protection round the economy. The government concedes or cannot prevent quasi-monopolistic conditions which make for monopoly prices and profits. Without such profits, foreign investment would go elsewhere. The cost of all this cannot be properly estimated. But MacNamara of the World Bank—certainly no disinterested source—has estimated that in 1965, the backward countries spent $2,100 million in domestic resources to manufacture automotive products with a world market value of $800 million. The "loss" of $1,300 million is just about the amount in aid advanced up to that time by the World Bank in the 23 years of its existence.[28] Of course, "liberalization" of the backward economies would merely break down the flimsy barriers at present protecting them, and Western industry would be able to wipe out much of what industry exists in backward countries. But the costs of protection cannot be dismissed.

Why do many of the socialist accounts of modern imperialism argue that the advanced capitalist countries are increasingly dependent upon the raw material exports of the backward countries? It is usually an attempt to explain the exigencies of US

[28] Robert MacNamara, Address to the Annual Meeting of the World Bank and the International Monetary Fund, 29 September 1969, reported *Financial Times*, 30 September 1969. On foreign company profits in India, cf. Michael Kidron, *Foreign Investment in India*, London, 1965, III, 5 and 6.

foreign policy, to explain the scale of military intervention in, for example, Viet Nam. To say: "the United States is just doing it for the money," is part of an old Liberal-Populist—muck-raking—tradition. But it appears to be quite false. The truth is somewhat more brutal.[29] On the other hand, many of the accounts of modern imperialism turn out to be descriptions of the domination of the rest of the world by the United States, without simultaneously showing the rivalries between advanced capitalist States. But the increasing dependence of the United States on imported raw materials (demonstrated, for example, by Harry Magdoff),[30]

[29] So far as can be seen, the known resources of the whole of southeast Asia would hardly compensate the US Government for the enormous costs of the war, and the markets concerned are trivial for American capitalism because the income level is so low. What market has developed, is result rather than cause of US military intervention. What the US Government pursued in Viet Nam were its global interests—and therefore, the location of the war in Viet Nam was relatively "accidental," for it could have been fought anywhere for that purpose. In Viet Nam, the American ruling class asserted its Paramount Chieftaincy of the world, at the same time as warning China, the Soviet Union, Cuba radicals in Latin America, Asia and Africa, and not least, potential rebels in Europe. Although the war bred a host of economic interests, each with its fingers in the pork barrel, the American ruling class as a whole was against the war—because of the resulting high taxation, the high commodity prices Defence Department purchases created at a time when American business was threatened both abroad and domestically by foreign competition. The truth is thus nastier than many of its opponents admit, for at least the pursuit of raw materials presupposes some specific interest. Whereas there appears to have been little economic interest at stake at all—so many people were slaughtered as a terrifyingly gratuitous display of barbarity.

The history of imperialism has similar examples, although nothing on the scale of the Viet Nam war. Take, for example, the Pacifico incident. In 1850, Lord Palmerston despatched British warships to blockade the city of Athens. This was a reprisal for the Athenians maltreating a certain David Pacifico, an Athenian moneylender. Pacifico, born in Alexandria, was a British subject, and therefore, Palmerston argued, entitled to the full protection of the British State. This was not a prelude to the seizure of Greece, nor the Balkans. There were no raw materials or markets involved. The action was no more than forcefully "showing the flag," or, what is the same thing, "flashing the knife," not merely for the benefit of the Greeks, or even the more important Turks, but for the edification of the whole of Europe.

[30] *The Age of Imperialism The Economics of U.S. Foreign Policy*, New York, 1969.

does not show an increasing dependence by advanced capitalism on the backward.

(ii) The Left Post-Independence Alternative

The weakness of the Left position is shown most clearly in what is suggested as the alternative strategy for backward countries. If only the constricting control of the world market can be ended, it is argued, then development can be pushed ahead with great rapidity by the State. Autarchy and State enterprise will be able to break through the impasse. Yet hitherto, the main forces pushing development have been transmitted by the world market. The demand for raw materials stimulated the opening up and exploitation of whole new areas of the world, creating an exchange system —imposed and regulated, certainly, in the interests of metropolitan capital—between the advanced and the backward. Today the exchange is weakening, and foreign capital no longer plays its former role in pushing industrialization. The advanced drain resources out of the backward without contributing significantly to real industrialization—in terms of repatriated profits, interest on loans,[31] the net advantage in the exchange between manufactured and primary commodities and, not least, in the drain of skilled manpower.

Nevertheless, those backward countries with the highest growth rates are all ones which are tightly knit into the world market.[32] The highest *per capita* income growth is in those countries which are major exporters or related directly to an advanced capitalist power. It may be that the country is parasitic upon some large nearby market—as Spain, Greece and Turkey are on the periphery of the European Common Market, Mexico and Jamaica close to

[31] For example, between 1961 and 1968, the net capital inflow to Latin America was $11,493 millions; the outflow in income from investments remitted abroad was $14,749 millions. Latin America lost $3,256 million. cf. *Annual Report*, Inter-American Development Bank Social Progress Trust Fund, Washington, 1970.

[32] "The growth rates of individual developing countries since 1950 correlate better with their export performance than with any other single economic indicator. If the expansion of world trade were to flag, the development effort would undoubtedly be retarded"—*Partners in Development, op. cit.* p. 45.

the North American market, South Korea and Taiwan to Japan. They may command an important raw material, as do the oil-producing countries, or as Malaya (with tin and rubber). Or they may, by the accident of strategic geography, be favoured client States, with an inflow of foreign capital servicing a defence programme, as is the case with South Korea, Taiwan and Thailand. And in the case of the last three, the pork barrel of the Viet Nam war is important in recent growth.[33]

But "growth" may not mean "development." The statistics may show a rising national income, even a rising average income per head, at the same time as unemployment is increasing, there is no change in the distribution of the occupied population between agricultural and non-agricultural employment, and in the distribution of non-agricultural employment, between manufacturing and other sectors. In human terms, nothing very much may have happened, and things for the majority may even have got worse.

Yet at least there is *some* growth, and that is more than is ordinarily promised by economic autarchy, by cutting the local economy off from the world market. Even if the economic links can be severed—and they can never be broken comprehensively and with impunity—military and political threats keep even the largest backward country snared in the concerns of the powerful. China is an excellent example of the limits imposed by the system itself. For its entire development is governed by the necessity to maintain a defence capability far in advance of its level of economic development, including a missile programme.

Yet where there is integration into the world economy, what growth takes place is determined by the demands of the system, the preponderant element of which is advanced capitalism. The backward economy's development is shaped into that specialization which ensures its dependence upon the external market and sustains its backwardness outside the area of its specialization. The difficulties faced by Cuba in trying to industrialize and diversify its output are a vivid illustration of the power of the world system in shaping its constituent parts. Cuba could not for a moment make itself self-sufficient. The only way to pay for the imports of capital equipment and industrial raw materials was

[33] cf. "The Far East and Neo-colonialism", The Notebook, *International Socialism*, 34, Autumn 1968, pp. 7-8.

to *increase* Cuba's specialization in sugar, to make it more of a mono-cultural economy than it was in the pre-revolutionary period. Cuba also is governed by the generalization advanced by those socialists who have outlined the neo-imperialist or neo-colonialist identification of the modern world: the present relationships between the advanced and backward countries continue, and indeed, make worse, some of the most oppressive features of colonialism.

The Left has excelled in the critique of what happens when a backward economy is bent to fit the world market. It has been less sensitive to the problems arising out of isolation from the world market. As a result, economic nationalism has been used as a substitute for international socialism. Today, the weakness of economic nationalism as a real alternative is becoming clearer, particularly because the model of Soviet development appears increasingly to be a unique case. Soviet economic nationalism was not a matter of choice. It was forced upon Russia by the inter-war collapse of the world economy, a collapse which forced all the major capitalist powers into a greater or lesser degree of defensive autarchy. To make of this necessity a virtue only obscures discussion. The waste, the terrible cost imposed upon the Russian population,[34] the continuing backwardness of the Russian economy, particularly in its agricultural sector, do little to convince one of its universal desirability. Even more, Russian conditions were the most favourable for autarchic development. Tsarist Russia had the highest rate of economic growth in the whole of Europe in the last two decades of the 19th century, and this process created both a stable working class with the required skills, as well as heavy industry and an infrastructure of important services (for example, railways). Russia was certainly backward by the standards of advanced capitalism, but in 1913 it was already well in advance of those countries containing the majority of the population of the backward countries.

There are—sadly—no magic cures for poverty and backwardness. Rhetoric does not wish away the terrible and brutal process of capital accumulation which scarred the capitalist powers and

---

[34] On the agrarian costs—and so some of the industrial and development effects—cf. M. Lewin, *Russian Peasants and Soviet Power*, London, 1968, and review, "Agriculture, Peasants and Accumulation," *International Socialism*, 40, Oct./Nov. 1969, p. 37.

the Soviet Union. Capital accumulation is the aggregation of a surplus. The surplus can come from abroad, on trade, in aid or loans, or from savings out of current consumption by the population at home. In the absence of the first, there is only the second. And if the level of current livelihood of the population is low, and the political and administrative machine weak, then any surplus from this source is likely to be small. If the population is simultaneously growing, what surplus there is may only provide a basis for standing still rather than actually improving the situation. On the other hand, only a very powerful army and police force can snatch the surplus for national investment between the peasant's hand and mouth. The obstacles in the way of development constantly grow larger as the advanced countries come to dominate even more the world market from which formerly backward countries could gain some advantage. Implicit in modern efforts at development is police tyranny, for rational men will not otherwise make the sacrifices asked of them and their families.

In countries where the material problems of survival are great, the prospects for development are grim, let alone the prospects for creating a free and equal socialist society. Freedom and equality depend upon the problems of sheer survival having long since been overcome. Those problems could be overcome in the modern world, but not without the transformation of world capitalism. One isolated country, sooner or later, is forced backwards by its own poverty into a new stringent division of labour. For the motive force of early capitalism was not human greed, but the logic of scarcity, of poverty. It is backwardness itself which reshapes the social relationships men think they have created, leaving the words and phrases intact, but giving them a new practical connotation: the reassertion of class rule.

Despite the rhetoric, none of the backward economic autarchies —China, Cuba, Viet Nam or North Korea—has yet been able to demonstrate the superiority of its mode of economic development. And this fact, as much as any other, makes the appeals of Stalinism weaker. Economic independence does not in itself overcome the problem of backwardness. An economist, summarizing the experience of Latin American countries in pursuing economic independence, recently concluded that "it must be recognised that economic independence cannot be the magical consequence of an heroic political act. Rather it will be the medium, or long term result—depending on the case—of the construction of a national economy which is both efficient and flexible, and also capable of generating a large and rapidly increasing surplus of resources for investment."[35] The conclusion is interestingly in error. For economic development does not, apparently, produce economic independence. No advanced country today has much viable economic independence. All are enmeshed in the world market, and would stagnate or decline without it. It follows that an *independent*, diversified developed economy is today a utopian aim, whether to be achieved through autarchy or integration into the world market. For the backward countries, in the short term, one or other of these two alternatives—and they are not necessarily open to choice—may ameliorate certain problems, but neither holds out much hope of development, and neither are substitutes for the essential task: transforming the world market itself.

II. The agency of revolution

(*a*) *Classes and Politics*

Lenin's account of imperialism assumed that industrial workers as a class were the people who alone could lead the socialist revolution, the overthrow of imperialism as a world system. Among Marxists of his day it hardly needed saying since it was so much taken for granted. Indeed, the assumption was central to being a Marxist, rather than some other kind of revolutionary, socialist or anarchist. Without the industrial working class, Marxism became *Hamlet* without the Prince.

But, although it was taken for granted, it was not a gesture of faith. It was the conclusion of an argument. Capitalism was, Marx had argued, the first system in history which compelled its rulers to accumulate capital as the basis for their very survival, and on an increasing scale. As a result of the accumulation, of the competitive dynamic of the system, for the first time the conquest of all the major problems of material scarcity lay within the grasp of mankind. And as a result of this, the possibility of freedom for all, of socialism, also became possible. It was not that socialism

[35] cf. Sunkel, *op. cit.*, p. 37.

depended simply upon the wishes and intentions of the socialists; it depended upon the solution of a range of problems of material survival, upon a prior accumulation of capital. Without it, the scarcity that had forced upon society a division of labour between rulers and ruled would exercise the same influence as before.

But in creating capitalism, the capitalists also created for the first time a subordinate class which had within its power the transformation of capitalism and the establishment of freedom for all. This class, by its labour, created the accumulation of capital, created and sustained capitalism. Workers were not just exploited —exploitation had existed for thousands of years—but exploited ever more systematically, and the more systematically they were exploited, the more they ensured an even greater rate of exploitation in the future. They were exploited, not in the sense that they were impoverished, but in the sense that a greater and greater share of their increasing productivity was appropriated by the capitalist.

In creating the working class, capitalism had to concentrate it physically in the cities. And the cities were simultaneously the source of the power of the capitalists, and the place where for the first time the collective power of the working class could be expressed. Capitalism had also to educate its labour force in order to operate its industry, to break down the inherited customs of the past and make the workers continuously responsive to the dynamic of an advancing technology. In the great concentrations of the industrial working class, skilled by its daily work in interdependent collective action and the techniques of production, lay the promise of political power, of workers' control and workers' power. The possibility was created of the self-emancipation of the working class, rather than its emancipation by sundry enlightened reformers of other classes.

By contrast, other exploited classes which, in many cases, had existed long before the creation of capitalism, were kept on the margins of society. The peasants were widely dispersed geographically, trapped in the most backward, non-collective, forms of production. Nothing in their way of life compelled them to comprehend society as a whole, as a system, let alone formulate an alternative industrial society. Egalitarian and visionary they might be, but within their grasp lay neither the vision of, nor the power to achieve, a free expanding interdependent industrial society. Without industry, the world returned willy-nilly to the poverty and barbarism of a pre-capitalist past[36] and inevitably scarcity would restore class society.

Yet if much of the Left today accepts some version of Lenin's account of the economic relationship between the metropolitan and backward countries, and of "finance capital," many socialists reject Lenin's assumptions about the role of the industrial working class. Analysis and strategy come apart, and there is apparently no force created within the system capable of transforming it. As a result many socialist writers concentrate simply upon a critique of capitalism, rather than framing a serious strategy. In this, they retreat from Lenin's account of imperialism to Hobson's, leaving out any systematic treatment of how the world is to be changed. The separation of analysis and strategy is not so much the result of an argument, as a reaction to the failure of the industrial working class in the capitalist countries actually to challenge the system on a political basis. Facts spoke louder than "mere theories."

On the other hand, in the backward countries themselves— where, in many cases, the industrial working class was very small and rarely of much political significance—radical opponents of foreign political or economic control found in Lenin's arguments the most searching available condemnation of imperialism. Less frequently were they aware of Lenin's strategic assumption about the agency of change, the proletariat. Even more important, Lenin's perception of the class conflict *within* each and every society, backward or advanced, was scarcely understood at all except as a division between those who opposed foreign influence (whatever their class), and those who supported it (whatever their class). Inevitably, the struggle for national independence superseded and, indeed, for many nationalists, eliminated the need for the emancipation of the industrial working class. Internal class divisions were dismissed in the search for national unity, and nationalism was rebaptized as socialism.

Leaving out the industrial working class as the agency of the socialist revolution left a vacancy. In some cases, it was filled by the conception of the nation, and even by a conglomerate of nations, the "Third World." The working class was to lead the

[36] For a fuller discussion of these issues, see the preceding chapter, "The Revolutionary Role of the Peasantry."

revolution because of its position within society. Its substitute, the nation was now supposed to lead the world. Trotsky once warned against "that national revolutionary Messianic mood which prompts one to see one's own nation-State as destined to lead mankind to socialism."[37] The working class was said to have no vested interest in the geographical boundaries of any particular State; it was internationalist. The "Third World" expressed the— at least aspirant—internationalism of the new candidate for agency of the revolution. An international alliance between the working classes of different countries against their respective ruling classes was replaced by an alliance between backward countries against the capitalist countries. Alliances of States replaced the alliance of workers against all States. And the States in alliance were identified by their level of poverty, of oppression, even though oppression is at least as divisive as it is unifying.

In the alliance of States, the language of classes was still used to describe the States. There were "proletarian States" and "bourgeois States." But the bourgeois States include no proletarians. To the workers of the advanced capitalist countries, the advocates of this position have nothing to say, except that they are guilty of living off the proceeds of the exploitation of the backward countries, and therefore cannot be considered even as allies in the attack on imperialism. The theory of the bribe—that Western workers have been silenced by higher wages—never carried a great deal of credibility, and certainly cannot be made consistent with Marx's theory of exploitation. But even if we ignore these aspects, mutual recrimination is hardly productive. James Connolly, the Irish revolutionary, answered the reproaches of the Irish against English workers in this way:

> We are told that the English people contributed their help to our enslavement. It is true. It is also true that the Irish people contributed soldiers to crush every democratic movement of the English people . . . . Slaves themselves, the English helped to enslave others; slaves themselves, the Irish helped to enslave others. There is no room for recrimination.[38]

[37] Cited by Isaac Deutscher, *The Prophet Armed, Trotsky 1879-1921*, London, 1954, p. 238.

[38] James Connolly, cited by Sean Matgamma, *Socialist Worker* 11 December 1969, p. 4.

(*b*) *The Orthodoxy and the Unorthodox*

In practice, the anti-imperialist struggle has been led by people who were neither from the industrial working class nor identified with its interests. If it is the case, as many socialists today assume, that the anti-imperialist struggles, once victorious, have introduced what Marx meant by socialism, then the whole Marxist scheme comes unstuck. Socialism can be, and has been on this account, achieved by forces other than those of the industrial working class.

Those socialists who positively identify with Marxism have been most troubled by this inconsistency. For example, in China, the Communist Party tends to call itself "the leadership of the proletariat," even though industrial workers played scarcely any role at all in the Chinese revolution. By a verbalism, the tradition persevered. Others have argued, more radically, that the industrial working class was only "the proletariat"—that is, the agency for the socialist revolution—in the peculiar conditions of the 19th century. And this was because at that stage the workers were exploited, propertyless, poor, and politically militant, whereas now the class which possesses these characteristics is the peasantry of the backward countries.[39] In fact, the interpretation of Marx and of the 19th century worker is wrong. If being poor and property-less were the main criteria, much of the peasantry of the 19th century were significantly worse off than the industrial workers. On the other hand, there is no real evidence that the differential between peasants as a class and workers as a class in backward countries today is greater than it was in the advanced countries in the 19th century. Nor was the 19th century worker notably politically militant. Many socialists have an idealized picture of the Victorian

[39] cf. the statement of Fanon, for example: "In colonial countries, the peasants alone are revolutionary, for they have nothing to lose and everything to gain. The starving peasant, outside the class system, is the first among the exploited to discover that only violence pays. For him, there is no compromise, no possible coming to terms"—*The Wretched of the Earth*, London, 1965, p. 48.

Paul Sweezy writes: "The masses in the exploited dependencies constitute a force in the global capitalist system which is revolutionary in the same sense that Marx considered the proletariat of the early period of modern industrialization to be revolutionary"—"The Proletariat in Today's World", *Tricontinental*, 91/1968, p. 33.

worker as someone who was heroically unselfish, unconcerned with the details of daily life. It is romantic nonsense as any serious history book will show. Workers then as now fought on a daily basis for specific economic gains. Western middle class opinion today chooses to accept that those battles were justified then, but are *not* justified now. But to accept such an opinion is both to distort the past and identify oneself with one side in the class argument now. The relationship between "high ideals" and immediate concrete issues is not some enormous abyss as those with an adequate income like to think. Grubby selfishness and absurd heroism are necessarily part of the same act, then as now. In the same sense, the heroic battles fought in backward countries are about specific issues—not just about freedom, but also about this little bit of land, that foreign bully, this man's hunger and that man's job, about issues of status and standing. The battles are not just about the heroic posturing which the more naive revolutionary posters portray. Particularly when people are far away fromt he scene of the action, they miss the complexities, the wrinkles, the real men struggling under heroic concepts. In doing so, they do no justice at all to the real victories which are won.

But are the backward countries more exploited? In the sense of "impoverished," this is clearly so. But this tells us little about the system involved. For Marx, the most exploited are those who proportionately produce the most surplus value appropriated by the capitalist. The transformation of capitalism has created a phenomenal increase in labour productivity in the capitalist countries, and has thus permitted an even greater increase in the rate of exploitation. For the poorest are rarely the most exploited: their subsistence takes too high a proportion of their output to permit much "surplus." If the basis of the system is the creation of surplus value, embodied in capital accumulation, then clearly the most exploited are the Western working classes, and within those classes, the most productive workers. The Western car worker is among the most exploited of all, and, for the same reason, among the best paid. The Left account concentrates on consumption levels, not on production, so that it is then suggested that low consumption is the index of exploitation. Of course, the relative level of exploitation does not tell us who is likely to be most rebellious. Where the system breaks is not necessarily determined by who is most exploited. The complexities of oppression and discrimination overlay and distort the stratification imposed by relative exploitation.

Those closest to the Marxist tradition have felt most poignantly the inconsistency between what actually happened in the independence movement and the Leninist prognosis. For some Trotskyists the dilemma was resolved by agreeing that, for example, the Chinese Communist Party was composed of people in the main not drawn from the industrial working class, but that the "proletarian character" of the party was guaranteed by its adherence to "proletarian ideology." Isaac Deutscher adds to this criterion[40]— if I understand his argument correctly—two others. Since China is allied to a "proletarian power," namely the Soviet Union, it is again of proletarian character. And since the Chinese Communist Party is committed to industrialization, it is committed to *creating* a proletariat, and thus again qualifies as a proletarian power.

The curiosities of this argument illustrate the oddities which arise when revisions are only piecemeal. For if any regime which commits itself to industrialization is thereby "proletarian," the Victorian bourgeoisie must also qualify for the term. And if an alliance with the Soviet Union (*if* China can seriously be said to be allied with the Soviet Union) has the same effect, then Britain and the United States were presumably "proletarian" during the Second World War. More to the point, two of the criteria turn entirely upon the "proletarian" nature of the Soviet Union. Once we hesitate there, the case collapses. In any case, the "proletarian ideology" in question is the Stalinism of the 1930s[41] and we are to assume that somehow it survived intact independently of any real live workers in China. The ideas have become independent of the men whose ideas they were supposed to be; the smile is independent of the Cheshire Cat.

However, it is more common on the Left today for there to be no illusions about the role of the Soviet Union or its "proletarian"

[40] cf. Isaac Deutscher in *The Socialist Register 1964*, London, 1964, p. 23 *passim*.

[41] For an attempt toi dentify some of the main differences between Stalinism and "Mao Tse-tung thought" and more extensive discussion of the evolution of Marxism in China, see the following chapter, "Marxism : Leninism-Stalinism-Maoism."

character. Orthodox Stalinism proved incapable of containing the new revolutionary forces created by the problems of backwardness and foreign domination. Even in the case of China where, in theory, an orthodox Communist Party led the struggle to free the country from foreign influence and control, it did so only by operating independently of the Soviet Party or the Comintern. Elsewhere, there was scarcely even a nod in the direction of Moscow.

Yet if many of the new revolutionaries have rejected the dogmatism of Soviet orthodoxy, they have not created a framework of theory to put in its place. Indeed, for some, it is a point of principle to reject all "ideologies," and stress instead spontaneous popular action. Since radical forces have for so long been curbed by Moscow, it is, at least initially, a healthy reaction to demand action rather than debate. But action is self-limiting and can be self-defeating unless it takes place within some sort of strategy. Society is not always and everywhere dry tinder that requires but a spark to set it ablaze. To find out whether it is tinder, requires an analysis and clear purposes. The resources of the *status quo* to resist isolated action are much greater than the instant activist allows. In the long haul, theory and organization conserve the revolutionary forces and build them, directing them towards the final aim. Without them, the rebels become merely society's gadflies, irritants which are tolerated because they are relatively harmless.

For the new revolutionaries, the agency of revolution is less a social class at all than a small body of armed idealists fighting a guerrilla war against the *status quo*. Urban guerrilla warfare, in conjunction with the organization of a working class mass political party, may or may not be a useful tactic to pursue, but urban guerrilla warfare in isolation has few political implications. Societies have been able to support individual terrorism without this having any political implications except to keep the revolutionaries well away from those who actually produce the wealth on which the power of the ruling class is based. And this observation is even more true of rural guerrilla warfare. In the Debray scheme, the small band of revolutionaries create a rural base from which they begin to demonstrate that the ruling class is not invulnerable. They are protected by their remoteness from the centres of the country, and immunized against infection by the germ of urban corruption.[42]   Slowly, they grow, until finally they are in a position to march on the cities and conquer power.

This was not the sequence of events in Cuba, nor in any other known successful guerrilla war. Nor indeed, in the Cuban case, did the success of Fidel Castro's forces depend upon his techniques of guerrilla warfare (important though they may have been for sheer survival). What was vital in Castro's assumption of power was the collapse of the Batista regime, strongly assisted by the attitude of benevolent neutrality on the part of the mass of the population towards Castro's challenge. The politics, not the military technique or the guerrilla strategy, of Castro made him important. And in any imitation of the Cuban events, it will be the politics of the existing regime and the attitude towards it of the population which will determine the outcome, rather than merely guerrilla activity. In any straight military confrontation, Castro's forces would have been destroyed, as those of Guevara were destroyed in Bolivia.

But to assess the significance of a political challenge returns us to the task of social analysis and the identification not of where a rural base is to be established but what popular forces are to play the leading political role. Mere guerrilla warfare is often a matter of pure luck, depending on the existing regime. For every Cuba, there are a dozen contrary examples. To take only one series of examples: between 1948 and 1950, the Communist parties of Burma, Malaya, Indonesia and the Philippines, all launched armed struggles of guerrilla warfare. In all cases, they were disastrous,

---

[42] The "anti-urbanism" of the new revolutionaries is more powerful than their positive identification with the rural population. On the first, cf. Fidel Castro's opinion that "The city is a cemetery of revolutionaries and resources," and Debray's view: "the forest proletarianizes the bourgeois and peasant elements, and the city can bourgeoisify the proletarian" (note that the first relationship is apparently unconditional). Why the city is so destructive is not convincingly explained, although it is the main justification for selecting a rural area to wage war in. Not that the peasants, Debray says, can be wholly trusted until the guerrillas are strong enough to dominate the villages. The guerrillas must always keep themselves quite separate from the rural population—"The guerilla force is completely independent of the civilian population, in action as well as in military organisation; consequently it need not assume the direct defence of the peasant population." Citations from Regis Debray, *Revolution in the Revolution?* Pelican, London, 1968, pp. 67, 75 and 41.

isolating the party from the main centres of population and destroying its political credibility and relevance. In Indonesia, it took ten years for the P. K. I. to live down this abortive episode. In Burma, the Communists became irrelevant rural fragments, as much bandits as revolutionaries. In Malaya, the nationalist forces were pushed into the arms of the British in self-defence, the Left was isolated, and the achievement of independence postponed. In the Philippines, the party disappeared into the Huk revolt and its warring sects contained. Almost nothing of substance was achieved, except the advance of Western power in protecting the regimes concerned.

If the only choice were between armed struggle on its own and passively supporting the *status quo*, then choice of the first would have a clear significance. The role of the Soviet Union in emasculating the revolutionary politics of Communist parties has made it seem that only choice of the first alternative would be revolutionary. And the first puts a premium upon immediate action rather than building a mass political organization with a coherent strategy.[43] But Marxism is irrelevant to success in guerrilla warfare. Its words and concepts may add a decorative embellishment to what would otherwise be more easily understood in non-Marxist terms. Marxism as a method of the analysis of society dissolves into pre-Marxist populist socialism, the closest analogies to which occur in Narodnik thought in Tsarist Russia in the 1860s and 1870s. Narodnik thought is amorphous and fertile. Some of its offspring followed Marx, some Bakunin, some Kropotkin and Tolstoy, and some even returned to the Russian Orthodox Church. But

---

[43] Debray is nothing if not cavalier about the political significance of guerrilla warfare. He says, implying praise: "During his two years of warfare, Fidel did not hold a single political rally in his zone of operations" (p. 53, *ibid*). In Moscow's account of revolution, politics—that is, the creation of a viable Communist Party—is necessarily prior to any action. And for other Marxists, the definition of purposes in a strategy, with appropriate organization, is similarly prior to action to achieve the purposes concerned. For Debray, action—definedsimply as guerrilla warfare—is prior to finding the purposes or politics: "Eventually," he writes, "the future People's Army will beget the party of which it is to be, theoretically, the instrument: essentially, the party is the army" (p. 104, *ibid*). It emerges in his account that "the party" is in any case not the directing political force at all, so much as a public relations agency for the guerrillas among the local population.

mainstream Narodniks experimented both with trying to spread revolt among the peasantry and with urban terrorism. Many Narodniks were aware of the dilemma facing the dedicated minority: for if the revolution is created by a small minority, what justifies that minority in comparison with the old ruling class?[44] Might the elitism of the one seem little improvement on the authoritarianism of the other? Marx's formulation—that the emancipation of the working class can only be the act of that class itself—resolved the dilemma for Marxists. But self-emancipation requires that the revolution be executed by a class which is fully aware of society as a whole and its place within it, which has the power and knowledge to take over society. The most backward sections of the rural population are not in this category, even if their hostility to the *status quo* provides a springboard to catapult a dedicated band of revolutionaries into power.[45] In that case,

[44] Debray's account of Fidel Castro's answer to this question is no more than bland—or naive—assertion: "Fidel Castro says simply that there is no revolution without a vanguard; that this vanguard is not necessarily the Marxist-Leninist party (that is, the Communist Party, NH); and that those who want to make the revolution have the right and the duty to constitute themselves a vanguard, independently of those parties" (p. 96, *ibid*). Debray himself elsewhere argues that a guerrilla group is justified in assuming the leadership of the revolution by "that class alliance which it alone can achieve, the alliance that will take and administer power the alliance whose interests are those of socialism—the alliance between workers and peasants" (p. 109, *ibid*), a statement which comes close to perpetuating the error Debray chastises the Trotskyists for: expecting support merely because one declares oneself socialist. If Castro's answer expresses the perspective of the pre-socialist rebels of the Sierra Maestra, perhaps Debray's shows an eagerness to graft this onto the imperatives of the Cuban State's alliance with the Soviet Union.

[45] And they are also (*a*) less able to create a collective organization without outside leadership: "The guerilla force unites the peasantry. Unlike the workers, peasants don't have the facilities to organise concerted action; they are scattered, each one on his plot of land or in his village, surrounded by an enemy whose power is embodied in the army and other instrumentalities of repression. The guerilla force, going from village to village, from region to region, is the embodiment of the common struggle and of the common aspirations of the peasants to possess the land. And there is a key fact to be remembered: the *guerilleros* go with gun in hand"—Adolfo Gilly, "The Guerilla Movement in Guatemala", *Monthly Review*, May 1965, Part I; and (*b*) less critical of the guerrillas: "The peasant possesses a virgin mentality, free from an assortment of

self-emancipation turns into emancipation by proxy, and the heart of Marxism—the struggle for freedom—is extinguished.

The guerrillas are guided by their estimate of military tactics, not by the interests of a particular class. They are outside of popular control, isolated from the concrete interests of the members of a class (except in so far as they want popular support), and can therefore be as opportunistic as their tactics require. They are under no compunction to fight the daily battles on the factory floor or on the land, and so they have no need either for a popular party or for a detailed analysis of society. *Elan* and slogans, a stress upon individual morale rather than equally upon objective circumstances, replaces any systematic theoretical framework.

The dissolution of Marxism is common to a very large number of countries, some of which are ruled by Communist parties, the majority of which are not. The differences between countries where the struggle for independence was led by Communists, and those where it was not, come to seem relatively unimportant, despite the attempt of some socialists to make the two qualitatively distinct. The relics of Marxist terminology characteristic of one country appear to have little contribution to make to the battle. In Cuba, the Communist Party did not support Fidel Castro until he was virtually certain of winning power. And Castro himself, by his own account, was a radical liberal rather than a socialist or Marxist. The so-called "proletarian ideology," like the proletariat itself, had no active role to play in the winning of power in Cuba. The similarities and differences between the struggles in India and China are discussed later, but again, the qualitative distinction which Communists want to draw seems very doubtful. In the end, rhetoric makes up the credibility gap in the interests of preserving a tradition of orthodoxy. But rhetoric does not win revolutions, and, after the revolution, it does not wish away the problems of poverty and backwardness.

---

influences which poison the intellects of citizens in the city. The revolution works on these fertile intellects as it works on the soil."— Fidel Castro, *Obra Revolucionaria*; 7 March 1961, p. 24, cited Theodore Draper, *Castroism, Theory and Practice*, London, 1965, p. 75.

(c) Workers and Imperialism

The shift in emphasis was achieved by default. Socialists instinctively felt a warm sympathy for those struggling for national independence. New nations, for so long despised, abused, ignored, rose with amazing speed to cry defiance at their European overlords. The White Man's Burden was suddenly and plainly seen to be no more than the White Man's Jackboot. The sympathy of Western liberals and socialists for the Indian Congress and Indonesian Nationalists, for the Chinese Communist Party and the Vietminh, for the Algerian FLN, for Cuba's David struggling with the American Goliath, and for movements in a host of other countries, had the unintended effect of directing all attention away from the advanced capitalist countries. Many Marxist intellectuals assumed the final victory of Finance Capital in the West: the working class had sold its historic mission to liberate the world for a mess of television sets and washing machines. By contrast, the aspiration for change, the audacity and heroism of the struggle to be free, lived on only in some of the backward countries. The great traditions stretching back to 1789 and beyond to the Diggers and the Levellers, encompassing 1848 and 1871, 1905 and 1917, seemed to receive their only echo in China and India, Indonesia and Ghana, Egypt and Algeria, and in Cuba. And the scale of the movements in some of these countries dwarfed their puny European predecessors.

The fact that it was not the industrial working class which led these struggles, that there was no answering echo from the workers of the capitalist countries, only seemed to reiterate the fact that they had been neutralized by bribes from the "super-profits of finance capital." Marxism must remain "flexible": revolution defined its own character, whatever the inherited theology.

It was true that industrial workers did not lead—and in most cases, played no role whatsoever—in the struggle for national independence. But few tried to understand why. In China in 1927, in Cuba in 1935, and in Spain in the Civil War, workers did indeed play a crucial political role, but in each case, in the last analysis the interests of the working class were subordinated to those of other classes. The demand for the establishment of workers' power—for "the dictatorship of the proletariat"—was lost in a welter of other demands, and, in particular, lost in the guiding interests of Soviet foreign policy. "Betrayal" is too simple an explanation to cover such a diversity of different situations, but nevertheless it played a vital role in diverting worker support into class coalitions.[46]

Most Marxists before the First World War assumed that the role of the bourgeoisie in the bourgeois revolution had been exhausted. For the new bourgeoisies in "feudal" countries were too weak to break the power of the *ancien regime*, too deeply involved in foreign capital, and too frightened of the rising discontent of their own working classes, infected with the spirit of socialist revolution from the advanced capitalist countries. In Russia, Lenin saw the working class as the only force capable of executing the bourgeois revolution, of establishing a republic and the conditions within which capitalism could grow. If the workers did not play this role, then Tsarism and capitalism would reach an alliance in which the repressive features of both systems would be combined to the immeasurable loss of the developing working class movement. The militaristic and authoritarian capitalism of the Kaiser's Germany, rather than the democratic republican capitalism of the United States, would result.

What no one seriously entertained was that any other social groups could intervene to execute the bourgeois revolution. Not even Stalin adopted this position. Rather he argued that the working class, alone, in China was too small to lead the struggle against foreign domination. A class coalition—a Four Class Bloc—of all the major classes of China would be the agency to free China. Concretely, this meant an alliance between the Kuomintang, covering the nationalist landlords and capitalists, as well as the army, and the Communist Party, organized among peasants and workers. In the twenties, the Kuomintang was allowed to grow by borrowing on the popular work of the Communists. Worker and peasant support was delivered to the Kuomintang by the Communist Party. In 1927, when the armies of the Kuomintang swept northwards, when Chiang Kai-shek calculated that his military strength was great enough to dispense with popular support, his followers were permitted to fall upon the Communists and slaughter them. The class coalition came to pieces in Stalin's

[46] The reasons for the failure of independent political action by the industrial working class in the backward countries is explored in greater detail in the last chapter of this book.

hands. For the leadership of the coalition had ultimately determined the balance to be tolerated between social and Kuomintang interests. And the landlords and capitalists of the Kuomintang had only narrow limits of toleration for the social interests of the Communist workers and peasants.

Trotsky's perspective—that the workers must lead the struggle for independence—seemed triumphantly demonstrated. As the Kuomintang degenerated more and more into a corrupt military oligarchy, compromising with foreign interests to the point where Chiang refused to put up any serious military opposition to the Japanese invasion, his perspective seemed even more correct. If the workers had preserved their independence, they could have provided the only source of challenge to foreign domination that might have won.

But, contrary to Trotsky's perspective, the force which did finally challenge foreign domination and carry out the revolution, was not drawn from the Chinese working class. Nor was it drawn from the bourgeoisie. Its leadership came from miscellaneous sources, from the urban middle class and from the lower stratum of the landlords, from what Marxists had hitherto called the "petite bourgeoisie." This was true not just for the Chinese independence struggle, but around the world. In some exceptional circumstances, the movement was led by Communist parties, but in most cases, by non-Communist nationalist parties. But in almost all cases, the social composition of the movements was very similar— a middle class leadership, and a coalition following, drawn heavily from sections of the peasantry.

Far from raising the demand for the "dictatorship of the proletariat," the independence movements all concentrated upon cementing a class coalition, on keeping in tow poor and rich peasants, urban workers and capitalists, and even landlords. In China, the Communist leadership devoted its efforts to preventing class conflict surfacing within the coalition, lest some classes be alienated from the central task. Mao himself opposed the demand for radical land reform right up to the revolution lest this alienate landlords and rich peasants; and he assured the capitalists of their right to make a profit in the new China, lest they be frightened off by worker demands for expropriation.[47]

[47] cf. for example, Mao Tse-tung's *On Coalition Government*, 1945 —admittedly designed to woo the Kuomintang : the task of our New

This was not a peculiarly Communist tactic. For, although in very different language, Gandhi in India pursued the "harmonization" of interests, assuring both landlords and capitalists that they would have an important role in the new India. Indeed, if anything, Gandhi was more critical of industrialists than Mao, more "anti-capitalist" than Mao. In both cases, issues arising out of the class structure were damped down in order to highlight the anti-imperialist struggle. In both cases, peasant hostility to the landlords was diverted into opposition to those landlords who supported the foreigners. The struggle was for the eviction of imperialism rather than the anti-imperialist struggle being part of an attempt to transform the indigenous class structure. For the same reason, the struggle was nationalist rather than internationalist.[48] Of course, in both cases, promises were made to both

_____

Democratic system is...to promote the free development of a private capitalist economy that benefits instead of controlling the people's livelihood, and to protect all honestly acquired private property," *Selected Works*, 3, New York edition, p. 255.

[48] There were also, of course, important differences between the struggle in the two countries. The conditions of China made it necessary and possible to form a private army, and this military component made the Communists distinctively different from the Indian Congress. The Communists, as part of their different political tradition, organized a centrally controlled party with an army, and opposition within the party was firmly disciplined. The party was clearly quite separate from its popular support. Congress combined leadership and supporters in a large amorphous crowd in which open public opposition to Gandhi flourished. The military needs of the Communist Party necessitated it be located in a remote area, isolated and far from the main centres of population and power; Congress was the reverse. Gandhi would not have accepted the formation of independent military forces, even if it had been remotely practicable. Indeed, his opposition to Subhas Chandra Bose, who did ultimately favour this, included rejection of such radicalism. But the social base of the two movements was not so clearly different, even though in Congress the small town petite bourgeoisie was much more important. When the two came to power, both tried to reform the distribution of the land, to destroy the hereditary power of the landowners and landlords, to build a large and growing sector of State industry and to plan. Congress did not expropriate all foreign industry, but then the Chinese Communist Party did not have the opportunity to avoid expropriation, given the flight of foreigners. Both aimed at a mixed economy of public and private capital.

But in India, the aims disintegrated slowly in a resurgence of the old entrenched classes. In China, despite numerous vicissitudes, the process peasants and workers to ensure their support, but on the same basis as the promises made to other social classes: not as the representation of interests, as the embodiment of anti-capitalist or anti-landlord interests, so much as to induce support of bene-volent neutrality. Indeed, the welfare promises to workers made by Congress had the even more limited purpose of preventing Com-munists dominating the trade unions,[49] and the threat of Com-munist control made Congress intervention acceptable to the employers.

Thus, "petit-bourgeois" leaderships have filled the vacuum left by the failure of the industrial working class to lead the indepen-

went in the reverse direction, culminating in the collectivization of land in the mid-fifties, and the slow suppression of private capital (although, for example, interest and dividend payments to private businessmen continued through until at least the beginning of the Cultural Revolution in 1966).

It is clear that the degree of political autonomy achieved by the Chinese leadership was always much greater than that achieved by Congress. Congress included many different forces, and floated on top of them. Gandhi was as much victim as master of the movement he led. And the movement was integrally related to Indian society—the peasant members did farm land, the capitalists and workers did operate factories. Thus, the class conflicts of India were transmitted through Congress, and not resolved. By contrast, the Chinese Communist Party was a body of professional organizers, outside Chinese society, and dependent upon its military forces for its independent power. It could therefore inhibit the transmission of the conflicts of Chinese society, and seek, from outside, to resolve or use them. It was only able to do this because of the unique conditions of China, conditions of long-term social collapse over nearly one hundred years. The era of warlords was the seedbed for Communist survival, and the Japanese invasion the precondition for its success in championing the interests of Chinese nationalism. The autonomy of the party, carefully preserved against the infiltration of members who did represent class interests by purges and rectification campaigns, continued into the post revolutionary period. It was the precondition for sustaining the reforms pursued, for mobilizing the peasantry and so giving itself a new legitimacy which it had not created before the revolution. Yet even this independence slowly seeped away, making necessary the grand purge of the Cultural Revolution.

[49] For an account of the origin of the Bombay welfare legislation (Bombay was the leader in labour legislation), cf. Morris David Morris, *The Emergence of an Industrial Labour Force in India, A Study of the Bombay Cotton Mills, 1854-1947,* Berkeley and Los Angeles, 1965, Chapter X, pp. 178-198.

dence movement.[50] But this is not Marx's "petite bourgeoisie"—
small property owners, small town businessmen and property-
owning peasants—so much as the urban lower middle class,
employed in white collar jobs, highly organized by its bureaucratic employment on a collective basis and, most importantly,
propertyless. As the whole ideology of capitalism has decayed in
this century (as indeed the class of capitalists as private owners
has become weaker by the sheer process of concentration) its
appeal has weakened to the point where the bureaucratic lower
middle class has very little interest in the extension of private
property. Since the State is the biggest single employer of white
collar staff, the lower middle class is more concerned with the extension of the power of the State than of private business. In India,
the lower middle class was originally created to service the
bureaucracy of empire, and it dominated the independence struggle in the cities and was easily able to outbid the Communists for
worker support for most of the time. In China, elements of the
same class made up for its relative weakness (since the bureaucracy
of—at least, foreign—empire was insignificant) with independent
military power. In both cases, after independence, the interests
of this group almost inexorably extended the public sector unless
challenged by other entrenched classes. In India, those entrenched
classes were much stronger than in China after independence:
the capitalists were stronger from the start, and the landlords
were not subject to the long drawn out war which occurred in
China. The difference between the two countries shaped the post-
independence regime and its aspirations.

The language of "socialism" used in both countries—a language
inherited from the interests of the European working classes—
obscured the social realities. The debate was supposed to be between the proletariat and the bourgeoisie, the two classes dominating capitalism. But in India, the debate was rather between the
urban lower middle class—pressing for an extension of the State
and public employment—and the richer peasantry and small
town businessmen—pressing for the devotion of more resources to
agriculture. This is the heart of a struggle between State ownership

[50] This is discussed further in the last chapter here. For an example
of a similar process in Africa, cf. Claude Meillassoux, "A Class Analysis
of the Bureaucratic Process in Mali", *The Journal of Development Studies*,
6/2, January 1970.

—identified by the urban lower middle class as "socialism"—and rural capitalism.

If the extension of the public sector is socialism, the urban lower middle class is the class of socialism *par excellence*. But it is State socialism, the socialism of order and planning, not of freedom. And it is national socialism, not the international socialism argued by Marxists to be intrinsic to the situation of the industrial working class. The context of backwardness means that, even if the lower middle class becomes supreme—as has happened in a number of backward countries—the new State will be compelled to accumulate capital out of the surplus created by the working class. Exploitation must necessarily be increased, and the instruments originally seen as the means to emancipate the working class will be turned into new means to bind it.[51] For example, those instruments of worker interests, the trade unions, in all cases where the lower middle class rules the State, have been converted into instruments to control the workers.[52]

[51] The present fashionable argument that urban wages—and therefore, the trade unions—must be controlled in order to assist the rural population, is a good illustration of the kind of attack launched by the new regimes. There is, of course, no assurance that any savings made in this way will go either to the rural population or even to development, rather than to higher salaries for members of the new regime. The arguments used to justify the British Labour government's incomes policy had a very similar flavour.

As an example of the approach, cf. the speech by Kenneth Kaunda of Zambia, "Towards Complete Independence" (speech to the UNIP National Council, August 1969): "If you demand higher wages for the urban workers, the consequent inflation will inevitably hit the majority of our own relatives in the rural areas. We, the urbanites, will in the end have to pay the price, for, in the final analysis, our brothers and sisters, our uncles and aunts, will flock to the town to seek assistance to meet the basic necessities of life, the prices of which have become higher. This is why I emphasize that now Government is yours, industries are yours, the whole economy is yours...to run and manage effectively and successfully...it is against this background...that I find it imperative in the interests of the nation as a whole to announce a wages freeze until further notice...as a corollary, I also want to put an embargo on strikes, whether official or unofficial, as instruments of bargaining for higher wages."

[52] Consult the "Aims" section of the Constitution of the national trade union federation in any Eastern Bloc country. In China, trade unions exist "to strengthen the unity of the working class, to consolidate

III. The strategy

Trotsky's theory of permanent revolution outlined most clearly many of the points made here. In particular, he was concerned to answer Stalin's argument that socialism could be built in the Soviet Union in isolation from the rest of the world. The revolution, he argued, must be spread until it included a more or less significant section of the advanced capitalist countries. Without this, the new regime would inevitably degenerate, overwhelmed by the contradictions of backwardness. As he put it:

> Marxism takes its point of departure from the world economy, not as a sum of national parts but as a mighty and independent reality which has been created by the international division of labour and the world market, and which in our epoch imperiously dominates the national markets.... In respect of the technique of production socialist society must represent a stage higher than capitalism. To aim at building a *nationally isolated* socialist society means, in spite of all passing successes, to pull the productive forces backwards even as compared with capitalism... means to pursue a reactionary utopia. (LT emphasis)[53]

The hope of Liberalism—that securing economic independence was a sufficient condition for economic development—seems no longer valid. The world is one whole, and without the resources accumulated by the advanced capitalist countries by means

---

the alliance of workers and peasants, to educate workers to observe consciously the laws and decrees of the State, and labour discipline, to strive for the development of production, for the constant increase in labour productivity, for the fulfilment and overfulfilment of the production plans of the State"—cf. Constitution, 1953, in *Labour Laws and Regulations of the People's Republic of China*, Peking, 1956, p. 17. In Cuba, the Law of Union Organization (August 1961) lays it down that Cuban trade unions should "assist in the fulfilment of the production and development plans of the nation, to promote efficiency, expansion, and utility in social and public services"—cited James O'Connor, "The Organised Working Class in the Cuban Revolution", *Studies on the Left*, 6/2, 1966, p. 19.

[53] Trotsky, L. D., *The Permanent Revolution*, 1930, John G. Wright translation, revised by Brian Pearce, London, 1962.

barbarous and brutal, the process of primitive accumulation imposes upon any backward country intolerable strains. The rhetoric may lay claim to traditions of emancipation, but the practice is driven in the opposite direction. Soviet development illustrates what happens, even in conditions generally more favourable than those facing most of the backward countries today, when accumulation becomes a vital necessity for the survival of the State. Trotsky had feared the process would lead to the restoration of the bourgeoisie in Russia—up to that time, the necessary expression of the division of labour imposed by accumulation. He had hoped that what he saw as the only other alternative, the resumption of power by the Russian working class, would in fact result. But neither change took place. Behind the verbal facade of Marxism, a new class regime was created amid the turmoil and terror of industrialization.

But even the Soviet path seems ruled out for most backward countries today. World development has reached an impasse. The bourgeoisie dragged mankind out of pre-capitalist society, but it is now unable to complete the process by developing the whole world. The result is that, while the developed countries continue to grow, the rest stagnate. The impasse can be broken, not by establishing islands of nationalist autarchy—world imperialism is too strong to permit that to be a real threat—but only by breaking the world domination of capitalism, and thereby releasing the accumulated resources of world capitalism for a massive global development programme. Without this, every partial revolt is less a cure than a symptom of the crisis. The social composition of each national regime makes it impossible to unify the "Third World," and even if unified, a boycott of capitalism by the backward would inflict more damage on the backward than the advanced. And it would not destroy capitalism.

Unless the citadels of capitalism can be challenged from within, the global domination of the capitalist powers remains. The partial successes won in particular backward countries are vital if seen as the springboard to spreading the revolution. But alone, isolated, they inevitably succumb to the logic of backwardness in a world dominated by the rich.

At a whole series of different points in this critique of dominant opinion on the Left, we are led back to the original Marxist stress on the role of the industrial working class. It is here that the key to the global system lies. The lack of proletarian leadership in the struggle for national independence shaped that struggle in certain ways, and created post-independence regimes which positively exacerbated both the attempts to internationalize the revolution and to develop the countries concerned. The lack of a response from the proletariat of the West, to an even greater degree, converted the colonial revolution into a basis for new repressive class regimes. Meanwhile, capitalism had grown and transformed its relationship with the backward countries, making the new regimes even more dependent than before.

In the final analysis, the beleagured garrisons of China, of Cuba, of India, can only be relieved by a mutiny in the imperialist forces. Socialists must quite obviously support the struggle for national independence, but without thereby thinking all the problems are wished away. Once independence is secured, then our interest should be focused upon the creation of a proletarian alternative within each backward country, for that is one of the first steps in transforming the perspective. But even more, the creation of an independent proletarian challenge in the countries of advanced capitalism is the precondition for decisive progress. The two together are the beginnings of a new international class alliance. The development impasse, the resulting political and social instability, terrible poverty and hopelessness for the majority of the population of the backward countries: these are the symptoms of the inevitability of barbarism without international socialism.

Marxism: Leninism-Stalinism-Maoism

Men fight and lose that battle, and the thing they fought for comes about
in spite of their defeat, and when it comes, turns out to be not what they
meant, and other men have to fight for what they meant under another
name.   WILLIAM MORRIS

I. Marxism in Russia

Marxism-Leninism is a body of beliefs said to be the guiding
perspective of the dominant groups in Eastern Europe and the
Soviet Union. It is currently in a process of rapid change, or at
least, substantial parts of it are being relegated to unimportance,
so that a current definition of "Marxism-Leninism" would
be almost impossible. Historically, the subject is vast, and it is
proposed here only to examine briefly some of the background to
the work of Lenin, that work itself, that of Stalin, and a little of
what followed Stalin's death. The account cannot, for reasons of
space, be a history of modern Russia, nor even of the revolutionary
movements in Russia. It is only one narrow segment, which omits
the many perspectives of other groups in opposition, from the
Mensheviks to the workers' and Left opposition. This is a severe
weakness, since the few themes examined are separated from the
historical context which gave them specific content. In particular,
this is crucial for Bolshevism, for it is a very specific response to a
relatively narrow range of problems. A characteristic means of
vilifying Bolshevism is to present its themes without mentioning
the problems analyzed by those themes, to treat it as an atemporal
theology, generalizations on the nature of man and society in all

*Published earlier as two chapters: Ch. V, "Conservatism and the
East" and Ch. VI, "Nationalism in the South" in my *Beliefs in Society,
The Problem of Ideology*, C.A. Watts, London, 1968, pp. 142, 185.

times and places.

However, the justification for this account is that a discussion of the history of Marxism-Leninism most vividly illustrates a group of beliefs which began as radical, profoundly opposed to the existing *status quo*, but ended as conservative, in defence of the Soviet *status quo*. The theoretical framework for the transition was supposed to remain the same, and it is important to see the transition from one posture to its opposite within one apparent orthodoxy. The similarities at the end between Western conservatism and Marxism-Leninism are marked, although the two groups of beliefs are not the same, since the immediate conclusions are derived from different postulates, heirs of different inheritances, but the practical impact is the same.

Bolshevism, the viewpoint of that section of the Russian Social Democrat Party which assumed revolutionary power in 1917, exists essentially in relationship to the needs of revolutionary practice. Lenin's writings were always rooted in some immediate context, and most of them cannot be interpreted in relationship to general problems without severe damage to their meaning. He wrote very little "general theory," and even when he did, it was written in relationship to some immediate political purpose. It is thus impossible to understand what he wrote without understanding the charges to which he is replying. For Lenin, his theoretical work was a prelude and guide to his practical activity, a means to identify the right actions at the right time, and something which itself evolved with the experience of trying to do things. A continuing purpose and context gave general coherence and continuity to his work, but each part of his work must be seen, given these factors, relative to a specific task.

Lenin's successors did not need the same theoretical framework, did not need to guide their actions in the same way, for they were already in power. Already, the purposes that had guided Lenin were changing into new purposes. So tenuous did the relationship with Lenin's purposes become, that his words were increasingly used as a ritual, a theology, generalized so that they were said to be applicable at all times and places. The association of a perspective and the maintenance of authority had once more come to dilute and finally destroy the perspective. In Stalinism, Leninist theory was used as a means of justifying Stalin's practice, after the event. What Stalin chose to do, without clearly specifying his reasons (and so framing a theoretical context for his actions), was subsequently reconciled with an earlier tradition, so that the popularity of the second could conceal the unpopularity of the first.

The change did not occur because Lenin's successors were muddled, mistaken, or intellectually his inferior, but because their perspective on the world, their purposes, had been transformed. In this transformation lies the metamorphosis of Marxism from a means of so analyzing society that an obligation to change society is immediately incurred by all who accept the analysis, into the conservative ideology of a new class society, a body of formalized doctrine, designed to justify the existing nature of society and so leave complete freedom of action to its leaders. Comparisons have been made between Soviet ideology and various forms of theology, and this is, perhaps, an interesting exercise although it overestimates the static quality of the doctrines and is most plausible only for the heyday of Stalinism.

A continuing theme in this account will be the changing relationship of theory, held beliefs relative to immediate problems, to practice, what one does about the problems. The relationship was summarized by Marx for socialists in the term "sensuous practice." In seeking to change the world, "practice," men learn new lessons and adjust their theory accordingly, this adjusted theory then is subjected to the tests of further attempts to achieve the same ends. Implicitly, Marx is rejecting the conservative notion that men can achieve their aims without simultaneously attempting to be fully conscious of what they are doing, without analyzing the world and being "theoretical." Where the ideal is the real, as it is for conservatives, what they wish to achieve, day-to-day administration, can be achieved without general analysis, without being "theoretical." Thus Marx's prescription applies only to radicals, and even more narrowly, to socialists. But Marx is also stating that no theory can constitute alone an adequate means to change; it must be subjected to practical test, and if it secures success for those who make use of it in practice, then and then only is it "valid." For conservatives, the general social structure is not problematic, so general theory is not required, and the social structure, whatever it is, can be taken for granted. Of course, when the social structure comes under serious radical challenge, conservatives do have to frame more general positions to counteract radical theory, and in doing so, they may pass beyond conservatism—either identifying with the radical challenge, or offering a more militant counter-challenge. However, the sole point of interest here is that Marx's prescriptions are only for radicals, not for general purposes.

The Background to Bolshevism

Marxism was initially defined and shaped on a mass political level by the German Social Democrat Party, and this definition in the 1890s provided a framework for the union of the purposes of German socialists and the 19th century philosophic doctrine loosely described as positivism. Positivism, very roughly, can be described in this context as the contention that a deterministic knowledge of the world is possible, and is so, independently of any activity in the world. Indeed, some positivists maintain that knowledge is *only* possible if completely isolated from practical concerns and problems confronting men in their daily lives.

By implication, knowledge is atemporal—what constitutes knowledge is what concerns all men at all times and places, rather than what concerns a few here and now. The belief that Marxism was part of an atemporal and deterministic science was already emerging in the later writings of Engels, and Marx himself detected the same tendency among some of his followers when he declared that he was not a "Marxist"; his work, he said, was only an "historical sketch of the genesis of capitalism in Western Europe," not "an historico-philosophic theory of the *marche generale* imposed by fate upon every people, whatever the historic circumstances in which it finds itself."[1] The warning did not prevent Engels from generalizing some of the methodological principles Marx employed in the analysis of European history (where man was the sole creator) to the world of nature. Generalizations about man's activity came to be seen as merely particular applications of general "laws of nature." Man was therefore ruled by scientifically determinable laws which, Engels claimed, were embodied in a doctrine which came to be known as "dialectical materialism."

---

[1]Letter, November 1877, Karl Marx and Friedrich Engels, *Selected Correspondence*, Moscow, 1953, p. 354.

The implications of the shift were immense, for "dialectical materialism" could easily become a kind of religious doctrine, without reference to particular time or place, a theory of the cosmology, not a method of analysis for quite clearly specified purposes.

It was thus possible for men to look at society as a kind of natural organism, the evolution of which was "inevitable" and did not require the intervention of men. Within this determinist framework, the achievement of a socialist revolution was not so much the work of men as the inevitable result of natural evolution, much the same as the evolution of men from anthropoids. This version of Marxism as a collection of universal scientific laws was further developed by the two major theorists of Social Democratic Marxism before the First World War, Karl Kautsky and Georgi Plekhanov. Marxism had become less a philosophy of revolutionary action, and rather more an atemporal ideological system based upon faith in certain doctrinal postulates, called necessary and natural laws. This peculiarly stark form of economic determinism virtually excluded the opportunity for revolutionary action— since the revolution was "inevitable," nothing much need be done about it—and it also made theory redundant, since it was irrelevant to the day-to-day problems facing the Social Democrat movement. Marxism was restricted to the role of analyzing society for no particular purpose; it was not a guide to action in the here-and-now; it was "science": that is, it accepted reality as it was without seeking to examine that reality in relationship to the purposes involved in changing it. Inevitably it became conservative. In day-to-day practice, German Social Democracy was at one with the non-Marxist English Fabians, suggesting how little a different general theory mattered.

But even as Marxism, in the hands of Engels and Kautsky, reached the respectability of positivism, general European culture was itself reaching a state of almost explosive rejection of some elements of positivism. The era of the peaceful expansion of industry which had underpinned the complacent optimism of the Victorians in Britain, the assumption of society as a simple self-equilibrating machine, was giving way to open imperialist clashes abroad and increasing class conflict at home. But the domestic conflict took a new form, producing almost a division of labour between revolutionary theory and revolutionary practice, between "science" and activism.

There were a number of different responses to the schism. One philosophic response accepted the Engels and Kautsky version of Marxism at face value, saying that it was therefore a simple form of economic analysis which presented a scientific view of the world but did not suggest why the individual should also want what was inevitable. Edouard Bernstein, who became the best-known advocate of this view, argued that: "No amount of histori-cal materialism can get round the fact that history is made by men, that men have minds, and that mental dispositions are by no means so mechanical as to be entirely governed by the economic situation,"[2] Marx's economic analysis thus needed underpinning with a system of individual ethics, drawn in the main from the work of Kant. The movement became known as Revisionism, but neo-Kantianism had wider implications throughout Social Democracy and occurred in the work of perhaps the most impor-tant group of Social Democrat theorists, the Austro-Marxists. On a non-theoretical level, anarcho-syndicalism, important in France and Italy, can also be seen as a response to the central problem, an attempt to restore revolutionary practice in explicit isolation from what had formerly been revolutionary theory. Again, to some extent, Mussolini's evolution from orthodox Social Democratic Marxism through the phase of leading a Leftwing "ginger group" to stimulate greater radicalism by the Italian Social Democrat leadership, to Fascism (even though, Mussolini ended as profoundly anti-socialist), could be seen as also a response to the central problem.[3] However, the most important attempt to reunify theory and practice within Marxism, although not the orthodox version, was undertaken by Rosa Luxemburg and Parvus, and in Russia, by the Bolsheviks.

Marxist ideas began to circulate in Russia, mainly in academic circles, from the 1870s, hot on the heels of the Narodnik socialists who had themselves sought to rid Russia of Tsarism. Narodnik activity had shown how limited were the possibilities for any kind of radical politics. Some of those who have criticized Lenin for not behaving as if he lived in Victorian England or even the Kaiser's

[2] *Die Neue Zeit*, XVI, p. 749, cited by G. A. Wetter, *Dialectical Materialism, An Historical and Systematic Survey of Philosophy in the Soviet Union* (translated by Peter Heath), London, 1958.

[3] Ernst Nolte, *Three Faces of Fascism*, London, 1965, p. 151 ff.

Germany make too few allowances for the ruthlessness of Tsarist autocracy and the comprehensive influence of the Tsarist secret police. The conditions which allowed the development of a strong democratic labour movement in the West were not permitted in Russia, and special tactics had to be employed for any revolutionary even to survive. Similarly, the central problem for Russian radicals was not, as it was for west European socialists, how to create socialism, but rather how to permit capitalism, how to end Tsarism and create the conditions for a bourgeois republic which would simultaneously develop the economy and allow the growth of a free labour movement. When that was accomplished, socialism would become a feasible aim.

The first Social Democratic organization in St Petersburg dates from 1885, and the first, abortive, congress of the Russian Workers' Social Democrat Party from 1898. Georgi Plekhanov led the attack on the ruling Narodnik orthodoxy among socialists —that the peasantry could create socialism in Russia without the country developing capitalism—by asserting that the Russian proletariat was the sole agency for the achievement of socialism, and that capitalism was already well under way in Russia so that any thought that a peasant socialism was possible— let alone socialism without an intervening capitalist phase— was illusory. One of the earliest Marxists actually in Russia (Plekhanov was in exile), Struve, wrote the first manifesto of the RWSDP, and it is of interest that he there repeats an opinion common among European Social Democrats and one of some significance for Russian socialists who wished to precipitate a bourgeois revolution and thereby create a republic:

> The farther east one goes in Europe, the weaker, meaner and more cowardly in the political sense becomes the bourgeoisie, and the greater the cultural and political tasks which fall to the lot of the proletariat. On its strong shoulders, the Russian working class must and will carry the work of conquering political liberty.[4]

At least three main trends of Marxist thought emerged out of

---

[4] 1898, cited by E. H. Carr, *The Bolshevik Revolution, 1917-23*, London, 1950, p. 4.

this initial activity:

(i) A group of intellectuals, the best known being Struve, Berdyaev, and Tugan-Baranovsky, who, in conjunction with the Revisionists in Germany, saw Marxism as profoundly weak as a general philosophy, without any ethical code to justify its "inevitability" for the individual. The group avoided activity which might cross the censor or the Tsarist police, and thus earned the nickname Legal Marxists. Some of them subsequently pursued the ethical strand of thought into religious mysticism.

(ii) A slightly overlapping group, nicknamed Economists, who argued that the entrepreneurial middle class in Russia could and would overthrow Tsarism in due course once capitalism was fully established. Thus, workers should not worry about political matters but concentrate on improving their economic positions—the bourgeois revolution was coming, whatever workers did. The Economists placed heavy stress on the spontaneous activity of workers as superior to a consciously disciplined organization, despite the chaotic conditions of early industrialization in Russia and the pervasive watch of the secret police.

(iii) The Bolsheviks, who argued against the first that Marxism included its own ethical presuppositions, and that any revolutionary group must inevitably go beyond what was legal in the conditions of Tsarist Russia. The case against the second group will concern us below. Those subsequently called Mensheviks were members of all three groups at different times.

Lenin

Lenin was a man of great simplicity, severity and dedication, and he possessed that peculiar synthesis of the sense of freedom and of necessity, of practice and of theory, which characterizes the work of Marx. The economically "inevitable" and the ethically desirable are, in Lenin's work, once more one and the same in the "sensuous practice" of a revolutionary. Lenin's theoretical writings are not, by the standards of Marx and some of the other Marxist writers of his times, great, since they are not so comprehensive in scope nor fully worked out. However, they are essentially bound up with his activities, and the actual achievement of the first workers' revolution.

Like most of his contemporaries, Lenin was burdened with the inheritance of positivistic Marxism so that, despite his attempts to overcome that burden, his philosophic work as a whole is split between a crude and philosophically indefensible materialism, his clumsy version of "positivism," and his refurbished Hegelian dialectic. He used the analytical work done by other Social Democrats in Europe (for example, Hilferding's *Finanzkapital*) for his popularization of the theory of imperialism, but with a crucial difference. "Science" for Lenin was not passive contemplation by one individual of a world separate and unchangeable, but the study of the world by men who sustained that world and who by their action could change it. His view of capitalism accordingly stressed its continuing contradictory nature, the way those contradictions were resolved turning upon the choices and decisions men made. Thus, advanced economies were marked not just by cartelization stabilizing markets, but cartelization making competition between cartels that much more explosive; not just world unification through imperial conquest, but increasingly aggressive conflicts between rival imperialisms. The framework thus provided was the context for the strategy he designed for the Bolsheviks in Russia, and that practice was in its turn related back to the general European and world scenes.

Lenin was active in politics from the 1890s. Like many other Russian Marxists, he judged that the weakness of the middle class in Russia was the main barrier to the overthrow of Tsarism, without which a parliamentary republic, free political parties and the growth of the labour movement would be impossible: thus making a socialist revolution itself some time in the distant future also impossible. The State and foreign interests had developed capitalism in Russia, so that a proletariat proportionately larger than the native bourgeoisie had been created. The small bourgeoisie would be too frightened of the proletarian threat to risk overthrowing the Tsar, despite the restrictions Tsarism might place on the free growth of private industry. However, the proletariat itself was still very new and primitive, at that anarchic stage where its members could not analyze clearly their own position in society as the basis for realistic action. It wasted its collective strength in sporadic and hopeless battles. The intelligentsia which had sustained the fragmentary Narodnik assaults on Tsarism in the sixties and seventies, was radical enough, but equally anarchic. It could not supply the proletariat with a rigorous and continuing theoretical framework which would channel labour's manifest hostility into realistic activity: metaphysical talk, endless and fruitless, was all it seemed spontaneously capable of.

Thus, two related problems faced revolutionaries in Russia: (i) If the bourgeoisie would not overthrow the Tsar, could proletarian pressure or initiative prompt them to do so? And how could the proletariat, still a small minority in a country overwhelmingly peasant, act thus but avoid destroying itself in the process?
(ii) How could the proletariat, with its ignorance, but drive and strength, be welded to the intelligentsia, with its education but weakness?

Many of the Economists and Legal Marxists replied that these were pseudo-problems. Since the coming revolution would be bourgeois in both form and content, the proletariat should restrain itself to supporting the middle class, thus simultaneously lending the bourgeoisie the strength to overthrow the Tsar and not frightening it into his arms. At an extreme, of course, this position entailed restraining workers in their day-to-day pressures for wage increases or improvements lest such pressure alarm the capitalists too much—"economic" and "political" activity could only for short periods be plausibly separated.

Lenin accepted up to 1917 that "The democratic revolution will not extend beyond the scope of bourgeois social economic relations" (1905), but he insisted that workers must remain independent of the bourgeoisie. It was not feasible for workers both to fight and support capital. However, the 1905 attempted revolution against the Tsar radically changed the picture. For it seemed both that the proletariat could take independent action to secure the bourgeois revolution, and also the peasantry could play an important revolutionary role, at least in the early stages—until the peasants' demand for land was satisfied, when it would become conservative in defence of its new property. Lenin therefore argued that there must be an alliance between workers and peasants, and this could force the bourgeois revolution which the bourgeoisie itself would not initiate. If the proletariat did precipitate the bourgeois revolution, it would be able to carry out the main historic tasks of that revolution: the creation of a democratic republic, the confiscation of the estates of the large landowners, the introduction of the eight-hour day. If the revolution did not take place, then a hybrid regime would result from the alliance of the Tsar and the bouregoisie, an *etatiste* capitalism on the model of the Prussia of his day. The choice, Lenin said, lay between a landowner-capitalist regime and a proletarian-peasant "bourgeois" revolution, between the creation of a society modelled either on the militaristic despotism of Prussia or on the republicanism of the United States. However, if the second was achieved, the peasantry would immediately become conservative in defence of its new land ownership, and it would then ally with the bourgeoisie to oust the proletariat from political power.

A third view on the situation might also be mentioned, since, although it was not particularly important at the time, it proved in 1917 more accurate than Lenin's. The Trotsky-Parvus position accepted Lenin's judgment that the Russian bourgeoisie would not do the job, but it also maintained that the peasantry was a force too disunited between rich and poor to form a united party for long. Again, if the proletariat seized power, it would be impossible to make it execute demands solely in the interests of the bourgeoisie. Inevitably, it would meet problems for which it could frame only socialist answers: freeing industry from the constrictions of the Tsar would be superseded by nationalizing industry. Thus, there would be a "permanent revolution." The bourgeois would merge into the socialist revolution willy nilly; the phrase "permanent revolution" was taken from Marx's 1850 *Address to the Communist League*, outlining a strategy for a situation in Germany at that time not dissimilar to that in Russia. Trotsky argued—against straight economic determinism—that there was no direct correlation between the stage of development of a particular country, part of an international economic order, and the type of revolution which ensued. After all, the Paris Commune of 1871 had occurred in a country economically more backward than Britain and the United States which had experienced no such revolt. The revolution could occur on the edges of capitalist civilization, rather than in its main centres.

However, Trotsky went on, if the *attempt* at a socialist revolution in Russia was inevitable, it was impossible that the new order could survive long unless the revolution in Russia sparked off a general socialist revolution in the more advanced countries of western Europe. Russia was underdeveloped, its proletariat small and relatively backward. The revolution would not survive against the combined opposition of the Russian industralists and peasants, the overwhelming majority, unless both the numbers and the economic aid of western Europe came to its assistance. A European revolution would save the Russian proletariat and permit it to sustain the socialist revolution, despite the immense strains of development that must follow.[5]

Lenin, like most Social Democrats, rejected this view as going too far; such proposals would disillusion the peasantry before the alliance had even begun. He reiterated firmly that:

> The task of the Russian proletariat is to carry the bourgeois democratic regime in Russia to its conclusion, *in order* to kindle the socialist revolution in Europe. This task has today come very close to the first, but it nevertheless remains a separate and second task; for different classes are to co-operate with the Russian proletariat; for the first, our ally is the *petit-bourgeois* peasantry of Russia; for the second, the proletariat of other countries.[6]

Lenin maintained this position through the substantial fluctuations of Bolshevik support up to 1917. Only after the installation of the Provisional Government following the overthrow of the Tsar in 1917, and in response to the very radical mood of the St Petersburg workers, did he acknowledge the unrealistic nature of the proposal that the proletariat, having seized power, should quietly relinquish it in conformity with some "historical law," independent of the consciousness of men.

For the solution of the second problem—how to build a disciplined revolutionary group, intelligentsia and workers, capable of surviving in Tsarist conditions—Lenin's proposals were unoriginal. In 1902, he accepted the opinion common among Social Democrats, summarized in Kautsky's rather elitist statement that:

> ... socialism and the class struggle arise side by side, and not one out of the other. Modern socialist consciousness can arise

[5] L. D. Trotsky, *Results and Prospects,* St Petersburg, 1906, translated by Brian Pearce, London, 1962.

[6] V. I. Lenin, "Some Theses", *Collected Works,* 18, Moscow, 1960, p. 357.

only on the basis of profound scientific knowledge. . . . The vehicles of science are not the proletariat, but the bourgeois intelligentsia. . . . The socialist consciousness is something introduced into the proletarian class struggle from without, and not something that arose within spontaneously.[7]

Since, Lenin went on, a mass democratic party with open, public discussions, was impossible in Tsarist conditions (the members would be gaoled), the party must be a small secret organization, demanding absolute dedication from its members lest it be betrayed to the police. It would be, when it was small, inevitably overweighted by the "vehicles of science," the intellectuals, and it would have to be relatively undemocratic since it would have to choose its members carefully to avoid infiltration by police spies. It would demand great internal discipline and organization to avoid suppression. It would have to be composed of professional revolutionaries, not dilettantes or amateurs, since the weakness of one could endanger all.

There were implicit dangers in these proposals, as critics within the Social Democratic Party were quick to point out. The *elite*, sustained by the nature of Tsarism, could become a substitute for the force it claimed merely to represent. In so far as the Bolsheviks did do this, they courted political failure, and perhaps some of the criticisms of Bolshevik tactics during the 1905 revolution are just in this respect. But the mere enunciation of certain tactics in a minor document, *What is to be Done?*, does not on its own demonstrate very much about the Bolsheviks in practice. Many Western critics of Lenin have pounced upon this pamphlet as complete demonstration of all manner of evils. But the proposals are partly common sense in Tsarist conditions, partly unoriginal (some Narodniks had responded to Tsarism in a similar manner, inevitably so given their aims), and partly contradicted by Bolshevik practice. Lenin had no power to enforce his will upon his followers. He had only their voluntary adherence to the cause to ensure loyalty, and that feature meant that *What is to be Done?* could, at best, be an aspiration, not an accomplished fact. Instead of attacking the aims the Bolsheviks had, some anti-Communists

[7] V. I. Lenin, "What is to be Done?", *Selected Works*, I, London, 1937, p. 149.

have pursued the side issue of Lenin's organizational proposals, seeing in them the founding constitution of Stalin's tyranny. Yet Stalin could have been a tyrant without Lenin, and no inexorable railway lines were laid down in 1902 from which the train of Soviet history could not escape.

Bolshevik practice confirms the very doubtful validity of placing so much stress on one early document. Lenin and his followers changed their minds from time to time relative to changes in Russian political conditions. For example, in the 1905 revolution, with Tsarist control weakened by internal revolt, the party was able to open itself to mass membership. It was able to sustain an open public existence until Tsarist strength was sufficient once more to impose control and drive the party back into secrecy. On the other hand, Lenin quite clearly rejected Kautsky's dictum when he proclaimed excitedly after the 1905 revolt that "the working class is instinctively, spontaneously, Social Democrat." Lenin learned, and changed, much as most people do, and unlearned things over the passage of time. In 1917, the party was broadly opposed to the seizure of power, despite Lenin, and in the first instance, Lenin appealed directly to the St Petersburg workers *against* the party which had become relatively conservative and supported the new post-Tsarist Provisional Government. Thus, in this instance, his attempt to build a party which was more revolutionary than the ordinary workers of St Petersburg had failed—at the moment of crisis, the party was just like all the others. Within the party itself, Lenin was occasionally outvoted, so that it cannot realistically be seen as a one-man dictatorship. Indeed, any such picture of it would be unable to explain how it survived and was popular in 1917, for one man, no matter how attractive (and Lenin was certainly not an "attractive" man) cannot carry many supporters merely on his own personality, let alone a politically significant movement.

In his writings also he indicated both how important open discussion was, and what kinds of limitations were necessarily imposed by Tsarist conditions. "Democratic centralism," "free criticism plus unity of action" was not a mysterious and sinister doctrine until the time of Stalin, and the first element was vital for the party to achieve the best perspective possible—"without debate, conflicts, without a war between opinion, no movement, including the workers' movement, is possible at all. But without a merciless fight against the degeneration of conflicts into quarrels and squabbles any organization is *impossible*."[8]

What might be called "ideational determinism," the notion that once an idea is enunciated, it must continue for evermore to dominate men, has peculiarly afflicted Leninism. It is said that Lenin's assertions lead inexorably to Stalin's policies, as Plato's or Hegel's or Nietzsche's ideas "lead" to Hitler. Yet as many of Lenin's assertions can be interpreted out of context as democratic as can be seen as authoritarian. Lenin's successors were not bound to any inexorable track. They *chose* what was useful for their purposes (simultaneously abandoning other elements which did not contribute). In that choice a critique should begin.

The same remarks might apply to that hoary old chestnut, *partiinost* (literally, "party-ness," and meaning "party spirit"), beloved of Sovietologists. Lenin argued against Struve that someone with political convictions should behave in intellectual controversy in consistency with those convictions, he should be "committed" rather than sustaining perhaps contradictory positions—on the one hand, a Marxist, on the other, a conventional social scientist or historian.

It was a demand for responsibility, for consistency, for dedication, not for the posture of an idle bystander, someone who was uncommitted. However, critics have argued that this position, explicitly a recommendation to party members, is really the practical source of Stalinist censorship, interference in all cultural and scientific activities in society as a whole: again, as if Stalin needed such a relatively modest notion to create so tyrannical a weapon.

All that has been described so far derives directly from the actual circumstances of the Bolshevik attempt to survive as a disciplined party active in Russia rather than exiled to Siberia or Switzerland. Lenin was a hard man without the gifts of circumlocution and diplomatic courtesy. Inevitably he made many enemies, and most of the subsequent criticisms of him were made at the time by his contemporaries. But his vindication came in 1917, as Trotsky, who campaigned with the greatest bitterness against Lenin's ruthlessness (and earned, in reply, equally savage denunciation from

---

[8] V. I. Lenin, "Two Methods of Fighting and Disputing", *Collected Works*, 17, Moscow, 1960, p. 73.

Lenin), acknowledged:

> Only the highest concentration on the goal of revolution, free
> from everything pettily personal, can justify this kind of personal
> ruthlessness. . . . His behaviour seemed to me inadmissible, terri-
> ble, shocking. Yet at the same time it was politically correct and
> therefore indispensable from the point of view of organization.[9]

The most traumatic event in Lenin's political life was the failure
of the European Social Democratic Parties to prevent war in 1914.
For so many years, these parties had declared that they would not
fight each other, and that any war declared by their respective
governments would be promptly turned into revolution by the
Social Democrats, yet at the moment of testing, the overwhelming
majority opted for nationalism rather than socialism, and marched
off to slaughter each other. The whole precarious house of cards,
the theoretical inheritance of Social Democracy, collapsed in the
trenches. The hopes that the Second International would lead
Europe into a new society could no longer be sustained. The event
forced Lenin to re-examine his own beliefs and the Marxism he
had accepted for so long to see why those whom, even in criticizing, he had respected as his seniors in Marxism, had failed before
the decisive challenge. As a result of this re-examination, he revised much of what he had taken for granted from Kautsky and
German Social Democracy, so that although, in intellectual terms,
the revision remained incomplete, his life's work fits into two
inconsistent parts, pre- and post-1914. Thus, in philosophy, his
main pre-1914 work, *Materialism and Empirio-Criticism* (written
in reply to neo-Kantian Revisionism), merely repeats in clumsy
and philosophically indefensible terms the crude materialism of
Kautsky. But after 1914, Lenin's pursuit of the theoretical sources
for the failure of the Second International led to his rediscovery of
Hegel's dialectic and his assertion that no Marxist had understood *Capital* for a quarter of a century. For Lenin, the dialectic
both restored the primacy of human activity and threw a new
stress on the contradictory elements in the new capitalism, summarized in his popular pamphlet, *Imperialism*: *The Highest Stage of
Capitalism*.

[9] L. D. Trotsky, *My Life*, London, 1930, p. 188.

New events compelled the Bolsheviks to rediscover the theories associated with their own purposes. Bernstein had challenged the divergence between German Social Democrat theory and practice, by urging that the theory be revised to conform to the practice. Lenin identified the same divergence, but demanded that practice conform to the theory, the aims claimed in the rhetoric be systematically pursued rather than used as decorative elements on a basically conservative standpoint.

But if Social Democratic Marxism had extinguished the role of human activity and consciousness in its deterministic interpretation of Marx, it had also absorbed other matching elements from its environment: in particular, bureaucratism, a heavy reliance on the State, and an implicit nationalism. In restoring the primacy of human agency in history, Lenin, in like form, passionately reaffirmed freedom as the essence of Marxism and socialism in *State and Revolution*. The "withering-away of the State" was not, as it had been for German Social Democracy, to be relegated to some utopian limbo; it should begin immediately power was won. Lenin also rejected the alliance of socialism and nationalism that had destroyed the Second International and was embodied in the Social Democratic acceptance of the State as a substitute for popular participation and initiative. He affirmed that the aim of all radical socialist movements should be to *abolish* the State, and he accused Kautsky of censoring the writings of Marx and Engels which asserted that the State was necessarily an instrument of tyranny. When class domination ended, the administration of society must inevitably devolve so that all would participate and control society. Uncompromisingly, he concluded: "So long as the State exists, there is no freedom; when freedom exists, there will be no State."

Such an unequivocal affirmation of the necessity for freedom and the form it must take, could only lead to great pessimism or great optimism. In 1917 and 1918, optimism was the dominant motif—men could control society, the majority could be self-governing. In May 1918, Lenin promised his audience that those who were not over 35 years old would see the dawn of communism. Immediately after the October Revolution, he warned Russian workers that:

Remember, *you yourselves* now administer the State. Nobody

will help you if you yourselves do not unite and take *all affairs* of State into *your own* hands. *Your* Soviets are henceforth the organs of State power, organs of full power, organs of decision.[10]

In January 1918, he explained to the Congress of Soviets that "In introducing workers' control, we knew it would take some time before it spread to the whole of Russia, but we wanted the workers themselves to draw up, from below, the new principle of economic conditions." The affirmation of the necessity for freedom is too frequent and too passionate to be the cold calculation of a Machiavellian.

The revolution was the supreme moment of Lenin's career, both vindication of his work and test of his strategy. It was also, ironically, a critique of the elitism that sometimes appeared in his work and derived from the conditions for a revolutionary party in Russia (sanctioned by the authority of Marxism's "Pope," Kautsky). For Lenin could not rely on his party to champion popular demands of the moment that brought power in 1917. Organization had not been able to ensure that the party was always slightly ahead of popular wishes, was more revolutionary than the workers. For when the decisive moment came, the party had to be whipped into championing those demands—even to the extent of stealing its programme directly from them rather than advancing what the party had already decided.[11]

But the winter of 1917-18 saw the effects of the World War and the dissolution of the Tsarist armies, as well as the revolution, leaving the administrative machine in ruins, and food supplies exhausted. Once it had gained land, the peasantry no longer sustained the revolution, and there was not, as yet, a European revolution to fill the sails of the new Soviet craft. Lenin began retracing his steps, not by revising his general theoretical work, but by becoming deeply immersed in day-to-day administration, in mere survival. His statements have a tone of rising pessimism, a refusal to speculate on what had been achieved and what could be achieved, an identification of some of the central problems but without solutions. The civil war dealt a further staggering blow to the eco-

[10] V. I. Lenin, cited in Carr, *op. cit.,* p. 244.

[11] V. I. Lenin, speech, 11 November 1917, *Collected Works,* 22, London, 1960, p. 30.

nomy and the new government was compelled to take back into employment thousands of former Tsarist officials, so transforming the nature of the administration at the same time as its own followers, urban workers, were dispatched to the army to fight the White forces. Force had now become increasingly important as the means to win some food from the obdurate countryside.

Plekhanov once taunted Lenin with a quotation from Engels, and it became increasingly relevant from 1918 as the claimed social basis of the party drained away and no European revolution occurred to shift the balance of forces:

> The worst that can befall the leader of an extremist party is to be compelled to take over the government at a time when the movement is not yet ripe for the rule of the class he represents. . . . He finds himself necessarily in an insoluble political dilemma: what he *can* do is in conflict with his entire previous attitudes, his principles, and the immediate interests of his party; what he is *supposed* to do cannot be done . . . he is compelled to represent not his party, his class, but the class for the rule of which the movement happens to be right. For the sake of that movement he must act for the interests of an alien class, and must feed his own class with phrases and promises along with the assertion that the interests of that alien class are really their own. He who gets himself in that false position is irredeemably lost.[12]

The great hopes disintegrated in increasing gloom, only heightened by the revolt of the Kronstadt sailors (an earlier generation of Kronstadt sailors had been foremost supporters of the Bolsheviks), a wave of strikes and peasant revolts. It was clear the Bolsheviks no longer represented a majority of even the industrial working class; indeed, they represented nothing except themselves. Yet what alternative existed? Were they quietly to acknowledge their "mistake," abandon hope of a European revolution and give up power? Yet the White armies which would have inherited that power would show no such respect for any principle: they would probably have instituted the first Fascist regime in Europe, with an accompanying wave of terror that would surpass the brutality

---

[12] F. Engels, *The Peasant War in Germany*, 1850, Moscow, 1956.

of the Tsars.

Lenin did not make his peace with Marxist theory; he left it in suspension. He became preoccupied with how to develop Russia, how to drag it out of backwardness, ignorance and poverty in the face of international hostility. The day-to-day problems of the economy became the most important affairs of State, and any tactic to drive the economy along assumed major importance— "it is our task to learn State capitalism (not socialism, *NH*) from the Germans, to adopt it with all our might, to shrink from no dictatorial methods to hasten this transfer of Western culture to barbaric Russia, without hesitating to use barbaric fighting methods against barbarism."

But still no revolution in Germany appeared, so that there was no option but to relax the pace once the civil war and the phase of war Communism permitted. Requisitioning from the peasant was replaced by a fixed tax, with free trade for surplus foodstuffs; a number of small and medium industrial units were denationaliz- ed. Bukharin went even further and argued that, since the world revolution had failed, then the Soviet State must pursue a policy which would retain the "alliance" with the peasantry. The with- drawal was not simply a "tactical retreat," for the whole focus of attention was taken away from the international scene, the possibi- lity of an international revolution, and turned inwards towards the defence and development of Russia. Of course, the terminology did not change, but it was a fatal shift, for the territorial interests of the Soviet Union as a nation-State now superseded the interests of the wider international class—"the fight for Soviet Russia," the Second Comintern Congress resolved, "has merged with the struggle against world capitalism. The Soviet Russian question has become the acid test for all organizations of the working class" (1921). As German Social Democracy had merged its nationalism in the language of international socialism, the same tendency now emerged in the Soviet Union.

For Lenin, the theoretical problem remained unresolved. He offered no explanation for Bolshevik power, a socialist seizure in an underdeveloped country in the absence of a European revolution. In such a forthright man, that is a significant omission—for no peace with integrity was possible. He made do with piecemeal, pragmatic responses, with attacks on "bureaucracy" and Russian "barbarism," but with increasing pessimism:

> Can every worker know how to administer the State? Practical
> people know that this is a fairy tale. . . . The trade unions are a
> school of communism and administration. When they (the
> workers) have spent these years at school, they will learn, but
> it progresses slowly. . . . How many workers have been engaged
> in administration? A few thousands all over Russia, no more.[13]

The great trade union debate of 1921-22—where Trotsky's demand for the militarization of labour (that is, for an explicitly
tyrannical regime) faced the demand of the workers' opposition
for the abolition of the State and control of the economy by
workers' Soviets—is significant as an exhibition of Lenin's purely
pragmatic tacking between extremes, in which his reasoning becomes uncharacteristically tortuous—"Ours is a workers' government with a bureaucratic twist. . . . Our present government is
such that the proletariat, organized to the last man, must protect
itself against it. And we must use workers' organization for
the protection of workers against their own government."[14]
Lenin seems to have lost his moorings, the conceptual landscape
no longer provides the relevant landmarks—he is aware of the
problem, but sees no social force available to solve it:

> If we take that huge bureaucratic machine (the State), that
> huge pile, we must ask: Who is leading whom? To tell the truth,
> it is not they (the Communists) who are leading, they are being
> led (by the ex-Tsarist civil servants). (Or again) With the excep-
> tion of the People's Commissariat for Foreign Affairs, our State
> apparatus is very largely a survival of the old one, and has least
> of all undergone serious change. It has only been slightly re-
> painted on the surface, but in all other things, it is a typical relic
> of our old State apparatus.[15]

As a whole, then, Lenin's theoretical work is incomplete, but it

---

[13] V. I. Lenin, cited in Carr, *op. cit.*, p. 247.

[14] V. I. Lenin, "The Trade Unions, The Present Situation and the
Mistakes of Comrade Trotsky", *Selected Works*, 9, London, 1937, p. 9.

[15] V. I. Lenin, "How we should reorganise the Workers' and Peasants'
Inspection", *ibid.*, p. 382.

does constitute, in the conditions he faced, something of a brief
renaissance of the spirit of Marx's work. He did not undertake a
systematic or comprehensive critique of the religion Kautsky had
distilled from Marx, but he did demonstrate in his own life a very
considerable unity of theory and practice. From 1918, the validat-
ing conditions of his own position broke down in a way that
offered no possibility of solution: the unity had been so powerful,
it could not be restored again with honesty and integrity. The
tragedy of Lenin remained unrelieved. Around him, he could see
an entirely new and unenvisaged order beginning to emerge: he
could not possibly envisage how terrible that order would be.
He had no solutions to offer. The proletariat had gone, the European revolution had not occurred, and both together left the party
alone and isolated as the substitute for both.

Stalin

An entirely different range of problems faced Joseph Stalin,
finally to emerge as Lenin's successor. It is impossible here to trace
the nature of his diverse responses to 30 years in office. This is
particularly important since some of the canons of Stalinism are
not much more than the accidental positions of an internal party
faction fight, the sources of which have long since been forgotten.
Stalinism is essentially deducible from the practice of the Soviet
State, and Stalin's exiguous theoretical output is, unlike Lenin's
work, no longer any sort of guide to understanding the practice, but is rather a rationale offered after the event to justify it.
Theoretical analysis is not a guide to practice but is an historical
commentary. For the practice was brutal, and, for those subject
to it, irrational, a matter rather for concealment, disguise, than
theoretical illumination. As a result, Stalinism has an opaque
quality. We can no longer detect its direct connexion with the
acts of the Soviet State, and we are constantly aware of a background echo of real but unspoken purposes. Discussion within
Stalinism retreats into ritual, text-quoting, semantic quibbles,
terminological disputes and clear historical distortion. Trotsky
put it polemically thus: "Its 'ideology' (Stalinism) is thoroughly
permeated with police subjectivism, its practice is the empiricism
of crude violence. In keeping with its essential interests, the caste

of usurpers is hostile to any theory; it can give an account neither to itself nor to anyone else of its social role. Stalin revises Marx and Lenin not with the theoretician's pen but with the heel of the GPU (Secret Police, *NH*)."[16]
As a system, Stalinism is idealist, rather than materialist (in the philosophical sense). It begins not with the accomplished event, not with social reality, the facts of experience, but with ideas, the text and the axiom. Conformity with Leninist ideals is not achieved by action, but by redescribing what has been done. Lenin's writings came to be treated in a manner even more extreme than that in which the German Social Democrats treated Marx. Lenin's work became a corpus of theological doctrine, a ritual, a source of endless citations out of context, not theory as a guide to particular action by a particular group of people in a particular historical situation.

The texts of Stalinism itself are heavy with mechanical images of great clumsiness, with spurts of malevolence, with theoretical vacuity married to mindless militancy. Zhdanov's attack on Soviet philosophy in 1947 characterizes some of this empty militancy:

We have often used in our discussion the term 'philosophic front'. But where is this front? . . . does our philosophy resemble a real front? It resembles rather a stagnant creek, or bivouac far from the battlefield. The field has not yet been entered for the most part, contact with the enemy has not been established, there is no reconnaissance, the weapons are rusting, the soldiers are fighting at their own risk and peril . . . . [17]

The writing of Stalin is brief and poor in quality although of central importance for the history of the Soviet Union since it dominated the entire intellectual scene. Its most interesting tendency is a groping for the characteristic forms of conservative thought, and its most striking characteristic, an immense unresolved contradiction. It has no dialectic in any important sense, but it did provide the maximum scope for any action at all that Stalin might have wished to take. Stalin stressed both:
(i) A "material base" to society, the economic functioning of

---

[16] L. D. Trotsky, *Stalinism and Bolshevism*, Glasgow, mimeo, 1937.
[17] 1947, cited in Wetter, *op. cit.*, p. 27.

society, as almost independent of men. Ideas merely "reflected" material reality (a point from early Lenin), and political consciousness merely "reflected" the state of technology—put crudely, gasometers produce poetry via men. The actual lumps of the economic base—steel plants, cranes, factories and so on—seemed to possess a life of their own and to compel society to transform itself in conformity with this life. E. P. Thompson describes the relationship thus: "Ideas are no longer seen as the medium by which men apprehend the world, reason, argue, debate, and choose; they are like the evil and wholesome smells arising from the imperialist and proletarian cooking pots."[18]

There is little or no interaction between the base and the rest of society, the "superstructure," only the base dragging the reluctant superstructure along behind: "The superstructure is created by the base precisely to serve it, to actively help it to take shape and consolidate it, to actively fight for the elimination of the old moribund base, together with its superstructure."[19]

(ii) A crucial role for theory, for "the tremendous organizing, mobilizing and transforming value of new ideas, new theories, new political views and new political institutions." The embodiment of the role of ideas was the party offering leadership to the otherwise unliberated, confused masses. Stalin's stress on the role of theory embodied his demand that the party should reach a "correct" view of the world since its role was supreme in transforming society: theory was the one weapon of the party that it could acknowledge publicly.

The party's monopoly of theory symbolized the party's monopoly of power—like most rulers, Stalin implied that power was held solely because of the popular support for the ideas the party propagated. The monopoly of theory was heightened, stressed, by the contention that mass consciousness always lags behind correct theory. For Stalin, the lag of mass consciousness reached extreme proportions, for in 1937, 20 years after the revolution, he argued the ideological errors, contracted from the hostility of the "remnants of the old exploiting classes," would get *worse* the

---

[18] E. P. Thompson, "Socialist Humanism", *New Reasoner* I, 1, summer 1957.

[19] J. D. Stalin, *Concerning Marxism in Linguistics*, Moscow, 1950, pp. 9-10.

further Russia was from the time of the revolution:

> We must destroy and cast aside the rotten theory that with every
> advance we make the class struggle here would of necessity die
> down more and more, and that in proportion as we achieve
> success, the class enemy would become more and more tractable.
> This is not only a rotten theory, but a dangerous one, for it . . .
> makes it possible for the class enemy to rally for the struggle
> against the Soviet Government. On the contrary, the farther we
> advance, the greater will be the fury of the remnants of the
> exploiting classes, the sooner will they resort to sharper forms
> of struggle.[20]

Thus, although the present superstructure (that is, the mass of
the population) is totally subordinate to the base (that is, the
party), the superstructure of the past (Tsarism) could still operate
with increasing independence, could more and more play the
scapegoat when Stalin needed scapegoats. Through it all, the
narrow-eyed suspicion of the *muzhik* lurks behind the apparent
framework of Marxism.

The central contradiction in Stalinism is then between determinism and party voluntarism: determinism for the masses,
voluntarism for the leadership. The division is a class division
between the necessarily passive majority and the active ruling class,
enjoying a monopoly of legitimate initiative.

The contradiction was of no great importance to the advocates
of Stalinism, and was effectively resolved in practice through
Stalin's monopoly (crucially backed by force) of the right to define
at any given moment what the material base was or was becoming
and therefore what correct theory was. As a theoretical system,
Stalinism needed a Pope, needed the central defining role of one
individual or group to reconcile the whole, and it was not a system
which could be conceived as standing apart from the group that
created and used it. In Stalin's person is the necessary synthesis.
He is the substitute for the party as the party is for the Russian
working class and the international proletariat, the substitute for
the wishes of the majority.

20 J. D. Stalin, Report, Plenary Session, Central Committee of the
Communist Party of the Soviet Union, translated as *Mastering Bolshevism*, London, 1937.

A number of subsidiary elements are related within this framework, only a few of which can be cited here.

(i) *The State*. If Lenin had doubts about the future of the Soviet Union, about identifying what had been achieved and therefore what was to come, Stalin had no such doubts. He asserted firmly that socialism was possible in one country—that it was possible to create and sustain a proletarian dictatorship in an underdeveloped country where the proletariat was a small minority, not the great majority as in western Europe, and possible to do so without the aid of a European revolution. The statement which began as seeking to make a virtue of necessity in the faction fight with Trotsky who maintained that socialism was impossible without a world revolution, became for Stalin a general principle applicable to all countries. Whereas the bourgeois revolution occurred only where capitalism was already fully developed (as Marx had said), the task of the new socialist order was not so much to emancipate a highly developed majority proletariat, as to develop the economy, to "build socialism." This would thereby create a majority proletariat—the agent of the revolution only created itself *after* the revolution and through a process of industrialization which had historically been notorious for its brutality, Marx's "primitive capital accumulation." As Stalin put it:

> The main task of the bourgeois revolution consists in seizing power and making it conform to the already existing bourgeois economy, whereas the main task of the proletarian revolution consists in seizing power in order to build up a new socialist economy . . . in the proletarian revolution, the seizure of power is only the *beginning*, and power is used as a lever for transforming the old economy and organizing a new one.[21]

As for many arguments, some of Lenin's tentative and very qualified statements at the end of his life can be found to support a grain of this, but Stalin's version is unqualified, and plays upon the ambiguity of the term "socialist order," "socialist economy." For on the one hand, such phrases implied a society in which the proletariat were ruling; on the other, a society where the State owned the means of production. Hitherto, in socialist writings,

[21] J. D. Stalin, *On the Problems of Leninism*, Moscow. 1926.

the two were seen by and large as one and the same, but henceforth, after the experience of Stalin, increasingly the two diverged: democracy, the rule of a majority proletariat, was not a necessary precondition for the expropriation of capital. Stalin detached the agent of the revolution, the proletariat, from the society which created a proletariat, so that there was no meaning left for the phrase "socialist order" except "an economic order owned by the State." The class content of the phrase is extinguished, and socialism becomes no longer concerned with the emancipation of the industrial working class, but a tactic for forced economic development under State control: "socialist" means "State," regardless of who runs the State in whose interest.

The statement also portrays a political "superstructure" that has the power to shape and expand the economic "base," and which is "classless." The Short Course (*History of the CPSU(B)*, 1938), said to have been largely written by Stalin himself and used for many years as the standard textbook of Stalinism, describes the collectivization of agriculture in a similar vein. It was:

... a profound revolution, a leap ... equivalent in its consequences to the revolution of October 1917. The distinguishing feature of this revolution is that it was accomplished *from above*, on the initiative of the State, and directly supported *from below* by the millions of peasants who were fighting to overthrow *kulak* bondage and to live in freedom in the collective farms.

No doubt the Ukrainian peasants would have been pleased to know how they supported a process which destroyed so many of them, and which was for them quite clearly an external oppression.

For Stalin then, in contrast to both Marx and Lenin, the State in the Soviet Union was neither the embodiment of class tyranny nor the temporary feature of a transitional phase, but a classless and creative element. Both Marx (in *The Eighteenth Brumaire*) and Engels (in *The Origin of the Family, Private Property and the State*) had suggested that the State need not always embody the rule of a dominant class, for it could act as a mediating, initiating agency, where classes were locked in balanced equilibrium. This was a point Stalinism consistently rejected, since it could have constituted grounds for saying the Soviet State was not necessarily the agency of proletarian class rule.

(ii) *Nation*. The "classless" State implied also a change in the notion of class, a concept which is possibly the most important one of all in the work of Marx and Lenin. Stalin slowly replaced the idea with that of nation, for if the "proletarian class" was identical with the Soviet State, the Soviet State embodied historically the Russian nation, so that the role of the State corresponds to the stress on nationalism, a conjuncture Lenin had bitterly criticized in German Social Democracy.

The stress on *national* (not class) solidarity, embodying the necessary harmony of Soviet society, was slowly increased to reach its maximum during the Second World War. The change was extrapolated backwards in Soviet versions of Russian history also to iron out the class cleavages of Tsarist society that had been the central concern of Lenin's work. A decree of May 1934 condemned all previous accounts of Russian history and rehabilitated words like "homeland," "patriotism" and so on. From 1940, the Russian people's role in history was increasingly glorified, its origins were traced back to the civilizations of the Chaldeans and Assyrians of the second and third millennia before Christ (in similar fashion, the families of even minor gentry in England and France "go back to" Charlemagne). To its historical ingenuity all major inventions were attributed. Inevitably, since the basic historic unit was now identified not by its role in the social structure but by its ethnic descent, racialism appeared, for only "the blood" could identify who was part of the heroic people.

As Stalin was the sole active agent in the party, and the party in the Russian people, so the Russian people became the sole active agency in the historical population of the world—a pyramid or hierarchy of values that reflected the creation of a clear hierarchy in Soviet society. The Soviet Union remained the nation "for whom history has prepared the great mission of the liberation of mankind."[22] Even the intermediate layer, non-Russian subjects of the Soviet Union, received a special intermediate stratum in the hierarchy. The Russian people were superior to all non-Russian people in the Soviet Union, and should be acknowledged as such even by foreigners: "Love for the Russian people ... is not only

[22] *Pravda*, 6 June 1949, cited in F. C. Barghoorn, *Soviet Russian Nationalism*, New York, 1956, pp. 248-249.

one of the most important aspects of Soviet patriotism; it is a characteristic feature of every genuine proletarian movement, even in capitalist countries."[23]

(iii) *Class*. The Soviet Union was a "classless society," or rather a society in which the term "class" referred only to units which were functionally complementary, peasants and workers in harmonious interaction within an obvious division of labour, not competitive units locked in rivalry (as Lenin suggested peasants and workers would be after the revolution). Ossowski[24] notes that this conception is rather Adam Smith's than Marx's, and that Stalin comes close here to the gradualism favoured in, say, the United States, rather than any revolutionary perspective—"When the future of their own society is concerned, the ruling groups in both capitalist and socialist countries always take an evolutionary attitude." Of course, "remnants of the old exploiting classes" were kept on hand to offer some explanation of any domestic conflict that occurred, useful scapegoats perpetually in league with foreign powers (as they had to be to validate "basic national unity") and periodically infiltrating the party, even at its highest levels, as shown in the Moscow Trials of the 1930s. If the "remnants" were inadequate, spies were lacking, then scapegoats could be found in ethnic minorities, Jews and so on.

The main elements of conflict, the fragments of the notion of class struggle, were reserved not for domestic but for external use. Basic national harmony stood in sharp contrast to the real cleavages that lay abroad; indigenous strain was exported to the international scene where no basic loyalties were accepted except the national. Class was liberally attributed to groups or individuals according to the attitude they were thought to have towards the Soviet Union—thus, there could be a whole series of unlikely proletarians, or, if that term was really implausible, then "patriotic" would stand instead as in "patriotic African tribal chiefs," meaning chiefs who had perhaps been enthusiastic at a Russian Embassy cocktail party.

Ultimately, the struggle was said to be between "proletarian nations" and "bourgeois nations," a formulation also favoured

---

[23] *Problems of Philosophy*, 1948, cited in Wetter, *op. cit.*, p. 271.

[24] S. Ossowski, *Class Structure in the Social Consciousness*, London, 1963, p. 115.

by, for example, Rightwing nationalists in Italy after the First World War, operating in a context where Marxist terminology was important. The internationalism of Marx and Lenin dissolved into nationalism, the character of which was unimportant provided it included a favourable attitude towards the Soviet Union, for the "proletarian nations" were not proletarian at all. The phrase signified nothing about their domestic class structures. They were distinguished usually by their poverty and the overwhelmingly peasant character of their societies. And "bourgeois nations" were merely anti-Soviet rich industrialized countries. Of course, in fact, the first were usually involved in a nationalistic revulsion against imperialism, and the second were, to a greater or less degree, imperialist powers, but this factor should not conceal how little Stalin was seriously interested in the real social structure of the countries concerned. His interests were in international relations, between sovereign nation-States, not in international class struggle where national boundaries were of little significance. The most appropriate weapons for Stalin were primarily diplomatic, or professional warfare, for which agitation, cast in the language of class struggle, was occasionally an appropriate adjunct—much as it was for the Tsarist *agents provocateurs* or is for the American Central Intelligence Agency. Again, the loophole can be seen in some of Lenin's later formulations, heavily qualified and tentative in context, but no less a major shift. From a Russian revolution snapping the "weakest link in the capitalist chain," so precipitating a European revolution, focus shifted to China or India as the "weakest links in the imperialist chain." The end of the evolution arrived when the Comintern became not the leader of an international working class movement, of which the Soviet Union was merely one part, but a subsidiary agency of Russian foreign policy, of which the international working class movement was merely one small part. Foreign Communist parties became the rearguard of the Soviet Union, not the vanguard of world revolution, agencies, at least in their leadership, for the subversion of their local *status quo* in the interests of a foreign State rather than in the interests of the proletariat. The transition cost the lives of most of the old Bolsheviks, not "flexible" or "pragmatic" enough to convert themselves into all they had opposed for so long.

Occasionally, the transition did pose problems for Stalin; consider the following nimble hair-splitting: bourgeois nationalism is rightly condemned by Marxists since it has

> ... the object of doping the masses with the poison of nationa-
> lism and strengthening the role of the bourgeoisie. What is
> national culture under the dictatorship of the proletariat? It
> is culture that is *socialist* in content and national in form, hav-
> ing the object of educating the masses in the spirit of socialism
> and internationalism. It would be foolish to suppose that Lenin
> regarded socialist culture as *non-national*, as not having a parti-
> cular national form .... The period of the dictatorship of the
> proletariat and of the building of socialism in the U. S. S. R.
> is a period of the *flowering* of national cultures that are socialist
> in content and national in form. (Stalin goes on) It may be said
> that such a presentation of the question is contradictory, but
> is there not the same contradictoriness in our presentation of
> the question of the State? We stand for the withering away of
> the State. At the same time, we stand for the strengthening of
> the dictatorship of the proletariat, which is the mightiest
> and strongest State power that has ever existed .... Is this con-
> tradictory? Yes, it is contradictory. But this contradiction is
> bound up with life, and it fully reflects Marx's dialectic ....[25]

The General Secretary could rest assured that none in his audience
was brave enough to shout "Gibberish!" no child innocent enough
to say the emperor was naked.

After the great traumatic experiences of collectivization, industrialization and World War, after the immense sacrifices
demanded of the Soviet people were no longer needed, Stalinism
mellowed, permitting the more orthodox conservative tone of
tranquillity to emerge from the earlier harsh ritual. Stalin tied
together some of the ends of his practice in his two last works,
Concerning Marxism in Linguistics and *Economic Problems of
Socialism in the U. S. S. R.* The first, ostensibly designed to
answer certain problems in the narrow field of linguistics, in fact
goes much further by stressing the common elements of a nation
(pre-eminently its language) rather than its class elements which,
in Marxist terms, underpin internationalism. The second lays
down the economic conditions for the prelude to Communism;

[25] J. D. Stalin, speech, XVI Congress of the Communist Party of the
Soviet Union 1930, *Collected Works*, 12, Moscow, pp. 278-281.

its tone is cautious, conservative, and suggests almost indefinite postponement of what has clearly become a "utopian" aim.

What Stalin left of the terminology of Marxism was relatively useless for any specific purposes his successors might have, but this did not inhibit them in any way, any more than Stalin was inhibited by the pronouncements of his predecessors. Stalin's practice was not a series of pragmatic adjustments to new circumstances, the "logic of power" much favoured by conservative commentators, but rather the pursuit of purposes quite incompatible with those of Marx and Lenin—against their class internationalism he posed Russian nationalism. One cannot use "pragmatically" a general theory directed at destroying a certain kind of society for the purposes of *Blitzkrieg* economic development, any more than one can use an explosives manual for building a factory. Naturally, the terminology of freedom continued, but now to conceal a tyrannical reality, not to raise men's sights to the immense possibilities open to them. The terminology was decoration, not guide to practice, the sophistical arguments designed to make slaves not merely accept their slavery but kiss their chains as the symbol of their freedom. The regime never felt confident enough to dispense with police and army, any more than do Western regimes. The reality was such that the terminology, although it concealed much, also became a debased coin, the butt of cynics. "After 1929," Joravsky argues:

> ... the ideology actually at work in the minds of the chiefs is to be found much more in their intuitive judgments of practical matters than in the largely irrelevant texts of theoretical ideology .... Much of what passes for theoretical ideology in the Soviet Union is a traditional survival. It performs the same functions as Corinthian columns on modern public buildings, or the invocation of Jesus' name at the launching of a nuclear submarine.[26]

Thus, it would be a mistake to see Stalin's successors as having made difficult and daring ideological innovations since his death. What has happened is that they have permitted certain formulations to lapse (Stalin himself let some points of doctrine lapse in the later years of his life). Stalinism did retain some elements of

[26] D. Joravsky, "Soviet Ideology", *Soviet Studies*, Oxford, 1966.

radicalism. They were not of the Leninist variety—concerned with the emancipation of the industrial working class—but rather the radicalism required to industrialize a backward society, to explain and justify the ruthlessness of the process and the sacrifices required of the mass of the population. When that process was nearing completion, the Second World War and the following Cold War, kept alive certain elements of militancy.

But the logic of modern industrial society inevitably made itself felt in the organization of the Soviet Union once these three factors declined in importance. Indeed, the decline of the Cold War is part cause and part effect of that logic, in conjunction with the purposes of United States foreign policy. Stalin's death was rather the pretext for, than the cause of, the domestic relaxation in Russia. Narrowed wage differentials, raising the lowest pay rates, shifting slightly the industrial structure from heavy to light industry, from industry to services, placing a much greater stress on the consumption patterns appropriate to "affluence," these were all part of that logic of modern industrial society, and not held back by either curious ideological beliefs or the petulance of a bad-tempered old man.

The changes in modern Soviet leadership beliefs are, then, no more than a mellowing of the conservative features implicit in Stalinism. Soviet ideology is not a powerful and irrational constraint on the actions of the Soviet leadership. Ideology does not clash with the "facts," "reality." The adjustments—for example, polycentrism in foreign policy, the Libermann plan to charge interest on capital employed—were not belated recognitions of "reality," except if one believes that a conservative perspective is "reality."

What inhibits doctrinal innovation in the Soviet Union, as in the West, is not some preceding doctrinal position, but other people, people who feel rightly or wrongly that they stand to lose by the innovation or gain by opposing it, since in their estimation the innovation summarizes some changed state of affairs, some new purpose or intention. The conflict is between people, not ideas or ideas and "facts." Stalin's successors have had no need to make substantial changes in an on-going process—despite Khrushchev's Twentieth Congress speech in 1956, where Stalin was used as a convenient scapegoat for the errors of the past, errors in which the current Soviet leadership might also be implicated. This is so because they shared a basic tenet of Stalinist ideology, namely that the existing distribution of power in Russia should remain as it was. Existing ideology meets no great obstacles. The ideology, judged from a Western conservative position, merely seems to fade or is trivialized, since it no longer reasonably mediates between the purposes of the leaders and the desires of the led.

When the old soldiers of Stalinist ideology have faded away, then the "liberalization" of the Soviet Union can be seen for what it was. The adjustments were part of the attempted change of Soviet society, part of a transfer of increasing power from the old party to a new managerial *elite*, the new party.

This chapter has been burdened with relatively boring detail and a narrow focus of attention, but it has been necessary to pursue the limited themes properly. The aim has been to show the transformation of a group of radical beliefs into their opposite, how this was achieved in doctrinal terms, and the implications involved. Lenin has been described as an heir to Marx in a way German Social Democracy was not. He broke out of the constricting conservatism-in-practice of Social Democracy, rejected its failure to match behaviour and theory, and sought to restore the idea of the active agency of the industrial working class in the phase of history in which he lived. He defended the aim of freedom as the essence of Marxism against the bureaucratic, *etatiste*, and nationalist revisions implicit in German Social Democracy. Ironically, it was just this revision which Stalin revived in the new alliance of the Russian State and Russian nationalism.

The next section pursues the theme of Marxism, now transferred to a properly underdeveloped country under foreign domination (Russia was underdeveloped relative only to the European context). The legacy of Stalinism was important here, but again, new purposes created doctrines which are not strictly Stalinist.

II. Marxism in Asia

> Bismarck's "State socialism" was "the rennaissance of the Mercantilism of the seventeenth century, adapted to the benevolent and illuminated despotism of the eighteenth century and the conditions of a militarist State, remoulded by the phenomena of modern industrialism."
>
> C. G. ROBERTSON, cited in Issawi, *Egypt in Revolution, an Economic Analysis.*

The south, the "underdeveloped" (or "developing" or "backward," the alternative usages, like those for the poor, are numerous enough to illustrate people's embarrassment), includes the majority of the world's population and a far wider cultural diversity than exists among the developed. Many are neither in the south proper, nor "underdeveloped" to anything like the same degree. As a result, what can be said in general is bound to be superficial or false for at least some of the countries concerned. This account deals in the main with modern China, and touches briefly on a few other countries in Asia. Initially, the account examines what happened to Marxism when it arrived in China, and then what happened to it in the hands of Mao Tse-tung. This provides a means to illustrate some of the important features of underdevelopment and thereby the impact of underdevelopment on some important—hitherto—Western assumptions, Marxist or not. The ambiguity of purpose in some movements in underdeveloped countries permitted those movements to participate in groups of political ideas that in their original context would seem inimical to the immediate aims of those movements. Elements of orthodoxies remained intact, despite the transformed content. Yet events also changed the operative significance of well-known beliefs so far that they no longer seemed to be the same beliefs at all. The adjustment of meaning—typified in the transition from Marxism to "Chinese Marxism"—illustrates how far beliefs formulated in one context can be utilized in an entirely different one, how far contradictory purposes can lie behind similar terminology.

Marxism's Journey East

It would be wrong to see some of the characteristic forms of Stalinism as solely the creation of Stalin or the peculiar conditions existing in Russia in the 1930s, just as it would be wrong to pin the word "Stalinist" over all beliefs that seemed similar in some way to Stalinist doctrines. Because Stalinism was an authentic response to problems of development, a response by a ruthless development *elite* meeting an obdurate environment, one would expect to find similar ideas in countries which claimed to participate in the Marxist tradition and were underdeveloped, sometimes formulated before it was possible for the formulator to have contact with Stalinism, or, indeed, before Stalinism existed. The underdeveloped countries do not by definition, have the class

structure Marx described as appropriate to industrialized countries, so one would expect "class" to be a difficult issue. On the
other hand, the oppression of foreign imperial powers would
be a prime datum for all radicals in backward countries, and
that oppression could easily be seen in racial terms, given the
racial predilections of some of the imperial powers. Thus, the
substitution of "nation" for "class" is implicit (if not by any
means inevitable) in the situation, and perhaps of "race" for
"nation," without the influence of Stalin at all. One might reasonably expect that the social content of Marxist categories would be
blurred, the political implications stressed—anti-imperialism becomes very much more significant than anti-capitalism; proletarian movements become much less important than "popular"
movements, where the constituent elements of the "people"
remain unclear.

But there are deeper implications than this, for the underdeveloped countries are largely peasant, so that any significant
popular movement must include or have significant appeal for a
large number of peasants. Now Marxists identified the industrial
proletariat as the sole agency for achieving socialism. This is not
to say that Marxists did not incorporate peasant revolt in their
strategy for proletarian revolution. For example, Marx in *The
Eighteenth Brumaire* (1852 edition) estimated that a possible revolt
by the French peasantry against Louis Napoleon might precipitate
a proletarian uprising. But he also judged that peasant revolt
would ultimately have to be led by urban forces, by industrial
workers also in revolt. In societies where the peasants constituted
a majority of the population, a proletarian revolt could not succeed
without a simultaneous uprising of the peasants, so that Marxist
strategy in such countries must ensure a synchronized movement,
or both would fail separately. But the peasant revolt, of its nature,
could not be a substitute for the proletarian revolution, and could
not alone secure socialism as it was understood by Marxists.

Lenin, acting in a country, the majority of the population of
which was peasant, inferred from the Tsarist land distribution
that the Russian peasantry would be revolutionary in order to
secure land. Once secured, they would however become conservative in defence of their new land holdings and turn against the proletariat. However, at no stage did he conceive of the peasantry
as acting on a socially significant scale except under the "leader-

ship" of the urban proletariat, and even that was not for a "socialist revolution." One might reasonably infer that in countries where the urban proletariat was, proportionate to the peasantry, even smaller than in Russia, and where the Marxist tradition was relatively weak, radicals calling themselves Marxists might seek to use the peasantry as a substitute revolutionary force, making themselves—outside intellectuals—the crucial coordinating link between the otherwise isolated revolts in particular peasant localities.

The implication of this change is crucial for Marxism because it means that, even theoretically, "self-emancipation" is impossible —the intellectuals emancipate the peasantry, for the peasants cannot emancipate themselves. To summarize, then, one would expect a "regression" from Marxism to populism, even if this populism was expressed in Marxist terminology, a return to some of the themes Lenin and Plekhanov attacked when advanced by their Narodnik predecessors. It is of interest in this respect to note a recent comment on Li Ta-chao, one of the two main founders of the Chinese Communist Party: "In Li Ta-chao's conception of the peasant revolution there was that characteristically populist contradiction between a passionate faith in the spontaneous energies of the people and a conviction that the revolutionary intellectual must bring enlightenment and leadership to the mass movement."[27]

What would this "regression" entail? A belief that the intelligentsia plus peasants could produce a revolution; that that revolution could create socialism; that "nationalism" completely encompassed socialism; that the "people" encompassed the proletariat, and that the local national struggle was the key to the progress of mankind; that the country concerned could industrialize without undergoing capitalism; that socialism was a peasant way of life rather than an emancipated developed society. Li Ta-chao advanced many notions which, in the last section were identified as Stalinist, but long before Stalinism existed, many ideas which had occurred in Russia in Narodnik writings and which subsequently became identified with the name of Mao Tse-tung.

[27]Maurice Meisner, *Li Ta-chao and the Origins of Chinese Marxism*, Cambridge, Mass., 1967, p. 251.

Li tended to see the main revolutionary element as students and intellectuals, and urged them to go to the villages to enlighten the peasants, to strip back the corruption and reveal the inner goodness which would recreate a great China (apart from parallels with Narodnik thought, one can see traces of the same ideas in the work of such diverse thinkers as Rousseau, Gandhi and even Che Guevara). Li accepted the need for struggle but did not identify very clearly *class* struggle, and for him "struggle" was not something generated necessarily by the class structure, but was rather a campaign to change hearts and minds, to raise moral consciousness. Above all, he was a nationalist—Meisner says that it was ironic that "the first Chinese supporter of this profoundly internationalistic creed (Marxism) was a young intellectual who, even within a highly nationalistic milieu, was noted for his frankly nationalistic and even chauvinistic inclinations."[28] The identification of class struggle and national struggle against foreign domination produced, in 1920, the conception of China as the "proletarian nation" (a phrase noted in the last section in Stalinism and Italian nationalism in 1920), so that the national view became, by definition, a proletarian view, and national independence the signal for the emancipation of mankind.

No longer was the struggle to break the weakest link in the imperialist chain, so precipitating a revolution in the advanced countries (without which socialism was impossible). Socialism could be won in China by the Chinese themselves. Meisner[29] and Brandt[30] mention in this connexion also Tai Chi-t'ao, a prominent Kuomintang ideologist on the Right, who identified the class struggle as a struggle between nations, although he used this idea to deny the possibility of class struggle *within* China. Rather inconsistently, Li always excluded from the "nation" the largest landowners and those Chinese who acted as intermediaries for foreign capital.

Ethnic identification tends to follow intense national identification. Domestic ethnic diversity is conveniently forgotten in order to suggest a basic biological unity to the nation, to point up the contrast to the single enemy, the foreigner. In 1924, we find Li

[28] *Ibid*, p. 177.
[29] *Ibid*, p. 145.
[30] Conrad Brandt, *Stalin's Failure in China, 1924-1927*, Cambridge, Mass., 1958, p. 57.

arguing that "the race question has become the class question and the races, on a world scale, have come to confront each other as classes."[31]

Li's general views cannot be said to have been copied from Lenin's work, for Li seems, on Meisner's account, to have been imperfectly acquainted with this work. His Marxism came reasonably directly from some of the work of Marx and Engels. Ironically, although Li seems to have been a kindly and courteous man, the flavour of some of his work seems closest to Fascism, even if the social content of what he had to say was sharply different. Even though Li's intellectual evolution was not inevitable (Ch'en Tu-hsiu, the other main founder of the Chinese Communist Party, remained an internationalist and committed to the industrial proletariat), one can understand how that evolution came about, and see how effective the same ideas were in the hands of Mao Tse-tung.

The Marxism of Mao Tse-tung

Stalinism, it was suggested in the last section, recreated the dogmatisms which excluded popular revolutionary action and which Lenin had been so concerned to criticize in German Social Democracy. It has been necessary for *any* revolutionary movement to revise Stalinism and make some break with the Soviet leadership or operate independently in order to achieve a revolution. The Soviet perspective of stability, stable Cold War frontiers and peaceful co-existence between East and West, has meant in the post-war world that any revolutionary movement has had to act *in spite of* the Soviet Union, whether the movement was led by Tito, Mao or Castro. At best, a tacit agreement operated whereby the Soviet Union was formally accepted as leader but its suggestions largely ignored, as in China. In Cuba, the Communist Party only became a supporter of Fidel Castro when his victory seemed certain.

Thus, there has developed again almost a division of labour. Before 1914, it was suggested, that division separated ostensibly revolutionary theory in the hands of the Social Democrat leaders and revolutionary practice by the anarcho-syndicalists.

---

[31] Meisner, *op. cit.*, p. 191.

In the post-1945 world, revolutionary theory is supposed to find its home in Moscow, and practice, with scarcely any coherent and guiding general theoretical framework, in the "Third World." Of course, in fact, Moscow's revolutionary theory was revolutionary only in rhetoric. In reality, the Soviet Union relied on orthodox political relationships, aid and trade, to achieve its foreign policy ends. On the other hand, the restoration of "activism" in the underdeveloped countries had theoretical implications, although the more important of these were not specified—for example, what kind of revolution had been or was to be achieved, what the class content of such revolutions was, and so on.

The contribution of Mao Tse-tung to formal Marxist theory was relatively small and, by earlier standards, rather primitive; at most the loosening of a few themes, the omission of some major Stalinist points. However, Mao's practice does show substantial divergences from what Stalin suggested as appropriate for a revolutionary. The loose combination of agrarian populism and radical nationalism which constitutes Maoism in practice has its closest parallels not with ideology in the Soviet Union so much as with those doctrines advanced by non-Communist leaders in other underdeveloped countries.

Unlike the Soviet Union, China had neither a proletarian nor a Liberal heritage to overcome. Consistent with the absence of the class structure postulated in Marx's writings, and with the role of the intelligentsia, free from loyalty to a particular class which is tied necessarily to a particular role in the social structure, Maoism is essentially "voluntarist": that is, the aims of the leadership are seen as feasible provided they work hard, rather than provided the objective situation permits. The role of theory is thus changed from that suggested in Marx; for Mao, theory is a somewhat eclectically selected element in public relations work, in the propaganda necessary to change consciousness, rather than itself a more or less accurate analysis of reality to guide practice. Of course the role changed: it was not always—as it became after 1948—a doctrine with mystical-magical qualities, formulae to be manipulated by the leadership to achieve miraculous results (the *Thoughts of Mao Tse-tung*). In Mao's 1942 speech, *Reform in Learning, the Party, and Literature*,[32] he specifically warns his audience against

[32] Cited by Stuart Schram, *The Political Thought of Mao Tse-tung* London, 1963, p. 120.

the danger of seeing theory as magic—"It seems that right up to the present quite a few have regarded Marxism-Leninism as a ready-made panacea; once you have it, you can cure all your ills with little effort"; Schram notes that in the latest edition of this speech, the text has been changed so that it is only "isolated formulae drawn from Marxist-Leninist literature" which are dangerous, the implication being that Marxism-Leninism as a whole *is* a "ready-made panacea." Certainly, the sensible aphorisms of the "little Red Book" were not seen as anything but charms to ward off disaster or conjure success.

Mao renounced Stalin's heavy stress on historical necessity and the autonomous economic base, leaving alone and unhampered the complete voluntarism of the "people," the party and its leadership: activism in the nation has eliminated the need for theory at all. The "freedom" is freedom from association with any particular class, freedom for the leadership to do as it wishes. For Mao, unlike Stalin, retains no residual identification with the industrial working class. After the Kuomintang's shattering blow to the Chinese Communist Party (CCP) in 1927, "proletariat" in Communist writings came to mean little more than the party itself. The CCP scarcely involved urban classes at all after 1927, and the actual proletarian membership was less than one per cent in Mao's period of leadership before 1948. The cities in general became the rearguard of the revolution, not its vanguard.

More than this, for the actual vanguard was largely a *military* force, not a class embedded in the on-going social structure, and an army composed of heterogeneous elements—the remnants of the 1927 party (leaving their work-places for exile with the party), dispossessed peasants and labourers, professional soldiers, mutinous units of the Kuomintang or warlord armies, even bandits[33]— all moulded into an effective fighting force by members of the intelligentsia. The role of the army, separated from its disparate class origins over the long period in which it was not in power, constituted a separate force rather than the representative of a class, proletarian or peasant. So much was this so that Schwartz has argued that "the experience of Chinese Communism . . . casts a doubt on the whole organic conception of the relation of party to

---

[33] See Appendix, R. Harold Isaacs, *The Tragedy of the Chinese Revolution*, Stanford, 1961 (2nd revised edition).

class," [34] for it became clear that the voluntarist intelligentsia could in the conditions of inter-war chaos impose its will upon its followers, reshaping or even creating what the leadership called "proletarian class attitudes" regardless of what actual "class attitudes" existed. This approach was possible precisely because consciousness was the key element, moral attitudes, rather than the objective situation, the attitudes men imbibed from the particular role they played in the social structure. Thus, where "non-proletarian" attitudes persisted, phrased more accurately as opposition to the leadership, the cure lay less in changing the sociological composition of the army, more in intensified education and exhortation; for deserters from the other side, "The Red Army is like a furnace in which all captured soldiers are melted down and transformed the moment they come over"[35] (the phrase "melted down and transformed" in the 1954 New York edition of Mao's *Selected Works* is translated as "transmuted" in the Pekin edition.)

Nor did the actual experience of the party lead it to locate itself more securely in the class structure. The party had to adjust itself to a multitude of different administrative circumstances, not to one dominant social conflict. The productive and cultural level of the areas commanded by this kind of new warlord force permitted little radical transformation of the social structure—the party had to tack continuously between different social groups, including landlords, rich peasants and merchants, and had to do so in order to survive, for the primitiveness of the areas allowed little scope for anything except reliance on the existing *status quo*.

The resulting picture of the party before the Second World War is, then, of a fluctuating political force, rather detached from the Chinese social structure, ruling in the areas where it operated rather than expressing the aspirations of the ruled. Its power lay not in how far it embodied popular feeling in its own areas, but in its command of military force, and thus its political behaviour was not so central to its general position—policy could and did vary very widely, depending on local circumstances, and encompassing at different times the spectrum from radical land confiscation to the mildest amelioration of conditions. Since the army was

---

[34] B. I. Schwartz, *Chinese Communism and the Rise of Mao*, Cambridge Mass., 1958, p. 191.

[35] Mao Tse-tung, *Selected Works*, I, New York edition, 1954, p. 83.

the vanguard it became the essence of the revolution, and the dominant ideal after it, the substitute for a proletariat proper. This is very far from earlier conceptions of the class struggle—indeed, it cannot plausibly be seen as "*class* struggle" at all. It was struggle between different territorial political entities rather than struggle arising necessarily out of the nature of the social structure, a struggle which was military, not social.

Wherever possible, the party sought to bind the peasantry to itself by appropriate agrarian reform proposals directed at the larger landowners. Since the Kuomintang was reasonably consistently devoted to the interests of, among others, the landowners, political differentiation remained reasonably clear. But land reform for the party remained less its *raison d'etre* as a peasant party, more a useful means to win support as an outside body. If land reform lost important support, the party could temper its programme to the central aim.

The proletariat proper had little part to play except in an agitational role as a minor adjunct to the main military effort (the analogy in the relationship between Moscow and foreign Communist parties will be clear). Indeed, in the actual process of revolution, the proletariat always remained a potential danger, liable to diverge from the aims of the party and impede the military impetus, requiring constant discipline and supervision once the party had achieved power. It is interesting to note that, although Communists proper would not be so cavalier with their claimed traditions as to say that the proletariat was something of a nuisance in achieving revolution, others—less traditional—might. Che Guevara, for example, did see the proletariat as an inhibiting factor, and argued that "It is more difficult to prepare guerrilla bands in those countries that have undergone a concentration of population in great centres and have a more developed light and medium industry, even though not anything like effective industrialization. The ideological influence of the cities inhibits guerrilla struggle."[36]

In China, the controls were carefully spelt out. Workers were ordered not to take over their own factories as the revolution progressed, but to support their managers and await the party's consolidation of power. Factory committees of workers—created to represent the work-force—were always rendered subordinate

[36] Ernesto Guevara, "Cuba: Exceptional Case?", *Monthly Review*, New York, July-August 1961, pp. 65-66.

to the head of the factory. After the revolution, the new State trade unions were designed not as defensive representative organizations but as essentially disciplinary and propaganda agencies of management; the trade unions exist "to strengthen the unity of the working class, to consolidate the alliance of workers and peasants, to educate workers to observe consciously the laws and decrees of the State, and labour discipline, to strive for the development of production, for the constant increase in labour productivity, for the fulfilment and overfulfilment of the production plans of the State."[37] Special tribunals ensured that stringent sanctions were imposed on those who might diverge from the letter of the law in being negligent in behaviour or with materials or tools.

The implications of abandoning the conception of the proletariat in practice are decisive for Marxism. In abandoning the conflict within a particular social structure, a Communist Party abandons the only (Marxist) theoretical justification for its existence and embraces the elitism of the Narodniks. In addition, internationalism is jettisoned for nationalism. For Mao, as for Li Ta-chao, the first enemy was a foreign occupier, and he argued from the common interest of the Chinese nation against that foreigner, not from the common interest of the Chinese working class and foreign working classes against their own and each others' ruling classes. The nation becomes the most important operating concept in pursuit of a *national* revolution (class nature unspecified), and class merely a derogatory or commendatory term to apply to one's friends or enemies. Like Stalin's hair-splitting with form and content, Mao argues:

> A Communist is a Marxist internationalist but Marxism must take on a national form before it can be applied. There is no such thing as abstract Marxism but only concrete Marxism. What we call Marxism is Marxism that has taken on a national form, that is, Marxism applied to the concrete struggle in the concrete conditions prevailing in China.[38]

[37] "Constitution of the Trade Unions of the People's Republic of China", in *Labour Laws and Regulations of the People's Republic of China*, Peking, 1956, p. 17.

[38] Mao Tse-tung, *Report*, 6th Plenum, 6th Central Committee, Chinese Communist Party, October 1938. A version of this appears in *Selected Works*, 2, p. 209 (Peking edition).

Effective class internationalism does not arise out of the organization of international capitalism, but is relegated to the realm of sympathy, without any operational value in a peasant and non-capitalist China. Each ruling class is the problem solely of its own ruled; the historical accident of the borders of each nation-state provides the perimeters of operational consciousness.

Of course, in a national struggle, there is no crucial class to be emancipated. The prime tasks of the revolution become "classless": anti-imperialism abroad and industrialization at home, the two aims being, in a nationalist framework, distinguished in no crucial respect from those of any other nationalist movement in an underdeveloped country. As in Stalinism, "proletarian" refers to friends at home, so abroad it tends to identify whatever force opposes imperialism, and, in the nature of the case, those forces exist primarily in imperial or ex-imperial territories, in the underdeveloped countries. As a result, Mao has no role to offer to the people of the developed countries. They can merely support the "Third World." The scheme is a direct repetition of the lack of role for urban people in China during the revolution, and indeed the analogy has been explicitly made by Mao himself. Much earlier, the 1928 Comintern Programme included the observation that "Colonies and semi-colonies... represent the *world rural district* in relationship to the industrial countries, which represent the *world city*."

If the tasks are "classless" because the agency for the revolution is "classless," then any social forces willing to accept CCP leadership are equally relevant. Mao revived the strategy of a "Four Class Bloc," originally formulated by Stalin as the national coalition of forces required to achieve a *bourgeois* revolution in China (the agent of that revolution to be the bourgeois nationalist force, the Kuomintang, supported by the CCP). This had had disastrous results in 1926-27 when the Kuomintang nearly destroyed its ally, the CCP, but the strategy was appropriate for Mao's own perspective, provided the CCP rather than the Kuomintang could lead the coalition and it would achieve a "non-bourgeois national" revolution. More than this, Mao sought also to recreate the alliance with the Kuomintang itself before the Comintern made the pursuit of a united front mandatory on all its member organizations, again despite the terrible massacre of Communists in 1927. Mao showed no compunction about pursu-

ing this aim, and, indeed, went out of his way to flatter the Kuomintang and Chiang Kai-shek personally as one of the two "national forces."[39]

Capitalism as a social system was not the primary target. Mao's
1945 *On Coalition Government* proposed that the "task of our New
Democratic system is... to promote the free development of a
private capitalist economy that benefits instead of controlling the
people's livelihood, and to protect all honestly acquired private
property."[40] In the 1949 Constitution of the "People's Democratic
Dictatorship" (class content unspecified), the "national bourgeoisie" is part of the "people," but the "bureaucratic capitalists"
are not, since they are in league with imperialism. The means to
identify the "bureaucratic capitalists" are not, however, their role
in the structure of the economy or society, but merely whether or
not they support the CCP. In practice, the "national bourgeoisie"
came to include many of the very largest capitalists (fully as
much in league with imperialists when it suited their purpose),
including the "four families" of the Kuomintang period. Nor was
the subsequent gradual infringement of the prerogatives of private
industry pursued as a central political commitment, sustained by
the anti-capitalist feeling of a genuine proletariat, but rather was it
a subordinate element in the State's planning activities, much as
the extension of the public sector has been in other non-Communist underdeveloped countries. The CCP did not oppose the profit
motive *per se*, but rather opposed the State's deprivation of funds
for capital accumulation.

Mao's thought, then, places almost sole effective stress on
common national elements, rejecting the idea of a necessarily
divisive class system within China: China is effectively a "proletarian nation." Of course, the emphasis changes before and after
the revolution, and also, after the revolution in relationship to
different kinds of crisis, but by and large, the residue of class
terminology still utilized is a function of nationalist aims, describing those who are non-Chinese or linked to foreigners as
opposed to "true Chinese" people, a particular ethnic stock with a
particular attitude to the CCP. By implication, like Stalinism,
Maoism inherits, uses and identifies with a common national

---

[39] *Ibid.*

[40] Mao Tse-tung, "On Coalition Government", 24 April 1945, *Selected
Works*, 3, New York, 1954, p. 255.

heritage, with the pre-1911 achievements of the Emperors. It is implied that a common national culture links past and present and is more significant than temporary divisions. The marriage of this cultural tradition and the "alien" Marxism comes in the claim that Mao has created a "Sinification of Marxism," a Chinese or Asiatic Marxism. Of course, defining what constitutes true "Chinese culture" or Sinification is the prerogative of the party, and at different times different elements become appropriate according to short-term political requirements.

It is the nationalist emphasis which prompts the CCP to generalize its experience as the *only* model for future revolutions (and since the basic preconditions for this experience are lacking in developed countries, they cannot have a revolution) and as a profound "discovery," as if revolution were a matter of technique. "The tactics we have derived from the struggle in the past three years," Mao argued in 1930, "are indeed different from any other tactics, ancient or modern, Chinese or foreign."[41] Li Li-san, much more firmly, asserted in 1949 that "The working class definitely cannot fundamentally better its status and livelihood, not to speak of winning the revolutionary victory like that of today, without building a revolutionary army under its own leadership and waging a revolutionary war against the rule of imperialism and its lackeys, with the support of the broad masses of the people."[42]

It is unlikely that the CCP's conception of guerrilla warfare was so new, since guerrilla warfare is not uncommon, ranging from pure banditry to peasant revolt or terrorist campaigns for political ends. In any case, to put the stress on technique alone prevents one examining the CCP victory in a realistic light, seeing the accidents and good luck which contributed substantially to that victory and without which no amount of technique would have proved successful. The claim is the product of nationalist egoism, and is repeated wherever unorthodox conditions have, against prior predictions, produced success. The Viet Namese guerrillas today make similar claims (and firmly repudiate the idea that they are merely copying the Chinese, as if copying would work for guerrilla warfare which depends so crucially on unique conjunc-

---

[41] Mao Tse-tung, "Re-examination of Land Distribution in the Soviet Districts is the Central Task", *Red Flag*, 31 August 1933.

[42] Li Li-san, "Trade Union Work and Movement in China", *China Digest*, Peking, 1949.

tures of events), and the correspondence between the Yugoslav and Soviet Central Committees in 1948 shows the Russians ridiculing the Yugoslav claim to have invented the peculiar form of partisan warfare which, Belgrade claimed, had made a major contribution to the 1945 Allied victory in Europe. Of course, in China, the demand for national revolutionary autonomy embodied in the claim to have created a "Chinese Marxism" (as opposed to Moscow's presumably "Russian Marxism") tends to conflict with the claim that other countries have to follow China's pattern of revolution; the difference is between a party, out of power, seeking to establish its independence from Russian hegemony, and the party in power, commanding a position equal to the Russian and loyalty from other less succcessful Communist parties.

However, even if classes proper do not exist for the CCP in China (although Stalin's "remnants of the old exploiting classes" are kept in the wings for use in particular campaigns, as in the early phases of the current Cultural Revolution), disagreements do arise. The means to overcome disagreements, or rather to subordinate objections to the leadership, lie in party propaganda and education. In practice, the party can also adjust its own position: it is susceptible to a large range of social pressures. No domestic divisions (as opposed to divisions linked directly to imperialism) cannot be overcome provided the will is there, for society has no structure necessarily engendering certain sorts of conflicts. Conflicts depend on the *moral* nature of the opponent of the party, and that nature is as it is because the party has not educated (or indoctrinated) it. In principle, it is not a specific material reality which shapes certain forms of consciousness, but rather moral illiteracy, ignorance, and, in more traditional religious terms, backsliding.

In a country as disastrously poor as China, material reality cannot be changed in the short term, so that changing consciousness might seem a short-cut to security, for doctrine can be changed by the leadership. Fidel Castro, being less snared than the CCP in the orthodoxies of "Marxism-Leninism," has expressed this viewpoint more boldly in claiming that there is no ideology in a revolutionary struggle, only a road to power which "acquires" different ideological beliefs on that road (choosing them and abandoning them according to the immediate needs of the struggle for power). Theory has no role at all. Che Guevara acknowledged this when he described the Cuban revolutionary leaders as "only a group of fighters with high ideals and little preparation."[43] The concern should be to find the road to power, not to pursue the right political aims (for which power is to be used) or to locate those aims in an appropriate analysis of the situation. The assurance of success lies not in appraising the objective situation but in the group's spirit, morale, will, drive. The echoes of Sorel and pre-World War I anarcho-syndicalist activism without theory are here very strong.

In the Marxist position proper, by contrast, the analysis of objective conditions should indicate how the struggle should be undertaken. "Armed struggle" is only one of many possible means, not the "highest" or "real" one. Indeed, it was implied that the use of open or military (formal or guerrilla) force was likely to be only the very last stage when most of the issues had already been settled, not the first. Continuous guerrilla warfare means that military tactics replace revolutionary theory, that professional soldiers in battle replace a class struggle rooted in a real social structure, and that power is inevitably concentrated in the hands of generals, with mass consciousness being merely a subsidiary factor in morale rather than the dynamic of the whole. Soldiers need to obey orders, not appraise their daily experience in work relationships. It is necessary to stress the magic of guerrilla warfare where a popular mass movement does not exist, since the minority only can undertake action of this kind. With even smaller support, some Narodniks were reduced to individual terrorism for the same reasons. The emphasis does not explain the large number of failures—why the CCP took such an enormously long time to win power; why the Malayan, Philippine and Burma Communists failed to win; why the Telengana peasants, the Nagas and Mizos failed to win in India; why indeed the Khampa rebels against China in Tibet do not win. And if the CCP replies to this question that "ideology" is the distinguishing feature of successful movements, how was it that Castro won in Cuba as, broadly, a liberal, certainly not a Marxist-Leninist?

Armed struggle is supposed to create the objective conditions for winning power, and, in Castro's words, those conditions can

43 Ernesto Guevara, in *Hoy*, 16 July 1963.

be created in the "immense majority of Latin American countries" if between four and five dedicated men can be found to undertake it."[44] The CCP is not quite so cavalier about the role of theory as the Cubans but still it is seen as little more than a weapon to achieve obedience and thereby the free initiative of the leadership. "Socialist ideology becomes a weapon in mobilizing and organizing the masses and becomes a material force in society ... it becomes instrumental in establishing a socialist economic base by acquiring political power and by destroying the capitalist economic base with that power."[45] Another writer puts the point more sharply: "men are not the slaves of objective reality. Provided only that man's consciousness be in conformity with the objective laws of the development of things, the subjective activity of the popular masses can manifest itself in full measure, overcome all difficulties, create the necessary conditions, and carry forward the revolution. In this sense, the subjective creates the objective."[46] Allied with peasant superstition and belief in the power of magic, the magic of the formula, the text and the aphorism, it is hardly surprising that the works of Mao become elements of a popular religion, prescribed as a cure for any problem at all, from treating burns, selling water-melons or winning at table tennis (some of the few examples reported recently). We are here clearly in a world closer to that of medieval Christianity than of Marxism.

The elimination of specific class content, the stress on voluntarism and the role of an elite, automatically blurs distinctions earlier Marxists stressed, and makes it impossible to distinguish different countries in social terms—to distinguish, for example, between Egypt, based upon a *coup d'etat* by radical army officers, Algeria, with a military and guerrilla but non-Communist movement, and China itself. The classification of such countries is read off from the country's foreign policy stance, not its domestic class structure, even though that foreign policy might be based upon quite accidental or opportunist factors. For the CCP, the test of revolutionary

[44] Fidel Castro, speech, 16 January 1963; see also Ernesto Guevara, *Guerilla Warfare,* New York, 1961, p. 11.

[45] Hsu I-jang and Lin Ching-yao, 1959, cited by Maurice Meisner, "Li Ta-chao and the Chinese Communist Treatment of the Materialist Conception of History", *China Quarterly*, 24, October-December 1965, p. 168.

[46] Wu Chiang, cited by Schram, *op. cit.*, p. 80.

politics turned on one's attitude to the United States, and any sort of critical stance, even in a conservative authoritarian and private enterprise country like Pakistan (a member of United States alliances and recipient of United States aid) evoked fraternal warmth.

If the revolution abroad means opposition to the United States and little more, building the national economy at home for the purposes of national power makes the necessity of poverty a virtue. The seige economy dictates that tomorrow's abundance is forgotten and Communism converted into meaning common abstinence. Hobsbawm notes in another context that: "The pre-industrial poor always conceive of the good society as a just sharing of austerity rather than a dream of riches for all,"[47] and this seems to be the most prominent feature in the following reprimand by *China Youth* (31 October 1964): "The kind of life advocated by Comrade Feng Ting, which would provide good things to eat and wear, good places to live in, and cordial relations between husband and wife and between parents and children, does not conform with the Communist ideal." In the early phases of industrialization in all societies, the same flavour of puritanism seems to be repeated. Production becomes an end in itself. In China the apotheosis of Marxism as the instrument of primitive accumulation reaches its ironic conclusion. The modest "affluence" of the Soviet Union is a continuous threat to the need for common poverty, and periodic campaigns are one way of reviving the spirit of self-flagellation. Perhaps Mao might feel some sympathy for John Wesley when he complained:

.... I fear, wherever riches have increased, the essence of religion has decreased in the same proportion.... For religion must necessarily produce both industry and frugality, and these cannot but produce riches. But as riches increase, so will pride, anger and love of the world in all its branches.[48]

In conclusion, then, Mao has revised Marxism to such a degree that it cannot really be considered to be merely a local

[47] E. J. Hobsbawm, *Primitive Rebels, Studies in Archaic Forms of Social Movement in the 19th and 20th Centuries,* Manchester, 1959, p. 82.

[48] Cited by Max Weber in *The Protestant Ethic and the Spirit of Capitalism* (translated by Talcott Parsons), London, 1930, p. 175.

"application": the essence has disappeared. What constitutes revolution is not the most advanced urban masses securing their own emancipation by their own efforts, but guerrilla warfare by the least advanced rural groups, operating outside the ordinary social structure over many years, in order to seize power and begin industrialization. A would-be ruling *elite*, dispossessed and alienated from the *status quo*, within a decaying agrarian social structure, fits naturally into Maoism, although even more naturally into Castroism which was not part of Marxism-Leninism in its revolutionary phase in Cuba. Activism and populism provide the dominant themes. Outside the underdeveloped world, radicals may borrow the important activism of Maoism (particularly against the conservatism of Moscow), but its substantive principles can have little relevance, or rather, what relevance they have leads to inactivity, to waiting for emancipation at the hands of "Third World" peasant armies. The closest parallels to the "national revolution" in Marx's terms would be the bourgeois revolution, but this does not really fit, for the bourgeois revolution presupposes an established capitalism, a private economy the businessmen of which merely complete their power by appropriating the political sphere. By contrast, the national revolution does not take place in a predominantly private industrialized economy, and the political power gained is directly used to *develop* a backward economy. The issue of property has concealed the significance of the national revolution—since public property is seen as one of the dominant expressions of the new regimes, then it is described as socialist, whatever its specific content, whatever the diverse reasons for which different States may nationalize.

This section has tried to illustrate the continuing transition of basic Marxist themes—class, internationalism, proletarian revolution—in the Chinese context. The terms lost their original significance, and other, contradictory, concepts became much more important—nation, nationalism, and a peasant revolution. After the seizure of power, the imperatives of development, exacerbated most recently by continuous foreign threat from the most powerful nation in the world, the United States, have even further reshaped the dominant beliefs of the Chinese leadership. Both the internal and the external conditions are such that the CCP cannot pursue the same process of development in terms of beliefs that the post-Stalinist leadership took. China will remain underdeveloped for a very long period, and, indeed, there is nothing inevitable about its development. Its situation forces its leadership to pursue radical policies at home and abroad, and in pursuing those policies, the residual Marxism is even further lost in nationalism.

The conditions of China shaped the transformation of Marxism which the CCP undertook. But it was a transformation characteristic of most doctrines in the context of underdevelopment. Nationalism was the key focus for all anti-imperialist struggles and domestic class issues were subordinated to this struggle. It could only have been otherwise if events had occurred in accordance with the Leninist perspective, if the industrial proletariats of theWest had pursued a socialist revolution in the West, and thereby brought to the aid of the underdeveloped countries their strength and the accumulated knowledge and wealth of their societies. Thus, from many diverse backgrounds, some located in a specific Western political tradition, some not, the common logic of anti-imperialism and development reshaped the beliefs of the "Third World" in specific ways, even though each national leadership claimed to be as original as—many of them, indeed, even more original than—the Chinese Communist Party. The uniqueness was perhaps true in their own societies, but on the world plane it seemed less so.

The Nature of Underdevelopment

A significant number of underdeveloped countries have made a shift from their post-independence regimes to a new sort of politics. The new politics seem to be marked by an irresistible compulsion towards centralized State autocracy, embodied in a national dictator or one party which monopolizes all political initiative (military, nationalist or Communist), and advocates national planning, a steady expansion of the public sector and substantial State intervention in the economy. The general ideology is ultra-nationalist and anti-imperialist. We might provisionally describe it as *"etatiste* nationalism." Even those countries which do not undergo a radical social change find it useful to imitate aspects of *etatiste* nationalism and on occasions even execute it under the auspices of traditional rulers—Nepal, Bhutan, Afghanistan, are all monarchies, but all have national plans which involve expanding public initiative and a public sector. Even relatively conservative regimes follow suit, as for example Pakistan or Diem's South Viet Nam.

Historically, some aspects of a similar process have been visible during the development of European countries. A mild autarchic nationalism was seen in Britain, and a rather more radical version, involving extensive positive State initiative, occurred in the France of Louis XIII and XIV. Bismarck's "State socialism" is well known, and one historian's comment is put at the head of this section.

The example of Mehmet Ali (1805-42) is interesting in this respect, for—with the same pre-eminently military motives that inspired the European era of "Enlightened Despots"—he sought to shift Egypt from a subsistence to a modern economy ("modern" by the standards of the time). He revolutionized land tenure, expanded communications, established State monopolies to handle crops and begin industrial projects, all behind a wall of protection and operated by an expanded bureaucracy. The process was checked by outside intervention in 1841, and Egypt did not gain sufficient political autonomy to undertake another exercise in *etatiste* nationalism until after the Second World War. Military purposes, the aims of foreign policy, provided the main incentive to modern Egypt's second attempt, particularly after the Suez affair of 1956, but now the nature of modern industrialization itself exercised a powerful compulsion towards State direction—the concentration of resources and skills now required is much greater than ever before.[49]

Unlike the numerous earlier attempts (Bismarck's exercise apart), modern efforts usually acquire the label "socialist," and those efforts usually include a more explicit commitment to popular welfare. The "socialisms" present a luxuriant variety, apart from Chinese Marxism which we have already examined— Egyptian or Arab socialism, Burmese, Indonesian, Ugandan, and even Cambodia's "Buddhist Socialism within a nationalist framework." Sometimes explicit European influences are involved —Stalinism and Fabianism to mention only two—but important sources of the creeds are local, even if offered in "foreign" termino-

[49] Charles Issawi, *Egypt in Revolution, An Economic Analysis*, London, 1963, p. 21.

logy. This does not mean that they are proper expressions of an indigenous culture that predates development, but rather that there are common problems of development and independence which particular groups of beliefs seem to "fit." Some elements of Stalinism "fitted" the problems of China.

The most fruitful parallels with political ideas in modern underdeveloped countries can be found in Narodnik thought in the 1860s and '70s. The Narodnik terrorist tradition influenced both Chinese intellectuals immediately prior to the 1911 fall of the Ch'ing dynasty and Bengali aristocratic youth in the early part of the century. Gandhi found a major source of inspiration in the work of Tolstoy, and Li Ta-chao in Kropotkin. The Narodnik "To the People" movement of urban intellectuals had its parallels in Li Ta-chao's appeal for Chinese students to go to the villages and enlighten the peasants, in Gandhi's similar appeal to urban Indians, and in the Japanese *atarashika mura* (New Village) movement to promote village communities to practice rural Communism (Kropotkin's work was a direct influence here). All, in some measure, felt cities to be corrupt and corrupting, much as Guevara viewed urban influence.

One can also see close parallels in the condition of the intelligentsia itself at some stages, its proneness to "withdraw" from the troubled world when faced with major political obstacles (Li Ta-chao considered withdrawal to a Buddhist monastic sect for a time in 1913) Frölich[50] cites Rosa Luxemburg's account of the Russian intelligentsia in the 1880s when major Tsarist reforms were withdrawn:

> In this atmosphere of apathy and despondency, metaphysical and mystical tendencies began to make headway amongst the Russian intelligentsia.... The propaganda of 'non-resistance to evil', the condemnation of all violence in the struggle against the dominant reaction (which was to be opposed only by 'the inner purification' of the individual), and the general theory of social passivity developed....

It was an anarchic quality in the Narodniks which Lenin sought to discipline by his organizational proposals, and which others in

---

[50] Paul Frölich, *Rosa Luxemburg*, London, 1940, p. 20.

modern underdeveloped countries also seek to control through direct military discipline, through a one-party State, through successive limitations on individual rights, Preventive Detention Acts and executions. Those who pursue such courses of "discipline" for their opponents are not "copying" Lenin nor are they probably even influenced by him. But common problems generate solutions which are similar in form—with the difference that Lenin did not, when he framed his organizational proposals, have the power of the State behind him.

Poverty plus relatively meagre prospects alongside the urgency for development shape inherited culture in certain ways. For example, that wide range of social conflict, the issues of which do not permit compromise, grows as the alternatives become fewer. One cannot compromise between standing on a cliff and falling off it, and when the margins of survival are narrow, all decisions assume the form of either survival or death. Compromise, which even in other societies is often more limited than people think, depends upon the existence of choices other than the two mentioned. Where such alternatives are absent, it is not peculiar psychology or lack of education or an unfamiliarity with the preconditions for parliamentary rule which prompts men to fight, but the sheer need to survive. The climate of insecurity is such that it affects all. It is not the poor who are less compromising, but those who have further to fall in the social hierarchy. The truncheon is one way of silencing the struggle for survival.

We must not forget the crucial conditions for Liberalism in Europe (as well as the degree to which Liberalism was more or less qualified in practice). Its popular validity turned upon reasonably continuous prospects for expansion. Slumps and recessions were a constant source of anti-Liberal doctrines. Present sacrifice was sugared with hope for the future, and "compromise" became that much more possible—or rather, so the victorious claimed. Neither Liberalism nor "compromise" are possible in the conditions of poverty that exist in backward countries today.

The immensely expanded role of the State in underdeveloped countries today is a primary response to the intractable problems of development. Under imperial rule, it was the military State which wielded the truncheon, not the "logic of the market" nor the electoral contest; and it wielded the truncheon with little regard to the substantive axioms of Liberalism. It was this State against which any independence movement measured itself and which it inherited in victory—a State which was a conjuncture of political, economic. and military power overshadowing the rest of the society. It is hardly surprising that there were no social classes capable of resisting the State, as entrepreneurs were able to resist the British State in the early 19th century. The newly independent government became both business (to develop rapidly) and the regulator of business (both to underpin its own economic activities and to ensure some measure of protection for its supporters, real or potential); sometimes it was and is both employer and trade union and arbitrates between its two selves.

The drive to develop—mandatory as a means to survive in the modern world—combined with the needs of defence and the logic of modern industry, produces a powerful compulsion towards *etatisme* in the absence of counteracting factors. Indigenous capital is far too weak to resist this process and, where foreign capital continues to operate in the independent economy, it needs the State to protect it. That need is sometimes met at a high price for the line between "Indianization" (or Ceylonization, Egyptianization and so on) of business and its nationalization can become very fine.

The independence struggle has been, with some notable exceptions, a largely urban phenomenon, or at least under mainly urban leadership. Where the urban population has succeeded in overthrowing the old regime, the new State must take particular care to retain its loyalty. A higher proportion of national production must be devoted to urban working class consumption, or at least to the consumption of particularly crucial sectors of workers, which limits the surplus available for investment.

The cities are, by and large, the bearers of national feeling. It was suggested in the discussion on China why the peasants were unlikely to be nationalist, and Meisner argues that in China " 'mass nationalism' was not something that welled up from the elemental forces of the countryside and eventually reached Mao Tse-tung and his associates. It is more historically accurate to say that nationalism was brought to the peasants from without by an ardently nationalistic *elite* intent upon shaping history in accordance with its ideals."[51] For India, Bailey suggests that in Orissa, the Cong-

[51] Meisner, *op. cit.*, p. 266.

ress independence movement made relatively little progress among the peasants until it was pointed out that since many landowners supported the British, land reform would be one result of expelling the British: at which, a very large number of peasants became "nationalist."[52] The cities delineate the boundaries of the "nation," for city dwellers are aware of the geography between themselves, of the complex transactions that take place between themselves, of the need to control and administer the areas in between the cities. "Accidental" geographical areas are centralized not just by military conquest, and much less by the concept of "ethnic identity," but by the interaction of merchants and traders who supply an entire market, by bankers and moneylenders who supply the requisite credit for merchandizing, and, finally, by the great industries which are needed to supply the market. But if the economy is relatively backward or controlled by foreign business, then in reaction to that backwardness (and thus weakness) or foreign control, a substitute nationalistic agent must be found in the urban middle class, the intelligentsia, the clerks employed in the bureaucracy that make imperialism possible.

In newly independent countries, then, the State is the largest single institution, against which no other organized national group can stand. The State and nationalism are the creation of the cities, but the cities are a threat to the State once it is independent. It has happened in a number of underdeveloped countries that the political party which controls the government has sought to shift its support away from the cities to the countryside, in order to render its own power less subject to urban opposition. If the CCP began as urban intellectuals using peasant power to capture the cities, the Indian Congress has steadily found it difficult to control the cities since independence. However, the articulate public political arena remains urban and largely dominated by the educated national middle class, still by and large clustered round the State as employer or potential employer—a powerful attraction where higher educational facilities have been expanded under middle-class pressure faster than jobs for the educated are available. The middle class embodies both the most developed sense of nationalism and the greatest interest in the expansion of the State: State and nation are one.

[52] F. G. Bailey, *Politics and Social Change, Orissa in 1959*, Berkeley, 1963, pp. 172-173.

The need for intense national loyalty seems all the greater where countries are mere amalgams of different tribes and peoples that have not historically had any unifying feature except a common foreign invader. But schismatic trends are powerful even in countries with a relatively high degree of cultural or ethnic homogeneity and a common unified history. Schisms borrow on what Geertz calls "primordial" sentiments, "the 'givens' of social . . . existence: immediate contiguity and kin connexion mainly, but beyond them, the givenness that stems from being born into a particular religious community, speaking a particular language, or even a dialect of a language, and following particular social practices."[53] Groups can identify a common interest in multiple ways and some of the "primordial" loyalties are invented, or at least "discovered" by the new political situation. Invented or not, the climate of great insecurity generates immense tensions, "reduced" in the final analysis by the blunt and arbitrary intervention of the State. Since the trends to disintegration are so great, an accordingly heavier burden of compelling an unwanted nationality falls on the State and the national middle class.

So great is the need, so widespread and low the cultural level, that elements of "modernism" (of which nationalism is one constituent) towards which the national middle class is striving, tend to attain magical forms, to become fetishized—education, nationalism or Marxism can take on the character of an intense religion, a cure for all ills. This tendency is only one aspect of the continuity in an urbanized context of a number of elements of rural life—the values of the peasantry, still the majority class and the source of the new urban sector, pervade the atmosphere. Peasant society includes very strong kinship groups, and these provide the immediate context for all the activities of the constituent family unit. In the cities, by contrast, a multiplicity of alternative associations exist, and loyalties to any one of them can be very mild and limited. There are many people to depend upon lightly, and relationships are likely to be more strictly functional. The new rural immigrant, accustomed to intense and intimate personal relationships that spread out over all he does, is likely to feel lonely and alienated.

[53] Clifford Geertz, *Old Societies and New States*, New York, 1963, p. 109.

When large numbers of people move from village to city, it is likely that the "modern" elements in the city will become reformulated in rural terms and not just for the rural immigrant. One result is a romanticism, a nostalgia for a past golden age.

More concretely, workers tend to identify less with their fellow workers in the same occupational stratum or factory, more with their kinship group, caste or district. New urban immigrants inhabit urban areas already populated by people from their village, to take jobs where other villagers are employed, to form friends and marry within the same group. Thus, the *class* alignment is muted, and loyalty goes to a group which may include a number of members of different classes, or merely to authority.

With the middle class dependence upon public authority, this context inhibits the appearance of a clear and popular Liberal critique of authority, without which individual rights, civil liberties, become merely so much paper, a deferential gesture to foreign political traditions. Opposition oscillates between deference, often sustained by bribes or relatively vague promises, and outright opposition, ending perhaps in civil war. Among workers, when the hard conflict with an employer comes, fragmentation, the lack of solid organization, makes it sporadic, violent, anarchic—a sudden outburst of fury and frustration rather than part of a rationally disciplined campaign to achieve specific ends. In the underdeveloped countries, sometimes even in the act of opposing, the basic feeling of dependence is reaffirmed—strikers demand not so much their rights, as the satisfaction of their needs. Implicitly, the plea assumes powerful but kindly authority, a *deus ex machina* who will shoulder responsibility and permit workers to evade the responsibility for achieving their demands through their own efforts. This is one element in the absurd inflation of the role of particular leaders. Whether it be Stalin, Mao, Gandhi or Nasser, in a religious peasant-dominated society, such men come to play the role of God, intervening charitably in their omnipotence on behalf of the oppressed: to *give* them independence or economic development. However, the appearance of the Godlike figure should not mislead one into thinking popular commitment is necessarily to action for that person; the transformation in the fortunes of Sukarno or Nkrumah indicates just how shallow this "charisma" can be in practice.

For some among the educated urban middle class, identification with the State (as part of nationalist feeling) is both an incipient authoritarianism and part of a romantic reconstruction of rural society that serves both to compensate for the loss of presumed security and integration within the village group, and provides an effective justification for their own position. With the State as the pivot, society must be integrated like a village (naturally, real villages are quite unlike the romantic picture, and may be sharply divided in factions or kinship groups, locked in almost perpetual battle). Identification with the kinship group at the village level becomes identification with an ethnic group at the national, and is embodied in particular leaders upon whom one is dependent. What is at stake is not the detail of what the leader does or says he proposes to do, so much as his mere existence as a symbol of unity.

Just as the village (or the village faction) depends for its unity upon a shared hostility to outsiders which enforces common sacrifices on all members, the new nationalism depends upon sharp differentiation between in-group and out-group.

We noted earlier that the solidarity enforced by common hostility safeguards the positions of the existing leadership (although, to say this is not to imply that common hostility is invented by the leadership for the sole purpose of safeguarding its position). The former imperial power provides one target, and a target with more historical justification for hatred than many, but the target loses significance over time and needs replacement by more easily identified enemies; Israelis for Arabs, Indians for Pakistanis, Ethiopians for Somalis, Chinese for Indonesians, and vice versa. A sense of group honour is one symptom of group existence in the village, and the "honour of the nation" now becomes a practical political term. Men react with violent sensitivity to imagined slights on "their" national integrity, and personalized international relations portray the United States as an evil old man scheming with almost motiveless malignity the disaster of the virgin, the nation.

The presumed nature of armies conforms to some of the aspired ethics: order, security, hierarchy (where all accept their given place naturally and unquestioningly), each place in society carrying incumbent duties and rights that demand neither debate nor change, the whole coherently directed at one central purpose. In China Egypt, Pakistan, Algeria and so on, the role of the army in providing the civil population with certain kinds of ideals has similarities which overshadow some of the enormous differences between them. Actual armies, of course, are as likely to be riven with the same divisions as society at large, and soldiers will seek to maximize their returns and minimize their contribution as much as anyone else, with the difference that their activities are curbed to a greater degree by a system of pure force. The army embodies in its internal organization the coercion it is designed to exercise on others outside the army. The rural myth implies that unanimity and harmony spontaneously arise among villagers, but armies are straightforwardly commanded by generals at the top. The appearance of spontaneity is carefully created to hide the use of force. Armies themselves, (or rather their officers) foster the illusion of complete unity, for this is an element in the fear they seek to strike in those they oppose; they like to appear as outside the petty squabbles of mere politicians. They have no market interest (with some exceptions, as in Thailand), for their life depends on taxation, not sales, so that they seem honest and unselfish. In their natural attempts to control their own paymaster, and thereby their own existence, seizure or at least control of the State can answer a diversity of different needs.

This account has tried to suggest some of the features common to the nature of underdevelopment, or rather the early phase of development in modern terms. It is a dangerous exercise since one can quite mistakenly generalize a local peculiarity as a standard feature, and because it takes the discussion away from the hard reality which is its essential discipline. However, space does not allow more than a general account, designed to suggest that Western and Soviet accounts which separate Communist and non-Communist, or Communist, non-aligned, and Western-aligned, conceal some basic similarities which are problems ideology has to explain. Many of the features solemnly identified as essentially socialist in both Communist and non-Communist countries are no more than the historical concomitants of development, the conversion of harsh and unpleasant necessities into slightly more attractive virtues.

Nationalism, the belief in the population of a given politically defined area as the basic operating unit of consciousness, the source of all virtue and legitimacy, is the guiding thread, and inevitably the nationalism of the underdeveloped countries has very close similarities with nationalism in Europe—"And there has arisen ... blood against formal reason; race against purposeful rationality, honour against profit; unity against individualistic disintegration; martial virtue against bourgeois security; the people against the individual and the mass" (Ernst Krieck, leading National Socialist Philosopher at Heidelberg). National socialism can be a coherent doctrine for some of the population, even if its appearance in inter-war Germany and Italy makes it seem no more than an elaborate make-believe to conceal a personal dictatorship. Of course, it would be quite wrong to see such diverse beliefs as "Fascist," but intense insecurity for the urban middle class in an hostile international environment can recreate eerie echoes. Similarly the combination of the notion of struggle from socialist or Marxist sources and nationalism occasionally awakens old memories. Inevitably, nationalism is a minority cult, and as a result, it is misleading to infer a popular response from the behaviour of either a member of the urban middle class or one of the major leaders of society. Geertz comments on the nationalism of an Indonesian newspaper as a "sort of intensely felt but curiously abstract kind of ideological expression, part of a symbolic masking of real value conflicts within the society, a kind of cultural protesting too much, by means of which conflicts which threaten to upset the social equilibrium can to a degree be kept out of conscious awareness or at least from open expression."[54]

The sociological shallowness of the feeling engenders a similar kind of ideological shallowness (which is not to imply that the feelings expressed are shallow). The doctrines are loosely refined and relatively incoherent, drawn from apparently contradictory sources that are only united in the passionate faith of the believer. The examples of what is known as syncretism are diverse: the description of Burma as a "nation built upon a combination of Burmese national identity, Buddhist philosophy, British political organization and socialist economic theories—both Marxist and non-Marxist"; Nasser's suggestion that "Islam in its early days was the first socialist State"; Ben Bella's "Islamic socialism"; Nkrumah's remark that "I am a non-denominational Christian and a Marxist socialist, and I have not found any contradiction

---

[54] Clifford Geertz, *The Religion of Java*, New York, 1960, p. 370.

between the two"; Sukarno's Indonesian socialism, and the Indonesian Communist Party's Indonesian Marxism-Leninism; the Indian Praja Socialist's marriage of Marxist historical analysis and the Vedantist ethic. Nor is this just play with words, for as Lewis Feuer has pointed out, when Burma's U Nu and China's Chou En-lai signed a treaty on behalf of their countries, they did so at 5.50 P.M. on 1 October 1960, since that was the exact time which astrologers had indicated was the most propitious. But Stark[55] cites a somewhat tragic example of the synthesizing of past and present in the catechism of some Italian republican peasants:

> *Question:* What are the three distinct persons in Garibaldi?
> *Answer:* The father of the nation, the son of the people, and the spirit of liberty.
> *Question:* How did he make himself man?
> *Answer:* He took on a body and soul just like ourselves in the blessed womb of a woman of the people.

Yoking together apparently quite inconsistent threads of argument is a characteristic feature of the use of a doctrine in a place other than that in which it was formulated. Economic development is a "Western process," and the cultural forms hitherto associated with development are derived from Western sources. There is nothing intrinsic in this, but as a matter of historical fact, the Western development process, including in this that of the Soviet Union, has dominated the field. For the moment, at least, developmental efforts borrow from this cultural inheritance and "Third World" leaders try to marry it to selected elements of indigenous culture. The marriage is imperfectly consummated by Western standards, since the doctrines derive from incompatible sources— to achieve any conjuncture at all involves small or large redefinitions of both elements, so that in the end, one is sometimes left with no more than a play on words. Putting together traditional practices and "foreign" doctrines is part of the attempt to carry contradictory audiences, the local peasant and the Westernized *elite*.

It is also a form of special pleading, for in the "foreign" doctrines, there are often criteria publicly available for appraising whether

---

[55] Werner Stark, *The Sociology of Religion*, I, London, 1966, p. 175.

or not the words are being used reasonably correctly. "Ruritanian socialism," however, is carefully concealed from such inspection, for any criticism is dismissed as being made by a person who does not "really" know the peculiarities of the local situation. Sometimes this is true, sometimes it is merely an evasion of an embarrassing criticism. In the examination of the new orthodoxy, one must also ask the opinion of those members of the indigenous society who are in prison.

Syncretism is a major and important feature of political ideas in underdeveloped countries. Very few people are actually involved in political debate of the kind which borrows "foreign" doctrines, so that the political implications of syncretism are possibly not as great as one might imagine. Often the syncretist formulations are framed deliberately for foreign consumption, or are no more than part of the discussion between members of the small *elite*. For the average peasant, Marxism is—quite reasonably—as remote as the society in which it was originally formulated. Indeed, in the larger "Third World" countries, the peasant's own State is almost as remote. Thus, one must keep a strict sense of proportion in appraising the new orthodoxies, for probably they do not go very deep, and even where they do go deeper, they are almost certainly reformulated in entirely traditional terms. Mao, to an average Chinese peasant, probably seems less like a champion of Marxism-Leninism, and more like an emperor-cum-prophet.

Nor should one underestimate the groping pragmatism which the new orthodoxies are merely late attempts to rationalize. We have already noted how Fidel Castro did not become a "Marxist-Leninist" until after he came to power; his Marxism-Leninism was not a revolutionary aid so much as the indication of a certain foreign policy alignment. In Egypt, the army officers who seized power in 1952 had no clear philosophy, no clear programme of what they intended to do beyond "clean up." They were initially rather conservative, and it was really only with the events of 1956, that they moved towards a much more radical transformation of the economy and society of Egypt. Thus, "Egyptian Socialism" evolved relative to a series of determinate challenges, rather than from any inner force of its own. The combination of elements we have called "*etatiste* nationalism" are not the expressions of national souls, but rather the contingent adjustments of peoples striving to survive in a world dominated and, indeed, exploited by the most advanced countries.

Common problems in the "Third World" shape a similar response, although the differences that also exist in both the problems and the responses have here been ignored in order to emphasize some of the common elements. The terminology has been borrowed from many different sources, so that, in terms of language alone, the differences seem very great—between "free enterprise" in those countries directly subject to American domination, through the Fabian "mixed economy" of India, to the Marxism-Leninism of China, North Viet Nam and North Korea. Yet, beneath these labels, similar processes are concealed, a common combination (to different degrees) of *etatisme*, nationalism and voluntarism. The closest actual parallels in European history come from populist and nationalist regimes, rather than from Fabian or Marxist traditions themselves. The countries of the "Third World" have to fight for survival in conditions far harsher than those that governed the development of the Western countries—indeed, the Western countries are the major obstacle to the development of the underdeveloped. The struggle for survival lends a radicalism to their orthodoxies which contrasts with the conservatism of the West, both capitalist and "socialist."

PART FOUR

Economic Development and the
Perspectives for Revolution

10

The Economic Development
of India and China

If the world was a place in which the interests of the majority of people directed the exercise of power, no doubt it would be perfectly feasible to raise the general standard of living to the same high level without industrializing anything like a majority of the world's countries. There is no peculiar magic about industry except in an unequal and violently competing world. Indeed, if men were seriously set upon the task of conquering poverty, it might well be considered a high privilege to *exclude* industry from the patch of territory where one lived. But in contemporary conditions, to rule out industry is to guarantee the perpetuation of economic backwardness.

"Backwardness" in this context has nothing to do with the lack of consumer durables. Some currents of Western opinion are now so remote from the serious problems of scarcity that they can muddle the satisfaction of world hunger with the provision of a second car to each household—and being against the spread of "consumer society." The problem is much cruder. Ensuring an adequate, not a lavish, diet; ensuring that a high and increasing proportion of children survive the dangers of childhood; that women survive childbirth; that all live to a reasonable and rising age; this nucleus of aims—with others—constitutes the claim to progress that industrialization has made possible. Some say it is not everything (there is much idle chatter about not living by bread alone); but if you are denied these things, they are everything. For most of the time, the spiritual verities pale into insignificance beside the sorrow and hardship which are the results of stifling economic development.

The cases of economic development without industrialization are insignificant. Despite much bold talk, there is no evidence that there is another road to economic development other than through industry. To be without industry today is to be without power, to be the creature of forces beyond one's control. Externally, the predatory imperialist powers depend upon the weakness of all the rest to sustain their position of dominance, their monopoly of much of the industrial capacity and most of the industrial technology of the world. At home, small ruling elites can offer their people virtually nothing without industrialization, and so are prey to the harvest, the peasants, the urban workers, other factions in the ruling class. To industrialize, or even to survive, they must squeeze resources out of their people—the precondition for their survival is simultaneously the possible means of their destruction. It could only not be so if the world were unified, one whole in which the riches of one part came to the aid of the development of the other. Then there would be no necessity to squeeze out resources. To unlock the historic accumulations of wealth in the advanced capitalist countries, the product of the systematic and very long drawn out exploitation of both the rest of the world and their own people, would offer some hope of substance to the majority. With the world divided into petty principalities, with poverty locked up inside the national boundaries of each backward State, each ruling class must devote itself to the economic development of its own territory as the price of its survival.

Industrialization of a country requires either a relatively high level of surplus wealth available for investment at home for long enough to create a modern economy; or an inflow of investible resources from abroad, as revenue on the sale of domestically produced goods, grants, or aid from foreign countries or foreign investment, or some combination of these elements. Historically, virtually all the industrialized countries of the world depended upon foreign trade as a primary engine of industrialization for a more or less extended period of time. That does not mean that the main source of investment was trade, but the main force pushing the economy, pushing elements of the ruling class into increasingly intensive exploitation of the home population, came from involvement in commerce abroad. Even the United States and Russia, countries which subsequently depended least upon foreign trade, in the early phases of development were powerfully stimulated by foreign trade and an inflow of foreign capital. Indeed, in the case of the United States, foreign investment in the US economy was larger than US investment abroad right up until 1950. Of course, the general process shows only what actually happened, not what must always happen.

However, while the crude precondition for industrialization— the availability of investment resources—remains constant, the scale, conditions and implications are constantly changing. With increasing speed, the price of the initial phase of industrialization is rising. Take steel, for example. The production of iron suitable for most industrial processes in the Britain of the first quarter of the 19th century was still within the financial capability of individual businessmen. The production of steel today is not. It is open only to the largest concentrations of capital, State or monopoly, only in the largest economies. Even then, steel production must be protected and enhanced by the government if it is to survive. In 1948, the economic-sized steel plant produced up to two million tonnes each year; now it is closer to six million tonnes, and the forward projections already plan plants of 12 million tonnes. The concentrated cost involved is staggering and beyond the capacity of virtually even the largest backward countries (and many of the industrialized ones as well).

The implication of the rise in costs is that no individual businessman can alone aspire to develop a significant industry, nor can any private business class aim to develop any significant backward country. Private business concentrates on the declining number of fields which are "profitable"—consumer goods for the small high income market. It is left to the State to develop the country, or make some passing imitation of such an exercise. For only the State has the power and position to squeeze resources out of the whole of society, and even then—pursuing policies of deliberate and ruthless coercion to mobilize, direct and sustain investment—it will probably not be enough.

This is so not just because the price is so much higher than it was in the past, nor because the price is rising so quickly and discontinuously. But also because the majority of the people who live in backward countries today exist on an income per head too low to provide much of an investible surplus. The impoverishment of the backward countries by imperialism in the past has reduced the ability of their peoples to support industrialization at the same time as the industrialized countries were withdrawing the opportunity. In Europe in the 18th century, it seems, income per head was higher, skills much closer to those required in industry, and colonies available to support the capital accumulation process.

Easily accessible surpluses from other sources are not available to the majority of backward countries on a scale sufficient to make up for the deficiency in income per head. The opportunities to export an increasing volume of the commodities in demand on the world market are declining, with a few exceptions of which oil is the most notable. Foreign investment is too small to make much difference and, in any case, has interests at odds with the imperatives of national development.

Even those countries which appear to be developing—the prize cases in the permanent exhibition of capitalism's singular merits—are most often cheated in the statistics. It may indeed be the case that an increasing proportion of their national income is generated in the industrial sector, or—more often—in the "mining and manufacturing" sector. But that is not necessarily "development," the structural transformation of an economy. The source of the national income does not show the distribution of the labour force, and it is this which constitutes the structural change of an economy. It is not at all absurd to conceive of a country in which the oil industry, employing one per cent of the labour force, generates 70 per cent of the national income. Meanwhile, the other 99 per cent of working people remain as they were before the advent of the oil industry; when the oil wells run dry, everyone returns to where they were before. Development must mean the transformation of the structure of the labour force—moving workers out of low into highly productive activities—not just an increase, steady or not, in wealth, nor an increase in the generation of wealth from particular sectors.

On that criterion, the evidence since the Second World War suggests very few countries are developing, and even those that have had some significant structural change, are finding it increasingly difficult to sustain it. For most countries, economic development has become impossible. On the employment criterion, for example, the Latin American statistics show that between 1925 and 1960, employment in manufacturing as a proportion of the non-agricultural labour force declined from 35.4 to 27.1 per cent; furthermore, between 1950 and 1965, employment in manufacturing as a proportion of the *total* labour force declined from 14.2 to 13.8 per cent. A similar picture is repeated in one form or another round the world. The import-substitution boom which everyone took to be development is now being succeeded by relative stagnation, by—in employment terms—"deindustrialization."

The intractability of the core problem was for long concealed by the enormous growth of the world economy following the Korean war boom. Yet the steady elimination of the mass of backward countries from any substantial position in the world economy, their further subordination, continued all through the high growth phase. The proportion of world exports held by the backward declined from 30 per cent in 1950 to 21 per cent in 1960 and 17 per cent in 1970 (if the expanding proportion of this total held by oil is excluded, the figure falls to 10-11 per cent). The flows of capital are heavily concentrated in the advanced sector of the world economy; by 1968, the US cumulative investment stake in the industrialized countries had reached 45 billion dollars, in the backward countries, 17 billion dollars. Within the backward, investment was increasingly concentrated in the richest countries— Latin America attracted more foreign investment than the whole of Asia and Africa together, despite the wildly disproportionate distribution of population. Even more, foreign investment—like private investment generally—is increasingly concerned with offering luxuries to the small high income market in the backward countries, less and less with general development.

The downturn in the world economy in the last half of the 1960s brought the scale of the problem to light so far as "liberal opinion" was concerned. The so-called gap between the industrialized and backward countries was widening—in the 1960s, income per head increased by $650 in the advanced, and $40 in the backward countries. Balance of payments crises and rising unemployment were the most immediate signs of the development impasse. The rash of military *coups*—ruling classes reaching for the bayonet as the sole means of collective survival—and spreading corruption—individuals seeking private exits to the public *cul-de-sac*—were two of the less immediate signs. Each ruling class, having been offered by world imperialism its own Bantustan and told to get on with development, found itself increasingly unable even to assure its survival, let alone advance.

There was little that ruling classes had left open to them except to arm themselves against their "own" people. But, just as industrial equipment is increasingly expensive, so also is the armament now required for modern military purposes. It is also of a type which is more likely to burden the balance of payments than stimulate indigenous industry. The cost escalation can be enormous. For example, a burst of aerial cannon fire used to cost about $20; its contemporary equivalent—an air-to-air missile—requires $100,000 each. Per "unit of defence," military expenditure eats more deeply into development resources than ever before. The scale and type of defence cannot be determined in relationship to local resources, only relative to "the threat," and ultimately that means the most powerful military force in the world. The technology and standards are hardly variable—ultimately they are imposed by the US defence sector. Of course, in practice no country can aspire to the US scale of operations except the largest industrialized powers, but nevertheless all must try to go as far as they can in that direction—technology-capital-skill-intensive, heavy imports, everything least conducive to the proper utilization of local resources for development.

In Asia, the poorest zone and the one with the most severe problems, the effects are substantial. Excluding China, Asia increased its military spending in real terms by 84 per cent in the 1960s; China by 161 per cent (in the backward countries as a whole, by 114 per cent). The backward countries had 13.5 million men under arms (the advanced, 10.5 million), eight million of which were in Asia. If we include civilian defence personnel, the Asian total of those engaged in "defence" is probably over 24 million. The cost per man was rising far more rapidly than most other elements of national expenditure. Defence in the 1960s has proved a far more dynamic growth industry than most others, far more effective than any other in its call on the attention of ruling classes and the national exchequer. Against the roughly $215 billion expended on arms each year, the spending on aid— $16 billion—was not much more than a joke.

These were topics remote from the minds of many of those supposedly concerned with economic development. Military expenditure is only rarely part of the analysis of an economy; more often it is seen as a marginal amendment, as indeed it was for many countries in the 19th century for much of the time. Military expenditure is as marginal as cancer to the dying patient so far as economic development is concerned. The orthodox wisdom preferred to see hope in all manner of technical adjustments to the world economy—lowering the tariffs in the advanced countries in order to facilitate the exports of backward countries, increasing world liquidity (with a more than proportionate increase in the reserves of the backward countries), more intensive technical advice and assistance, an "intermediate technology" that adjusted technical advance to the specific resource endowments of a particular backward country, increased trade between backward countries themselves (regional trading areas and so on), a larger scale of aid on less harsh terms, and even more contraceptives so that, one day, the statistics per head do not look so sick as output increases. The proposals either touched too seriously issues of the power of the industrialized countries to stand much chance of being conceded, or were too impractical to achieve much effect.

Yet other reformists continued to see hope in national economic autarchy and planning. If, it was argued, a country could establish its complete independence, sever all except the most carefully controlled relations with the world economy, then it would be possible for the State to reorganize the national economy and direct all resources to the task of development. The development of the Soviet Union from 1929 seemed to be a clear demonstration that this strategy was practical. By implication the main factors preventing development in most backward countries were the drain of resources out of the country, the waste and duplication of private capitalism, the irrationality of a market system. The "crisis of development" was only a crisis of the private capitalist system, not of the world system as a whole: escape was possible.

Despite the example of the Soviet Union, this perspective itself is now exhausted. Yet it remains singularly attractive to many people, not least aspirant ruling classes in backward countries. That brand of radical nationalism which today goes under the name "Marxism-Leninism" remains wedded to the notion of gradualist economic development, without the precondition of this being the transformation of the world economy. The evidence does not suggest there is any such route out of the impasse.

India and China

Today in Asia, the case for State capitalism depends upon the dramatically superior economic performance of the People's Republic of China over that of other backward countries. Very often, it seems to many people that so great is the gap between China and the rest that the case is scarcely even worth arguing. Indeed, China's excellent economic record seems to be a fact so well established that contrary evidence can only be counted as CIA propaganda or deliberate and wilful perversity—like the man who insists that tropical temperatures are lower than arctic.

In particular, this attitude is strong on the Indian Left. China and India, by reason of their very great size, are only strictly comparable with each other. Each is or could be more nearly a full "economy"—that is, with the entire range of economic activities present in each country—than smaller countries where each is to a greater or lesser extent intrinsically dependent on others. In India, the affirmation of China's qualitative superiority seems beyond reasonable dispute. And of course, anyone familiar with Calcutta who visits Canton or Shanghai cannot but be most powerfully struck by the stark differences. The appearance of appalling decay and human misery in the one, the austerity but adequacy in the others, this is indeed beyond question. The poor in India are physically distinct to the naked eye—smaller, thinner, more fragile. Men die on pavements. And the rich are so ostentatious in their consumption—palaces, foreign cars and so on—the contrast is sharp. There does not appear to be anything so ugly in China.

However, this "evidence of the eyes" is not evidence that China is developing economically at a much faster pace than India. It is partial evidence that a much larger volume of resources is devoted to popular welfare in Canton or Shanghai than in Calcutta (leaving aside the question of whether all three started at the same point in terms of popular welfare). For many people, that is enough. For those many Liberals sympathetic to China, it is enough that China is a fairer society than India (although not enough that British capitalism seems domestically "fairer" than Indian). For a poor man in India, this consideration must appear decisive.

But the argument is not complete. How secure is the achievement of a fairer society in China? What is the direction of its growth: towards or away from greater equality? Can China also raise the very low standard of living of its people (high though that might seem relative to the poor in India), and defend its borders against all comers? The original argument made much higher claims than the achievement of a fair distribution system—by autarchic State organization, rapid economic development could take place so that China could simultaneously meet the rising demands of its people and preserve its national independence. This means, among other things, that the gap between the industrialized countries and China must be closing to the point where the People's Republic can unequivocally show that its system is the only way forward for the majority of the world's people; there is hope without world revolution.

If we leave aside all the other aspects of contemporary China, what has the economic record been in comparison to India? It should be said at the outset that, despite the confidence of the Maoists, China's claims rest more on the audacity of its propaganda than the available statistical evidence. India's economy is known in some detail and within known limits of accuracy. China's cannot be. No continuous series of statistics on the national economy or on individual sectors have been published by Peking since 1959. That omission is not at all evidence of sustained economic success: the People's Republic has never been afraid to boast of its achievements when it felt the need. The published population figures date from the census of 1953 (since then, there have been two complete censuses in India). Nor was the 1953 census necessarily reliable—preparatory work was poor, the census takers were often barely literate, there was much resistance to being counted because many people thought it a means to tax them, the registration of children was thought to be unlucky, and so on. However, despite this evidence of underenumeration, there is little other firm evidence to go on. Yet the projections of population from the 1953 figures to 1973 can show wild variations, depending upon what rate of population growth is assumed. It is these shaky extrapolations which nevertheless underlie estimates of income per head, food per head, and so forth, the indices of China's progress.

So far as the government is concerned, a number of estimates are employed. The Ministry of Commerce seems to use the figure of 830 million population, the Ministry of Food 800 million, the planning department "less than 750 million," all presumably based upon 1953's 582.6 million. In 1972, Chou En-lai spoke vaguely of the present rate of growth of population being "around two per cent," a figure which could be based upon an unpublished count in the sixties or just a repetition of the 1953 figure. It could represent a change to under two per cent, or something virtually the same as India's 2.47 per cent (1971 census). The working figures of population growth—roughly 40,000 per day, 15 million per year—have to be taken as most rough and ready approximations.

For other statistics, the picture is sometimes a little better. A combination of the statistics available up to 1959, of what is known in terms of the broad proportions of the Chinese economy, of hints or isolated facts mentioned publicly by Chinese leaders, out of this some rough view of the course of economic growth is possible. Since US imperialism has had the most powerful interest in analyzing modern China, the most attention to studying China has been in America, and most often, the most reliable estimates are American. Of course, some of these estimates are prejudiced, but provided the sources, assumptions and calculations are available, they can be adjusted and used. Certainly, serious estimates of this kind are not lies, any more than Chinese Government estimates are lies. The American ruling class needs reliable information for its policy calculations, not propaganda: the popular press may indeed publish the most absurd distortions, but the advice given to the US Government is a different matter altogether. The most optimistic views of the Chinese economy are also American. However, the most important consideration is to examine those series most clearly based upon official Chinese evidence.

India and China start from very different base points. British imperialism left independent India with a much more elaborate system of communications and an infrastructure much superior to China's (with the exception of Manchuria). This was not a charitable gesture: the British Raj needed roads and railways to move troops. On the other hand, China's people seem to have been significantly richer than India's for a very long period of time. Buck argues that the crop rotation pattern operating in China

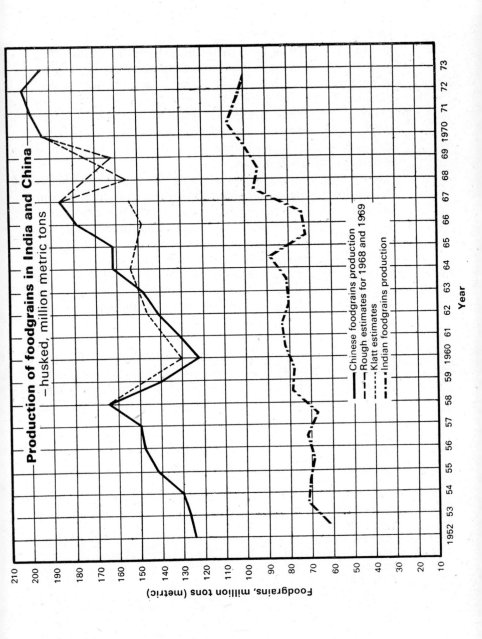

Production of foodgrains in India and China
— husked, million metric tons

Foodgrains, million tons (metric)

210
200
190
180
170
160
150
140
130
120
110
100
90
80
70
60
50
40
30
20
10

Year

1952 53 54 55 56 57 58 59 1960 61 62 63 64 65 66 67 68 69 1970 71 72 73

Chinese foodgrains production
Rough estimates for 1968 and 1969
Klatt estimates
Indian foodgrains production

in the 1930s was basically the same as that which existed in the 10th century and supported significantly higher rice yields per hectare than in India throughout the period.[1] The paramount position of foodgrains in total output figures and the higher level of productivity in China ensured higher income per head figures than India throughout modern times—"*per capita* income (in China) in the 1930s and 1950s was well above that in India in the 1950s.... In particular, grain output *per capita* in China in the 20th century was roughly comparable to that in the grain-surplus countries of South-East Asia."[2]

If we take a sample of the available information on what is overwhelmingly the largest sector, foodgrains production, we can get some idea of the relative performance of the two economies.[3] The preceding graph portrays the respective output of China and India. Apart from the inherent difficulties of accuracy in the figures (some of these are suggested in the sources), there are problems of comparability: for example, the Chinese figures exclude soyabeans but—unlike the Indian—include potatoes. However, the *direction* of the plotted lines is not affected in any significant respect by this factor.

One of the conclusions from the graph is that, over two decades, the contrast in the performance of the two countries is slight. China's grain output was roughly double India's in 1952 and, despite fluctuations, the ratio remained roughly the same throughout. Some people have argued that India's grain performance after the recent growth in wheat output has been better than China's. Sinha[4] cites compound rates of growth of "food production," 1957 to 1970, of 1.3 per cent for China and 2.7 per cent for India (per year), but these figures seem far too heavily influenced by the

---

[1] J.L. Buck, *Land Utilization in China*, New York, 1937

[2] D.H Perkins, in *China in Crisis* (edited by Ping-ti Ho and Tang Tsou), Chicago, 1968, 1, 1, p. 200.

[3] "In assessing the performance of the Chinese economy, no single indicator is more significant than the annual harvest of grain"—Thomas Rawski, Recent Trends in the Chinese Economy, *China Quarterly* 53, January-March 1973, p. 3.

[4] In the *Times* (London), 4 December 1972, after a visit to China and on the basis of *People's Republic of China, Economic Assessment, Compendium of Papers*, 92nd Congress, Washington, 18 May 1972; UN *Statistical Yearbook*, New York, 1971; and Government of India, *The Fourth Plan Mid-Term Appraisal*, December 1971. His comparative figures for

last years of India's performance. Bardhan,[5] on the basis of the data included here for the period 1952 to 1967, argues that the annual rate of growth of foodgrains production was 1.9 per cent for China and 1.7 per cent for India; because the broad direction of grain output is heavily distorted by a major downturn in the case of both countries, he also calculates the annual growth rate after excluding the two worst years (1965-66 and 1966-67 for India and 1960 and 1961 for China)—2.5 per cent for both countries, barely a hair's breadth ahead of the likely rate of population growth.

China's grain output seems to grow much more strongly than India's when it does grow, but it also falls much more drastically when it falls. Contrary to the popular argument about the superiority of "socialism," the fluctuations in China's output seem to have been much greater than India's.

Including other major items of agricultural production reduces the differences between the two countries since China seems to have had a slightly poorer performance in major non-grain crops than in grain, whereas India's has not (or, at least, not to the same extent). Bardhan estimates the annual compound growth rate for agricultural output from 1953 to 1965 at roughly three per cent for both countries. Rawski,[6] relying on the combination of grain and cotton (since relatively little is known in most recent years of the output of subsidiary Chinese crops such as edible oilseeds, sugar, tea, vegetables and livestock), argues that between 1957 and 1971, China's average annual rate of growth of agricultural output was 2.1 per cent (or 1.2 per cent, 1957 to 1965, and 3.4 per cent, 1965 to 1971; Ashbrook[7] for the same two periods estimates 0.1 and 2.2 per cent).

China and India, 1957 to 1970, are for selected elements as follows:

Compound rates of growth :	*China*	*India*
Gross National Product	3.1	3.6
Gross National Product, *per capita*	1.0	1.0
Industrial production	6.0	6.0
Agricultural product	1.2	2.6
Population (in 1960s)	1.8—2.4	2.5

[5] Pranab Bardhan, "Recent Development in Chinese and Indian Agriculture", in *Comparative Development of India and China* (edited by Kuan-I Chen and J.S. Uppal), London, 1971, p. 46.

[6] Rawski, *op. cit.*

[7] A.G. Ashbrook, "China : Economic Policy and Economic Results, 1949—71", in *People's Republic of China, op. cit.*

Production of Foodgrains, Husked, Million Tonnes
(figures rounded)

India		China	(a)	(b)
1952-53	62	1952	125	
1953-54	72	1953	127	
1954-55	71	1954	130	
1955-56	69	1955	142	
1956-57	72	1956	148	
1957-58	67	1957	150	
1958-59	79	1958	165	166
1959-60	77	1959	138	
1960-61	82	1960	122	130
1961-62	83	1961	131	
1962-63	80	1962	141	146
1963-64	81	1963	148	
1964-65	89	1964	162	154
1965-66	72	1965	162	
1966-67	74	1966	178	146
1967-68	95	1967	186	154
1968-69	94	1968	(155)	
1969-70	100	1969	(162)	
1970-71	108	1970	194	
1971-72	104	1971	199	
1972-73	100 (estimate)	1972	203	
		1973	194	

Sources :

1. *India:* 1952-53 to 1960-61 data are the officially revised index numbers of agricultural production; 1960-61 to 1970-71 are the official production figures, contained in Table 1.5, *Economic Survey, 1971-72*, Government of India, 1972, p. 80.   1971-72 is the provisionally estimated official figure; 1972-73, an early guess (cf. *The Economic and Political Weekly*, 17 February 1973, Bombay, p. 366).

2. *China:* (i) The figures from 1952-1967 are derived from estimates for the total production of unhusked grain (employing a reduction factor of 0.81 for processing, following S. Ishikava, *Factors Affecting China's Agriculture in the Coming Decade*, Institute of Asian Economic Affairs, 1967, unpublished) by Pranab Bardhan, "Recent Development in Chinese and Indian Agriculture," in Kuan-I-Chen and J.S. Uppal, *Comparative Development of India and China*, London, 1971, p. 45, from the following sources.

(a) 1952-57—from official Chinese sources (State Statistical Bureau, *Ten Great Years*, Peking, 1960).

(b) 1958 and 1959—no official revisions of the inflated official figures for these years have yet been published, although it is officially accepted that the original estimates were incorrect. The figures given here are those cited in E.F. Jones, "The Emerging Pattern of China's Economic Revolution," in US Congress, Joint Economic Committee, *An Economic Profile of Mainland China*, VII, 1, 1967.

(c) For the sixties, there are no official estimates of the grain output available, although there are indirect references and suggestions from official sources. The figures for 1960-65, are from Jones, *ibid.* The 1966 figure is mentioned by Han Suyin in *China in the Year 2001*, London, 1967, p. 54 (220 million tons), and the 1967 total by Anna Louise Strong in *Letter from China*, 15 January 1968, the difference between the two years being confirmed by Vice-Premier Hsieh Fu-chih's statement that unhusked grain production increased by 10.5 million tons between 1966 and 1967. In 1965, Chou En-lai confirmed the figure for 1964 (200 million tons).

(ii) The alternative series (b)—every two years—is included merely to indicate some of the diversity of estimates that have been made. These figures are taken from the full annual series, 1957 to 1967, for unhusked foodgrains, prepared by Werner Klatt, *The China Quarterly* 35, July-September 1968, p. 155.

(iii) The 1968 and 1969 figures are not officially supported and can only be treated with great reservation. The 1968 figure, suggested by very poor weather in some ten provinces, was estimated by the China Association, London, and reported in the *Financial Times*, 28 May 1969. The 1969 figure was reported by the Tanjug correspondent in Peking.

The 1970 figure is reported by Edgar Snow from his interview with Chou En-lai (240 million metric tons; cf. "Ciu En-lai ci parla della potenza Cinese," *Epoca*, Milan, 28 February 1971, p. 21). The 1971 figure is included in *Peking Review*, 1, 1972, p. 10 (246 million metric tons) and New China News Agency, 1 January 1971. The last two figures are attributed to Chou En-lai by a group of Scandinavian journalists who interviewed him in November 1972, reported from Stockholm radio in *The China Quarterly* 53, January-March 1973, p. 196. *Note*—The figure is attributed to the year 1973, although it clearly refers to what can have been known about 1972-73.

Given the difficulties in estimated China's population, comparing the grain per head of the two countries compounds the difficulties. However, for what they are worth, some of the figures can be given. Bardhan, on the official basis of a Chinese population of 575 million in 1952, estimates the annual production per head of processed foodgrains at 237.3 kilograms, in comparison to India's 164 kilograms in 1952-53 (32 per cent below China); on a Chinese population of 728 million in 1965, the comparable figures are 222.3 kilograms for China and 182 kilograms for India, 1964-65 (22 per cent lower). Others have calculated China's *per capita* foodgrain figures at significantly higher levels. For example,

O.L. Dawson[8] offers for 1960 to 1965 a range of 237 to 275 kilograms, much further in advance of India.

However, the broad conclusion—that, given the differences in starting points, the differences over time are relatively slight— remains. This is surprising since China has been significantly in advance of India in increasing inputs in agriculture. Chinese chemical fertilizer is said to have increased to nearly 17 million metric tons in 1971 (of which, nine million tonnes came from the modern sector); in India, consumption barely reached 5.5 million tonnes (all from the modern sector). Tractor use had reached 135,000 in China in 1956; 31,000 in India by 1961. The fragmentary holdings in India must have impeded the expansion of output and further exaggerated its relative disadvantage. Chinese agriculture also has always been more intensively cultivated, the irrigated area is larger, and the per hectare rice yields consistently higher. The explanation of China's relatively poor performance lies in the interruptions to production rather than the force of its growth. If expansion could be sustained over a long period, then China ought to be able to draw ahead of India much more rapidly than in the past; if the periods 1958 to 1964 and 1967 to 1970 could have been avoided (and they were not at all simply determined by natural conditions), this relative superiority would have become rapidly apparent.

Agriculture, where it is the major sector and there are no external sources, provides the main source of capital accumulation for the industrialization of any economy. Agriculture's growth is closely related to the possibility of industrial expansion, and fluctuations in the fortunes of agriculture can have a powerful effect on the "modern economy." Both the Indian and Chinese governments have in practice chosen to subordinate their respective economies to the short-run fortunes of agriculture, to the power of dominant rural groups. Perhaps there was no option in the given circumstances—income per head was too low to risk a more thorough-going attempt to overcome the rural elites and drain an increased proportion of resources out of the land. Whatever the reasons, the result is that a sluggish agriculture or agricultural fluctuations periodically curb the expansion of industry in the

[8] Irrigation Developments under the Communist Regime, in J.L. Buck, O.L. Dawson and Y.L. Wu, *Food and Agriculture in Communist China*, New York, 1966.

present framework of policy. In the long term, it seems, the rural surplus is too small to support sustained growth.

The rough picture of Chinese grain production is reflected in an exaggerated form in Chinese industrial growth. When Chinese industry has grown, it has done so with great speed, only to be checked and plunged downwards. Indeed, in contrast to India, the Chinese industrial economy seems to exhibit the wildest symptoms of capitalist instability. For example, the official index of industrial production (including handicrafts) rose from 100 in 1956 to a claimed 258 in 1959 (and, from one official source, to 332 in 1960), only to fall back to 184 in 1963 and 212 in 1964.[9] Field's index[10] moderates the amplitude somewhat—to 189 in 1960, 110 in 1962 and 121 in 1963. In the machine building sector, Cheng has constructed an index[11] (1957:100) which registered a dizzy 305 in 1960 and 122 in 1962.

By contrast, India's progress has been slower but has suffered from less drastic falls in production. Thus, the 1956:100 index reached 130 in 1960 and 166 in 1963. The 1960:100 fell only once (in 1966, by 0.7 per cent) although it was exceedingly sluggish in some years. India's overall rate of industrial growth, 1957 to 1970, is put at some six per cent annually (6.6 per cent for the modern industrial sector, but some four per cent if the small-scale sector is included[12]). The sustained growth of the second and third five year plans has not been restored in the late sixties and early seventies: the rate of growth has tended to decline, the more recent the year.[13] China's industrial growth rate is less easily quantified, but it is clear that there has been a relative decline from the extremely high rates of growth in the first five-year plan (19 per cent per year).

[9] Figures presented in the State Statistical Bureau's *Ten Great Years*, Peking, 1960, pp. 87, 94; 1956-58 and thereafter, from various official Chinese sources, compiled by Robert Michael Field, Chinese Communist Industrial Production, in *An Economic Profile of Mainland China*, Studies prepared for the Joint Economic Committee of Congress, Washington, 1967, Vol. 1, p. 273.

[10] Field, *ibid.*

[11] C.Y. Cheng, *The Machine Building Industry in Communist China*, New York, 1971, p. 108.

[12] From Ruddar Datt and K.P.M. Sundharam, *Indian Economy*, New Delhi, 1969, reprinted in an abbreviated form in Chen and Uppal, *op. cit.*, pp. 75-76.

[13] See Chapter 1 for further discussion of this.

This high rate was related to the existence of much unutilized capacity at the end of the civil war, whereas in India the problem was the overutilization of capacity during the Second World War without proper replacements and repairs. Some of the estimates of Chinese industrial growth since the first plan are as follows: Richman[14] proposes 5.5 to 6.5 per cent for 1957 to 1966; Field[15] five to six per cent, 1957 to 1965, and 5.4 to 6.6 per cent for 1957 to 1970: Rawski[16] nine to 10.8 per cent, 1957 to 1965, and 9.9 per cent, 1965 to 1971.

China's performance on the most optimistic account is considerably better than India's, and on the less optimistic, slightly better, but even at best, the overall rate of growth is not dramatically different. Technically, India's productive capacity is almost certainly more advanced than China's and the modern units on a larger scale; the diversity of India's output is probably greater and more sophisticated. But both economies have made very considerable advances—both now have important programmes in the fields of aerospace and nuclear energy, in electronics and computers. China still depends on imports for much of its needs in heavy trucks, special steels, ocean shipping, modern aircraft, chemical, metallurgical and oil refining equipment; India's dependence on imports of complete units is probably less than China's, but its dependence on imported components in a much wider range of manufacturing output is much greater. India's physical output is much smaller than China's and, relatively, growing smaller (in steel, the contrast is most dramatic: China's output of steel in the modern sector is some 14 million tonnes, with another seven million tonnes (1971) from the "traditional" sector; India's total output is about seven million tonnes).

In neither case has the performance had the sort of wide ranging effects in transforming both societies which were seen earlier during development. It is now nearly a quarter of a century since both countries began to attempt systematic capital accumulation, a period comparable perhaps to that in the Soviet Union between 1928 and 1951. The base line poverty of India and China and the rising price of development are strongly underscored in the com-

[14] Barry M. Richman, *Industrial Society in Communist China*, New York, 1969, p. 596.

[15] Field, *op. cit.*

[16] Rawski, *op. cit.*

parison with Russia. China's *per capita* grain availability in 1952 is said to have been less than half that in the Soviet Union in 1928.[17] The rulers of Russia pillaged agriculture to sustain a break-neck pace of industrialization regardless of fluctuations in agricultural output. In China and India, there has been relatively little significant increase in the marketed surplus of agriculture in the long term, and downturns in agricultural output have been allowed to affect the course of industrial growth decisively.

However, all this concerns growth in output, industrial or agricultural. Output bottlenecks are one of the key factors restricting growth in a backward economy. But expansion in output does not show what changes are taking place in the overall distribution of employment. It is here that the grounds for real pessimism for the ruling classes of India and China appear. Neither economy has shown any sustained capacity to utilize its available labour force. Even in China where more efforts have apparently been made to lower the capital-labour ratio, the same emphasis on labour productivity in industry minimizes employment. The rural areas are constantly used as a place to exile surplus labour in order to minimize urban labour costs and preserve low industrial output prices. The maintenance of police controls round China's cities shows how far the mass of the rural population willingly accepts this state of affairs.[18] Estimates of unemployment in China probably do not exist; assessments of Indian unemployment scarcely mean anything (because of the methodological difficulties in measuring anything so unequivocal as "unemployment" among casual labourers). Yet the rate of growth of employment in relationship to the estimated growth in the labour force gives us some conception of the gap. The expulsion of young people from China's cities gives us another.

While the rate of growth in gross national product in China may even be as high as it was in the Soviet Union in its first two five-year plans (1928 to 1938)—roughly six per cent per year (10-14 per cent rate of growth of industrial output)—the effects on Chinese society have been slight in comparison. It is possible at present levels of technology, for a very large backward country to aggregate resources from a very poor population on a scale sufficient to sustain

[17] Bardhan, *op. cit.*

[18] This is discussed in more detail in my review article, "China's Cities", *Economy and Society*, London, 1/1, February 1972.

for a given period a relatively high rate of growth in output. But this still leaves the overwhelming mass of the population much as it was before, at levels close to subsistence. China has not pursued industrialization by any new method, nor is it clear what a "new method" would mean. Nor, in following the "old methods" of industrialization, has there been much evidence that China has made some qualitative breakthrough. Indeed, China's national leadership has always been far more cautious in the perspective it has suggested for future economic development than its foreign supporters. The specific peculiarities of Chinese economic development flow rather from its relative backwardness in the middle of the 20th century than any conscious and deliberate shaping. As always, what is forced upon the Chinese leadership is portrayed by them as virtue (a characteristic not at all confined to the leadership of China). The more backward a country, the *less* possibility it has of any voluntary redirection of its economy—and breaking the back of the material problems of a society is the precondition for freedom of action for the ruling class, let alone freedom for the mass of the people.

The propaganda of the Chinese regime—and to a lesser extent, that of the Indian ruling class—implies that *organization* is a basic factor in stifling economic development. Reorganization can therefore release the resources which will make possible development, and reorganization essentially on a national basis. It is the argument of this chapter that this is not so. The organization of the Chinese economy and the morale of the Chinese people are not the basic factors in this question. Decentralization is rather the *product* of relatively poor long-term economic development (poor in relationship to what is needed in terms of transforming the country)—a response to stagnant employment—than the explanation of what growth has taken place.[19] Indeed, decentralization positively restricts the possibility of the economy growing at its full potential, disperses resources that should be concentrated. It is quaintly ignoring abundant historical experience to describe this as a "Chinese model" of development.

The central problem facing China and India is the gross shortage of resources in relationship to the price of development, contemporary technology and its poor employment capacity.

---

[19] See Chapter 5 for further discussion of this.

Redistributing poverty definitely brings all sorts of valuable results, but speeding development is not—other things being equal—one of them. Reorganizing the economy temporarily alleviates a basic scarcity, but it cannot ultimately overcome it. Nor indeed can the reorganization be sustained when growth is poor if it does not correspond to the material reality of the society concerned—poor growth has generated successive convulsions of the leadership in China; in both India and China, it has led to the dilution of the practices of State planning to the point where the government scarcely seems to play much of a directing role at all. Of course, there are supporters of both governments who praise this "increased flexibility" of planning!

The short-term immediate prospects for each economy are very different—at the time of writing, Indian industrial output is, relative to the past, in recession, and agricultural output is again in crisis; Chinese industrial output is expanding rapidly, but the growth of agriculture has been quite severely checked. But the short-term prospects could be reversed quite quickly. In neither case does this necessarily show the long-term tendencies. The sustained import-substitution boom of the fifties has now been exhausted, and the sixties have been marked to a greater or lesser degree by faltering performance. The governments of both countries have responded—or have been compelled to respond—in not dissimilar ways to this problem. One element in this response has been an expansion in external links to strengthen the national government against its domestic opposition. China's grain purchases,[20] increasing diplomatic links and commercial purchases, India's periodic grain purchases and foreign borrowing, all are part of the attempt by the respective leaderships to right their balance on a slippery slope by leaning on outside forces. In China's case this has assumed, in comparison to its "self-reliance" propaganda, surprisingly large proportions—estimates of China's foreign trade put it at roughly $4,200 million, or just slightly more than that of India in 1970-71 (preliminary figures: $4,164 million). Of course, India's external borrowing is now reaching the stage where the servicing and repayment of cumulative debts is becoming a crippling burden on its external payments. China does not bear this burden, although it is almost certain that the Chinese

[20] On this, see Audrey Donnithorne, *China's Economic System*, London, 1967.

Government will soon accept foreign credits and loans in order to make up with cheaper imports what is lacking at home.

However, much the most powerful external discipline on China is not its involvement in foreign trade but its maintenance of a defence programme, the main lines of which are necessarily determined by foreign technology. This calls, on a massive scale, upon all the scarcest resources of the Chinese economy and produces few significant benefits for the civil economy. It imposes upon Chinese peasants and workers the staggering cost of the technology of Soviet and American arms production. Almost certainly, that drain on resources also helps to reduce China's economic performance closer to India's, despite so many favourable contrary factors. The defence programme imposed on China is not of its choice. More vividly than any other factor, this illustrates how a country cannot cut itself off from the world system in order to devote itself to its own development. The world—global imperialism—imposes its imperatives upon each segment of the system, regardless of the wishes of the people concerned. Through the defence programme, the whole of the modern industrial sector is reshaped in accordance with priorities outside the choice of China's leadership.

There is very little room to manoeuvre between the internal pressures of a peasant society and the external vice of imperialism. In both India and China, the internal pressure has shifted the balance of each economy towards the restoration of a flourishing peasant economy;[21] the external forces, operating partly through the defence programme, shift the balance towards reintegrating each economy back into the world system, recolonizing it as a subordinate part. The millstones grind finely. The longer the present situation lasts, the more powerful the forces of reintegration become. Of course, Chairman Mao may well strive with might and main to reconcile his people to austerity and equality, but the struggle against material backwardness without the requisite resources is a labour of Sisyphus. At each turn, backwardness restores the inequality,[22] restores the overt privileges that reflect the covert power system. For ruling classes are created

[21] See Chapters 1 and 5.
[22] See Chapter 4 here. On the accepted inequalities in household income between communes, cf. Shahid Javed Burki, *A Study of Chinese Communes*, Cambridge, Mass., 1969.

not by selfishness, by some corrupt or unreformed psychology—if it were so, psychotherapy would be a revolutionary activity—but by backwardness. No number of good intentions can conquer objective reality just by wishing.

Yet "objective reality" need not play this role if we step out from the constrictions of one merely nationalist perspective. The problem is as it is because backwardness is locked up inside national boundaries. What Stalin called "Socialism in One Country" has become "Development in One Country." The second was possible in the 1930s for the Soviet Union; the first was not. Now even the second has become impossible. Development can now take place only on a world scale—the vast accumulated resources of the industrialized countries must be brought to bear on the development of the rest of the world. The perspective of national development in isolation has become essentially reactionary. What national development takes place is merely in the interests of the local national ruling class, purchased at the cost of the sacrifice of the interests of the majority. What is now almost a quarter of a century of development experience in India and China demonstrates that imperialism has made the nationalist and gradualist perspective entirely utopian.

11

International Socialism and Perspectives for the Backward Countries in the Seventies*

I. Where we stand

The position of International Socialism on the backward countries in the past has been in essentials a reiteration of the points advanced by Trotsky in *The Permanent Revolution*. The heart of this position is a declaration that only through the agency of the industrial working class in the backward countries can imperialism be decisively defeated in the backward countries and can socialism become a possibility. But if, in the unstable conditions of a backward country, a minority proletariat can defeat imperialism by establishing workers' power, the dictatorship of the proletariat, that dictatorship can only survive and provide the basis for socialism if it is able to spread the revolution to the imperialist countries themselves. If the revolution does not spread, then the dictatorship of the proletariat is likely to be defeated or wracked with the internal contradictions of a backward society in an imperialist-dominated world. On the other hand, if any other class leads the onslaught on imperialism, then the perspective of the revolutionary movement will be nationalist rather than internationalist. Thus, the contradictions of isolated backwardness will be enshrined from the very beginning in the movement; the movement will not be able to break fully with imperialism; and ultimately

* First published in *International Socialism*, 42, February-March 1970, "Prospects for the Seventies", p. 20.

the post-revolutionary regime will turn upon the working class itself.

II. Introduction

(*a*) Events since 1917 have continued to demonstrate the long-term attrition of the world bourgeoisie. On the one hand, in the advanced capitalist countries, the position of the mass of private owners of the means of production has been successively limited by two interdependent processes: (*i*) the concentration of production has continued to separate the mass of small powerless owners from the largest owners and managers of companies; (*ii*) the alliance between the largest companies and the State, embodied most clearly since the last World War in the permanent arms economy, has further concentrated power within a minority of the owning class. Without a solid core of State capitalism, private capitalism in the advanced capitalist countries cannot survive. Finally, the accumulation of capital in a whole new area of the world economy, the Eastern bloc, has not been undertaken by private capitalists but by the State. On the other hand, in the backward countries, the native bourgeoisie is too small—because its role is circumscribed by imperialism—and too integrated into imperialism itself, to constitute an independent national class. To survive, it also needs a more or less extensive public sector to protect it and make profitable enterprise possible. Thus, on a world scale, the bourgeoisie has proved progressively less capable of reproducing itself. The dominance of private ownership has been steadily weakened, without this weakening in any way the dominance of capitalism as a system or the dominance of the world ruling classes.

(*b*) The integration of the parts of the world economy has also continued at an increasing pace since the First World War. But this integration does not signify increasing interdependence. Contrary to Lenin's account of imperialism, the evolution of the world capitalist system has not led to the advanced countries being the purely consuming segment and the backward countries the producing segment of the world economy. On the contrary, the advanced countries have concentrated an increasing proportion of *both* production and consumption, thereby making themselves less, not more, dependent upon the backward countries. This asymmetrical integration means that any socialist strategy that relies *solely* upon a revolt in the backward countries producing a major economic crisis in the advanced countries is doomed to failure. This is not, however, to say that the *political* implications of a revolt in one or more backward countries could not be important in the advanced countries. Around the European bloc of advanced countries, there are numerous "weak links" which, if broken, could perhaps precipitate a political challenge within the advanced countries. Ireland is one of the more obvious examples, but there is also Spain, Greece, Turkey, Algeria and the European countries under Soviet domination. These are among the same selection of countries seen by the Bolsheviks as important for the development of the European struggle. Lenin himself carefully distinguished between the different implications of struggles in near and distant backward countries:

> The struggle of the oppressed nations *in Europe*, a struggle capable of going to the lengths of insurrection and street fighting will 'sharpen the revolutionary crisis in Europe' infinitely more than a much more developed rebellion in a remote colony. A blow delivered against the English imperialist bourgeoisie by a rebellion in Ireland is a hundred times more significant politically than a blow of equal weight delivered in Asia or Africa.[1]

[1] *Selected Works*, V. p. 304. Lenin's 1920 theses, although applicable to the whole colonial world, were primarily directed at the Middle East, Turkey and Iran in particular. The subsequent Comintern Congresses were similarly more concerned with nearer backward countries than distant. The Fifth Congress in 1924 was mainly concerned with prospects in the Balkans. Despite US attempts to demonstrate an irrepressible Soviet desire to control all the backward countries from the very earliest times, in fact Stalin undertook only the barest intervention in the Far East, primarily in China to offset possible Japanese intervention in Siberia, and usually through orthodox diplomatic means (fostering one warlord against another). Very briefly—from 1925 to 1927—he undertook a more systematic intervention through the Kuomintang, but the debacle of 1927 cut short this interest. In any case, the interest had existed in part to defeat Trotsky in the internal faction fight within the Russian party, and that interest ceased after 1927. Up until the Second World War extensive Soviet intervention was inhibited by Russian military weakness. In the case of India, Moscow's interest was so weak, it delegated responsibility to the British CP (Palme Dutt); similarly, the

On the other hand, it would be quite wrong to underestimate the *indirect* effects of a struggle in a more remote backward country. Thus, the strain of the Viet Nam war on the US Government has precipitated important conflicts within the United States. The tension between expenditure on defence and on urban renewal and welfare payments brings the Viet Namese struggle into the middle of the internal American political debate.

(c) The regimes in the backward countries face three inter-related problems.

(i) The national question—that is, securing or preserving the national independence of the country concerned.

(ii) The agrarian question—that is, transforming agriculture so that the rural population secures rights in the land and an adequate livelihood from agriculture, at the same time as there is an agricultural surplus capable of supporting the cities and the drive to industrialization.

(iii) The development question—that is, raising the rate of the accumulation of capital to the point where a long-term transformation of the economy takes place. This transformation is embodied in a rapid expansion of national output at the same time as the share generated in agriculture is declining, and the proportion of the population employed in agriculture is declining.

The impossibility of solving permanently any of these three problems arises directly from the failure of the world proletariat to present a revolutionary challenge to the system as a whole. Of major importance in this respect is the failure of the proletariat in the advanced countries to challenge their respective ruling classes, and thereby make possible—at a minimum—the destruction of the strait-jacket of Stalinism on the one hand, and Social Democratic reformism on the other. A revolutionary proletarian response to the rise of Nazism in Germany, to the Civil War in Spain, to the Second World War, to the carve-up of Europe after the war, to the Hungarian revolution, and so on, would have laid down a series of political alternatives with major implications throughout the world. Without the example of a proletarian alternative from the most advanced and experienced

---

Philippines was given to the US CP, Viet Nam to the French CP, and so on. This lack of direct control made possible the development of independent Communist parties.

sections of the proletariat, the field was left open in the backward countries to other political alternatives.

III. The class struggle in the backward countries

(a) Stalinism and Social Democratic reformism were the two faces the proletariat of the capitalist countries presented to the rest of the world. They were also the active forces on the Left organizing within the proletariats of the backward countries. In practice, Social Democracy was much less important than Stalinism, and less clearly distinguished from it, than in the advanced capitalist countries. Thus, at no stage in the struggle for independence, did the major political alternatives available encourage an authentic, independent proletarian response, an explicit demand for the dictatorship of the proletariat, workers' power. Moreover, changes within the capitalist countries and between the imperialist powers and their colonial dependencies made it possible in a large number of cases for political independence to be granted without a major social struggle. The damping down of a domestic social struggle inhibited the formation of politically distinct classes and permitted a heterogenous class coalition to wage the battle for independence.

(b) But these two "external" circumstances—the internationally available political alternatives on the Left, and the reaction of imperialism to the struggle for independence—were also matched by certain objective features in the new working classes of the backward countries. These objective features would not have inhibited a proletarian movement had it appeared, but, in the circumstances, they fitted closely the political priorities of Stalinism. Very briefly, these features were:

(i) Telescoped economic development created new working classes in the backward countries which are much more sharply differentiated within the class. The working class simultaneously includes both the most advanced strata of technically highly skilled workers in—by world, not local, standards—the most sophisticated industries; plus an important block of unskilled or semi-skilled workers in industries important in earlier phases of development (for example, cotton textiles) both large-scale and small; plus an enormous mass of workers, many of them illiterate, in small-scale shops, household and traditional craft industries; plus an even larger number, partially employed in petty trading and miscellaneous services.

The old working class of western Europe in the early phases of capital accumulation was, by contrast, concentrated in the second of the four groups listed above—a small group of highly differentiated skilled workers, along with a mass of unskilled labour, both employed in what are today backward industries, with a much smaller section in the last group (petty trading and miscellaneous services).

Again, the speed of the development of working classes has tended to prevent the slow development of forms of working class organization. The pattern in Europe where skilled workers were able to organize craft unions, which then provided the stable leadership for mass unions, has not been possible in most backward countries. In many cases, the leap to mass industrial unions has been made, without the sinews of organization within the factories being capable of sustaining such units.

Furthermore, the proportions between production workers and other workers within the working class in backward countries has changed significantly. New investment has the modern technical characteristic that enormous additions are made to output with relatively little new employment (in comparison to 19th century European industrial investment). This relative decline in productive workers within the working class in part changes the nature of the class. Thus the pivotal role played by a concentrated mass of productive workers in the history of west European capitalism cannot be repeated in exactly the same way. On the other hand, the modern economy—even in backward countries—is a much more interdependent process, so that the effects of a relative decline in productive workers are offset by the interdependence of all segments of the modern economy.

On the other hand, social differentiation seems also to be more pronounced in the working classes of some of the backward countries. In British working-class history, the conflicts between workers from different parts of England, between English, Irish and Jewish workers, were factors which inhibited class solidarity, but these seem of less significance than the open communalism among, for example, Indian workers or tribalism among African workers. Imperialism itself deliberately played upon these divisions in order to maintain its control, and the newly independent ruling classes have not been averse to pursuing the same tactic. However, this factor cannot be assessed independently of the available political alternatives which stress class solidarity. In the absence of such a political alternative, the social fragmentation of the working class continues to reflect the fragmentation of the peasantry between different districts (since many of the new workers are rural migrants). This fragmentation, left to itself, can be very restrictive for a very long period of time, and is ultimately only superseded by the unified attack of the ruling class.

(ii) Imperialism and full or partial State capitalism has created a much larger urban petite bourgeoisie. For Marx, the petite bourgeoisie was pre-eminently the mass of peasant small-holders, the shopkeepers and independent artisans or small businessmen in small towns—that is, all *small property owners.* By the nature of its mode of production, such a stratum was incapable of collective political leadership and, as a result, oscillated between the two major classes, the proletariat and the bourgeoisie. By contrast, in the backward countries today (and, for that matter, in the advanced capitalist countries) the urban "petite bourgeoisie" is *property-less,* pre-eminently engaged in large-scale bureaucratic employment, especially in the agencies of the State. Its material conditions of life are very poor, particularly in comparison with its aspirations to a fully middle class way of life. On the other hand, its employment subjects it—as was not the case with the Victorian petite bourgeoisie—to large-scale collective organization, although not to direct organization in the production process (that is, the sources of the generation of material wealth remain outside its activities). Yet, being propertyless, this stratum has no vested interest in the private ownership of the means of production, nor is the bourgeoisie proper large enough to be a major point of attraction for this stratum. Because it is heavily concentrated in the cities, it dominates urban politics, particularly on the Left. And for obvious reasons this stratum is primarily interested in an extension of the power of the State.

(*c*) Thus, as a result of this changed class structure—of the weakness of the bourgeoisie proper, of the failure of the proletariat to raise an independent political alternative—the central debate in many backward countries is not that between the proletariat and the bourgeoisie, but between the urban petite bourgeoisie—pressing for an extension of the State and of public employment—and the rural petite bourgeoisie—pressing for the devotion of more national resources to agriculture. This is the heart of a struggle which appears in its external form as a political debate between State ownership—identified by the urban petite bourgeoisie as "socialism"—and rural capitalism.

The bourgeoisie proper is too weak to survive on its own, and the index of its weakness is shown in its dependence upon the State, the public sector and national planning. Thus, the bourgeoisie may, for limited purposes, ally with the urban petite bourgeoisie against the rural challenge of landowners, landlords and kulaks, but it is more likely in the long term to ally with the rural petite bourgeoisie in defence of private property. In any case, the role of the bourgeoisie is, at every stage, qualified by its intimate involvement with foreign capital, by its role as a fifth column of imperialism within the politically independent State.

(*d*) The perspectives of Stalinism appeal directly to the urban petite bourgeoisie. The mass of Communist Party members is most often drawn from this section of the population. The upper stratum of the working class is often better off than the mass of the bureaucratically employed petite bourgeoisie, and it has not in the past identified its interests separately. Indeed, the organization of the working class itself has most often appeared, not as the action of the skilled workers, part of the self-activity of the class itself, but as a by-product of the struggle of the urban petite bourgeoisie for dominance. Urban petit-bourgeois political parties created trade unions as ancillary supports for their politics, rather than workers creating unions to defend their interests. In the independence struggle, as in Bismarck's Germany, the workers traded their political loyalty for the promise of welfare legislation and improved wages once independence had been won. After independence, where full State capitalism was not achieved, the urban petit-bourgeois political parties continued to use sections of the working class as supporting forces in their struggle for power, but at each stage ensuring that these forces did not assume any kind of independent role (thus, for example, the bribe for worker loyalty in the independence struggle was in part a body of labour laws; since independence, labour courts have become a major institution in mediating the class struggle; the law is introduced by the State, itself the bastion of the urban petite bourgeoisie; its existence demands that trade unions be operated by lawyers, that is, members of the urban petite bourgeoisie, and that only trade unions "recognized" by the State be permitted to fight in the courts). Again, however, the lack of an independent proletarian challenge makes possible the role of the urban petite bourgeoisie. If the challenge existed, then it would not be possible for the urban petite bourgeoisie to play the role it has done.

(*e*) Thus, the objective characteristics of the industrial working class and its relationship to other classes have provided an important basis for the success of Stalinism or perspectives close to Stalinism. This in its turn has inhibited the appearance of an independent proletarian politics. And this in turn has left the national stage vacant to purely nationalistic forces, and in particular, to the struggle for State capitalism by the urban petite bourgeoisie.

IV. The role of the petite bourgeoisie

(*a*) However, whether or not a genuine national bourgeois revolution is possible or the proletariat fails to begin the permanent revolution, the central questions facing any particular backward country remain. The vacuum has been filled by different types of petit-bourgeois leaderships, borrowing at different times on the grievances of different sections of the population in order to build and lead a coalition of classes. The existence of the vacuum has lent a degree of autonomy to sections of the urban petite bourgeoisie that was not envisaged by Trotsky (indeed, this possibility was explicitly ruled out by Trotsky in *The Permanent Revolution*).

But if there are great similarities between the sections of the urban petite bourgeoisie in different countries, there are also striking differences in the degree of autonomy with which such sections have been able to act. For example, both Mao Tse-tung in China and M.K. Gandhi in India built movements of class coalition. Mao warded off the demands of poor peasants in order to keep the rich peasants and small landlords in his coalition, stressing always that domestic issues of class conflict must be subordinated to the central task of evicting foreign imperialism. Likewise—although in very different language—Gandhi consistently opposed class demands within Congress, stressing the need for "harmony" in the common struggle against the British. In

China, social disorder and military organization in a remote geographical area underpinned the supremacy of Mao within the Communist Party, and the relative independence of the party from class interests; as a result, Mao was scarcely ever openly challenged by a class-oriented opposition. In India, the struggle was waged in the centres of power, and Congress was a coalition of interests wider than those used by the Chinese Communist Party. Gandhi's attempt to secure the adherence of large landowners to his cause, and keep loyal the largest capitalists, brought him under continuous attack from the urban petit-bourgeois elements within Congress. Both Mao and Gandhi claimed that it was really the peasantry which was the basis for the movement, but in practice both relied heavily on sections of urban classes— the small town petite bourgeoisie and the rich peasantry. What most sharply differentiates the two movements is Mao's use of military force. The army gave the CCP its independence of class interests; the lack of military force made Gandhi as much victim as master of the class coalition he led. But the possibility of using independent military force was a function, not so much of CCP politics or subjective wishes, as the concrete circumstances of the struggle in China.

Thus, the clearest difference between the two movements is in the degree of autonomy available to the leadership. Where the autonomy was greatest, as in China, the circumstances of the national independence struggle were particularly unique. In the spectrum of independence struggles, the Indian example is much closer to the norm than the Chinese. Again, in China the final victory of the revolution led to a much more decisive break with the old order. In India, Congress tends constantly to resubmerge in the remnants of the pre-independence society, to fight out in its midst the unresolved social struggle.

(*b*) In the case of China, nearly a hundred years of social disorder, including the disintegration of the country, a major foreign invasion, and waves of a long drawn out civil war, preceded the Communist Party's victory. This background of long-term social collapse is essential in understanding how the leadership of the Chinese Communist Party was able (*i*) to achieve a role independent of the entrenched classes of pre-revolutionary China; and (*ii*) to secure a much more decisive break with the old order, and to undertake a much more radical attempt to solve both the national and agrarian questions.

But the social basis of the Chinese regime and the failure of the international revolution to relieve beleaguered China of its national isolation also demonstrates that the Chinese leadership cannot finally answer the development question and, as a result, cannot therefore achieve long-term stability. In the period since 1948, the great efforts to accelerate the accumulation of capital in China have done little more than keep pace with the rate of growth of the population. The poverty of the population severely restricts the possibility of extracting a substantial surplus consistently over a long period of time. Without that surplus, only foreign assistance, itself only forthcoming on a significant scale in the event of a proletarian revolution in the capital-abundant countries of the advanced world, could relieve the inner contradictions of the regime. But without development, the regime tends to stagnate or disintegrate into warring factions, which even further inhibits the national accumulation rate. And if the development question cannot be answered, then the other two questions will reassert themselves in new forms—concretely, for example, by peasant seizures of the land once more in order to secure a stable livelihood and throw off the yoke of the State's demand for the agrarian surplus; or by foreign encroachments on China's territory, encroachments which China can do little to prevent in conditions of backwardness.

(c) The Communist parties have been, in the past, able to act as the most radical and disciplined wing of the urban petite bourgeoisie. Ironically, they borrow from the historical experience of the proletariat under capitalism in order to organize the urban petite bourgeoisie, and champion a coalition of interests. In the presence of an independent political proletariat, such organization would be no more than a shadow, but in its absence, it has in a few countries—in conditions of long-term social crisis—been able to play a major role. But it is *only* in a few countries. In India, the non-Communist urban petite bourgeoisie proved fully capable of leading the independence movement and resisting Communist takeover. The CP in India never came even remotely near to assuming a monopoly of the nationalist cause. In Indonesia, the nationalists were similarly easily able to control the movement, despite having to wage a bitter and sustained war against Holland, and they prevented PKI domination up to long after the achievement of independence. The same is true in Burma where the urban petite bourgeoisie was much weaker, and in the Philippines and Malaya. Indeed, Viet Nam, where the Communist Party was able to secure an almost unchallenged hegemony of the nationalist movement, seems the exception rather than the rule.

Nor was it the Communist willingness to use armed force which secured their leadership. Between 1948 and 1950, the Communist Parties of Burma, Malaya, Indonesia and the Philippines, all launched armed struggles and campaigns of guerrilla warfare, sparked off by the victory of the Communist Party in China and the advent of the cold war. In all cases, the struggles were disastrous, isolating the cadres from the centres of power and population, and destroying their political credibility. In Indonesia, it took ten years for the PKI to live down this abortive episode. In Burma, the Communists became irrelevant rural fragments. In Malaya, the nationalist forces were pushed into the arms of the British in self-defence. In no case, did the armed struggle bring to the Communist parties the hegemony of the nationalist movement. The failure of the advocates of universal guerrilla warfare to analyze this disaster indicates the lack of seriousness in their perspective.

(*d*) However, in those exceptional conditions where the Communists have been able to lead a majority of the petite bourgeoisie, victory has made possible a more radical attempt to overcome the three central questions facing backward countries. But this attempt is necessarily conditioned by world circumstances, by the demands which those circumstances make upon the new regime. The demands, with domestic material conditions, circumscribe at every stage how far the three central questions can be met. In failing to meet the three questions, the stability of the State capitalist regime is immediately placed in jeopardy. To form a stable ruling class—that is, a class the members of which recognize a common interest against the subordinate classes as more important than the interests which divide sections of the ruling class—requires both a long period of stability and a relatively high rate of growth of the national economy. Russia provides a good model in this respect. Without a high rate of economic growth, the rulers of Russia would have tended to disintegrate into warring factions, each competing to displace the other. High growth, expansion sustained in the armaments industry, gave

Stalin the power to mobilize the majority against minority opposi-
tiow nithin the party, to create out of a socially heterogeneous
group, an homogenous ruling class. In this sense, China today
does not possess a stable State capitalist ruling class. It has the
embryo of such a class. Whether the Chinese leadership can
create a class, at the same time as sustaining the rate of economic
growth and warding-off foreign threats, turns upon the behaviour
of the rest of the world, upon the imperialist powers.

(*e*) In all the post-colonial backward countries, the stability of
the new regime, of the urban petite bourgeoisie, is circumscribed
by the existence of other entrenched classes—a land-owning class
and rich peasantry, an urban bourgeoisie and proletariat. In the
new regimes led by Communist parties such is the autonomy of
the new order, they have been able to liquidate over a period of
time the exploiting classes, simultaneously expanding their own
material base, the public sector. Thus, in China, first the land
owners were eliminated, then the rich peasantry, and finally, the
national bourgeoisie (although in this case, interest and dividend
payments to the *rentiers* were not eliminated until the Cultural
Revolution, nearly 20 years after the revolution). This leaves,
of the former entrenched classes, only the urban proletariat.
In China, the regime has tried to keep the proletariat in alliance
with the regime, but the demands of capital accumulation constantly push the regime towards diluting the working class—the
"worker-peasant system"—to cut labour costs. External threats
impel the regime to expand its defence efforts which in turn force
it to raise the rate of accumulation, which in turn increases the
pressure on the subordinate classes and the likelihood that the
"alliance" will break down. If it does, the urban working class
could once more raise an independent challenge to the regime.[2]

(*f*) On the other hand, in those countries where the urban
petite bourgeoisie was unable to secure as much autonomy as in
China, the role of entrenched classes is much more powerful.
For the sake of simplicity, two separate cases can be identified:

(i) Countries where the urban petite bourgeoisie was able to
terminate the independence struggle, and thereby inherited a
major position of power in the post-independence regime. In

[2] cf. an attempt to reconstruct the behaviour of the Shanghai working
class during the most radical phase of the Cultural Revolution, in VI,
The Workers, Chapter 4 above.

India, Congress tried to expand its autonomy by liquidating the traditional rulers, undertaking a land reform programme, and pursuing an industrialization strategy for massive expansion of the public sector. In this way, it was hoped to secure the same result as that in China. However, while the traditional rulers were deprived of political power (based upon the old Princely States), and universal suffrage in the short-term undercut traditional power, nevertheless, the old rulers and the richer peasantry infiltrated Congress to the point where it was possible for them to nullify the land reform and, indeed, expand their power by milking the State of development funds. On the other hand, within the organs of the State, the national bourgeoisie was able to protect and enhance its position, limiting the State to those industrial activities directly of need to private capital. In Egypt, the military origin of the new regime lent it greater autonomy than that secured in India, and it was able to make much greater encroachments upon national capital, but not to eliminate private land ownership. In both Egypt and India, a "mixed" system prevails, that is, an unstable struggle between the urban petite bourgeoisie and entrenched classes, between a public sector and a majority private one. Again, the movements of the world economy in terms of changes in trade, capital, direct political manipulation, heavily determine how far this struggle can be won by one side or the other, and how far the accumulation process is raised or lowered.

(ii) Countries which did not go through an independence struggle at all, and therefore, ones in which the urban petite bourgeoisie was never able to the same degree to achieve some political autonomy. In some cases, the State in these countries plays the role of a classically Bonapartist regime—as, for example, in Brazil—balancing between entrenched classes which ultimately control the main basis of power. Again, however, external events—like the role of foreign capital—can push even this kind of State into creating a public sector, which, in its turn, can sustain a separate interest striving to dominate the society.

(g) The fragmentation endemic in the petite bourgeoisie does not cease to exist in modern conditions. Particularly is this so given that the urban petite bourgeoisie only really creates its material basis *after* the revolution, and can only do so in conditions of rapid industrialization. The main target of the urban petite bourgeoisie is the State, and therefore *national* power is its sole aim.

Conceptions of international solidarity obviously threaten this national power (unless "international solidarity" is seen as *subordination* of foreign countries). Thus, the domestic fragmentation of the leadership is matched by the impossibility of an international alliance of petit-bourgeois regimes. Not only, therefore, is domestic instability one result, external disunity in the face of imperialism is equally disastrous. Given that many backward countries are primarily commodity producers for imperialist powers, the class nature of the regimes involved makes consistent collaboration between them in order to control their markets impossible. Thus, for example, faced with a monopoly buyer of oil, the disunity of the oil-producing countries is the trump card in imperialist control. Individual backward countries are in this way vulnerable to complete manipulation by the advanced capitalist powers. The only available response is an attempt at national economic autarchy, attempting to cut links with the world market. But this in its turn only makes even more difficult the process of capital accumulation, only "drags backwards" the productive forces, as Trotsky says in *The Permanent Revolution*. The costs of this regression are enormous. One calculation estimates that in 1965 the backward countries spent $2,100 million in domestic resources to manufacture automobile products which had a world market value of only $800 million. The backward countries paid this price in order to avoid importing these products from abroad. But the "loss" of $1,300 million is just about equal to the amount in aid advanced by the World Bank in the 23 years of its existence.

On the other hand, where the State capitalist regimes also intervene internationally, they do so, not to create an international class alliance which will wage a common class struggle within a number of countries against those countries' ruling classes, but merely to imitate the tactics of the imperialist powers, to establish "friendly" countries by offering aid and diplomatic assistance to the ruling classes. Thus, China's assistance to Zambia, or to Pakistan, at no stage includes even mild criticism of the existing regime, and thus aids the existing ruling classes against their own masses. In the case of Pakistan, China merely "ignored" the popular revolt of 1970-71, remained loyal to Ayub right up to the end (much as the Soviet Union remained loyal to the Kuomintang right up to the Chinese Communist

Party victory in China) and then merely transferred its support to the new military ruler, Yayha Khan.

(*h*) The instability endemic in the urban petite bourgeoisie forces the leadership of each regime to employ extraordinary measures to enforce loyalty. Imitating the State capitalist regimes, one-party States are used to enforce a common discipline on the disparate elements of the ruling class. Any criticism at all threatens to open Pandora's Box, to release the stifled class struggle. To eliminate all forms of opposition by using the mechanisms of party control, backed by liberal use of police truncheon, political murder and gaoling, describing the whole as "real" socialism, corresponding to the "classless" nature of the people, is one way to enforce stability. Another is to make the army the regime, so that to party discipline is added military control. The central contradictions of backwardness which impel army rule have been seen most recently in Indonesia, the Sudan, Libya, Somalia, Brazil, Bolivia, Argentina. On the other hand, the impossibility of the ruling class surviving without the bayonet is starkly matched by the impossibility of the bayonet solving the central contradictions. In Nigeria, Egypt, Pakistan, Burma, militarism is like a dangerous drug: the more it is taken, the more it is needed. Even the high rates of economic growth in Turkey and South Korea do not remove the instability. In Turkey, the army glowers in the wings, waiting only to return to power. In South Korea, the translation of the military leadership into civilian disguise only conceals the real balance of power. The prize for the year 1969 goes to Dahomey, clocking up its sixth *coup* since independence in 1960.

Again, the domestic instability provides an essential basis for imperialist manipulation—whether it be the French in Chad, or the Russians and Americans in the Middle East and south Asia. Urban petit-bourgeois leadership simultaneously exacerbates the conditions of backwardness and strengthens the domination of imperialism on a world scale.

(*i*) Any ruling class or clique reduced to dependence upon its armed forces—as in China—or reduced to making the armed forces the core of the ruling class—as in Egypt—is in a state of grave weakness, of endemic instability. Since the question of political power cannot be settled decisively, and there is little possibility of relief from abroad, it is impossible for the regime to answer the development question. And this means that there can also be no permanent answer to the national and agrarian questions. Thus, the perspective becomes one of insoluble stagnation. It is the paucity of political alternatives which permits the long-term crisis to continue, the paucity arising from the failure of the proletariat to intervene.

V. The development question

(a) Hitherto the most important engine of growth, forcing the most rapid rate of capital acccumulation, has been the world market. With the partial exceptions of American and Soviet development, virtually all other countries which have developed have done so by means of their relationship to the world economy, primarily by exporting goods but also by importing capital or, at least, capitalists. Today, there is no evidence at all that the exceptional conditions within which Russia and the United States developed (the land available, size of population, nature of external markets and technology) are shared by any of the currently backward countries. However, while integration into the world market appears to be a necessary condition of long-term growth, it is not a sufficient one. On the contrary, whereas in the 19th century, foreign capital went to backward countries to exploit raw material sources, thus expanding the export flow of the country concerned and making possible a major import flow of development equipment, now much of the direct foreign capital entering backward countries is interested in exploiting only the internal market and expanding its *imports* from its parent company in a metropolitan country. In the absence of large-scale exports from other sources within the backward country concerned, the balance of payments is a consistent restriction on the expansion of the economy, both in terms of importing new capital equipment, and also in importing raw materials and spare parts for existing plant (given a sluggish agriculture, the import of foodgrains may also exacerbate the working of the economy). On the other hand, to cut off all links with the world market (or at least, what links can be cut) is to force the economy back to an even more primitive stage, to base the accumulation process on what can be squeezed out of the local population. The problems involved in economic autarchy are greater than the benefits which accrue from ending foreign exploitation, although quite clearly foreign exploitation must be curtailed. In the absence of an international revolutionary alternative which will break the stranglehold of world imperialism, the contradictions of backwardness—for example, that increased exploitation by the world market is the precondition for an increased rate of domestic accumulation—are insoluble. It seems clear on the evidence since 1948 that none of the backward State capitalist countries has been able to sustain a rate of accumulation fast enough to constitute rapid development (there are few statistics on North Korea, but impressions suggest it has sustained the most significant growth). On the other hand, the most rapidly growing backward countries in the past decade are almost all in some way or other favoured client States (South Korea, Taiwan) satellites of a geographically close advanced market (Greece, Turkey, Spain; Jamaica and Mexico) or economies geared to export of one or more strategic commodities (Malaysia, Venezuela). Yet the growth that has taken place has not been rapid enough to subsume some of the central problems, to expand jobs as rapidly as the labour force and food as rapidly as the population and accumulation needs. In Venezuela, after a decade of a ten per cent rate of growth each year, unemployment is still as high as before. In India, unemployment and underemployment may cover as many as 30 or 40 millions. Meanwhile, the advance of world technology, monopolized at source by the advanced capitalist powers and designed for their needs, continually lowers the possibility of employing the population as output expands. As a result manufacturing continues consistently to employ a smaller proportion of the non-agricultural labour force. On the other hand, the fastest rate of growth stimulates very rapidly the development of a proletarian opposition which itself seeks to divert resources into wages—South Korea's ability to attract foreign capital is already under threat from the pressure of skilled labour for higher wages. Even in the most "favourable" conditions, the petit-bourgeois leadership is caught between the millstones of the world market and the proletariat, and its hopes of independent national power become increasingly illusory.

The symptoms of the crisis are: increasing financial dependence (an outflow of resources in repayment of aid, loans, dividends and interest); a relatively slow rate of growth, continually subject to restrictions from the balance of payments and fluctuations arising from oscillating or declining commodity prices; output expanding far more rapidly than employment, creating, as population and labour force increase, a growing army of under-employed and unemployed; the threat of the urban masses, subjected to conditions of the utmost misery. If the alternatives available are socialism or barbarism, the second has been the choice of the ruling groups in the backward countries today.

(b) There is little or no choice open to the leadership in the backward countries. Either they already command a part of the world market in a strategic commodity, or they are compelled just to hold on. The oil producers command the commodity in highest demand, and therefore possess the most advantageous economic position. But their disunity, and the feverish search for oil resources or substitute energy sources within the developed countries (most recently North Sea gas, Alaska, etc.) ensure that any individual oil producer cannot command his own price. This is even more true of other strategic commodities—copper, nickel, iron ore. If the price is too high, the capitalists of the advanced countries will find other sources, or create substitutes. Thus, even commanding a strategic commodity gives only short-term and strictly limited bargaining power to a backward country, let alone the weakness of commanding a commodity which is not strategic (coffee, tea, cocoa, jute, raw cotton). On the other hand, without a strategic commodity for export, a backward country has only its internal market to offer as inducement to foreign capital.

(c) Closing the national borders in order to stimulate industrialization so that formerly imported goods can then be manufactured domestically is only a short-term palliative. For, on the one hand, foreign companies already within the economy are likely to become monopoly suppliers to the domestic market, making dependence on foreign companies even greater; and on the other, the ability of domestic companies to compete abroad is reduced since they now have a protected home market, and export earnings are a first casualty. Latin America is a good example in this respect. Import-substitution industrialization has left most of the Latin American countries even more dependent than they were before. The intensity of US investment and intervention in South America makes these countries in certain respects an extreme phenomenon. They did not participate in the colonial revolution of the 20th century (although, aspects of the revolution occurred in Mexico and Cuba, and abortively in Bolivia), and thus remain in some respects colonies without colonialism. On the other hand, the much longer phase of growth witnessed in some Latin American countries makes them the most backward of the advanced rather than the reverse. In class terms, such countries (Argentina, Chile, Uruguay) already have the class structure of a fully capitalist country, with a developed proletariat and dominating bourgeoisie. The role of the petite bourgeoisie is accordingly much more restricted. In such countries, the agrarian question is much less serious (although, extreme in some areas of each country) but the national question much more so. Given the size and significance of the proletariat, the prospect of the dictatorship of the proletariat is, in purely objective terms, much more promising. The degree to which that promise is realized, however, turns upon the available political alternatives and how far these raise the question of the dictatorship of the proletariat.

(*d*) Just as in the period 1880 to 1914, so in the period since 1948 world trade has expanded very rapidly and, as one of its by-products, permitted the growth of a number of backward countries. The growth that takes place is distorted to fit the priorities of a world market dominated by advanced capitalism, but nevertheless it is growth. The expansion of world trade is essentially a function of the expansion of the advanced capitalist countries. In the earlier period, world trade was much more centrally an exchange between capitalist and backward countries, but today the most dynamic sector is the exchange between capitalist countries themselves. Thus, the growth in the backward countries that has taken place is at a slower rate than the growth of world trade itself. The long-term viability of the growth of world trade turns upon the rate and pace of growth of the metropolitan countries. Even if this were to remain high, the share of the backward countries in world trade is likely to continue to decline as it has done since 1950. The advanced capitalist countries are less and less dependent upon the backward majority, even though the domination of the backward by the advanced grows heavier. The drain of resources out of the backward grows larger, but that drain of resources is less and less significant for the growth of the advanced. Through a complex series of mechanisms governing aid, trade, foreign investment, as well as direct and indirect political means, the advanced powers continue to drain resources from the backward. Indeed, debt repayments in the immediate future will increasingly consume a larger proportion of the export earnings of the backward—when Shylock forecloses, all growth is likely to be paralyzed. Given a prospect of relative stagnation in the advanced countries, the effects on the backward are likely to be extreme.

(*e*) In the attempt to overcome the crisis, particular ruling cliques will inevitably be forced "Leftwards"—that is, they will be forced to make more or less substantial encroachments upon entrenched social groups in order to buy popular support for their own survival. Nasser's role in Egypt between 1956 and 1966 is an important example of this process. The fate of Nkrumah in Ghana and of Sukarno in Indonesia illustrates also, however, how fragile this Leftward movement is, how it is unable ultimately to honour its promises in conditions of intractable backwardness. More recently, General Ovando Candia in Bolivia and General Velasco in Peru have similarly moved "Leftwards" by nationalizing major US oil interests in their respective countries. General Candia was one of the people involved in the murder of Guevara, which has not prevented some of the Fidelistas rallying to his support as a Leftwinger. Velasco has followed up his measure with what looks like a radical land reform proposal.

Of course, in the world-wide struggle against the domination of the capitalist powers, socialists must support every move against that domination, whatever its source. But they must do so without illusions, that is, while seeing that this blow against imperialism does not break the contradictions of backwardness. Indeed, it may make some of them worse: without the oil cartel, Bolivia is already finding it extremely difficult to sell its output. As the first blow in an international strategy to destroy imperialism, expropriation of foreign capital is vital. But without that strategy—a strategy which is open to the international proletariat alone—expropriation is merely a measure to fortify the national power of a national ruling class. Nationalization as a legal change of ownership has *no* socialist implications; it is only socialist if it represents a change in class power, a victory for the working class (and in the Bolivian case, the Bolivian workers will remain as they were before nationalization). Of course, the struggle of a national ruling class for independence does have political implications. On the one hand, it can stimulate elements in ruling classes in other countries to imitate the process—thus, the Bolivian and Peruvian changes prompted an Argentinian General, Eduardo Labanca, immediately to proclaim an attack on all US investment in Argentina. On the other, workers, at first no doubt diverted by the "Leftward" shift, also see how easy it is to make a major change of this kind, despite countless earlier arguments about its impossibility, and about how empty such a shift is in the absence of real class power.

The same kinds of considerations arise in appraising more or less radical regimes in backward countries. Socialists must support men like the late President Nasser, both against imperialism and against the reactionary regimes of Saudi Arabia and the Gulf Sheikhdoms (themselves, much more clearly creatures of imperialism itself) but without identifying the regime in Egypt as "socialist" or pretending that Nasser could win that struggle. The Nasser regime itself depended upon subventions from Saudi Arabia, the by-product of the activity of the international oil cartel. Without any kind of international class perspective, Egypt could do no more than operate as just another national unit trying to dominate other national units. Nasser could not challenge Saudi Arabia on class and political grounds, and thus he could not provide any ultimate perspective for Arab unity. Alone and isolated, Egypt's *ad hoc* responses to the contradictions of backwardness are the symptoms of crisis rather than means to solve it. Thus, the Leftward shifts have to be supported, but with critical insight into the preconditions for a real solution. The Leftward shifts are no more than stopgaps in the long-term crisis, itself generated by the impossibility of solving the development question in contemporary conditions. Certainly, they are no substitute for a proletarian internationalist strategy. As Fidel Castro is reported to have told a group of Brazilian revolutionaries: "It is five times more difficult to develop a country than to win a war." His pessimism clearly focuses on the fact that both radical reforms and a popular *coup* by guerrilla forces do not in and of themselves overcome the contradictions of backwardness. The stalemate of development arises directly from the failure of the proletariat to present an independent internationalist alternative. The perspective for world trade makes it look as though the crisis will get worse, leading to greater differences within and between backward countries, greater obstacles to collaboration between backward countries, and greater domestic instability.

VI. The preconditions for a socialist movement

(*a*) The failure of the proletariat has isolated the Left, leaving socialists with no alternatives other than intellectual or actual guerrilla warfare. In the advanced capitalist countries, the memory of a strong political movement of the working class still in many cases remains. The ruins of that movement still mark the political landscape. But in many backward countries, there is not even the memory, only "foreign" theories. Thus, it is not at all surprising that the first steps of opposition in backward countries learn little or nothing of the lessons of the working-class movement—except some of the rhetoric—and, usually unconsciously, revive pre-Marxist utopian socialist thought. For many revolutionaries in the backward countries, as with the utopian socialists, the working class is not the agency for the achievement of socialism, and the "proletariat" can be any force which happens to be in opposition to the *status quo*. Given stagnation in the backward countries such forces multiply—the unemployed, the urban lumpen proletariat, sections of the richer or middle peasantry, tribal groups on the very fringes of society. As the society decomposes there are possibly many such groups, each capable of adding a little to the decomposition, but none capable of constituting an alternative ruling class. The political revolutionary, student or urban petite bourgeois, sees his role as using such groups in order to seize power, and on this basis create an independent national economy and accelerate the rate of accumulation. The pre-revolutionary strategy depends for success on an available vehicle to transport the revolutionaries to power, and a *status quo* sufficiently rotten to collapse without serious struggle. The post-revolutionary strategy is entirely utopian economically, although important short-term advances can be made in terms of popular welfare.

The only example of success with this pre-revolutionary strategy occurred in Cuba. In the case of China, as argued above, not only did a major foreign invasion intervene, a World War, but also the Communists waged a struggle for nearly 18 years before coming to power. Similarly, the struggle in Viet Nam is directly related to the peculiar—indeed unique—overlapping of the decolonization struggle and the Cold War. In the case of Cuba the decisive element in the confrontation between Castro and Batista was the collapse of the Batista forces rather than the size and significance of the Castro threat. To generalize the Cuban case requires us to believe that many regimes are as vulnerable as Batista's. Yet regardless of the brutality and corruption of numerous regimes, there are few countries of substance where there is any evidence of such vulnerability. Even Haiti has so far proved impregnable. In the countless rural guerrilla revolts which have marked modern history—and earlier mention was made of the 1948-1950 Communist insurrections of South-East Asia—the surprising feature is how few, not how many, have been successful. Numerous regimes appear to be perfectly capable of tolerating rural revolt, even sustained like the Huks in the Philippines or the Malayan Communist Party, over many years, without this having any political implications for the country at all.

More than this, the actual politics of the revolutionaries concerned are essentially Narodnik, elitist and anarchist. Owing allegiance to no major class, such revolutionaries are responsible to no one. Therefore their political analysis turns not upon the nature of society and the class struggle, but upon their individual elan, their morality and dedication. They are, in all but name, Liberal nationalists of the 19th century with the difference that the problems facing them are much more intractable, and that they require a social programme to attach their movement to the dynamo of the grievances of heterogeneous social groups. Many nationalists in backward countries have certainly understood that the national revolution cannot today be achieved without a socialist programme. The success of the Chinese Communist Party in securing the hegemony of the Chinese nationalist movement has demonstrated that. In this sense, all revolutionaries are necessarily socialists today. But most of them have not understood that the national revolution is impracticable and utopian without an international revolution. All programmes—the Liberal for national independence, and the socialist for world revolution—have thus become one, all stages have become telescoped. The demands of 19th century Liberalism—of Garibaldi and Kossuth—for national independence, cannot be achieved this side of the world socialist revolution.

Without an international class strategy, each isolated revolutionary becomes no more than a nationalist. Political States replace classes. The "Third World" becomes a unified revolutionary class, despite the bitter class struggle running right through each member State of the "Third World." And the advanced capitalist world similarly becomes a unified ruling class, despite the class struggle which racks its vitals. The political squabbles, leading to war, which divide the ruling classes of the backward countries are forgotten. And at its worst, the world's solitary enemy becomes the United States, a unified class of oppressors. In this scheme, there is no need for class at all, no need for a political party to embody the politics of a class, no need for the scientific analysis of society as the basis for strategy. Only that revival of anarchist mythology, The Deed, undertaken by the saints, is required to set the world tumbling. And for the deed, individual morale, not class solidarity and clarity of political purpose, is the precondition. Nor are advocates of this position in any way susceptible to argument. The countless failures of The Deed are as nothing to a solitary success. The failures are explained as those of individual dedication, not of the objective situation. Society is thus always a bonfire, and the revolutionary's sole function is that of spark.

In practice the truth is less heroic and simple. Of course, in certain circumstances the spark is vital, but alone it is certainly not enough. The dedication of revolutionaries is also vital, but alone it is not enough. Dedication untempered by a clear knowledge of reality is mere stupidity—the tiny socialist forces can be completely eliminated, and the movement set back for many years as a result. In practice, Mao was among the most cautious political leaders of any revolutionary movement, which is why he took so long to come to power and did so unhampered by loyalty to any specific class. Castro is much more clearly the model for revolutionary audacity, but even in his case the lack of a class movement which emancipated itself crucially weakened his challenge to Batista and his post-revolutionary attempts to build a strong State. The fate of Guevara in Bolivia is the more standard result. Yet it would be quite wrong to denigrate the heroism and sacrifice of these populist revolutionaries. Their defeat is a defeat for the Left. That they are misguided is a product of our failure to create a proletarian movement which is a viable alternative to the solitary national *coup*.

However, whatever the role of populist socialists in backward countries, their effects in the advanced capitalist countries can be dangerous, both by diverting the centre of revolutionary attention away from the proletariat, and by substituting elan for theory.

More to the point, the muddled class orientation of such socialists makes them easy victims for shifts in the politics of particular ruling classes. Maoist foreign policy occasionally favours particular capitalist classes—for example, the French, because de Gaulle was seen as "anti-American." "Anti-Americanism" thus becomes the key criterion of a revolutionary. Within each capitalist country, one segment of backward national capital is struggling against advancing international capital, and an alliance between backward capital and the "revolutionaries" around a programme of radical nationalism might have some success. Servan-Schrieber's account of US domination of Europe, in defence of the existing European ruling classes, could thus come close to Maoists or Fidelistas. Given the stagnation of capitalism, the rising threat of proletarian challenge, the need by ruling classes for diversifying politics—racialist and nationalist—the way would be open for some political alliance in which the rhetoric of revolution is married to the politics of conservatism. When Hitler came to power in Germany a number of important Social Democrats thought it was a major advance to socialism. Some of the Maoists and Fidelistas could go the same way. The class nature of any possible future socialist movement is the only protection against individuals pursuing this path—working-class power is the aim, not radical action or institutional reform.

Populist socialism today embodies despair at the intractability of the contradictions of the world as well as the rebirth of hope that change can be achieved. If the class is dormant, then at least one individual will strive to bear witness to what he believes. If he is successful in attaining power, then he will begin to describe the unique way in which he came to power, his technique, his contribution to science. Thus, in China, an account of military technique replaces class politics. But this substitution saps any possibility of serious social analysis, of locating revolt *within* existing society rather than on its margins. It means also that analysis takes its frame of reference as the national borders, and "internationalism" is not class solidarity across frontiers, but merely sentimental dogmatism that, for example, *only* armed struggle on the Viet Namese, Chinese or Cuban "models" (and each is seen as exclusive of the others) can lead to socialism. Again, nationalism dominates even this semblance of internationalism, reformulating the Stalinist contention that defence of the Soviet Union is the defining characteristic of a true proletarian internationalist. An essential part of any attempt to overcome the populist position involves necessarily coming to terms with the Russian experience. The Maoist muddle about Stalin is a good example of their failure in this respect. The Maoists in Britain today are not Stalinists, but they do not know it, and if they did they would not know why.

(*b*) In terms of the perspective facing us, the strategy of rural guerrilla warfare remains very strong among socialists in the backward countries in the absence of any other. But, in Latin America, the failure of Che Guevara in Bolivia has been a major blow to the credibility of this strategy. One of the first results has been a return in many countries to the earlier, pre-Cuba, urban guerrilla action, on the model of the Tupamaros of Uruguay. This is an important change, although it still leaves the socialists acting out mass resentment before a passive audience, rather than building an organized class movement. Nevertheless, the socialists are forced back into the areas where the proletariat is concentrated, are forced into political argument rather than self-imposed isolation. The change occurs at a moment when military rule in much of Latin America is curbing the possibility of economic and political advance by the working class. Of course, as earlier noted, there are pressures on some of the generals "Leftwards" which could give them a breathing space in Peru and Bolivia. But this is likely to be a temporary respite. The combination of urban guerrillas and widespread economic stagnation could do more than usual to jell out a coherent proletarian force—provided the politics or the example are available.

There are some small possibilities of a reunification of the socialists and the working class, a reunification which, to be successful, must transform both sides and place in the centre of any strategy the dictatorship of the proletariat.[3]

[3] Both the volatile nature of the perspectives on much of the Left and the relative shallowness of its roots are amply illustrated by the fact that this section, originally written in 1970, contains no mention of what has since become the main hope of the Left, and in particular, of the Cuban and Chinese Governments: the Allende government in Chile. In the first chapter of this book, it was argued that guerrilla warfare and parliamentary reformism are two sides of the same coin, Allende has now provided

(c) In Asia the signs of the possible creation of an independent proletarian politics are smaller. Certainly economic attrition is taking a terrible toll of the mass of the population, but this alone is as much demoralizing as capable of precipitating revolt. In 1969's upheaval in Pakistan, there seemed to be briefly the possibility of a proletarian intervention when the textile and railway workers of West Pakistan went on to the streets. The movement then seems to have disappeared in the common struggle of the urban petite bourgeoisie. But possibly the attempt by the Pakistan army to stabilize ruling-class political power and the instability of the urban petite bourgeoisie proper could be very clearly demonstrated in the coming period, particularly if there is a partial return to parliamentary politics. The exhaustion of both the military and parliamentary alternatives could force the creation of an independent political proletariat. If this were the pattern of events, then the political situation in India could be transformed for the first time since independence. There would exist a new alternative to the squalid wrangling of factions within and without Congress. And a change in India would transform Asia, particularly if conjoined with an upsurge in the Middle East which simultaneously rejected Zionism, the Arab monarchies, and Nasserite reformism. The transmission effects of the permanent revolution—the twisted reflection of which appears in the Washington image of "the dominoes"—would once more become effective, arising out of the despair of backwardness and directed at the chains of oppression in capitalism itself.

But the shift away from rural guerrilla warfare for socialists in Latin America has not been clearly matched as yet in Asia. In India the revolutionaries of the fragments of the Communist Party remain focused upon such a perspective the (abortive "Naxalbari movement"). Certainly, the experience of the CPI State Government in West Bengal and Kerala (although both were officially coalitions) will be salutary in robbing both the "parliamentary road" and the urban petite bourgeoisie of credibility.

---

the opposite face to Che Guevara for Fidel Castro and Mao Tse-tung. Unconditional support for Allende's struggle with US imperialism should not persuade anyone that Chilean socialism is any more possible than Indian socialism is likely by the election of a CPM government in West Bengal.

But this lesson has not been matched by the development of an independent proletarian politics. In Indonesia, the opposition still appears to be concentrated among the depressed peasant strata of central Java, although the student enthusiasts of Jakarta who originally assisted the army to throw out Sukarno have now long since swung into opposition to the military regime. Until the rural struggle and the urban petit-bourgeois opposition evokes an answering movement of urban workers, it will almost certainly pose no major threat to the regime. For the ruling classes have also learned lessons from China, Viet Nam and Cuba. On the other hand, the exhaustion of all other strategies—Stalinist, both Moscow and Peking varieties, the Sukarno Left reformism, and the military, limit the possibilities of evading the formulation of a proletarian strategy. In particular, Peking's role in encouraging the Indonesian Communist Party in its reformist support of Sukarno, in direct contradiction of its claimed politics, may have robbed Maoism of much credibility as a revolutionary alternative.

(*d*) But the Asian perspective is predicated on a very narrow basis. The proletariat exists, but its politics do not. In Africa, the proletariat is the newest in the world, and the degree of development lowest. Nevertheless, Lagos and Accra workers have already made their mark. Africa is increasingly sucked into the whirlpool of the world market, manipulated on each side by the imperialist predators. The results in the Congo, and now in Nigeria, in the increasing rash of military coups, are the same as those in other regions. Yet so far no trace of an independent proletarian politics has made its appearance. A primary target must obviously be the lynch pin of southern Africa, where racialism and class struggle combine. A proletarian revolt which sparked off an answering movement in southern Africa would shake the entire *status quo* of Africa. The European revolution was stopped on the borders of Germany and bottled up in backward Russia. In Asia, India and China are the Germanies of today, and in Africa, South Africa and Rhodesia. These countries are not the sparks, but the boosters without which the rocket will not go beyond the stage reached by the Russian revolution.

(*e*) In the past Stalinism in its prime exercised power against all revolutionary action, whatever type of action it was. Now Stalinism is weakening throughout the world, fragmented between different nationalisms—Russian, Chinese, Cuban—and increasingly unable to unite a popular politics with the exigencies of orthodox diplomacy. A mark of the disintegration is the contradictions within the external politics of each national Stalinism. Mention has already been made of the Chinese position on Pakistan, Indonesia and France, and the same contradictions exist in Chinese policy towards Egypt and the Middle East. The Cubans are less able to manoeuvre than the Chinese, but nevertheless their oscillation between accepting Moscow's direction (on, for example, Czechoslovakia), and the reverse, illustrates clearly that their foreign policy is less a function of their politics and more a bargaining counter against Moscow. Quite rightly, Havana is afraid of a deal between Moscow and Washington which will completely isolate Cuba and make any foreign policy worthless. Given Cuba's economic dependence on Soviet sugar purchases and equipment supplies, Moscow's abandonment of Havana could be the spark for a counter-revolution. The instability of Cuba's situation underlines the necessary limits on any Fidelista policy going beyond Cuban nationalism.

A greater danger than these contradictions is the complete dissolution of Marxism altogether into a vague populist socialism. At each stage in this account, the main weakness of a proletarian challenge has been seen as its lack of theoretical equipment to deal with its crisis. The dissolution of Marxism makes this situation worse, even if it also clears the board of diversionary "socialisms." However, simultaneously, the non-proletarian alternatives are becoming increasingly limited in concrete terms. The alternatives—a revival of proletarian politics, or stagnation and crises—remain.

VII. International Socialism and the struggle in backward countries

(*a*) What is centrally lacking in the backward countries today is a clearly expressed strategy to establish the dictatorship of the proletariat. Without this aim the sporadic involvement of workers in broader movements has no specific political implications except as a possible prelude to proletarian independence. Isolated and alone in one country, the proletariat can only, through major crises, very slowly begin to move towards an independent strategy, and it is unlikely in modern conditions to have the opportunity. Thus, the role of the international situation (proletarian revolts in other countries) and of class-conscious socialists is vital. Yet the socialists themselves are, by and large, not committed to the dictatorship of the proletariat so much as the urban petit-bourgeois aim of purely nationalist State capitalism.

The task of revolutionaries in backward countries is thus clear: to raise the slogan of the dictatorship of the proletariat and organize around it. Given the aim, a broad coalition of forces is available to wage the struggle, a coalition that must include large numbers drawn from the urban petite bourgeoisie and the peasantry, but more important, must be based essentially on the separate organization of the working class and, in particular, those sections of it employed in large-scale modern industry. An authentic proletarian organization would immediately change the terms of the debate, and begin the long task of working towards the permanent revolution. That task would be immeasurably shortened by a sustained proletarian revolt in an advanced capitalist country.

(*b*) In certain limited respects the prospects today are more promising for the development of a proletarian movement than for the past 20 years.The limits of the State capitalist alternative are more clearly apparent, as also are the limits of the strategy which leads up to State capitalism, rural guerrilla warfare. The scale of oppression by the advanced countries grows steadily heavier and more clearly apparent, so that both the alternatives of national independence in conditions of backwardness and integration into the existing world market—the alternatives of the urban petite bourgeoisie and the national bourgeoisie respectively—are shown to provide only temporary solutions. In such a context, an internationalist and proletarian strategy could come to be seen as a more *practical* alternative.

(*c*) IS's role in assisting this process is obviously, if regrettably, limited. Organizationally and financially, IS is scarcely equipped to do very much outside of Britain. However, our theoretical position could be of particular importance in what help we could give. In particular, our critique of Stalinism and our consistent stress upon the role of the proletariat could be important in clarifying perspectives for some socialists in some backward countries.

(*d*) So far as our work in this country is concerned, we must at the same time as describing clearly the class content and direction of movements in the backward countries, clearly and strongly affirm that we are always and everywhere on the side of the oppressed against the oppressor. Whatever the nature of the opposition to imperialism in the backward countries, as socialists we must be clear in supporting it. The international linkages of revolt do not follow the distinctions of economics. In 1968-69 the sparks which flew between Berkeley, Peking, Paris and Karachi came from different fires, but their ignition power in the student revolt was the same. The qualifications we have about petit-bourgeois revolts concern *not* whether we support them or not—we must always and everywhere support them against imperialism—but how far such revolts can be a substitute for the struggle of the proletariat and the achievement of socialism. But our basic position is quite clear. As Lenin put it: "If tomorrow, Morocco were to declare war on France, or India on Britain, or Persia or China on Russia, and so on, these would be 'just' and 'defensive' wars, *irrespective* of who would be the first to attack; any socialist would wish the oppressed, dependent and unequal State victory over the oppressor, slave-holding and predatory 'great' Powers" (*Socialism and War*, 1915).

Index